The Diary
of Virginia
Woolf

Volume One:
1915-1919

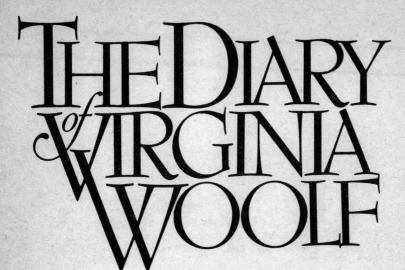

THE DIARY of VIRGINIA WOOLF

Edited by
Anne Olivier Bell
Introduction by Quentin Bell

VOLUME ONE

1915-1919

A Harvest/HBJ Book

Harcourt Brace Jovanovich

New York and London

Printed in the United States of America

LIBRARY OF CONGRESS CATALOGING IN PUBLICATION DATA

Woolf, Virginia Stephen, 1882–1941.
The diary of Virginia Woolf.
(A Harvest/HBJ book)
Includes index.
CONTENTS: V. 1. 1915–1919.
1. Woolf, Virginia Stephen, 1882–1941—Diaries.
2. Authors, English—20th century—Biography.
I. Bell, Anne Olivier. II. Title.
[PR6045.072Z494   1978]   823'.9'12   [B]   78-23882
ISBN 0-15-626036-0

First Harvest/HBJ edition 1979

A B C D E F G H I J

CONTENTS

The Diary

EDITOR'S PREFACE

On Sunday, 3 January 1897, Virginia Stephen, then nearly fifteen, began to keep a record of the new year; on 1 January 1898 she writes '*Finis*' to ' a volume of fairly acute life (the first really *lived* year of my life)'. This diary was maintained without a break until October, save for the day following the death of her recently married half-sister in July. But after that disaster it dwindled, and on 14 September she remarks on the moribund condition of her poor diary, but says 'Never mind, we will follow the year to its end & then fling diaries & diarising into the corner—to dust & mire & moths & all creeping crawling eating destroying creatures.'

Between 1898 and 1915 Virginia kept, at different times, at least five notebooks having something of the character of diaries but consisting largely of literary exercises or essays arising from events, people, and places that she observed; only in the first months of 1905 did she again keep a brief day-to-day journal. On 1 January 1915, now married to Leonard Woolf and lodging in Richmond upon Thames, she once more resolved to make a daily record of her doings and reflections. This diary was terminated six weeks after it was begun by a breakdown more appalling than those she had already suffered, and one that lasted longer. However, by 1916 she was again leading a comparatively normal life at home in Richmond and at Asheham, her house in Sussex. It was at Asheham in August 1917 that she began yet again to keep a journal, noting in summary form each day's happenings and weather, and her observations of natural phenomena. On returning to Hogarth House, Richmond, in October that year, she began the much fuller record which, in one form or another, she was to maintain until the end of her life in 1941.

It is these diaries—written from 1915 onwards in thirty separate books—which it is the intention to publish complete in five volumes, of which this is the first. They are now, together with all the earlier diaries and essay-journals save one, the property of the Henry W. and Albert A. Berg Collection of English and American Literature in the New York Public Library (Astor, Lenox and Tilden Foundations). That they are so is due in large part to the enterprise of those percipient dealers in literary manuscripts, the Misses Hamill and Barker of Chicago. In 1956 they obtained from Leonard Woolf (who had already published selected extracts under the title *A Writer's Diary* in 1953) an option on the manuscript originals provided that they were able to ensure their acquisition by a major university or public collection, and provided that he (Leonard) might retain possession during his lifetime. Negotiations were entered into with Dr John D. Gordan, Curator of the Berg Collection, and on his undertaking to purchase the diaries for $20,000 when they they should become available, Leonard Woolf chose to look upon the Berg as the appropriate repository for the greater part of his wife's literary remains. It was thus, through the agency of the Misses Hamill and Barker, that the Berg Collection obtained its unrivalled Virginia Woolf archive.

Leonard Woolf received payment for the diaries in 1958; he lived until 1969, and it was not until 1970 that the transaction was completed and the diaries entered the Berg.

The 1915-1941 series of diaries which thus eventually reached New York comprised twenty-seven volumes—1918 was in two books, and there was none for 1916. The three further books which are included in the present publication were detached from the main series: one—a third book for 1918, which includes Virginia Woolf's first impressions of T. S. Eliot—was found after Leonard's death, and was offered to the Berg Collection by his executor; the other two (the Asheham Diary, because of its different nature, and one kept for three weeks in September 1919 soon after the move to Monks House) were grouped with the early diaries and essay-journals rather than with the main series, and entered the Berg Collection much earlier. The entire series of manuscript volumes concerned is itemised in Appendix I on p. 321.

At the invitation of the copyright holders and of the Hogarth Press, I have undertaken the task of preparing these diaries for publication with great and I hope proper diffidence. My qualifications for the undertaking rest partly on luck and partly on assiduity. I was born, geographically speaking, in Bloomsbury during the First World War, and was largely educated in London; to some extent my parents' world was contiguous with that of Virginia Woolf's. (I saw her only once.) I am married to her nephew and biographer Quentin Bell, and we live in Sussex half-way between Rodmell and Charleston, a mile distant from Asheham. So much for the luck. I have spent the best part of the last ten years on the documentation of Virginia Woolf's life, assisting my husband with this side of the biography of his aunt, published in 1972. My assiduity in this respect caused him some despair; it may well cause readers of these volumes despair too. Whether they are sensible of a corresponding benefit it must be for them to decide. As editor I start from the position that I should make it my business to be able to read what Virginia Woolf wrote, and to understand what she was writing about, in these diaries, in order to present a clear and comprehensible text. I do not find much difficulty in the reading and transcribing (and here it should be said that this was first done for, and with, Leonard Woolf by Kathleen Williams, and it was from her typescript that he made his selections for *A Writer's Diary*. It has formed an invaluable basis for my revision.) The elucidation of the text has been much more demanding. Virginia Woolf's interests and observations range over so wide a field—art, literature, politics, people, and her surroundings—that some supporting explanation seems necessary. In deciding how much annotation is appropriate, I have to take into account the probability that—for reasons of cost and copyright—there is not likely to be another edition of these diaries for perhaps half a century. In that time much pertinent information that I have acquired from within the circle of family and friends will have vanished for ever unless it be recorded now. Moreover, the obstacles and obscurities born of time and distance will become increasingly impenetrable; names that are household words to some may become—may already be—Greek to others. When Virginia Woolf wonders whether to stretch out her hand for Rob Roy or says she saw a painted lady near Glynde, can we be sure that she will be understood?

Then I feel that the readers of what will inevitably be expensive volumes ought not, if they do pause to shift their focus from text to footnote, to be fobbed off with only an abbreviated reference to some other expensive book. So at the risk of overdoing it, I have (though as concisely as I can) given what I judge to be essential and interesting information to illuminate or elucidate Virginia Woolf's rapid flow of words. I must beg those who find such explanations superfluous to ignore the footnotes, remembering that others may find them helpful.

Virginia Woolf wrote a distinguished and elegant hand which in general it is not difficult to read, though the speed at which she wrote, the instruments she used (for preference a dipping pen and ink), and her habitual position—seated in an easy chair with a board on her lap—do frequently give rise to irregularities and obscurities. She also wrote a very pure and grammatical English, and although her choice and use of words often appears almost miraculous, it is never eccentric or jarring. The transcription of her diaries is in intention complete and entirely faithful, although I have made one or two concessions to common sense and production costs. The most obvious of these concern dates. Virginia Woolf dated her diary entries with every possible combination and abbreviation of day, date, and month. I do not think sufficient light is thrown upon her state of mind or habit of thought to justify the typographical difficulties and expense involved in reproducing her variations; the essential thing is to give the reader a clear and accurate point of reference. So in these volumes the date is invariably set out: day, date, month, and italicised, thus: *Thursday 14 January*; the months are repeated in the running headline on each page, together with the year. When there is a difference—Virginia sometimes mistakes the date—this is noted; her errors, when they do occur, have been rectified by reference to Leonard's laconic but exact pocket diaries, to her own and her correspondents' letters, to internal evidence and to external events.

Another departure from Virginia Woolf's autography arises from her manner of forming abbreviations such as M^{rs}, Sq^{re}, 2^d, 19th, and even Sh^{re} (Shakespeare); the superior letters are lowered, and the stops and dashes, if any, omitted. Her inconsistent abbreviation of names to a capital letter followed—or not—by a colon—particularly in the case of L:—or other stop, is not reproduced as it becomes irritating on the printed page; a simple full stop is used. On the other hand her almost invariable use of the ampersand has been retained; it suggests the pace of her writing, and gives point to the few occasions when she does choose to spell out the conjunction.

Her spelling is so consistently good that the rare eccentricities are perpetuated (*lovabilility* is a lovely word); obvious inadvertencies have been silently corrected. Her spelling, often phonetic, of proper names is less reliable, but is retained, and the correct version given in a square bracket or footnote.

Punctuation: it is not always easy to determine whether a single mark made at speed is intended as a comma, a full stop, or a dash; or two marks as a colon or a semi-colon. In cases of real uncertainty I have leaned to the side of orthodoxy. Usually her punctuation is perfectly appropriate if inconsistent, though apostrophes in the possessive case and inverted commas tend to stray or fall by the wayside; I have made minimal adjustments in such cases without calling attention to them. I *do* call attention, by means of square brackets and question marks, to doubtful readings or to words added to complete the sense.

There is remarkably little crossed out or altered in these pages, considering the speed at which Virginia wrote; indeed the pace at which she wrote precluded those corrections and additions which are so striking a feature of her more pondered manuscripts. Where she has corrected herself, her corrections are followed. Very occasionally, her first thoughts or hesitations seem of enough interest to repeat, and they appear within angled brackets: ⟨　⟩.

The annotations are given at the foot of the page to which they relate, and are numbered in sequence *within each month*. This is a compromise between many possible methods, all of which have disadvantages, but it is hoped that this one will prove generally convenient.

The essential biographical information about people mentioned in Virginia Woolf's diary is normally given at the foot of the page on their first appearance, although when they are merely named in passing it is sometimes postponed to a more appropriate page; the index will indicate where it is to be found. Whenever possible full names and dates of birth (and death) are given, since temporal relationships were of interest to Virginia; and the origin of the connection with her (for instance, her parents', or her brothers' Cambridge, circle) is suggested. In general, details concerning someone's later history are not given, unless they appear to throw some light on his present character or situation.

Virginia frequently makes passing reference to articles or book reviews she must write or deliver; these are identified in the footnotes according to B. J. Kirkpatrick's invaluable *Bibliography of Virginia Woolf*, her numbers prefixed by Kp. On p. 328 is a list of names and publications cited in abbreviated form in the footnotes; other books are referred to by author, full title, and date of publication in England, except for Virginia Woolf's own works, when reference is made to the *Uniform Edition* and the 4-volume *Collected Essays* published in London by the Hogarth Press, and in New York by Harcourt Brace Jovanovich.

Acknowledgments

This volume could not have been produced without the help and encouragement, moral, intellectual, and material, of a very large number of individuals, officials, and representatives of various bodies. First of all I would like to acknowledge the fundamental support of the curator of the Berg Collection in New York, Dr Lola L. Szladits, of the Leverhulme Trustees who granted me a Research Fellowship, of Norah Smallwood and Ian Parsons of the Hogarth Press, and of the copyright holders, Quentin Bell and Angelica Garnett.

I am particularly beholden to Barbara Bagenal, to my cousin Angela Richards, and to Norman MacKenzie, for their ever-readiness and resource in answering questions. George Spater, who, like me, enjoys the pursuit of elusive facts, has been both a stimulating and a most generous collaborator. Trekkie Parsons has allowed me to make use of Leonard Woolf's pocket diaries, an invaluable help. I have also had the great advantage that Nigel Nicolson and Joanne Trautmann's edition of *The Letters of Virginia Woolf* precede the publication of her Diary; I am especially grateful to Nigel Nicolson for making their volumes available to me before publication.

The lines from T. S. Eliot's poem quoted on p. 219 are reprinted with the permission of Mrs Valerie Eliot, Faber & Faber Ltd., London, and Harcourt Brace Jovanovich, Inc., New York.

I wish also to thank the following for their help:

Lord Annan; R. Page Arnot; Virginia Bell; Mary Bennett; Noel Carrington; Dr Martin Ceadel; Lady David Cecil; Mr E. R. Chamberlin; Dame Margaret Cole; Miss Adeline Croft; Edward Croft-Murray; Arthur Crook; Adam Curle; Pamela Diamand; David Erdman; John Fuller; P. N. Furbank; David Garnett; C. H. Gibbs-Smith; the Ven. Max Godden; Mr & Mrs Ronald Gosden; Cecil Gould; Duncan Grant; Lady

(Hubert) Henderson; George Holleyman; Michael Holroyd; Judith Hubback; Miss Virginia Isham; John Jones; B. J. Kirkpatrick; Paul Levy; Lord Llewelyn Davies; Dr Dermod MacCarthy; Richard Morphet; Lucy Norton; Lord Norwich; Frances Partridge; Denis Richards; Professor Sir Austin Robinson; Mr R. R. Robinson; Professor W. A. Robson; Angus Ross; Carol Rudman; Lucio Ruotolo; Richard Shone; Graham Speake; Julian Trevelyan; The Hon Mrs Fred Uhlmann; Dame Janet Vaughan; Daniel Waley; Dame Veronica Wedgwood; and Professor G. P. Wells.

A very large part of my research has been done in the recesses of the London Library, for which establishment and its staff I feel an almost devout gratitude. I have received great courtesy and help from librarians and officials in respect of enquiries addressed to the following institutions and businesses:

The Autotype Company; George Allen & Unwin Ltd; the Libraries of Emmanuel, Girton, Gonville & Caius, King's, and Trinity Colleges, Cambridge; Caslon Ltd; The Thomas Coram Foundation for Children; East Sussex County Record Office, Lewes; the Electoral Reform Society; The Fawcett Society; Charles Frodsham & Co. Ltd; the Guildhall School of Music; The Library, Hatfield House; the Department of Health and Social Security Records; Hull University Library; the India Office Library & Records; Isola Bella Restaurant, Frith Street; The London School of Economics; Morley College, London; the *Morning Star*; The National Gallery; The National Portrait Gallery; the *New Statesman & Nation*; the Library of Nuffield College, Oxford; the Borough Architect & Planning Officer, Richmond upon Thames; The Royal Academy of Arts; The Royal Commission on Historical Monuments; The Slade School of Fine Art; the University of Sussex Library; The Tate Gallery; *The Times*; *The Times Literary Supplement*; The United Nations and The United Nations Association; University College, London; the Library, the Indian Section, and the Departments of Ceramics, Sculpture, and Textiles of the Victoria and Albert Museum.

Imogen Scott and Pauline Hillman have done the essential typing for this volume with noteworthy accuracy. Michèle Barrett was my assistant in long exacting tasks and did invaluable research on political, social and local matters; Andrew McNeillie has more recently undertaken equally exacting tasks of checking, searching, and indexing. I have relied very much, and with grateful confidence, upon them both. But above all I have depended upon the unfailing and happily accessible knowledge, judgement and assistance of my husband.

Did I not feel it presumptuous, I would dedicate this publication of his wife's diaries to the dear memory of Leonard Woolf.

ANNE OLIVIER BELL

INTRODUCTION

This is the last of Virginia Woolf's major works to be offered to the public.

In calling it a major work I wish to imply not merely that it is a large work of major historical and biographical importance (which it certainly and obviously is) but also that, considered as a whole, it is a masterpiece.

And if further definition be required I would say that in calling it a masterpiece I mean to indicate that it is a literary achievement equal to though very different from *The Waves* or *To The Lighthouse*, having the same accurate beauty of writing but also an immediacy such as one finds only in diaries; it is in fact one of the great diaries of the world.

When, therefore, the last of these volumes comes from the press, the *œuvre* of Virginia Woolf will be complete and the critics may, if they so wish, sit down and assess it as a whole.

It may be thought that this would have been an appropriate task for the writer of this introduction and furthermore that he should begin by justifying his assertion that this is a masterpiece. I shall do no such thing. The assessment of Virginia Woolf's work cannot fairly be made until the reader has all five volumes at his disposition; nor does it seem very useful to discuss a valuation which cannot possibly be justified and which cannot be disproved. Let it stand, together with my affidavit that this is my sincere and considered opinion.

Considering the diary not as art but as history, we should perhaps try to answer the question: Is it true?

To this no completely unequivocal answer can be given. Virginia Woolf's reputation for truthfulness was not good. She was supposed to be malicious, a gossip, and one who allowed her imagination to run away with her. At least one of her friends, foreseeing the publication of her letters and of this diary, tried to warn posterity that it must not believe everything that she might tell it.

Sooner or later Virginia's diaries and letters will be printed. They will make a number of fascinating volumes: books, like Byron's letters, to be read and re-read for sheer delight. In the midst of his delight let the reader remember, especially the reader who itches to compose histories and biographies, that the author's accounts of people and of their sayings and doings may be flights of her airy imagination. Well do I remember an evening when Leonard Woolf, reading aloud to a few old friends extracts from these diaries, stopped suddenly. 'I suspect', said I, 'you've come on a passage where she makes a bit too free with the frailties and absurdities of someone here present.' 'Yes', said he, 'but that's not why I broke off. I shall skip the next few pages because there's not a word of truth in them.'*

One would like to know which passage it was that Leonard Woolf censored. I do not think that there is any substantial part of the diary of which it can fairly be said that 'there's not a word of truth' in it. Certainly there is much which is dubious gossip, much that is exaggerated, much that is inaccurate, and there may be some pure fantasy. This is more true of the letters than of the diary. In her letters she certainly invents; sometimes she invents in order to amuse, knowing very well that she will not be believed by the recipient. But in her diaries she is not trying to be entertaining, and such fantasies are rare. She certainly is untruthful in her assessment of people: that is to say she is true only to her mood at the moment of writing, and when the mood changes she often contradicts herself, so that when she writes a great deal about one person we frequently end with a judgement balanced between extremes. But although she is biassed and at times misinformed or careless, she does not consciously tell lies to herself, or even for the benefit of some future reader. The editor has frequently had occasion to correct her upon points of detail but never, I think, has she discovered a complete fabrication.

In general it may be said with confidence that the reader will find in these pages a true account of Virginia Woolf, together with a reasonably accurate, and in many ways intensely perceptive, account of her friends and family, her life and times.

In addition to this assurance the prospective reader requires—if indeed he requires any kind of introduction—the kind of information which will enable him to understand the text. In fact, he must be put in possession of facts which the diarist took for granted and, writing for herself alone, could leave unmentioned. This information may be supplied by means of a recital (as succinct as possible) of the lives of Leonard and Virginia Woolf up to the time at which the diary begins, and also some account of the character of Virginia's social environment.

Leslie Stephen, a writer of some eminence, married twice: Laura the child of his first wife, was feeble-minded. By his second wife, *née* Julia Jackson, he had four children: Vanessa, Thoby, Virginia and Adrian. But before becoming Julia Stephen, Julia Jackson had been Julia Duckworth and in this first union she bore three children—George, Stella, and Gerald.

* Clive Bell, *Old Friends: Personal Recollections*, 1956, p. 97.

All these, including Laura (who had later to be sent to an asylum) lived at No. 22 Hyde Park Gate, Kensington and, in summer, at Talland House, St Ives, Cornwall, for which place Virginia retained nostalgic memories for the rest of her life.

Virginia had decided to be a writer, as her sister Vanessa had resolved to be a painter, in the nursery. A considerable part of Virginia's childhood, and it seems to have been a secure and very happy childhood, was spent in writing for her own pleasure and amusement.

In May 1895 Julia Stephen died and that was the end of all security and of most happiness. The shock drove Virginia out of her mind. She had barely recovered from this first bout of insanity when it was followed by the death of her half-sister. Then came tragedy of another kind; Jack Hills, Stella's widower, addressed himself with passionate indiscretion to Vanessa who, being his deceased wife's sister was, in the eyes of the law, taboo. Meanwhile the master of this cheerless house became increasingly odd, irritable and deaf. Virginia herself was almost insanely shy; she had a sharp tongue, but she also had qualities which won and for many years retained the friendship of intelligent women such as Madge Vaughan, the daughter of John Addington Symonds, Janet Case the Greek scholar, Lady Robert Cecil and, above all Violet Dickinson, a woman of large moral character who was at once surrogate mother and—in a purely sentimental fashion—the lover of this very difficult and complicated young woman. When, in 1904, Sir Leslie (knighted in 1902) died of cancer, Virginia again went mad and it was Violet above all who devoted herself to the invalid.

Virginia's recovery seemed to be the beginning of a happier epoch. Vanessa made a new home for her brothers and sister at 46 Gordon Square, Bloomsbury, a more cheerful environment than 22 Hyde Park Gate and one more appropriate to the free existence that the Stephen children now sought. Virginia's brother Thoby brought his Cambridge friends and notably Saxon Sydney-Turner, Lytton Strachey and Clive Bell to Gordon Square. Virginia was at first very critical of these young men but she learnt presently to enjoy conversations of a kind that were entirely new to her. She had had no formal education, but her father had given her the run of his library—she was a voracious reader—and a few excellent words of advice. Cambridge, having as it were come to Blooms-bury, could supply the dialectical teaching of which she had felt herself to be deprived. At the same time she continued her own education as author by writing reviews.

Then, once again fate mauled the Stephen family. In 1906 after travel-ling in Greece, both Vanessa and Thoby fell ill. Thoby died (20 November 1906). To Virginia it seemed not only that she had lost a much loved and much admired brother but that she had also lost a sister, for Vanessa then married Clive Bell. This seemed almost like treachery; her sister was the most important person in her life. She did not think Clive worthy of his good fortune.

The ensuing years were not all unhappy but they contained much unhappiness. Virginia set up house in another Bloomsbury Square with her surviving brother, Adrian. They made an inharmonious couple. Moved by what one may almost call a spirit of revenge, Virginia soon embarked upon a reckless flirtation with Clive which gave little but pain to everyone concerned. Men were a new interest; she found time for some other flirtations and was momentarily engaged to Lytton Strachey. In 1908 she began to write a novel which was eventually to become *The Voyage Out*.

In 1910 she had another breakdown. This resulted in a friendship with Miss Jean Thomas who kept the nursing home in which she was hospitalised. In 1911 she moved to a new home, again in Bloomsbury; with Adrian she set up a collective establishment (it was considered a scandalous thing to do). The other subscribers were two comparatively new friends: Duncan Grant and Maynard Keynes; in December 1911 Leonard Woolf became a member of this commune.

Leonard Woolf was born in 1880, one of a large Jewish family; his father Sidney Woolf, Q.C., was able, hard-working and prosperous; but not sufficiently prosperous to leave his family much to live on when, very suddenly and in the prime of life, he died, leaving a widow and nine children. The Woolfs met this catastrophe with the supple fortitude of their race. Somehow the children were given a good education. Four, of whom Leonard was one, gained scholarships to Cambridge, and it was there that he formed the friendships which were to determine the course of his life.

The Cambridge Conversazione Society, usually called 'The Apostles', had been founded at the beginning of the nineteenth century and in its time it had enlisted a great many of the most brilliant undergraduates, or rather of the most gifted, for I think the 'Apostles' slightly mistrusted brilliance; the term suggests superficiality whereas the ideal Apostle, although of course he had to be intelligent, had also above all things to be serious and of a ferocious integrity; it was something in his favour if he were rather unworldly, almost, in fact, a prig. Leonard came fairly near to that ideal and for him Cambridge remained always a spiritual home and 'Apostolic' purity the proper aim of an intellectual.

At that time the Society could be regarded as a kind of freemasonry of the intellect. Its existence was supposed to be a secret; there were phrases, ceremonies, allusions and jargon not understood by the profane and in consequence it offered a fair target for ridicule. Those of Leonard's contemporaries who had not been members of the Society poked fun at the secrecy and the ceremony, they delighted in stories of pretty numskulls smuggled into the Apostolic fold by Lytton Strachey. Behind their censure there was some envy, the envy of those who have been tried by their peers and found wanting. There were several of Virginia's friends who never quite got over the chagrin of having not been Apostles. Correspondingly Leonard himself, arriving at Trinity conscious no doubt of his own intellectual powers but conscious also that certain barely visible but still sensible barriers remained in English society to impede the passage of members of his race, must surely have found in his membership of a powerful society which was morally and intellectually superior to the conventions and prejudices of the age, a cordial and a reinforcement.

When Leonard came down in 1904 and found himself without money, without an outstanding degree and with no better prospect than that of going to Ceylon as an apprentice civil servant, he certainly needed some such reassurance. To descend from the rarefied atmosphere of Trinity to the solitude of the jungle and the loud convivialities of the white man's club was a sad transition. However, he was made of uncommonly stern stuff; he managed not only to survive but to prosper and to rise in his profession. When he returned to England on leave in 1911 it was clear that he had a great future before him in the colonial service. He decided to throw it away, to stay in England and to marry Virginia.

It was a programme which could not be realised without hardihood. He had to deal not only with the Colonial Office but with Virginia and, while the former very much wanted to keep him, the latter was half inclined to let him go.

After a period of long and agonising doubt Virginia did in fact marry him on 10 August 1912 and the marriage, despite the fact that Virginia was not sexually enthusiastic, was both happy and durable. Almost at once it was subjected to the most exacting tests, for within a year Virginia was struck by the third of her bouts of madness. In September 1913 she tried to kill herself. The recovery from this attack was painfully slow, for a long time she had to be watched day and night by nurses, for a long time she tried to starve herself to death. It was not until the autumn of 1914 that she could again begin to lead something like a normal life.

The Woolfs had discovered a house called Asheham in a valley of the Sussex downs and it was here that Virginia passed her convalescence. She herself would no doubt have wished to return to London and Leonard, who was getting more and more involved in political work, needed to be near the capital, but he feared the effect that it would have upon Virginia's health. They compromised by settling in Richmond, about half an hour by train from central London, and it was here that Virginia began to keep this diary.

'I, Virginia Woolf, am a lady.' So far as I know Virginia never said or wrote those words, and yet I do not think that she would have denied that, if we could interpret it properly, the phrase would describe one of the assumptions which she makes in writing her diary; and it is an assumption of which we ought to be aware even though it might never have occurred to her to state it. The difficulty is that we can hardly know what such words imply in the mouth of one who was born in 1882, brought up in Kensington, ready to contemplate marriage with a self-confessed sodomite at the age of twenty-seven and at thirty to exchange the name of Stephen for that of Woolf. Her situation was one of considerable social complexity and to describe it adequately is nearly impossible. Nevertheless an attempt to do so could be helpful to the readers of these diaries and should be made.

Many people, if asked now to describe Virginia's social environment, would answer with one word: 'Bloomsbury'. But that word, howsoever liberally it may be defined—and indeed it does bear a great many meanings—could never properly describe the great number of social groups with which Virginia was concerned, and of course the statement would ignore the very obvious fact that Virginia was a social being with strong affiliations to other people long before 'Bloomsbury' ever existed.

Her parents belonged to the upper middle class. People of their kind worked for their living but they did not work with their hands. They did not belong to the leisure class or to the hereditary ruling class; they were neither landowners nor industrialists, nor were they engaged in any sort of commerce. They were 'professional' people, lawyers, civil servants, dons, men of letters, a few were physicians, a few were clergymen; their culture was almost entirely literary, and they were only to a slight extent concerned with the other arts, hardly at all with music or the theatre.

For this class success was the fruit of intelligence and hard work. The education of their sons was a very important matter; they were sent to 'good' schools and then to Oxford or Cambridge and so into some kind of legal, literary or administrative work which, not uncommonly, took them to India. From India they returned to an area which may, very loosely be termed 'Kensington'. Here they lived in tall dark overfurnished houses on the walls of which hung large dark pictures in heavy gold frames. They employed a very large number of servants.

The education of the daughters followed a much less clearly defined pattern than that of their brothers. On the one hand they were trained to cultivate the graces, on the other there was an increasing tendency to give them a more serious education. There were schools which could provide something more than the rudimentary knowledge, the French, Music, Drawing and Deportment, that could be learnt from a vast and needy army of governesses. In 1870 the Universities had left their doors slightly ajar so that, even in an age of bustles, an intelligent young woman might squeeze her way through. Virginia's generation was to see the first results of that invasion, the brilliant and stout-hearted sisterhood of Oxford and Cambridge. But there was nothing in the least odd about the fact that neither Virginia herself nor her sister or half-sister received any form of systematic education. A lady was, in a refined way, a domestic animal; it was her duty to devote herself to the home and to her relations, to be an obedient child, an unpaid companion, an amateur nurse and, in effect, a kind of upper servant. Marriage was the grand aim of her youth, it enabled her to escape from the tyranny of the home and to exchange a lower for a higher form of servitude. It was a transaction to which she, at least, was expected to bring the gift of purity, a term of imprecise meaning but of enormous importance to the Victorian middle classes.

Once married, the girls found themselves pregnant again and again. The vast broods that were thus engendered, the strong sense of family solidarity, a solidarity reinforced by the heavy casualties of nineteenth-century disease and nineteenth-century medicine, the fact that the survivors naturally tended to repeat the educational pattern of their parents and usually had sufficient ability to rise to a fair height in what became 'family' professions, meant that certain branches of administration were largely in the hands of a relatively small number of families. When one begins to examine the history of this class at this period one discovers a dense and complicated network of family connections; the ramifications seem endless and everyone, it appears, knew, or was related to, or at least had been at the University with, everyone else.

Looking back across a century, one tries to imagine what a gathering of Mr and Mrs Leslie Stephen's friends would have been like. The picture is dim and confused. One may reasonably situate the party in a large house built about the middle of the century or rather earlier; these were people who altered but did not build houses and who, on the whole, were uncomfortable with modernity. The decorations would have been sober—dark crimson curtains relieved by dusky bronze, black shiny furniture picked out with a narrow gold line. In a draped alcove a marble bust by Marocchetti, Watts quoting from Titian in a heavy gilt and stucco frame, a large photograph of the Ansidei Madonna on a bed of purple velvet, glazed and framed in gilt and darkly japanned wood, a great many small photographs of gentlemen wearing resolute expressions and a lot of hair, ladies with fine eyes and bare shoulders and everywhere books, books treated with respect and clothed in leather or at the very least in cloth.

When one tries to populate this scene the mind settles too easily on the agreeable images of du Maurier. His social types are so very familiar: the tall military Adonis of the ballroom, the infinitely distinguished diplomats, professors, actors, bishops, and Royal Academicians, the superbly caddish cads, the abundant bevy of beauties. The temptation is all the greater because du Maurier was a not infrequent guest at Hyde Park Gate and could well have found some of his models in Julia Stephen's drawing-room—not the diplomats, actors, bishops, guardsmen and cads—but the intellectuals, the beauties of the family and Leslie himself—it is possible to discover them all in the pages of *Punch*, which did indeed hold a flattering mirror to their class. But it is a too flattering glass; du Maurier's pencil beautifies or caricatures. Neither is that other image of 'the Cimabue Browns' anything like the realities that Virginia might have known in her youth. On the maternal side her aunts were indeed 'aesthetic'; they did not follow the fashions of the day at all closely; but the peacock feathers and sunflowers of du Maurier's aesthetes, if they existed at all, would not have been found at Hyde Park Gate. As for the Stephen ladies, they, I suspect, were simply dowdy.

When the aesthetic movement of the 'eighties and 'nineties began to exert its influence Virginia's parents were too old to be affected by it. The wit, the brilliance, the naughtiness and the mysticism of the late century passed them by; they were the characteristics of a very different social group. This is particularly true of Leslie, whose second marriage had been made comparatively late in life and who looked always to the past, to the social and intellectual ideas of the mid-century.

Considered *en masse* such a party would have been respectable rather than fashionable. To consider them in any other way is hard. Certainly it would be wearisome to provide a catalogue of individuals but I will mention two who may be thought of as representing opposing elements. Fitzjames Stephen, Leslie's elder brother, a big, solid man, tightly buttoned into a frock coat and armed with a massive intellect, may be considered the outstanding representative of the Stephen family. It was a family which, in a century, had risen from very humble origins to positions of power in the British and Australian legal systems. Fitzjames himself was a lawyer, formidable in cross-examination and terrible when, as a hanging judge, he sat upon the bench. He was not only a forensic and political theorist but a man of letters, and in this at least he resembled Anne Thackeray Ritchie. She was the novelist's elder daughter, her sister Minny had been Leslie's first wife and she was herself the author of a number of novels which radiate sweetness, light and confused thought (Virginia drew her portrait as Mrs Hilbery in *Night and Day*). In conversation she was vague, charming, and optimistic to the point of absurdity and quite overwhelming in the gaiety of her enthusiasms. She knew 'everybody' in the world of letters and found just the kind of qualities that she valued in the lovely, benevolent, impetuous and imperious daughters of James Pattle, Virginia's great-grandfather, who with their abundant families formed a large section of the society in which the Stephens lived. Virginia had seven first cousins on the Stephen side of the family and sixteen on the Pattle side. Amongst these maternal relations we may notice Countess Somers, who had been Virginia Pattle, the most beautiful of the sisters—'Elgin marbles with dark eyes' Ruskin called them. Lady Somers left her class by marrying an aristocrat; she also married both her daughters to the sons of Dukes and in so doing helps to define the limits of what was otherwise a decidedly middle-class group.

As Victorian society went the Stephens, their friends and their relations were not socially compact, they wandered fairly easily over an extensive field of acquaintance. But there were frontiers. It is probable that the Duchess of Bedford, Lady Somers' daughter, would have been slightly out of place at a party at No. 22 Hyde Park Gate; one imagines that she would have been a little too 'good' for her company. Her sister Lady Henry Somerset, having, although perfectly innocent, been at the centre of a sexual scandal, presented a more serious social problem, for there were a great many people of her own class who refused to speak to Lady Henry. At the opposite end of the community one of Julia Stephen's nieces had married a farmer's son and he too would have been hard to include in a Kensington party.

These then were the extremes. Between them, as I have said, there would have been no remarkable barriers. The important Stephen contingent was different but not radically different from Mrs Ritchie and her numerous connections. They were all middle class, they were all very literate. The Stephens all wrote books and so did many of their friends. Meredith, Henry James, J. R. Lowell (Virginia's godfather) were frequent visitors at 22 Hyde Park Gate or at Talland House, St Ives, and there they might have found Hardy, Gosse, Froude and also many other Victorian men of letters whose names are now forgotten. The Stephens had little to do with politics, although in his youth Leslie had been an ardent supporter of his friend Henry Fawcett; John Morley was always a close friend, but Morley was as much concerned with literature as with the Liberal Party. Even Charles Booth, their only link with the world of industry, was the author of books on social questions. The Pattle connection brought with it an interest in the fine arts of which the Stephens knew nothing; Watts and Val Prinsep (Julia Stephen's cousin), the Holman Hunts and the Burne-Joneses were fairly close friends.

At Mrs Stephen's Sunday Afternoons, which were small, unambitious social gatherings, there would have been very few guests who would have missed a quotation from Dr Johnson, from Shelley or from La Rochefoucauld; there would have been even fewer guests who had ever heard the name of an impressionist painter.

By our standards their manners were formal. 'Damnation' would have been the strongest imaginable expletive in mixed company. The coarser passages of Swift and Sterne would have been perfectly familiar to Leslie Stephen, but he could no more have quoted them than he could have alluded to a visit to the lavatory. He was a man who was ready to lead a revolution against God, who would not have been afraid of political innovations, but who so completely accepted the conventions and prohibitions of his age and class that he was ready to regard them almost as laws of nature. In this he was not peculiar, only a little old-fashioned, for it was a sedate, elderly atmosphere in which Virginia was reared and this no doubt magnified the distance that she was to discover between herself and her parents' generation. But even when one allows for this distortion, the difference between Kensington—and in that term we may include the great majority of Virginia's coevals—and Bloomsbury is immense. The manners, the moral assumptions, the language of Bloomsbury in 1910 were not really very unlike that of the permissive generation of our own times; it was of course different but it was not radically different. Or, to put the matter in another way, the Kensington of 1900 would hardly have been more horrified by us than it was by the Bloomsbury of 1910. If it be possible to fix a date for such things then it is in that year that the modern world, considered as an ethical, social or aesthetic entity, may be said to have been created, but created within a very restricted circle.

The move from Kensington to Bloomsbury was a social as well as a geographical departure. It was a departure from a 'good' to a bad address, from social propriety to social heterodoxy. I have little doubt that it was Vanessa Stephen who was the prime mover in this exodus; she was always the enemy of propriety. At 46 Gordon Square, in a young and un-chaperoned household, she hoped to achieve liberty. Her hope came true.

The liberties which the Stephen children and their friends took were not, at the outset at all events, very outrageous. Certainly they would not seem so today. But almost immediately they elicited a startled murmur of disapproval. The Stephen girls were failing to cultivate the social graces, they did not dress or behave in a decorous manner, their days were given to the desk and the easel, they largely neglected the duty of accepting or dispensing tea, of leaving cards, of paying calls or even of dressing for dinner. Family obligations were ignored, social opportunities missed, not only were there no chaperones and no small talk but there were grave positive evils in the form of quite ineligible young men and conversation on quite unsuitable topics. Painters of dubious reputation and their women, whose reputations were not even dubious, were received in Vanessa's drawing-room and, as the first decade of the century ended, rumours of a more horrifying nature began to circulate: coarse words, wholly unmentionable subjects and utterly abandoned behaviour were, it was said, of common occurrence at 46 Gordon Square. It was hardly a surprise when these same young iconoclasts played a disrespectful prac-tical joke on the Royal Navy, affected an admiration for the daubs of Cézanne, and sneered at the patriotic emotions of a nation at war. These of course were later developments, but almost from the first, Kensington was sure that the Stephen children had forgotten their breeding and there were some who expressed their resentment in the most direct form of social hostility known to them, 'the cut direct'.

To Vanessa this seemed the crowning mercy. It meant that all pretence at intercourse might be abandoned. To her it appeared that there was nothing to be said for the old way of life in which they had been brought up. It was stuffy, dull, pompous and limited; the jokes were as heavy as the furniture and the list of things that a girl might not discuss was even longer and more discouraging than the list of things that she was expected to do. Bored by their manners and revolted by their morality she could dismiss even the aesthetic values of the tribe, finding in their admiration for Watts and the pre-Raphaelites the trivial enthusiasms and dangerous sentimentality of a vanished epoch.

Virginia agreed, but she did not agree entirely. She was much slower to break with Kensington, in fact with her there never was a complete break. She was more attached to her father's memory, much more inclined to look for that which was good in the ethos of their youth. She practised an art less dramatic in its revolutions than the art of painting; Henry James and Meredith were not to be dismissed so easily as the deities of Ruskin's Pantheon, nor was there for her, as for Vanessa, a deeply impressive revolutionary tradition to which she could turn.

Moreover I think that it seemed to Virginia that there was a case to be made even for the formalities and restraints of Kensington. The cult of the family might lead to excesses but it was not wholly bad; there was a real virtue in that unquestioning solidarity of the clan. The Stephen devotion to truth and clarity might take an arid legal form, but it had also a certain austere beauty; the proconsular character of the family had also its admirable and its romantic side.

No less beautiful, heroic indeed, was the service of those vestals of the tea urn. The long tedium of a life devoted to courtesy, the constant polite endeavour to soothe the vanity, repair the composure and ensure the comfort of guests—usually male guests, who arrogantly took such endeavours for granted—might be futile but it was also touching. Virginia was glad that she had finally and successfully murdered the 'angel in the house'; her art left no room for angelic ministrations. But she was glad also that she and Vanessa had received a training in civility.

Kensington was a region from which she could make occasional raids upon another territory which may perhaps be described as 'Mayfair'. She never seems to have sought out or been in any serious way concerned with her ducal relations but, through Violet Dickinson whom she loved and Kitty Maxse whom she did not love, she did get to know the Marchioness of Bath and her daughters, Lady Beatrice Thynne and Lady Cromer, and some of their friends and relations and there, amongst people who needed no social assurance, who were above the gentilities of Kensington, she was able to enjoy a freer, less stuffy atmosphere. Theirs was a society which permitted eccentricity to flourish and with it a refreshing sincerity. Apart from Violet Dickinson, Virginia's chief attachment here was to

Lady Robert Cecil, for she was seriously engaged in and loved the art of writing.

She had indeed a very catholic collection of friends, for in addition to Bloomsbury and Kensington and Mayfair there were several intermediate figures who can hardly be classified. Such were: Janet Case who had taught Virginia Greek and became a lasting friend; Miss Sheepshanks who had enlisted her to teach working men and women at Morley College; Hilton Young, the son of an old friend of Leslie's but more than half infected by the heterodoxies of his generation; and above all Lady Ottoline Morrell who herself lived in a social world as various as that of Virginia. Though obviously very unlike the Cecils and the Thynnes, she had something of the same disregard for the minor social conventions and had in the highest degree that capacity to behave oddly, but at the same time with natural dignity and even with grandeur, which may fairly be called aristocratic. Ottoline lived in many worlds and was, for a time, influential in Bloomsbury. She made it more worldly or, as Virginia put it: 'filled the place with lustre and illusion'.

Exactly the opposite tendency was represented by a younger set, almost a second generation of Bloomsbury, for it was also largely derived from the intellectual middle class and from Cambridge. Rupert Brooke, Ka Cox, Frances Darwin, Jacques Raverat, Brynhild, Margery, Daphne and Noel Olivier, shared many of the tastes and ideas of Virginia's generation; but they were much less interested in the ethical doctrines of G. E. Moore and in the Post-Impressionists; they were much more concerned with politics, more strenuous, more uninhibited. These Neo-Pagans delighted in physical exercise, in the simple pleasures of the countryside and in poetry. Rupert Brooke stood at the centre of this group and, when he left to fight in the war and died at the beginning of the Dardanelles campaign, Neo-Paganism seemed to die with him. But several of its components, and especially Ka Cox, who had cared for Virginia in her madness, remained as friends.

Thus the circle to which Leonard was introduced when he married was sufficiently heterogeneous. Many of Virginia's friends were already his; he had belonged to the original nucleus at Cambridge from which Bloomsbury grew. He returned from Ceylon to find a different society, one in which painting had become important as it had not been important at Cambridge, in which Clive Bell played a larger and more central role, and which had been augmented by Roger Fry and Duncan Grant. Leonard himself had to introduce his wife to the Woolf family. Virginia found them strange and very foreign; they must be alluded to because they played an important part in her life, but the outsider speaks with diffidence. The impression that one gained from her was of a family with few friends, or at least there were few known to her; there were a great many brothers and sisters dominated by Leonard's mother, a woman capable of heroism but usually perceived as timorous and sentimental, continually demanding proofs of affection from her children and, I think, receiving them. Leonard, who was clearly a rebel and determined to escape from this matriarchy, was at the same time conscientious in his performance of what he saw as his filial duties—too conscientious for Virginia; and the claims of the Woolfs (like the claims of Virginia's family) were a cause of some dissension in the home.

> Leonard Woolf . . . is the son-in-law of our old friend Leslie Stephen, having married Virginia. I have never had any communication with him . . . a perverse, partially educated alien German, who has thrown in his lot violently with Bolshevism and Mr Joyce's "Ulysses" and "the great sexual emancipation" and all the rest of the nasty fads of the hour. It is no use for us to strive with such a man. He would only redouble his sarcasms and gibes. What he hates in R.L.S. [Robert Louis Stevenson] is radically what we love—the refinement, the delicacy, the beauty. You cannot argue with a type like that. You can only let it pass by, and, on the next possible occasion, say once more that R. L. S. was a beautiful writer and a beautiful soul.*

Thus Gosse, writing to Sidney Colvin in 1924. He exhibits very nicely the difference between two generations of literary men, but his letter is also interesting because it contains so much misinformation. This is all the more remarkable because, by 1924, Bloomsbury had begun to make its weight felt in the republic of letters and elsewhere. Ten years earlier such ignorance would have been very natural, for at that time, the time when this diary begins, Bloomsbury was almost a non-entity. E. M. Forster was the only writer of the group to have established a reputation and Forster stood rather at the confines of Bloomsbury. Lytton Strachey, like Virginia, had written reviews; his only book was a useful but hardly an earth-shaking guide to French literature. Desmond MacCarthy was also a journalist. Everyone had expected that he would write a great novel, but somehow it never got written and his friends were beginning to think that it never would. As for Saxon Sydney-Turner he was, even more clearly, taking a road which would lead him away from worldly success; from his desk in the Treasury he produced minutes which were models of all that a minute should be, but he did not produce decisions; his life was increasingly devoted to obscure intellectual parlour games. Maynard Keynes was also in the Treasury and, as they say, 'a coming man', although nobody at that time could foresee how conspicuously and how scandalously he would arrive. Virginia's brother Adrian had married Karin Costelloe, a marriage which neither of his sisters welcomed and he,

* National Library of Scotland, MS 3355, ff 56-7. I am indebted to Mr Alan Bell for calling my attention to this letter.

like Saxon, seemed to be in search of obscurity rather than of fame. In fact he had not yet discovered a profession which suited him.

In the area of the fine arts Bloomsbury had indeed begun to make its mark, although Vanessa was practically unknown as a painter and had never had a one-man show. Clive, with whom she could barely be said to be living but who remained and always was to remain an affectionate friend, had caused a considerable stir by publishing *Art*, an attempt to give systematic expression to aesthetic formalism (this was in 1914), and two years previously he had helped to organise the second Post-Impressionist Exhibition; he was, by the outbreak of war, becoming known as a critic. Roger Fry was his senior and to some extent his mentor. Fry had indeed made a name for himself before the first Post-Impressionist Exhibition startled London in the last weeks of 1910. He had since then been Vanessa's lover and was now, very slowly, learning to live without her and at the same time, like Clive, becoming her friend. Duncan Grant, who had replaced him in Vanessa's affections, was just beginning that long professional and emotional partnership which was to endure while she lived; as an artist he was highly valued by the small circle which knew his work, but he too had attracted no large degree of public attention.

It has to be remembered that although Fry was a central figure in the avant-garde revolt of the years 1910-1914 and had, with some éclat, created the Omega Workshops, he and his friends in Bloomsbury were but one element in a wider movement, and perhaps the greatest publicity went elsewhere. It is significant that the word 'futurist' was generally used to describe all forms of pictorial modernism in this country and that this remained the case long after Futurism, Vorticism and the abstract phase of Bloomsbury painting had come to an end in the war.

The people whom we call 'Bloomsbury' were those whom Virginia knew and loved best. What kind of people were they? Certainly they were all intelligent, although the intelligence of Duncan Grant, Vanessa Bell or indeed of Virginia herself had none of the lightning celerity which made the mind of Maynard Keynes so dazzling, nor had it much in common with the forceful and erudite but sometimes slow and erring wisdom of Roger Fry. It cannot even be said that they all enjoyed the pleasures of discussion: while Desmond and Maynard, Clive and Lytton and Roger would argue happily about almost any topic that was not utterly trivial, Duncan would make drawings and Vanessa as often as not would fall asleep. Virginia indeed affected, not quite seriously, to consider the painters as little better than cretins and quite desperately ignorant. But she would not, in cold sobriety of spirit, have accused any of her Bloomsbury friends of stupidity. In all she found a liveliness of mind, a felicity of humour, which depended upon some kind of intellectual strength; in all there was a robust sense of balance which led them to value intelligence. They felt that the emotions should never be allowed to govern reason, so that now, with the catastrophe of war upon them and despite the fact that they held a great variety of views and were at some points diametrically opposed, they could none of them admit, as did some of their friends, that 'this is something about which I will not argue. I feel too deeply to listen to reason. I love, I hate, and I will not discuss.' In Bloomsbury there had always to be the possibility of discussion.

The obverse of this respect for the intellect was a certain lack of respect for customary morals, traditional wisdom and popular enthusiasm, an almost instinctive distrust for the passions of the multitude, which readers of this diary will notice in several entries when Virginia finds herself confronted by some large demonstration of national joy, grief, or courage.

And yet I think it may fairly be argued that the cohesive power of Bloomsbury had moral rather than intellectual origins. Virginia, Vanessa, Clive, Saxon and Lytton were united in friendship, kinship and love; it was their mutual affection which provided the solid nucleus around which Bloomsbury grew. That affection received its unbreakable astriction from a common sorrow, the death of Thoby Stephen in 1906; it was at this time that Vanessa and Virginia, who had only too much experience of the maudlin formalities of Victorian grief, discovered in these brilliant, argumentative, theory-spinning young men from Cambridge a depth of feeling which did not need to be advertised by black crape or high sentiments. The strength of their union was not, in the end, based upon a similarity of ideas and outlook. It was based on affection.

The solidarity of Bloomsbury was strong enough to withstand a great deal: the furies of jealousy and thwarted lust, the almost sadistic tedium of Saxon's conversation, the back-biting and fault finding, the insincerities and teasing of literary rivals, all the jars and gibes that intelligent and sensitive people can inflict upon one another. And yet, in the end the friendships always did survive. Some members of the group might wander away from the rest or become deeply involved in exogamous adventures; but there was never a break, never a lasting quarrel. The friends remained friends for as long as they lived.

At the time when this diary opens Bloomsbury was a misnomer. The old propinquity was gone, there was no more pleasant easy visiting between neighbours. Maynard still lived in what had been the Bells' house at 46 Gordon Square, but Vanessa was away in the country for most of the time and Duncan with her. Lytton was also usually out of London; Ottoline retired from Bedford Square to her country house at Garsington; there she was joined by Clive and some other pacifists. Virginia herself was living very quietly in Richmond.

The persistence of old friendships would draw them together again, Bloomsbury would be reformed, but with a new aspect. Meanwhile Virginia was living in a kind of vacuum and was still barely recovered from her bout of insanity. Since she did appear to be getting well again and was able to work and to enjoy Leonard's company she may be considered happy. But in other ways her state was not enviable; she had reached middle life without any great achievement to her credit, and all around her were younger people rapidly advancing towards fame. She was poorer than she had ever been. She almost certainly knew that her mental health was precarious. She had hardly begun to find the fictional form that suited her, the great literary adventure of her life still lay unseen in the future, and she awaited with dreadful anxiety the publication of her first novel.

QUENTIN BELL

1915

1915

This part of Virginia Woolf's diary is a kind of prelude to the main work. After almost six weeks of conscientious reporting, the diary ends. Why she began this record we do not know; but we do know why she stopped: from the middle of February she plunged into madness. This was the second phase of her longest breakdown, an aggressive and violent period very different from the melancholic and suicidal mania which had preceded it in the latter half of 1913. This 'Prelude' therefore describes the end of a fair interval between two fearful tempests of lunacy.

Virginia's first novel The Voyage Out *had been accepted in March 1913; its publication was delayed until March 1915. She only mentions it once, but it would not be wise to suppose that it was absent from her thoughts; the knowledge that it was so soon to appear may well have been the cause of her renewed insanity.*

This is Diary I (see Appendix 1); each entry is dated on a small oval, lozenge-shaped or circular label gummed to the top of the page; the first eleven dates are typewritten.

Friday 1 January

To start this diary rightly, it should begin on the last day of the old year, when, at breakfast, I received a letter from Mrs Hallett. She said that she had had to dismiss Lily at a moments notice, owing to her misbehaviour.[1] We naturally supposed that a certain kind of misbehaviour was meant; a married gardener, I hazarded. Our speculations made us both uncomfortable all day. Now this morning I hear from Lily herself. She writes, very calmly, that she left because Mrs Hallett was 'insulting' to her; having been given a day & nights holiday, she came back at 8.30 A.M. 'not early enough'. What is the truth? This, I guess: Mrs H. is an old angry woman, meticulous, indeed as we knew tyrannical, about her servants; & Lily honestly meant no wrong. But I have written for particulars —another lady wanting a character at once. Then I had to write to Mrs Waterlow about the chimney sweeping charges foisted on us, such a

1. Lily, a simple-hearted Sussex girl who had had a baby, was house-parlourmaid to the Woolfs at Asheham in 1914, and then went, with a 'character' from VW, to work for Mrs Hallett. She returned to the Woolfs when they moved to Hogarth House in March 1915, but left voluntarily and contritely after being surprised with a soldier in the kitchen. See *III LW*, 173.

letter as comes naturally to the strong character, but not to the weak.[2] And then we tramped to the Co-ops. in rain & cold to protest against their bookkeeping.[3] Manager a bored languid young man, repeating rather than defending himself. Half way home we heard "British warship . . . British warship" & found that the Formidable has been sunk in the channel.[4] We were kept awake last night by New Year Bells. At first I thought they were ringing for a victory.

Saturday 2 January

This is the kind of day which if it were possible to choose an altogether average sample of our life, I should select. We breakfast; I interview Mrs Le Grys.[5] She complains of the huge Belgian appetites, & their preference for food fried in butter. "They never *give* one anything" she remarked. The Count, taking Xmas dinner with them, insisted, after Pork & Turkey, that he wanted a third meat. Therefore Mrs Le G. hopes that the war will soon be over. If they eat thus in their exile, how must they eat at home, she wonders? After this, L. & I both settle down to our scribbling. He finishes his Folk Story review, & I do about 4 pages of poor Effie's story;[6] we lunch; & read the papers, agree that there is no news. I read Guy Mannering upstairs for 20 minutes;[7] & then we take Max [a dog] for a walk. Halfway up to the Bridge, we found ourselves cut off by the river, which rose visibly, with a little ebb & flow, like the pulse of a heart. Indeed, the road we had come along was crossed, after 5 minutes, by a stream several inches deep.[8] One of the queer things about the suburbs is that the vilest little red villas are always let, & that not one of them has an open window, or an uncurtained window. I expect that people take a pride in their curtains, & there is great rivalry among neighbours. One house had curtains of yellow silk, striped with lace insertion. The rooms

2. Helen Margery Waterlow, *née* Eckhard (1883-1973), in 1913 married Sydney Waterlow (see January 1915, n 15) as his second wife. They had rented Asheham from the Woolfs from mid-October 1914; their tenancy was extended to July 1915.
3. The Richmond branch of the retail stores operated by the Co-operative Society.
4. The British battleship HMS *Formidable* was torpedoed by a German submarine early on New Year's morning, with a loss of some 600 lives.
5. The Woolfs' Belgian landlady at 17 The Green, Richmond, where they occupied furnished rooms from October 1914 until March 1915.
6. LW's review of *Village Folk Tales of Ceylon*, vols II and III, collected and translated by H. Parker, appeared in the *TLS*, 7 January 1915. 'Poor Effie's story' was to become *Night and Day*, and Effie, Katherine (see below, 16 January 1915, n 54).
7. By Sir Walter Scott, published 1815.
8. The Thames is tidal from its mouth to Teddington lock, upstream from Richmond; a conjunction of spring tides and exceptionally heavy rainfall could produce flooding.

inside must be in semi-darkness; & I suppose rank with the smell of meat & human beings. I believe that being curtained is a mark of respectability —Sophie used to insist upon it.[9] And then I did my marketing. Saturday night is the great buying night; & some counters are besieged by three rows of women. I always choose the empty shops, where I suppose, one pays $\frac{1}{2}$[d] a lb. more. And then we had tea, & honey & cream; & now L. is typewriting his article; & we shall read all the evening & go to bed.

Sunday 3 January

It is strange how old traditions, so long buried as one thinks, suddenly crop up again. At Hyde Park Gate we used to set apart Sunday morning for cleaning the silver table.[10] Here I find myself keeping Sunday morning for odd jobs—typewriting it was today—& tidying the room—& doing accounts which are very complicated this week. I have 3 little bags of coppers, which each owe the other something. We went to a concert at the Queen's Hall, in the afternoon.[11] Considering that my ears have been pure of music for some weeks, I think patriotism is a base emotion. By this I mean (I am writing in haste, expecting Flora to dinner) that they played a national Anthem & a Hymn, & all I could feel was the entire absence of emotion in myself & everyone else. If the British spoke openly about W.C's, & copulation, then they might be stirred by universal emotions. As it is, an appeal to feel together is hopelessly muddled by intervening greatcoats & fur coats. I begin to loathe my kind, principally from looking at their faces in the tube. Really, raw red beef & silver herrings give me more pleasure to look upon. But then I was kept standing 40 minutes at Charing X Station, & so got home late, & missed Duncan who came here.[12] Moreover, London on a Sunday night now,

9. Sophia Farrell (c. 1861-1942), cook to the Stephen and related families from the 'eighties onwards. See unpublished TSS by VW, MHP, Sussex, MH/A 13d and e.

10. 13 Hyde Park Gate, Kensington (which became no. 22 in 1884), was VW's birthplace and her family home, with some sixteen others including servants, until the death of her father Sir Leslie Stephen in 1904.

11. The Queen's Hall, Langham Place (destroyed by bombs in 1941), was London's principal concert hall. As was customary, the concert opened with the National Anthem; it was followed by 'O God our Strength', a hymn by the conductor, Sir Henry Wood, and works by Bach, Handel, Beethoven and Wagner.

12. Duncan James Corrowr Grant (1885-1978), painter, only child of Major Bartle Grant whose sister was Lady Strachey; Duncan spent much of his youth with the Strachey family. VW probably met him in Paris in 1907 with the Bells. He became their neighbour when she and her brother lived in Fitzroy Square, and in 1911 an occupant of their house in Brunswick Square. He had for some time been Vanessa Bell's lover; they were companions until her death in 1961. For VW's letter of exasperation and regret at missing him on this occasion, see II VW Letters, no. 717.

with all its electric globes half muffled in blue paint, is the most dismal of places. There are long mud coloured streets, & just enough daylight & insufficient electric light, to see the naked sky, which is inexpressibly cold & flat.*

*The Times today has an article upon the "Stars of London"—"We may gain from them a serviceable impulse to that steady concentration on enduring issues of which stars are a true symbol, & the glare of London is not". So be it. (5th Jan).[13]

Monday 4 January

I do not like the Jewish voice; I do not like the Jewish laugh: otherwise I think (in Saxon's phrase) there is something to be said for Flora Woolf.[14] She can typewrite, do shorthand, sing, play chess, write stories which are sometimes accepted, & she earns 30/ a week as the secretary of the Principal of the Scottish Church in London. And in doing these various arts she will keep lively till a great old age, like a man playing with five billiard balls.

The outside world burst in upon us with a clamour this morning. 1. I had a letter from Mrs Hallett. 2. I had a letter from Lily. 3. L. had a document from Sydney Waterlow.[15] According to Mrs Hallett, Lily hid a soldier in the Butler's pantry; she also met soldiers at the gates; & thus Mrs Hallett's house got a bad name in the village, besides which Mrs Hallett herself was alarmed 'there being ladies only in the house'. Lily confesses merely to one brother, but adds that Mrs H. is very ill, as well as very old. As for Sydney's letter—I am so sick of it that I can't describe it. The house was dirty—4 people scrubbing for a fortnight only succeeded in making it tolerable; & so & so on—all of which would have been suffered in silence but for my note. So I wrote to him, & I wrote to Lily—& after spending some time in phrasing virtuous sentiments nobly, I see clearly how official skins grow thick & shiny. To Lily I said that she must promise to behave better, if I gave her another character—for I am

13. The Times, 5 January 1915, p. 9, 'Stars in London'.
14. Flora Woolf (1886-1975), the youngest of LW's three sisters. Saxon Sydney-Turner was a long-standing friend of both VW and LW. See below, 14 October 1917, n 17.
15. Sydney Philip Perigal Waterlow (1878-1944), scholar of Eton and Trinity College, Cambridge. In 1900 he entered the Diplomatic Service, and served in Washington. In 1905 he resigned, but on the outbreak of war was re-employed by the Foreign Office on a temporary basis; he was re-appointed in 1920 after assisting at the Paris Peace Conference, and finally retired in 1939 as British Minister in Athens and KCMG. VW met him through the Clive Bells, probably in 1910; in 1911 after the breakdown of his first marriage, he proposed to her. He married Margery Eckhard (see above, 1 January 1915, n 2) in 1913.

sure poor Mrs Hallett & her trembling old sister heard soldier voices whenever there was a wind in the laurels. Philip came after luncheon, having 4
days leave.[16] He is sick to death of soldiering—told us tales of military
stupidity which pass belief. They found a man guilty of desertion the other
day & sentenced him; & then discovered that the man did not exist. The
Colonel says "I like well dressed young men—gentlemen" & gets rid of
recruits who sink below this level. In addition to this, the demand for cavalry at the front is exhausted, so that probably they will stay at Colchester
for ever. Another dark, rainy day. An aeroplane passed overhead.

Tuesday 5 January

I had a letter this morning from Nessa, who calls Mrs Waterlow a
German hausfrau, & advises us not to pay a penny— Cleanliness is a
fetish not to be worshipped, she says.[17] Certainly, neither of us do worship it; I suppose Mrs W. ran about with a duster, & dabbed her finger
under beds. I can imagine the list of discoveries she gave Sydney, sitting
smoking over his philosophy, & how she cursed that dreadful slut
Virginia Woolf. At the same time, it is a point of honour among servants
to find the house they go into filthy, & to leave it bright as a pin. But
enough of Waterlows & their slop pails. We worked as usual: as usual it
rained. After lunch we took the air in the Old Deer Park, & marked by a
line of straw how high the river had been; & how a great tree had fallen
across the towing path, crushing the railing beneath it. Three bodies were
seen yesterday swiftly coursing downstream at Teddington. Does the
weather prompt suicide? The Times has a queer article upon a railway
smash, in which it says that the war has taught us a proper sense of proportion with respect to human life.[18] I have always thought we priced it
absurdly high; but I never thought the Times would say so. L. went off

16. Philip Sidney Woolf (1889-1965), youngest of LW's five brothers, was, with Cecil
    the next youngest, serving with the Royal Hussars. He was wounded and his
    brother killed by the same shell at the Battle of Cambrai in November 1917. (See
    below, 3 December 1917.) He had wished to be a painter, but after the war became
    manager of the Waddesdon Estate for James de Rothschild, a cousin by marriage.
17. Vanessa Bell, née Stephen (1879-1961), painter, VW's elder sister and, after LW,
    the most important person in her life. She married Clive Bell in 1907, but the
    marriage was now a matter of convenience and friendship; from about 1914 and
    until her death she was, in terms of sentiment, the wife of Duncan Grant. A curri-
    culum vitae and brief bibliography is contained in the catalogue of the Arts Council
    Exhibition: *Vanessa Bell: a Memorial Exhibition of Paintings*, 1964, with intro-
    duction by Ronald Pickvance; see also S. P. Rosenbaum, *The Bloomsbury Group*,
    1975, p. 420.
18. On the morning of 1 January 1915 a local train at Ilford, Essex, was cut in two by
    an express from Clacton; ten people were killed and over thirty injured. See *The
    Times* leader, 5 January 1915.

to Hampstead to give the first of his lectures to the Women's Guild.[19] He did not seem nervous: he is speaking at this moment. We rather think that old Mr Davies is dying—but I have an idea he'll resist for years to come, although he wants to die, & his life prevents Margaret from much work.[20] I bought my fish & meat in the High Street—a degrading but rather amusing business. I dislike the sight of women shopping. They take it so seriously. Then I got a ticket in the Library, & saw all the shabby clerks & dressmakers thumbing illustrated papers, like very battered bees on very battered flowers. At least they are warm & dry: & it rains again today. The Belgians downstairs are playing cards with some friends, & talk—talk—talk—while their country is destroyed. After all, they have nothing else to do—

Wednesday 6 January

The Waterlows again: Lily again. Mrs W. writes to Leonard this time, about the oven, & ends by being very much distressed to think we are annoyed—seeing how delightful they find Asheham. It is a queer thing that both the ladies in this correspondence write to both the gentlemen—feeling instinctively, I believe, that if they wrote to each other, the whole affair would become much more acid. Lily's letter continues the story of the hidden soldier. It brings her very clearly before me, with her charming, stupid, doglike eyes, quite incapable of hurting a fly or thinking a coarse thought, & yet bound eternally to suffer for the sins of stronger characters. In this case, she was at the mercy of a parlourmaid, who invited the soldiers, & Lily had neither the strength of mind to be rude to them when they came, nor to 'tell tales of a fellow servant'. 'I would rather do anything than that'—& that, I imagine, was how she had her baby too. Anyhow, I have 'spoken' for her again, & she has promised to have no more to do with soldiers. L. went off at 10 A.M. to give his second lecture at Hampstead. The first was a great success, as I knew it would be. He finds the women much more intelligent than the men; in some ways

19. The Women's Co-operative Guild, founded in 1883, was a self-governing body within the Co-operative movement. Its headquarters were at 28 Church Row, Hampstead. For VW's impressions of the Guild, see her introductory letter to *Life As We Have Known It*, 1931 (Kp B11).

20. Margaret Caroline Llewelyn Davies (1861-1944); Girton College, Cambridge, 1881-83; General Secretary of the Women's Co-operative Guild, 1889-1921. Only daughter of the Rev. John Llewelyn Davies (1826-1916), theologian, Christian Socialist, and early supporter of Co-operative and Women's movements, successively Rector of Christ Church, Marylebone, and Vicar of Kirkby Lonsdale. He had for a time tutored VW's father Leslie Stephen before the latter entered Cambridge University. Of his six sons two, Theodore and Crompton, were Apostles. For the last eight years of his life he lived in Hampstead with his daughter.

too intelligent, & apt on that account, not to see the real point. He has another to give this afternoon, so he is staying up at Hampstead, lunching with Lilian, & perhaps seeing Janet.[21] No one except a very modest person would treat these working women, & Lilian & Janet & Margaret, as he does. Clive, or indeed any other clever young man, would give himself airs; & however much he admired them pretend that he didn't.[22]

I wrote all the morning, with infinite pleasure, which is queer, because I know all the time that there is no reason to be pleased with what I write, & that in 6 weeks or even days, I shall hate it. Then I went to London, & asked at Grays Inn about Chambers.[23] They had a set vacant; & I at once envisaged all sorts of charms, & let myself into them with a thrill of excitement. But they would be perfect for one, & impossible for two. There are 2 perfect rooms, looking over the gardens; & that is about all. Grays Inn Road thunders behind one. Next I saw a flat in Bedford Row, which promised divinely, but on asking at the agents, was told they had just been instructed to let it furnished only— And now, of course, I am convinced that there is no flat in London to equal it! I could wander about the dusky streets in Holborn & Bloomsbury for hours. The things one sees— & guesses at—the tumult & riot & busyness of it all— Crowded streets are the only places, too, that ever make me what-in-the-case-of-another-one-might-call think. Now I have to decide whether I shall go up again, to a party at Gordon Sqre, where the Aranyis are playing.[24] On the one

21. Lilian Harris (d. 1949) from Kirkby Lonsdale, friend and companion of Margaret Llewelyn Davies (see above, 5 January 1915, n 20), Cashier (1893), then Assistant-Secretary (1901-21) of the Women's Co-operative Guild. In VW's impressions of that body (see above, 5 January 1915, n 19) she figures as Janet Erskine. Janet Elizabeth Case (1862-1937), the youngest of six sisters and a contemporary of Margaret Llewelyn Davies at Girton College, Cambridge, was now living near her at 5 Windmill Hill, Hampstead, with her sister 'Emphie'. A classical scholar who had taught VW Greek from 1902 and had become a close friend, she was also an active supporter of women's, liberal, and pacifist causes.
22. Arthur Clive Heward Bell (1881-1964), art critic, married Vanessa Stephen in 1907 and, as VW's brother-in-law, played a notable part in her life, being at various times both her literary confidant and her flirt. At Trinity College, Cambridge, he was a close friend of VW's brother Thoby Stephen; both were interested not only in the things of the mind but in field sports; neither was an Apostle. Clive was now living at 46 Gordon Square, on affectionate but not on conjugal terms with Vanessa. See above, 5 January 1915, n 17.
23. The northernmost of the four great Inns of Court which housed the legal profession; it was sometimes possible for private individuals to rent residential chambers.
24. 46 Gordon Square, Bloomsbury, to which the four Stephens had moved after their father's death in 1904 and which, from 1907, was the home of the Clive Bells. The d'Aranyi sisters, Adila (1886-1962), Hortense (1887-1953), and Jelly (1893-1966), great-nieces of the renowned Hungarian violinist Joachim, were concert musicians who remained in England during the 1914-18 war.

hand, I shirk the dressing & the journey; on the other I know that with the first chink of light in the hall & chatter of voices I should become intoxicated, & determine that life held nothing comparable to a party. I should see beautiful people, & get a sensation of being on the highest crest of the biggest wave—right in the centre & swim of things. On the third & final hand, the evenings reading by the fire here—reading Michelet & The Idiot, & smoking & talking to L. in what stands for slippers & dressing gown—are heavenly too.[25] And as he won't urge me to go, I know very well that I shant. Besides, there is vanity: I have no clothes to go in.

Thursday 7 January

No—we didn't go to the Gordon Sqre party. Leonard got back too late, & it rained; & really, we didn't want to go. The lectures were a great success. One old lady told Leonard that they should consider him a personal friend for life; another said that he was the only gentleman who spoke so that working women could understand. He explained Bills of Exchange & so on for an hour; & then answered questions, which again, were amazingly intelligent. I started off after lunch today, first to go to the Foundling Hospital & ask whether they would let us have Brunswick Square—or half the house; then to the Omega to buy Janet a shawl, & then to tea with Janet.[26] Mr Chubb opened the door to me at the Hospital.[27] He was sitting at a writing table in a very warm comfortable room, looking on to the garden; while a clerk drew plans of houses on a very high desk. Mr Chubb is growing fat. He recognised me & became immediately extremely courteous. Brunswick Sqre is already practically let to a retired Ceylon Civil Servant, called Spence, who may however be willing to let the two upper floors, which would suit us very well. I became, of course, possessed with a passion to have Brunswick Square. Mr Chubb, who has infinite leisure, & likes conversation, discussed every possibility. He did not himself admire Adrian's frescoes, but said that most

25. In December 1914 VW had asked Clive Bell to lend her the first two volumes of Michelet's *Histoire de France* (see *II VW Letters*, no. 713); Constance Garnett's translation of Dostoevsky's *The Idiot*, 1913, inscribed 'V. from L.', is among the books from the Woolfs' Library now in the Library of Washington State University. (See *Holleyman*, MH II, p. 7.)

26. The Omega Workshops, 'Artist Decorators', 33 Fitzroy Square, were founded in 1913 by Roger Fry with the object of providing a source of income and a new field of activity for young artists.

27. The Foundling Hospital was a charitable foundation owning considerable property in Bloomsbury, including 38 Brunswick Square where VW had lived in 1911-12. Mr Chubb, the Hospital's Surveyor, also acted as its estate agent.

people do.[28] The Ceylon gentleman proposed to cover them with a curtain, being apparently of opinion that they were too good to destroy, though not nice to look upon. He is a bachelor, perhaps rather a crusty bachelor, once Chief of the Colombo Lunatic Asylum—[29] At this point a Secretary came in, also excessively polite when he heard my name. "Mrs Woolf certainly has a very strong claim to the house" he said. "And I myself don't think Spence is quite right"— "I do" Mr Chubb replied firmly "I've looked him up in the Medical Directory—besides, he seems all right." "He looks all right certainly" the secretary agreed, "but I don't know— However it wouldn't be playing the game to refuse at the eleventh hour." "The twelfth you may say" said Mr Chubb. At last I left, shaking hands all round, & having begged Mr Chubb to do his best & let us know. They advised me to see a house in Mecklenburgh Sqre, which I did. It is a vast place, with a great hall, a sweeping staircase; & we could have a flat at the top—the only objection being that Grays Inn Road is at the back— When I got out, it was raining. I walked to the Omega however & bought my stuff from a foolish young woman in a Post Impressionist tunic. I went to Hampstead, found some elderly lady there already, went to the station, in order to avoid tea with Emphie; & then was allowed up to Janet. She is in bed, & will have to stay in bed for weeks. Her nerves are thoroughly wrong. She can't read, or do anything—I can guess what she feels like—& how miserable she must be very often—especially since she is growing old, & Emphie must be wearisome with her repetitions, & general enthusiastic vagueness. & then, the fag end of life— Still she is trained to be brave, & so unselfish by nature that other people really interest her. We talked about Leonard, & Lily, & life in London & Hardy's poems which she can't re-read— Too melancholy & sordid—& the subjects not interesting enough. I don't agree. It grew late; & she suggested that I should dine there & go with L. to the Peace Debate at the Women's Guild. I couldn't face dinner, so I retreated to the Public Library. On the way I walked through one of the worst downpours I have ever been in. It was more like a shower bath than natural rain. My shoes squeaked so with wet as I walked up the Library that I was ashamed. Then I dined at a cabmans eating house—the only dining place, & very good. Coarse, but clean & sober. At 8 I met L. at 28 Church Row. The rooms are old white pannelled rooms; one was full of working women. It was a comfort (after reading more terrific letters of childbirth) to see how the women roar with

28. VW's younger brother (see below, 14 January 1915, n 48), had occupied the first floor rooms of their joint household at 38 Brunswick Square (now demolished) in 1911 and, with Duncan Grant, had decorated his sitting-room with life-sized nude figures of tennis players.

29. Dr John Buchan Spence, sometime Medical Superintendent, Colombo Asylum.

laughter, like schoolgirls.[30] Mr Hobson spoke[31]— It was very good—
The women impressive as usual—because they seem to feel, & to have
such a sense of responsibility. Another letter from Mrs Waterlow.

Friday 8 January

Sydney Waterlow came to lunch with us today 'to make sure' as he put
it 'that we had not quarrelled over these wretched matters'. We discussed
little else for the first hour & a half. My first letter had given him a sleepless night, he told us, though Mrs Waterlow in spite of pregnancy, slept
sound. As far as we could make out, Mrs W. acts & writes impulsively;
when Sydney bestirred himself to think, he was appalled to realise that
their behaviour was not ethically sound. He cogitated for long, devoted a
whole morning to his reply, & has taken the advice of several friends; who
happen to agree with him that chimneys are usually swept by landlords.
"But then we should have asked your leave—I entirely yield that point—
only" & so on & so on; all in the solid simple style, which is so like him.
His fat pink body always seems to me boneless & hairless like that of a
gigantic child; & his mind is the same. But there is a charm about him.
He & L. went for a walk. I went to Chancellors, to ask whether there was
any news of Hogarth.[32] At first the man said no. When I told him that we
might take a house in London, he at once confessed that he had twice seen
Mrs Wontner, the present tenant, & that she does not like the house. Is
this invented, &, if not, is there some good reason why she does not like
it? It seems likely that we shall have to choose between Brunswick &
Hogarth—unless both fail us. Sydney came back to tea, & told us how
Alice had been to see them, & how he had at once regretted her "as one
might regret a very fine walking-stick— She was so pretty & happy with
a great fat baby. The house was full of our furniture—like a house of
death to me."[33] But when I suggested that the present Mrs W. had been
uncomfortable he was amazed. "She isnt that sort of person at all" he said.
"She's perfectly sensible. . . . ." Still, if she saw Sydney coveting the
walking stick, I thought— Sydney replied that Marg. (as he calls her)

30. A selection of Letters entitled *Maternity: Letters from Working Women* was
 published in 1915 by G. Bell & Sons for the Women's Co-operative Guild as part
 of its campaign for a national scheme for maternity and infant care.
31. John Atkinson Hobson (1858-1940), humanist, economist and publicist, a noted
 supporter of the Union of Democratic Control, Women's Suffrage, and the League
 of Nations.
32. The Richmond estate agents acting for the owner of Hogarth House, Paradise
 Road, which the Woolfs hoped to lease.
33. Alice, the only daughter of the eminent jurist Sir Frederick Pollock, had been
 Sydney Waterlow's first wife. They were divorced in 1912, and she married
 Orlando Williams, a House of Commons clerk.

was so infinitely more to him than the walking stick that she couldn't feel anything of the kind. He went off to Asheham. They want to take it on for another 6 months— He has no work to do, but Asheham is so delightful that he is perfectly happy doing nothing.

Saturday 9 January

At two o'clock this morning several barges moored in the river broke loose. One crashed into Richmond Bridge, & knocked off a good deal of stone from one of the arches— The others went to the bottom, or drifted down stream. All this I mention, not because we saw or heard anything of it, but because we noticed the damaged Bridge as we walked to Kingston this afternoon. The stone is yellower inside than out, which makes it more obvious. We had a very good walk. The purplish fields outside Kingston somehow reminded me of Saragossa. There is a foreign look about a town which stands up against the sunset, & is approached by a much trodden footpath across a field. I wonder why one instinctively feels that one is complimenting Kingston absurdly in saying that it is like a foreign town. On the towpath we met & had to pass a long line of imbeciles. The first was a very tall young man, just queer enough to look twice at, but no more; the second shuffled, & looked aside; & then one realised that every one in that long line was a miserable ineffective shuffling idiotic creature, with no forehead, or no chin, & an imbecile grin, or a wild suspicious stare. It was perfectly horrible. They should certainly be killed. We found a market going on at Kingston, as if it were Marlborough. We bought a pineapple for 9d. The man said they had all ripened on his hands, &, as he expected another boatload on Tuesday, he had to sell at a loss. We had a bad tea in a very pretentious place. We came back by train with a working man & two small boys. The working man began to tell us about the Lyons meat contract scandals;[34] & told us that he was attached to the flying department at Hounslow. He was very clever, & should have been an M.P. or a journalist at least. I see Will Vaughan quoted in the Times to the effect that teachers neglect the grammar of modern languages, & talk too much about style & literature; but nothing fortifies the character & mind so much as grammar.[35] How like him!

34. In January 1915 Messrs J. Lyons & Co. were summoned for supplying troops in training with beef unfit for human consumption. On 5 March they were found guilty and given the maximum fine of £50.
35. William Wyamar Vaughan (1865-1938), VW's first cousin, Master of Wellington College and later Headmaster of Rugby School. As President of the Modern Language Association he had been speaking at a conference of Education Associations. In 1898 he had married Margaret (Madge) Vaughan, third daughter of John Addington Symonds and an object of VW's youthful veneration.

Sunday 10 January

I was sitting typewriting this morning when there came a tap at the door; & someone whom I thought at first was Adrian, appeared: it was Walter Lamb however, fresh from the King.[36] Whenever he has seen the King he comes to tell us. He insisted that we should go for a walk with him in Richmond Park. What did we talk about? We forgot about the King, & Walter told us a long inexpressibly dreary story which Professor Houseman had told him, about the inefficiency of the French soldiers.[37] Whatever Walter says, has the same flat, smooth, grey surface; & his voice alone would dull the fieriest poesy in the world. Nor does he deal in fiery poems. His life now lies among respectable, semi-smart, rich people, whom he half despises, so that his accounts are always a little conde-scending. The one passion of his life is for eighteenth century building. All the time this morning he was bidding us admire a moulding or a window frame or even a 'fan light'. He 'sees over' any house that is to let, apparently, & notices the internal decorations. He knows who now lives in big houses, & who once lived in them. He is perfectly suited by Kew, & the Royal Academy, & the Royal Family. On our doorstep he burst at length into an account of the last Royal visit, when the King, who now treats him as a friend (or rather, as Leonard says, like a superior footman) suddenly stopped admiring the pictures, & asked Princess Victoria where she gets her false teeth.[38] "Mine, George exclaimed, are always dropping into my plate: they'll be down my throat next. My man is a rascal. I'm going to leave him." Victoria then gave a tug to her front teeth, & told him that they were as sound as could be—perfectly white & useful— The King then went back to the pictures. His style of talk reminds me of George 3rd in Fanny Burney's diary—& so one must bless Walter for something—[39] He refused to lunch with us, saying that he had lived on pheasants all the week, & rhubarb was forbidden him, on account of his acidity. It rains hard, all the afternoon, & now Marjorie Strachey who was

---

36. Walter Rangeley Maitland Lamb (1882-1968), a contemporary of LW and Clive Bell at Trinity College, Cambridge, where he had read classics. He had proposed to VW in 1911. In 1913 he became Secretary to the Royal Academy of Arts, an office which enabled him to develop his talents as a courtier. At this time he was living at Kew, not far from the Woolfs at Richmond.

37. A. E. Housman (1859-1936), poet and classical scholar, was Professor of Latin at Cambridge University, 1911-36.

38. The Princess Victoria (1868-1935), second daughter of King Edward VII and Queen Alexandra, was King George V's favourite sister.

39. Frances Burney, Mme d'Arblay (1752-1840), whose later *Diary and Letters* gives an account of the domestic life of royalty at the court of George III and Queen Charlotte, to whom she was second Keeper of the Robes.

to dine with us, cant come because of a cold.[40] I heard last night from Mr Chubb that old Spence wont let any part of Brunswick Square—

Monday 11 January

Leonard was in his bath this morning, & I was lying in bed, wondering whether I should stretch out my hand for Rob Roy,[41] when I heard a commotion next door, & then someone rushed downstairs crying in a strange, unnatural voice "Fire! Fire!" As it was obvious that the house was not on fire, to any large extent, I put on my waterproof & slippers before I looked out of the window. I then smelt paper burning. I then went into the passage, & found smoke pouring from the open door of the next room. There was clearly time to escape, so I withdrew; & heard Lizzy return with the lodger; & heard her begin "I only put a bit of paper to draw the fire—" from which I guessed what had happened.[42] "In ten minutes the room would have been ablaze" said the lodger. L. came back; & we looked out of our window, & saw a large Japanese screen, all in flames, burning on the grass plot. Later, I heard that the paper had caught; the draperies on the mantelpiece had caught; the screen had caught; the woodwork had caught. As every room in the house is lined with dry old wood, loosely papered over, 10 minutes I think, would have put the fire beyond water jugs— The lodger was in terror, too, for his priceless rugs: 'worth hundreds & hundreds' according to Mrs Le Grys. The wonder is how we have escaped so far, considering Lizzy. Yesterday she smashed two very nice bits of china for us.

We went up to London this afternoon: L. to see the editor of the New Statesman about an article on Diplomacy—I to go over a flat in Mecklenburgh Square.[43] We met unexpectedly in M. Sqre. When we reached the house, however, the occupier refused to let us see it. So we had to apply to the owner, who lives a few doors off. We were shown into a beautiful room, which was disfigured horribly with velvet curtains, gigantic purple cushions, & the usual swarm of gilt & lemon coloured objects. The woman herself sat in an invalid chair, arranged, like a childs high chair, with a bar across it. Her hair (a flaxen wig) was plastered on either side of her head, & she had the usual powdered plump rouged look of Bloomsbury ladies. This always makes us both physically uncomfortable. She

40. Marjorie Strachey (1882-1964), teacher and writer, the youngest of Lytton Strachey's five sisters; frequently referred to as 'Gumbo'.
41. By Sir Walter Scott, published 1817.
42. Lizzy (or Lizzie) was Mrs le Gry's feckless maid of all work at 17 The Green, Richmond.
43. Clifford Dyce Sharp (1883-1935), first editor of the New Statesman, 1913-1931. (See III LW, 129.) LW's article 'The Diplomatic Service' appeared on 16 January 1915.

was very sensible however, a business woman, I suppose, owning several houses, & running them, I'm sure, at a profit. She made us see over her house, instead of the other one. We were taken over by a small, wizened, very amiable old lady, who had disfigured her part of the house until it was scarcely recognisable— The drawing room, in particular, where she had lavished her skill, made your eyes start with its innumerable, discordant, hideous small things—two clusters of flags displayed on the tables chiefly impressed me. There were all the flags of all the nations, I should think; all the photographs of all the royal families. It was like looking into a kaleidoscope, because of the innumerable separate dots of colour—& yet they weren't colour. I went on to Days Library & L. to the London Library.[44] He has to write an article of 1200 words by Wednesday noon, on Diplomatists— A wonderful subject anyhow.

Tuesday 12 January

Today did not begin with a fire. Leonard however had to take Mrs Le Grys to task for Lizzie's sins. The poor woman could only agree. Since she knows she is going, she doesn't mind how many plates she breaks— if she would only go. Mrs Le G. finds it impossible to get a servant; she pays them only £16 a year however.

Cecil came to luncheon, in mufti, I observed.[45] In fact they are both entirely sick of the army, & see no chance of going to the front. Nevertheless, Cecil thinks of being a permanent soldier, because the life is better than a Barrister's life. On the other hand, he & Philip may go to the colonies. The odd thing about the Woolf family, to me, is the extreme laxness of it. In my family, the discussions & agitations that went on about the slightest change in one's way of life were endless; but with the W.'s it doesn't much seem to matter whether they turn farmer, run away with another man's wife, or marry a Polish Jew Tailors daughter. I remember how elaborately Aunt Mary concealed the fact that Hervey's young woman was a kind of shopkeeper, & how indefatigable she was until the engagement was broken off.[46] Perhaps the W.'s haven't a family tradition.

44. Day's Library, 90 Mount Street, Mayfair, was a circulating library mainly devoted to fiction. The London Library, a private institution supported by membership subscription, was and is at 14 St James's Square. Sir Leslie Stephen, VW's father, had succeeded Tennyson as its president in 1892.

45. Cecil Nathan Sidney Woolf (1887-1917), fourth of LW's five brothers. A Fellow of Trinity College, Cambridge, he became an officer in the Royal Hussars on the outbreak of war, and was killed at the Battle of Cambrai. (See below, 3 December 1917.)

46. Aunt Mary was Mrs Herbert Fisher (1841-1916), sister of VW's mother. Hervey (1873-1921) was the seventh of her eleven children; he never married. The identity of the socially undesirable young woman remains unknown.

It gives a sense of freedom anyhow. From all this, obviously I have nothing to say. L. & Cecil walked to Kingston after lunch; I pottered about buying small fragments of meat & vegetables, & got some books out of the Library. I believe we shall find it more useful than the London Library, as no one, save ourselves, reads solid books. L. is now writing his article upon diplomacy, & I must go & typewrite. An entire fine day for a wonder.

Wednesday 13 January

I caused some slight argument (with L.) this morning by trying to cook my breakfast in bed. I believe, however, that the good sense of the proceeding will make it prevail; that is, if I can dispose of the eggshells. L. went off to the New Statesman office this morning with his article. I lunched here, & then went to Days, to get more books. Days at 4 in the afternoon is the haunt of fashionable ladies, who want to be told what to read. A more despicable set of creatures I never saw. They come in furred like seals & scented like civets, condescend to pull a few novels about on the counter, & then demand languidly whether there is *anything* amusing? The Days' assistants are the humblest & most servile of men— They tow these aged Countesses & pert young millionairesses about behind them, always deferential, & profuse of "Ladyships". The West End of London fills me with aversion; I look into motor cars & see the fat grandees inside, like portly jewels in satin cases. The afternoons now have an elongated pallid look, as if it were neither winter nor spring. I came back to tea. L. arrived—having seen Gordon Sqre & Maynard (who says German finance is crumbling) & Saxon, who is recovering from Influenza.[47] He had a headache, so, instead of going to the Co-op. meeting, we are staying at home.

Thursday 14 January

We were woken this morning (I see this is going to become a stock phrase like 'Once upon a Time' in a Faery story) by a thumping throbbing sound as if a motor omnibus were on the roof, endeavouring to start. Experience told now, however, that Lizzy had merely made a huge kitchen fire, when there was no water in the pipes. When L. turned on the tap, steam issued, as if it were Siegfried's dragon at Covent Garden, & then came floating bits of pipe, & the water was rust red— Nobody, however, seemed to think that the boiler might burst. We wrote all the morning. I

47. John Maynard Keynes (1883-1946), scholar of Eton and of King's College, Cambridge, Fellow of the College and University lecturer in Economics. In January 1915 he was appointed to a post in the Treasury. A member of the Apostles; in 1911, with Duncan Grant and LW, he became one of the 'inmates' of Adrian and Virginia Stephen's house at 38 Brunswick Square.

heard from Adrian, by the way, who has gone into rooms in Cambridge without a single sheet.[48] Now, I begin telephoning & writing about sheets, just as the Waterlows are silent. After lunch, we set off to Kingston in order to buy some charming cups, which are to be had there for 1d each. If Lizzie doesn't go, & continues to behave as though each day were her last, we must give her something cheap to break her rage against. We came home on the top of a bus; making up phrases in the manner & tone of Walter Lamb. Leonard is going up to hear the Fabians discourse;[49] I think I shall indulge in a picture palace—but why? I shall certainly come out saying to myself, "Nothing will induce me ever to go to a picture palace again". I also heard from Annie, who evidently intends to be our permanent cook, for the excellent reason, I think, that ours is the easiest place in England.[50] The Waterlows say that her young man has removed to—or been replaced by one—at Willesden. L's article on diplomacy is to come out on Saturday. He was, of course, convinced after sending it that it would be rejected (this is a note, for future use & quotation).

Friday 15 January

I went to my picture palace; & L. to his Fabians; & he thought, on the whole, that his mind & spirit & body would have profited more by the pictures than by the Webbs, & the doctors, who were talking about their etiquette.[51] There were 2 or 3 superb pictures; one of a barge laden with timber floating past Bagdad—another of an eastern palace, overrun with apes & pariah dogs—another of a sunken yatcht. But as usual, the drama

48. Adrian Leslie Stephen (1883-1948), VW's younger brother, with whom she had lived, not very harmoniously, at 29 Fitzroy Square after Vanessa's marriage in 1907, and then, in 1911 until her own, at 38 Brunswick Square. After attending Trinity College, Cambridge (1902-05), he studied Law, but remained without profession or vocation until five years after his marriage in 1914 to Karin Costelloe, when he and his wife became medical students. (See below, 18 June 1919.) He was a committed pacifist and active in the work of the No-Conscription Fellowship; after the introduction of conscription in 1916 he was directed to land work. In 1914-15 his wife held a Research Fellowship at Newnham College, Cambridge.

49. On 14 January at their new headquarters at 25 Tothill Street, Westminster, the Fabian Research Department met, with George Bernard Shaw in the chair, to hear Dr F. Lawson Dodd speak on the organisation of the medical profession.

50. Annie Chart, the Woolf's cook at Asheham, had worked for the Waterlows when they rented the house; she and Lily (see above, 1 January 1915, n 1) returned to work for the Woolfs when they moved into Hogarth House in March 1915.

51. Sidney Webb (1859-1947) and his wife Beatrice, *née* Potter (1858-1943), social reformers and twin pillars of the Fabian Society, founders of the London School of Economics and the socialist weekly *New Statesman*. After the meeting on 14 January, Mrs Webb was 'At Home' in the Fabian Common Room at Tothill Street.

is very boring. I wish one liked what everyone likes. The Hall was crowded, roars of laughter, applause &c.

I heard from Emphie Case this morning, who wishes me to find out about the Home at Lewes where Lily had her child—as she knows a young woman who also wants to have a child. I wonder how Emphie comes across these things. Janet much the same.

We walked to Hogarth this afternoon, to see if the noise of school-children is really a drawback. Apparently, it would only affect Suffield.[52] Well—I wonder what we shall do. I'd give a lot to turn over 30 pages or so, & find written down what happens to us. We walked into the Park, & saw Territorials flogging & spurring their carthorses;[53] also a great fallen tree. We are dining early, & going to a Hall—an unheard of dissipation—though there was a time when I went out to operas, evenings concerts &c, at least 3 times a week— And I know we shall both feel, when its over, 'really a good read would have been better'. L. continues to read diplomatists; I read about 1860—the Kembles—Tennyson & so on; to get the spirit of that time, for the sake of The Third Generation.[54] They were immensely scientific—always digging up extinct monsters, & looking at the stars, & trying to find a Religion. At this moment, I feel as if the human race had no character at all—sought for nothing, believed in nothing, & fought only from a dreary sense of duty.

I began today to treat my corn. It had to be done for a week.

Saturday 16 January

I think the Hall (Coliseum) last night *was* worth while—in spite of draw backs. What I like in Halls are 'turns'—comic singers, or men imitating Prima Donna's, or Jugglers. I don't like one act plays. It takes me a whole act to get into a play, & so one act plays are mostly sheer boredom. Therefore I was disappointed to have 3 one act plays; one the Barrie Der Tag—sheer balderdash of the thinnest kind about the German Emperor; then a play about a woman who means Parrot when she says Pirate; third Dr Johnson. To begin with Johnson spits bread & butter through his nose to end with he is paternal, sentimental & as tender as a woman—which is of course what he was bound to be on the stage. However, there was a man who sang like a Prima Donna; & a patriotic Revue—people clapped Grey more than anyone. We left, just as an Eastern jar, coloured grey &

---

52. Hogarth House was one half of what had been built about 1720 as a single residence; the other half was called Suffield House. See *IV LW*, 9-12.

53. Soldiers of the Territorial Army, a volunteer force created before the war and still in existence.

54. 'The Third Generation' and 'poor Effie's story' (see above, 2 January 1915, n 6) were to become *Night and Day*. (See Elizabeth Heine in *VW Miscellany*, no. 9, Winter 1977).

violet, shot up in the middle of the stage;—& I didn't see my war pictures, but departed mildly as a lamb.[55]

We wrote this morning. L's article by the way reads very well in the New Statesman. I had a request from Adrian for silver, glass, kitchen things. They seem to have set up house without a single article. He wrote by a candle light, stuck in a saucer. L. went to the L. Library; I took Max along the River, but we were a good deal impeded, by a bone he stole, by my suspenders coming down, by a dogfight in which his ear was torn & bled horribly. I thought how happy I was, without any of the excitements which, once, seemed to me to constitute happiness. L. & I argued for some time about this. Also about the worthlessness of all human works except as a means of keeping the workers happy. My writing now delights me solely because I love writing & dont, honestly, care a hang what anyone says. What seas of horror one dives through in order to pick up these pearls—however they are worth it.

Sunday 17 January

The morning was unremarkable—in the afternoon, Herbert came & took L. for a walk. I went to a Queens Hall Concert, stayed for three beautiful tunes, & came back, to find Herbert who stayed on till dinnertime.[56] M[arjorie]. S[trachey]. came to dinner; changed, somehow, at the first glance. Improved, I thought, though noticeably thinner. She complained of sleeplessness, & in the usual S. way of 'being shattered'; & life being 'too fearful'. But she talked of ordinary things until after dinner she began to harp very markedly on marriage—(I should say that for no reason at all, she said to us "I've a friend who thinks me rather beautiful, & very stupid"—& half suspecting something odd, I said "O he's a working man, & you mustn't marry him". Well, she pressed us more & more with questions about married life, & whether she should marry, & how she wanted to marry; & sometimes I thought she was only talking as so many unmarried people do, & sometimes I suspected there was more. At last one of us (I, perhaps) said "Well but Marjorie, what d'you want to be?" "A married woman" she answered tragically. "But is there someone you want to marry?" "Yes!" "Does he want to marry you?"

---

55. The one-act plays VW saw were *Der Tag* by J. M. Barrie, with Irene Vanbrugh as the Spirit of Culture and Norman McKinnel as the Emperor; *Longshoreman Bill* by Fred Rowe; and *Dr Johnson* by Leo Trevor. The patriotic revue consisted of excerpts from sea shanties, songs by Elgar and National Anthems sung by Arturo Spizzi; and the eastern jar formed part of the act of the Ko-Ten-Ichi troupe of oriental entertainers.

56. The 'tunes' were Bach's 4th Brandenburg Concerto, the Symphony in D by César Franck, and three movements of Lalo's *Symphonie Espagnole*. A. Herbert Sidney Woolf (1879-c.1950), LW's elder brother, was a stockbroker.

"Yes!!"—"Who is he?" She buried her face in her hands, & then exclaimed "A married man! Jos Wedgwood!" We both gasped, in silence.[57] And then we discussed nothing else for an hour or two. It is about the oddest business I ever heard of—this being more or less what has happened. Last summer, Jos left his wife, or she left him, this point being doubtful. Since that, he has lived alone in London, & complained bitterly to Philip Morrell among others of his loneliness. Philip recommended a prostitute. Ottoline thereupon procured Marjorie.[58] They asked her to dinner, & after dinner, Ottoline danced behind the folding doors, & left Marjorie to a tremendous tete a tete with Jos. Although this was their first meeting, he told her his history & his sorrows. Next day he called on Lady Strachey.[59] They met constantly, &, a week or so before Xmas he proposed to her at Lockeridge.[60] By this time she was much in love & accepted him—but what are they to do? She refuses to let him get a Divorce, on the ground that a divorce is ignominious; he, moreover, says that a Divorce would ruin him politically. He is tremendously ambitious. She wishes to live with him as his wife; but this of course means utter political ruin again. To be an ordinary mistress is out of the question for her. Lady Strachey again complicates the question, because she would be horrified at any unconventionality, & cannot be told of it. Then there is the fear of Mrs Wedgwood. If she hears, will she try to get Jos back? Will she succeed? Half of the Stracheys (Lytton among them) advise M. to think no more of it. She is obviously in love; & also quite distracted & worn out. She is going to the South of France; Jos meanwhile is going to the Front. Well— what can one make of it all? Seeing M. in love, & her love returned, I felt that the only course was the extreme one; but when I reflected, particu-

57. Josiah Clement Wedgwood (1872-1943), a member of the famous Staffordshire family, politician, MP for Newcastle-under-Lyme from 1906 until 1942 (when he was raised to the peerage), successively as a Liberal, an Independent, and finally as a Labour Party representative. He married in 1894 Ethel Kate Bowen, who bore him seven children but left him in 1913; their divorce, attended with considerable unwelcome publicity, was delayed until the end of the war. He was badly wounded at Gallipoli in May 1915 and received the D.S.O.

58. Philip Edward Morrell (1870-1943), Liberal MP 1906-18, married in 1902 Lady Ottoline Violet Anne Cavendish-Bentinck (1873-1938), half-sister of the 6th Duke of Portland. She was a notable patroness of artists and writers, and a catholic hostess, entertaining at 44 Bedford Square, Bloomsbury, and from June 1915 at Garsington Manor, near Oxford, which became a refuge for many conscientious objectors after the military service (conscription) act came into force early in 1916.

59. Jane Maria Grant (1840-1928) wife of Lt.-Gen. Sir Richard Strachey (1817-1908). They reared ten children, including Oliver, Lytton and Marjorie. See 'Lady Strachey' by VW, *The Nation and Athenaeum*, 22 December 1928 (Kp C307).

60. The Lacket, Lockeridge, near Marlborough, Wiltshire, a cottage rented from 1913 to 1915 by Lytton Strachey from his Cambridge contemporary Edward Hilton Young.

larly upon the way in which the thing has happened, the shortness of it, &
Ottoline's manoeuvres, I had doubts—about Jos, mostly. Isn't it a case
of Sydney Waterlow over again?[61] Will his feeling last, even if hers does?
He was married for 20 years to Ethel, & they have 7 children. Leonard is
pessimistic, & right, I expect. He thinks that M. is going the worst way
for her own prospects, & points out the horror of her position as a mistress, without any tie upon a man who admittedly cares more for his
career than anything, & has been supplied with her to gratify wants which
may quickly pass— But for some time now they will be apart, & so things
may settle themselves. For her, I feel it is the great affair of her life, one
way or the other. This morning, obeying a nocturnal command, I wrote
to Thomas Hardy! thanking him for his poem about Father, & his works![62]

Monday 18 January

We were still a good deal under the influence of Marjorie this morning.
All night (it seemed) people were banging boxes next door. The lodger
has got a wife back from New York. This afternoon we went over the
houses in Mecklenburgh Sqre; which has led to a long discussion about
our future, & a fresh computation of income. The future is dark, which is
on the whole, the best thing the future can be, I think. L. went to the
Webbs, & I came home—nor has anything happened since to be worth
putting down save that, as I began this page, L. stated that he had determined to resign his commission to write a pamphlet about Arbitration—&
now I shall stop this diary & discuss that piece of folly with him.[63] It is
partly due to my egoistical habit of always talking the argument of my
book. I want to see what can be said *against* all forms of activity & thus
dissuade L. from all his work, speaking really not in my own character
but in Effie's. Of course it is absolutely essential that L. shd. do a work
which may be superbly good.

Tuesday 19 January

L's melancholy continues, so much so that he declared this morning
he couldn't work. The consequence has been rather a melancholy day.
Outside it is very cold & grey too. We walked in Richmond Park this

61. In December 1911 Sydney Waterlow, parted but not yet divorced from his first
wife, made a declaration of love to VW, which she had gently rebuffed.

62. See *II VW Letters*, no. 719. The poem was 'The Shreckhorn, June 1897, with
thoughts of Leslie Stephen', printed in *Satires of Circumstance*, 1914.

63. This pamphlet—undertaken at the instigation of Sidney Webb nominally as a
report to a committee of the Fabian Society—was not abandoned but grew into
LW's influential book *International Government* (1916) used by the British
Government in its proposals for a League of Nations. See *III LW*, 183-89; Philip
Noel-Baker, *The Times*, 21 August 1969.

afternoon; the trees all black, & the sky heavy over London; but there is enough colour to make it even lovelier today than on bright days, I think. The deer exactly match the bracken. But L. was melancholy, as I say. All I can do is to unsay all I have said; & to say what I really mean. Its a bad habit writing novels—it falsifies life, I think. However, after praising L's writing very sincerely for 5 minutes, he says "Stop"; whereupon I stop, & theres no more to be said. When I analyse his mood, I attribute much of it to sheer lack of self confidence in his power of writing; as if he mightn't be a writer, after all; & being a practical man, his melancholy sinks far deeper than the half assumed melancholy of self conscious people like Lytton, & Sir Leslie & myself.[64] There's no arguing with him.

Well, I'm reading The Idiot. I cant bear the style of it very often; at the same time, he seems to me to have the same kind of vitality in him that Scott had; only Scott merely made superb ordinary people, & D. creates wonders, with very subtle brains, & fearful sufferings. Perhaps the likeness to Scott partly consists in the loose, free & easy, style of the translation. I am also reading Michelet, plodding through the dreary middle ages; & Fanny Kemble's Life.[65] Yesterday in the train I read The Rape of the Lock, which seems to me "supreme"—almost superhuman in its beauty & brilliancy—you really can't believe that such things are written down.[66] I think one day I shall write a book of "Eccentrics". Mrs Grote shall be one. Lady Hester Stanhope. Margaret Fuller. Duchess of Newcastle. Aunt Julia?[67]

64. Sir Leslie Stephen (1832-1904), VW's father; man of letters and first editor of the *Dictionary of National Biography*. See F. W. Maitland, *The Life and Letters of Leslie Stephen*, 1906; Noël Annan, *Leslie Stephen, His Thought and Character in Relation to his Time*, 1951. For Lytton Strachey, see below, 16 August 1917, n 17.

65. Frances Anne Kemble (1809-93), a member of the great theatrical family, published five autobiographical works between 1853 and 1891.

66. Alexander Pope's mock-heroic poem, published in its final version in 1714. 'Supreme' was a word much in favour with Apostles of LW's generation.

67. Harriet Grote (1792-1878), 'a Grenadier in petticoats', wife of George Grote the historian of Greece; her bizarre manner and appearance revealed to Sydney Smith the origin and meaning of the word 'grotesque'. (See F. A. Kemble, *Records of Later Life*, 1882, vol. II, p. 47 ff). Lady Hester Stanhope (1776-1839), niece of William Pitt, established herself in the Lebanon where she lived an increasingly eccentric life with a semi-oriental retinue. Margaret Fuller (1810-50), erudite American writer and feminist, married an Italian marquis and with him supported Mazzini and the revolutionaries in 1848-50. They both perished in a shipwreck. Margaret, Duchess of Newcastle (1624?-74), Pepys's "mad, conceited, ridiculous, woman", a prolific writer. Aunt Julia: Julia Margaret Cameron, *née* Pattle (1815-1879), VW's great-aunt, the pioneer photographer.

VW had already written on Lady Hester Stanhope, *TLS*, 20 January 1910 (Kp C42); on the Duchess of Newcastle, *TLS*, 2 February 1911 (Kp C46); and was later (1926) to write an essay on Mrs Cameron (Kp B5).

Wednesday 20 January

Having finished a chapter, I went off buying small fragments of things part of the morning— For one thing, I saw a mass of pinkish stuff in the fishmongers, & bought it—Cods' Roe. Then I made carbon copies of some notes of L's about Arbitration. The action of nature has relieved his spirits more than all the arguments of his wife—also the day was fine. Anyhow one may now hope he will get started, which is the main thing. He went to the School of Economics after lunch;[68] & I to Westminster. I want to see as many houses as possible. But in Barton St. the rent is £130—& that is low, on account of the war. Westminster, noiseless & shadowed by the Abbey is almost the heart of London.

By this time it was raining. I went to Days, & found my books already sent. When I tried to remember the name of one, I failed utterly; so one must feel in an examination. I read Essay upon Criticism waiting for my train at Hammersmith. The classics make the time pass much better than the Pall Mall Gazette.[69] Maynard Keynes came to dinner. We gave him oysters. He is like quicksilver on a sloping board—a little inhuman, but very kindly, as inhuman people are. We gossiped at full speed about Adrian & Karin (Adrian's lovemaking done in loud judicious tones)[70] & of course Marjorie & Jos. Here, though friendly & very amusing, I thought K. a little inhuman. He saw the queerness & the fun, but didn't seem to see that it might be serious. Nessa & Ottoline, he says, contrived the whole thing. Then we talked about the war. We aren't fighting now, he says, but only waiting for the spring. Meantime we lavish money, on a scale which makes the French, who are fearfully out at elbow, gape with admiration. We are bound to win—& in great style too, having at the last moment applied all our brains & all our wealth to the problem.

68. The London School of Economics and Political Science was virtually founded by Sidney and Beatrice Webb in 1895 with money left in trust to the Fabian Society to advance Socialism. It was never however under the Society's control, and since 1900 has formed part of the University of London.

69. *Essay on Criticism* was the didactic poem by Alexander Pope, published anonymously in 1711. *The Pall Mall Gazette*, a London evening paper, was amalgamated with the *Evening Standard* in 1923.

70. Karin Elizabeth Conn Stephen, *née* Costelloe (1889-1953), had graduated with distinction in Philosophy from Newnham College, Cambridge, where she now held a research fellowship. A stepdaughter of Bernard Berenson, niece of Logan Pearsall Smith and of Alys Russell (first wife of Bertrand Russell), her elder sister Rachel was married to Oliver Strachey; she married Adrian Stephen in October 1914. She suffered from deafness.

Thursday 21 January

Maynard last night was sceptical about the value of writing on Arbitration. He was sceptical about the value of almost all work, save for the pleasure it gives the worker. He works only because he likes it. This of course, depressed poor L. once more. He was very melancholy this morning, & had to spend the day at the British Museum, which was bad enough, even if one believed in one's drudgery. Still I believe it will be an enormous success, &, if it doesn't prevent another war, it will put him among the eminent young men, which isn't altogether despicable. I went to the London Library—a stale culture smoked place, which I detest. Here I read Gilbert Murray on Immortality, got a book for L. & so home, missing my train, & reading the Letter to Dr Arbuthnot on Hammersmith Station.[71] L. came in late, having been up to Hampstead & seen Janet, who seems still the same; but so I think it must be, for months. Emphie annoyed with Margaret, who advises a proper rest cure "which one doesn't do to the patient herself." Sylvia Milman came to dinner— After a good deal of bowing & scraping about China (which she has dutifully seen, in her endeavour to be advanced) we got on to memories of childhood which amused me, but bored L. I'm afraid.[72] No one ever had a duller home than she had; but by sheer hard work, without a scrap of talent, she has plodded after the Advanced i.e. Nessa, until she lives in a flat, saves money to travel, & helps at the Omega. Ida is nursing in France; Enid & Maud have a chicken farm. Clearly there was good stuff in the Dean; though never a spark of enthusiasm. She stayed on & on, until L. half rose from his chair.

Friday 22 January

When L. pulled the curtains this morning, practically no light came in; there was a kind of greyish confusion outside—soft swirling incessant snow. This has gone on all day almost, sometimes changing to rain. The Green itself is very lovely; & lights up the room with its pure white glare. But the streets became brown directly. Of course, in this House of Trouble, the pipes burst; or got choked; or the roof split asunder. Anyhow in the middle of the morning, I heard a steady rush of water in the wainscot; & Mr Le Grys, Lizzie & various people have been clambering about the roof ever since. The water still drips through the ceiling into a row of slop pails. Mrs Le Grys cries hysterically "O it'll be all right—you're insured".

71. Alexander Pope's *Epistle to Dr Arbuthnot*, 1735. The Gilbert Murray work was possibly his *Four Stages of Greek Religion*, 1912.
72. Sylvia Milman and her sisters Ida, Enid, and Maud, granddaughters of the dean of St Paul's, Henry Hart Milman (1791-1868), had been family friends of the Stephens since their childhood in Kensington. The reference to China has not been elucidated.

The plumber refuses to leave his house in weather like this. We are going to hear the Fabians at Essex Hall.[73] I daresay we shall be swept out of our beds tonight. Its a queer winter—the worst I ever knew, & suitable for the war & all the rest of it. I never said yesterday that I heard from Thomas Hardy! He wrote a very nice, very characteristic letter, & was much pleased that I wrote. So that my nocturnal impulse was from God.

Saturday 23 January

The Fabians were well worth hearing: still more worth seeing. Miss Atkinson drivelled at length about Peace—I could understand, always, & confute generally, all that she said; so that I think it must have been very bad.[74] The interest was watching Mrs Webb, seated like an industrious spider at the table; spinning her webs (a pun!—) incessantly. The hall was full of earnest drab women, who are thought 'queer' at home, & rejoice in it; & of broad nosed, sallow, shock headed young men, in brown tweed suits. They all looked unhealthy & singular & impotent. The only speech that was worth anything came from Squire, who wears a bright blue shirt & cultivates an amusing appearance. He said it was all very dull & sensible—which it was; & the idea that these frail webspinners can affect the destiny of nations seems to me fantastic. But it was well worth going,— & I have now declared myself a Fabian. We stayed in Richmond all day. We walked up the river, & were startled by the sudden fall of an avalanche of snow from a roof. It was very cold & misty. Jean asked us to go & hear some V.A.D.'s sing;[75] but the fire after tea was too tempting. Oliver & Ray dined with us.[76] Oliver as usual, very prompt impatient & rather

73. A meeting to discuss 'The Conditions of Peace' was held by the Fabian Society at the Essex Hall just off the Strand.

74. Mabel Atkinson (d. 1959), an active Edwardian Fabian and truculent member of the Women's Group, co-author with Margaret McKillop of *Economics, Descriptive and Theoretical*, 1911; she later married a Mr Palmer and emigrated to Natal. The other speakers were Beatrice Webb, Sir Sydney Olivier and John Collings Squire (1884-1958), poet and man of letters, literary editor of the *New Statesman*, 1913-1919, and an active member of the Fabian Society.

75. Miss Jean Thomas, the proprietor of a nursing home for nervous and mental cases at Cambridge Park, Twickenham, of which VW had more than once been an inmate. VW had known her, not only in her professional capacity, but as a devoted friend. V.A.D. = Voluntary Aid Detachment: a nursing service auxiliary to the armed forces.

76. Oliver Strachey (1874-1960), an elder brother of Lytton. He was educated at Eton and Balliol but did not graduate; he worked in India, studied music, and was now employed as a code-breaker by the Foreign Office. In 1911 he had married as his second wife Rachel Conn Costelloe (1887-1940), elder sister of Karin (see above, 20 January 1915, n 70) whom she preceded to Newnham College, Cambridge. She was an indefatigable worker for women's rights and causes.

testy. Ray solid & capable & soothing. We discussed the war, & Marjorie.
"I cant *bear* to think of it. Its *too* revolting" O. shuddered, after saying
that M. must of course live with Jos. as his mistress. Ray says she divides
the world into those who are nice enough to be in love with, & those who
aren't—& Marjorie is'nt. They think her in love—but in love too with
the drama of the situation. They share our fears too—but agree that anything in her case is better than nothing.

Sunday 24 January

In the middle of dinner last night, Molly rang us up to ask whether
she & Desmond might come to lunch today. Oliver exclaimed that
Desmond as he happened to know, had promised to lunch with Henry
James.[77] We told Molly this. It was news to her. So she came alone, about
12.30. We plunged of course into Gordon Square gossip. She has suffered
acutely this winter, owing to a series of embroilments with Clive, the
nature of which I can imagine; though whether he got bored first or she
disgusted, I don't know. Anyhow, as I could have foretold, after violent
scenes lasting almost 18 months, they have parted, & he abuses her, &
she abuses herself—for ever having listened. But she finds that an intermittent acquaintance wont do for him—'garden party talk' he calls it; &
she feels that intimacy in those circles leads to a kind of dustiness of soul.
So she has broken, & now takes Desmond off to Freshwater for 9 months,
to live cheaply & write a novel.[78] This is the very last attempt—& it
sounds a little desperate. He is to come up to town once in 6 weeks. She
is to manage 3 children & the house with only one servant. And she means
never again to come back into the whirl. Moreover they have quarrelled
with his Mother, & forfeited £100 a year; so they must live on £350,
which includes Desmond's weekly article in the New Statesman. She was
incoherent, inattentive, & fragmentary as usual; like a little grey moth
among machines. L. went to see his mother; I called on Jean, whom I
found sitting in black velvet in a room like a cheap restaurant with

77. (Charles Otto) Desmond MacCarthy (1877-1952), literary journalist and dramatic
critic, graduate of Trinity College, Cambridge, and an Apostle. His friends
expected him to be a great novelist, but his natural gift was for conversation. He
had known the Stephen family since before Sir Leslie's death; in 1906 VW had
attended his wedding to Mary (Molly) Josefa Warre-Cornish (1882-1953), a
daughter of the vice-provost of Eton and, like her, a niece by marriage of 'Aunt
Anny'—Lady Anne Thackeray Ritchie. (See *Bloomsbury Heritage* by Elizabeth
French Boyd, 1976, ch. 6.) Henry James (1843-1916), the American-born novelist,
had been domiciled in England for nearly forty years; later in 1915 he became a
British citizen.

78. Aunt Anny Ritchie lent her cottage, The Porch, Freshwater, Isle of Wight, to the
MacCarthys, who were chronically hard up.

brilliant lights. And there was old Mrs Thomas too, knitting incessantly: & we talked about waterpipes & soldiers; & so home, to a quiet evening thank God.

Monday 25 January

My birthday—& let me count up all the things I had. L. had sworn he would give me nothing, & like a good wife, I believed him. But he crept into my bed, with a little parcel, which was a beautiful green purse. And he brought up breakfast, with a paper which announced a naval victory (we have sunk a German battle ship[79]) & a square brown parcel, with The Abbot in it—a lovely first edition—[80] So I had a very merry & pleasing morning—which indeed was only surpassed by the afternoon. I was then taken up to town, free of charge, & given a treat, first at a Picture Palace, & then at Buzzards.[81] I don't think I've had a birthday treat for 10 years; & it felt like one too—being a fine frosty day, everything brisk & cheerful, as it should be, but never is. The Picture Palace was a little disappointing—as we never got to the War pictures, after waiting 1 hour & a half. But to make up, we exactly caught a non-stop train, & I have been very happy reading father on Pope, which is very witty & bright—without a single dead sentence in it.[82] In fact I dont know when I have enjoyed a birthday so much—not since I was a child anyhow. Sitting at tea we decided three things: in the first place to take Hogarth, if we can get it; in the second, to buy a Printing press; in the third to buy a Bull dog, probably called John. I am very much excited at the idea of all three—particularly the press. I was also given a packet of sweets to bring home.

Tuesday 26 January

L. went up to the School of Economics this morning: I wrote, as usual over the fire, with an occasional interruption by Lizzy, who is like a rough coated young carthorse, with muddy hoofs. After lunch, I met L. at the gates of Kew Gardens, & we walked back to Richmond through the Gardens, which are now one feels teeming with buds & bulbs, though not a spike shows. He has already grasped his Arbitration—such is the male mind—& will, I see, go through with it straight off & (here I make my

---

79. The German armoured cruiser *Blücher* was sunk, and their battle cruiser *Seydlitz* seriously damaged, at the Battle of the Dogger Bank on 14 January 1915; the British flagship *Lion* was damaged.

80. Sir Walter Scott's novel, published in three volumes in Edinburgh in 1820; inscribed 'V.W. from L.W. 25th Jan. 1915'. See *Holleyman*, VS II, p. 8.

81. Buzzard's Tea Rooms, 197-201 Oxford Street.

82. Leslie Stephen wrote a biography of Pope (1880) for the 'English Men of Letters' series; and an essay, 'Pope as a Moralist' was included in his *Hours in a Library* (new edition, 1892).

prophesy) it will be a great success, & lead to as much work as he wants. As Molly sighed 'It must be wonderful to have a husband who works!' I think it would be much odder to have one who didn't— Mrs Woolf & Clara are coming to dinner, so I must stop.[83]

Wednesday 27 January

Mrs Woolf & Clara came to dinner. I dont know what it is about them—I daresay I'd better not try to define it. Perhaps their voices partly?—partly their manners. Anyhow, they gave us flowers & chocolates. Mrs W. sat & knitted. Clara smoked. I think Jewesses are somehow discontented. Clara is. Mrs W. has the mind of a child. She is amused by everything, & yet understands nothing—says whatever comes into her head—prattles incessantly, now good humoured, now ill humoured. She seems to like everyone equally, as if they were all the same. She told us how she used to go to bed with a basket of socks by her side, so as to start darning first thing in the morning.

Leonard went up to the School of Economics today. I wrote, & then went to Janet. Emphie & the cook have influenza—I was met by an elder sister—a shrewd, sensible elderly woman, who has taken charge of things. Janet seemed better, & said she was better. We talked about my novel (which everyone, so I predict will assure me is the most brilliant thing they've ever read; & privately condemn, as indeed it deserves to be condemned.)[84] & about Shelley, & Poets & their immorality. She said that in her young days she would have disapproved of Shelley's relations with women— But the old sister dodged in & out, which made conversation about morality uneasy. Home & finished Pope, & so to bed.

Thursday 28 January

Leonard off again to lunch with the Webbs, & have his Committee meeting. Once more I wrote. All these days, I may remark, are semidark, lightening a little about 3 P.M. before their final plunge into darkness; & yet I think even this darkness is the darkness of very early spring, not winter darkness any more. I decided to go to London, for the sake of hearing the Strand roar, which I think one does want, after a day or two of Richmond. Somehow, one can't take Richmond seriously. One has always come here for an outing, I suppose; & that is part of its charm, but

83. LW's mother, *née* Marie de Jongh (*c.* 1848-1939), previously married to a Mr Goldstucker, widow since 1892 of Sidney Woolf, Q.C.; she had brought up nine children. Clara (1885-1934) was the second of her three daughters.

84. *The Voyage Out* had been accepted by Gerald Duckworth (VW's half-brother) in April 1913. Presumably because of her earlier breakdown, publication had been delayed; it was now in proof, and was finally published on 26 March 1915. This is the only mention of her novel in VW's 1915 diary.

one wants serious life sometimes. As I dressed, my watch fell on the floor; & sitting at tea in a shop in the Strand, I found that the hands pointed to 4.30 still, though it went on ticking. So I took it to Frodsham's, in South Molton Street, where I made great play with the name of McCabe, & the fact that the watch had been over 60 years in my family. Frodsham claims to be the only genuine watchmaker in London: the rest are jewellers.[85] I saw a beautiful woman in the Bus; who could hardly contain her laughter because a great military gentleman was thrown on to her lap, like a sack of coals, which seemed to tickle her greatly, & the more she laughed, the nicer I thought her. About one person in a fortnight seems to me nice— most are nothing at all. Home to find L. triumphant from his Committee meeting. He is to do as he likes: & Squire throws out hints that they would like him to edit the Blue book supplement for them.[86] Well 'I told you so'— A new servant has come today. Lizzy left, carrying a brown paper parcel & whistling loudly—I wonder where she has gone?

Friday 29 January

Shall I say "nothing happened today" as we used to do in our diaries, when they were beginning to die? It wouldn't be true. The day is rather like a leafless tree: there are all sorts of colours in it, if you look closely. But the outline is bare enough. We worked: after lunch we walked down the river, to that great mediaeval building which juts out into the river— It is I think a vast mill.[87] And we came back early, so that L. might have tea before he went to a Committee at Hampstead.[88] After that I bought our food, & did not observe much of interest. But the fact of the day for me has been a vague kind of discomfort, caused by the eccentric character of the new servant Maud. When one speaks to her, she stops dead & looks at the ceiling. She bursts into the room 'just to see if you are there'. She is an angular woman of about 40, who never stays long in any place. I

---

85. Charles Frodsham & Co. Ltd., clock and watch makers by Royal Appointment. The McCabe family were famous London watchmakers from 1778 to 1883.
86. Noting that the British Government was the largest (and in some respects the most unbusinesslike) publishing firm in the Empire, the early volumes of the *New Statesman* (no doubt at the instigation of Sidney and Beatrice Webb) carried a Supplement every five weeks or so listing, summarising or reviewing all Government publications ('Blue Books'). The frequency of its appearance diminished as the war progressed and that of 17 January 1917 appears to be the last. LW certainly contributed to these supplements.
87. Presumably Kidd's Mill (sometimes called Manor Mill) near Isleworth Church. Built probably in the eighteenth century, it was destroyed during the second World War.
88. LW went to see Janet Case, and then to a meeting with Margaret Llewelyn Davies and Lilian Harris at the offices of the Women's Co-operative Guild.

believe she lives in dread of something. She puts down plates with a start. Mrs Le Grys says that she herself is going mad, with Maud's peculiarities. She has just announced that she is the daughter of a Colonel. I am sure her brain is full of illusions, poor creature; & I shouldn't be surprised at anything. The only question is, how she contrives to exist.

Saturday 30 January

L. went to Chancellors this morning about Hogarth. They now volunteer that Mrs Wontner wishes to stay on—but will let us know on Monday for certain. It is a great nuisance. I have a nose for a house, & that was a perfect house, if ever there was one. We went to Wimbledon this afternoon, on the strength of Savages information that there was a beautiful house there to let.[89] Wimbledon is a dreary, high, bleak, windy suburb, on the edge of a threadbare heath. And Savage's house is an enlarged villa, with a rent of £150, furnished, overlooked by motor omnibuses, standing on the road. In all ways therefore utterly unsuited to us. We came home by Bus; & the world grew steadily nicer as we came to Richmond. Certainly it is the first of the suburbs by a long way, because it is not an offshoot of London, any more than Oxford or Marlborough is. It was icy cold; I had the grace to remember that many bus conductors are shivering today, but only stabs at my own comfort make me remember other people—unlike L. Maud's secret obsession, I believe, is that she is a lady. She attempts genteel talk, about the weather, as a Colonel's daughter very well might, & mutters something when she brings in the coal, about being accustomed to private work. She is certainly cleaner than Lizzie. I hope her mania wont develop. My corn is cured. I cannot get on with Michelet's middle ages. L. has Indian Blue Books to review. He was kept late at Hampstead: didnt get home till 10.15. when we had hot chocolate over the fire. He read Janet 'The Three Jews'.[90]

Sunday 31 January

O dear! We quarrelled almost all the morning! & it was a lovely morning, & now gone to Hades for ever, branded with the marks of our ill humour. Which began it? Which carried it on? God knows. This I will say: I explode: & L. smoulders. However, quite suddenly we made it up, (but the morning was wasted) & we walked after lunch in the Park, &

89. Sir George Henry Savage (1842-1921), a distinguished physician who specialised in the treatment of mental diseases. He had been both friend of the Stephen family and medical adviser, particularly on VW's problems, for many years.

90. LW's story 'The Three Jews' and VW's 'The Mark on the Wall', printed by themselves, were issued during the summer of 1917 as *Publication No. 1* of the Hogarth Press (Kp A2).

came home by way of Hogarth, & tried to say that we shan't be much disappointed if we don't get it. Anyhow, it hasn't got the Green in front of it. After tea, as no one came (we've hardly seen anyone this week) I started reading The Wise Virgins, & I read it straight on till bedtime, when I finished it.[91] My opinion is that its a remarkable book; very bad in parts; first rate in others. A writer's book, I think, because only a writer perhaps can see why the good parts are so very good, & why the very bad parts aren't very bad. It seems to me to have the stuff of 20 Duke Jones' in it, although there are howlers which wd. make Miss Sidgwick turn grey.[92] I was made very happy by reading this: I like the poetic side of L. & it gets a little smothered in Blue-books, & organisations.

Monday 1 February

I had to go out shopping this morning, so I called in on Chancellors. They say that Mrs Wontner makes conditions about taking on Hogarth, so that 'it is possible that she won't take it— So here we are on the seesaw again. Mrs Le Grys, also, told me this morning of a house on the Green, 3 doors off, which is to let in March. The rent is £65 & they want £75 premium. We went to look at it after luncheon, but, being a boarding house, couldn't see over it. What we saw was defaced in every possible way; but a nice substantial house, without the charms of Hogarth, but then with the addition of the Green. We went up to London—L. to the London Library: I to Days. I walked with him across the Green Park. In St James Street there was a terrific explosion; people came running out of Clubs; stopped still & gazed about them. But there was no Zeppelin or aeroplane—only, I suppose, a very large tyre burst. But it is really an instinct with me, & most people, I suppose, to turn any sudden noise, or dark object in the sky into an explosion, or a German aeroplane. And it always seems utterly impossible that one should be hurt.[1]

I was annoyed in the usual way at Days by the afternoon party of fashionable ladies, looking for books. We have just been rung up by Chancellors, who wish us to see the owner of Hogarth tomorrow, & possibly by our presence & respectability outwit Mrs Wontner, whose demands have annoyed Chancellors. In fact it seems quite likely at this

---

91. LW's second novel, *The Wise Virgins, A Story of Words, Opinions, and a Few Emotions*. Completed in 1913, publication was delayed until October 1914 owing to objections to certain passages by his publisher Edward Arnold. The book contains generally unsympathetic portraits based on LW himself, VW, and their families and friends; it was perhaps for this reason together with the state of her health that VW had not hitherto read the book.

92. Ethel Sidgwick, author of *Duke Jones, A Sequel to A Lady of Leisure*, 1914.

1. Cf. *Mrs Dalloway*, p. 16.

moment that we shall get Hogarth![2] I wish it were tomorrow. I am certain it is the best house to take.

Tuesday 2 February

Well, it is tomorrow; & we are certainly nearer to Hogarth than we were. We have done little else & thought of little else all day, so it is as well we have some profit—

There are no entries in VW's diary for the next ten days. According to LW's laconic record, they went to Chancellors about Hogarth House during the afternoon of 2 February; on the following two days they made an afternoon walk; on Friday LW went to the London Library—and VW probably went too. On Saturday morning, 6 February, they went to Rye, and stayed at the Old Flushing Inn. On Sunday they walked to Playden in the morning, and to Winchelsea in the afternoon. On Monday 8 February they had an afternoon walk, and on Tuesday went to Hastings for lunch and then returned to London, where he dined with Sydney Waterlow at the Cock Tavern in Fleet Street and, meeting Ka Cox and Gerald Shove there, they went afterwards to her rooms (which had once been his and VW's) in Clifford's Inn. On Friday 12 February the Woolfs again went to see Hogarth House.

Saturday 13 February

There was a great downpour this morning. I am sure however many years I keep this diary, I shall never find a winter to beat this. It seems to have lost all self control. We wrote; & after luncheon L. went to the Library, & I went to a concert at the Queen's Hall. I ran into Oliver Strachey, standing very like a Strachey in the Hall, because he dislikes sitting inside waiting for the music. I got by luck a very good place, for the Hall was nearly full—& it was a divine concert. But one of the things I decided as I listen[ed] (its difficult not to think of other things) was that all descriptions of music are quite worthless, & rather unpleasant; they are apt to be hysterical, & to say things that people will be ashamed of having said afterwards. They played Haydn, Mozart no 8, Brandenburg Concerto, & the Unfinished. I daresay the playing wasnt very good, but the stream of melody was divine. It struck me what an odd thing it was— this little box of pure beauty set down in the middle of London streets, & people—all looking so ordinary, crowding to hear, as if they weren't ordinary after all, or had an ambition for something better. Opposite me was Bernard Shaw, grown a whitehaired benevolent old man,[3] & down

2. On 25 February 1915 LW signed a five-year lease on Hogarth House; the rent was £50 p.a.
3. George Bernard Shaw (1856-1950), critic, Fabian socialist and playwright, was not yet sixty.

in the orchestra was Walter Lamb, shining in his alabastrine baldness like a marble fountain. I was annoyed by a young man & woman next me who took advantage of the music to press each other's hands; & read 'A Shropshire Lad' & look at some vile illustrations.[4] And other people eat chocolates, & crumbled the silver paper into balls. I went to the W.C. at the Tube station, & found a small party going on in that chaste recess. The old woman had a vast female dog which was drinking water out of a tumbler, & her daughters were paying an afternoon call, & we were all very friendly, in odd surroundings—I thought it very sensible to have no false shame. I met L. at Spikings & we had tea, & were very happy;[5] & stopped at Earls Court & called on his mother, but she was out. We were shown into a huge high sitting room, in which was a minute old lady, in semi darkness, sitting on the edge of a sofa. Nothing could have been more forlorn. L. has now got another book of Indian travels from the Times. He had just made up his mind that he was dismissed.[6]

Sunday 14 February

Rain again today. I cleaned silver, which is an easy & profitable thing to do. It so soon shines again. Philip came, & he and L. went for a walk. He lunched with us & stayed talking till 3.30. They despair more than ever now of getting to the front. All Regular officers are preferred above them. Cecil has a machine gun, which may lead to his going, &, if so, almost certainly to his being killed. Poor Philip was a good deal agitated, I thought, with his prospects. What is he to do after the war is over? He thinks he must emigrate. Cecil would like to stay on in the Army, which however, one can't do, unless one has money, & neither of them has a penny. Five hundred a year is considerably more valuable than beauty or rank. He stayed talking, wanting to talk about himself perhaps & had to go back to Colchester, where the only tolerable thing is the oysters. The men he declares never cease joking; & the worse things are the more they joke. Then we walked down the river, in the face of a cold gale (which is now raging outside) & gladly came home to tea; & now sit as usual surrounded by books & paper & ink, & so shall sit till bedtime—save that I have some mending to do, my entire skirt having split in two yesterday. L. is writing a review of his Indian book. I am now reading a later volume of Michelet, which is superb, & the only tolerable history. The people next door are singing the same song that they've been practising these 3 months—a hymn. From all this, it is clear that I don't want to mend my dress: & have nothing whatever to say.

4. A. E. Housman's volume of lyrics, 1896.
5. Tea Rooms at 45 Dover Street.
6. LW's review of *In the Lands of the Sun. Notes and Memoirs of a Tour in the East*, by H.R.H. Prince William of Sweden, appeared in the *TLS*, 18 February 1915.

Monday February 15

There is nothing to record of this morning, except my conviction that Mrs Le Grys is the best tempered woman in England, &, if she gets her 20 roomed house at Southampton, will make it a gigantic success. We have only to hint that we want dog soap, & she washes Max (who badly wanted it).

We both went up to London this afternoon; L. to the Library, & I to ramble about the West End, picking up clothes. I am really in rags. It is very amusing. With age too one's less afraid of the superb shop women. These great shops are like fairies' palaces now. I swept about in Debenham's & Marshalls & so on, buying, as I thought with great discretion.[7] The shop women are often very charming, in spite of their serpentine coils of black hair. (By the way, I met Walter Lamb at Dover Street station— A gentleman in frock coat, top hat, slip, umbrella &c. accosted me. I fairly laughed. It was old Wat. who had just been lunching with an M.P's wife, & seeing all the grandees. His satisfaction is amazing: it oozes out everywhere.) Then I had tea, & rambled down to Charing Cross in the dark, making up phrases & incidents to write about. Which is, I expect, the way one gets killed.

L. went to tea at Gordon Sqre where he saw Mrs Hutchinson, who is the present flame, but a very smoky one.[8] Clive anyhow approves our scheme of a Periodical, & he is a man of business, whatever he may be as an artist.[9]

I bought a ten & elevenpenny blue dress, in which I sit at this moment.

7. Debenham & Freebody of Wigmore Street, and Marshall & Snelgrove, Oxford Street.
8. Mary Hutchinson, *née* Barnes (b. 1889), whose mother was a first cousin of Lytton Strachey. In 1910 she had married St John Hutchinson (see below, 7 June 1918, n 3). She was for many years to come (according to Quentin Bell) "the most important person in Clive's life".
9. The Woolfs' dream of producing a magazine of their own was recurrent but never realised.

1917

1917

The last entry made by Virginia Woolf in 1915 was that of 15 February; on the 17th she had an appointment with the dentist, and she and Leonard went to Farringdon Street about a printing press. The next day she had a headache, and from then onwards, with increasingly sleepless nights and restless aching days, she slid inexorably into madness. By 4 March she was beyond Leonard's care, and professional nurses were called in. Leonard took possession of Hogarth House on Quarter Day, 25 March 1915, and Virginia was brought there a week later. Weeks passed during which she was incoherent, excited and violent, for many months more she was under constant surveillance. She took against Leonard, and for two months he dared not see her. It seemed that she might never return to sanity. But gradually in June she began to improve, and in November the last nurse could leave. Alternating between Hogarth House and Asheham House in Sussex—which she had rented since before her marriage—Virginia very slowly returned to normal life, shaken, older-looking and heavier.

For a long time there was no question of her writing at all, and then she was rationed, as it was thought to excite her. The diary she had broken off in 1915 seems to have been forgotten. In the spring of 1917 the Woolfs at last bought their printing press. After producing their Publication No. 1 that summer, they returned to Asheham, and Virginia began a journal which, though of a rather different character to her previous and subsequent ones, is included here.

The Asheham Diary is a small notebook (see Appendix 1, II); the date is written on the verso pages, opposite the text on the recto, each day's entry ruled off with a line across the page. This book remained at Asheham and Virginia added to it on later visits.

Friday 3 August

Came to Asheham. Walked out from Lewes. Stopped raining for the first time since Sunday. Men mending the wall & roof at Asheham. Will has dug up the bed in front, leaving only one dahlia.[1] Bees in attic chim[n]ey.

Saturday 4 August

Rained all the morning very hard. Newspapers sent on to Telscombe, but signalman lent us the Daily News.[2] To post at Southease in the after-

---

1. Will (? Attfield), a local man who did odd jobs for the Woolfs at Asheham.
2. The signalman at Southease and Rodmell Halt was Thomas Pargiter, Labour candidate for the Conservative stronghold of Lewes in the 1918 'Khaki' election. His surname was used in the original title for VW's book which became The Years. The Daily News was the most radical national daily paper then available.

noon. Back over the downs. Very wet. Corn beaten down by rain. L. made book cases.

Sunday 5 August

Dull morning, getting steadily finer, until it became a very hot & sunny afternoon. Walked on M.'s walk.[3] Saw 3 perfect peacock butterflies, 1 silver washed frit[illary]; besides innumerable blues feeding on dung. All freshly out & swarming on the hill.[4] Small flowers out in great quantities. Found mushrooms, mostly in the hollow, enough for a dish. Barbara & Bunny after dinner stayed for tea & dinner.[5]

Monday 6 August

Very fine hot day. (Bank Holiday). Sound of band in Lewes from the Downs. Guns heard at intervals. Walked up the down at the back. Got plenty of mushrooms. Butterflies in quantities. Ladies 6th Aug. 1918 Bedstraw, Round-headed Rampion, Thyme, Marjoram. eggs 4/6 doz. Saw a grey looking hawk—not the usual red-brown one. A few plums on the tree. We have begun to cook apples. Eggs 2/9 doz. from Mrs Attfield.[6]

Tuesday 7 August

Queer misty day. Sun not strong enough to come through. Went to Brighton after lunch. German prisoners working in the field by Dod's Hill. laughing with the soldier, & woman passing. Went to Pier; tea at Booth's;[7] horrible men at our table; staged at Lewes on way back. Bicycled

3. A walk which took its name from VW's private terms of endearment: Mongoose, signifying LW and Mandril, VW herself.

4. The four Stephen children, encouraged by their half-brother George Duckworth and his brother-in-law Jack Hills, had been ardent 'bug-hunters' or butterfly collectors. The Blues (genus *Polyommatus*) were once very common on the South Downs.

5. Barbara Hiles (b. 1891) studied painting at the Slade School 1913-14; very pretty, lively, and good-natured, she had attracted Saxon Sydney-Turner, and VW hoped he might marry her. At this time Barbara had installed herself in a tent at Charleston, but normally lived in Hampstead. David ('Bunny') Garnett (b. 1892) was by training a naturalist. He had served in France with a Quaker Relief Unit, but now he and Duncan Grant were living at Charleston and, as pacifists, working at nearby Newhouse Farm, Firle. He also kept bees. The previous year he, Barbara and another girl had broken in and spent a night at Asheham.

6. Mrs Attfield lived in one of the cottages, now demolished, at Itford, near Asheham House, of which she acted as caretaker, giving occasional domestic help.

7. Caterers and confectioners of 69/70 East Street, Brighton.

back from Glynde. N. & L. went to get mushrooms, & found several, also blackberries getting ripe, only have no sugar for jam.[8]

Wednesday 8 August

Mist again. Went to post at Southease. L.'s foot very bad. Saw wooden pews put into traction engine at Rodmell Church; a man without a hand, a hook instead. Met Mrs Attfield with dead chicken in a parcel, found dead in the nettles, head wrung off, perhaps by a person. Home over downs. Fair haul of mushrooms again, best in hollow. Alix came;[9] rain storm after tea, then fine.

Thursday 9 August

To get mushrooms with Alix: L. stayed down sawing wood, as his foot was bad. Bunny over, & climbed the roof to see bees; didn't take them: to be left till autumn.

Friday 10 August

L. up to Labour conference in London.[10] Fine day again. Alix & I to hills for blackberries. We found them in patches very plentiful. The servants got huge mushrooms called 'plate' mushrooms; the others 'natives' so the Woolers say.[11]

Saturday 11 August

To picnic near Firle, with Bells &c. Passed German prisoners, cutting wheat with hooks. Officer & woman with orderly galloped onto the downs. Rain came on after tea, so made a fire of wood. Henry followed us home, bit Will & frightened the servants.[12]

8. Nelly (or Nellie) Boxall and her friend Lottie Hope who, on the recommendation of Roger Fry, had started work as resident cook and housemaid to the Woolfs on 1 February 1916.

9. Alix Sargant-Florence (1892-1973), educated at Bedales and at Newnham College, Cambridge, 1911-14. VW first met her on 21 June 1916 when James Strachey brought her to dine at Hogarth House; by the following summer the Woolfs knew and liked her well enough to suggest she might work for them as an apprentice printer. (See below, 15 and 16 October 1917.)

10. LW and others in the Labour Party were attempting to organise an international conference in Stockholm to discuss socialist aims for peace; they failed, as passports were refused to the intending delegates. See also below, 21 and 22 August 1917. and 1 May 1918.

11. The Wooller family lived at Asheham Cottage.

12. Henry was a sheepdog belonging to the Bells.

Sunday 12 August

Walked up mushrooming. L.'s leg still bad. Saw a large green caterpillar in hollow, with 3 purple spots on each side by the head. Mushrooms old & black. Horse mushrooms out in great circles; but very few real ones. N. & Lot. to Charleston.

Monday 13 August

Went into Lewes with Alix: she left us in the High St. L. had his leg looked at; probably a strain. Market in Lewes.[13] Calves wrapped in sacking lying on platform. Walked back from Glynde. To get mushrooms before dinner; every grass almost had blues asleep on it. Found very few mushrooms, having seen the shepherd bring a bag down in the morning. Warned by Lottie that Will was going to blow up wasps nest after dinner, so we watched: much smell, explosion, wasps swarmed. This was done twice in nest near the hole in the wall.

Tuesday 14 August

To get mushrooms & blackberries; the rings of horse mushrooms seem to put an end to the others: we only get a few. Found G.L.D. when we came in.[14] Offered a bag of mushrooms by shepherd, but found them all horses, harmless, but too timid to try. Wall done about now—not a success.

Wednesday 15 August

Nessa, Mabel, & children came to tea.[15] Our pink flower she says is phlox: not stocks. Went into hollow without success; but Nelly found more mushrooms on the top. The Co-ops will allow more sugar, so we can now make jam. Gunn charges 4d quart for milk.[16] Duncan over for dinner. They walked home at 10 over the downs. Quentin ate till he was nearly sick at tea.

13. Monday was (and still is) market day in Lewes, the county town of East Sussex.
14. Goldsworthy ('Goldie') Lowes Dickinson (1862-1932), teacher, humanist, historian and philosophical writer; an Apostle; elected Fellow of King's College, Cambridge, in 1887; lecturer in Political Science there from 1896 to 1920. During the war he was actively working towards the foundation of a League of Nations and with others published in 1917 *Proposals for the Prevention of Future Wars*. (See E. M. Forster, *Goldsworthy Lowes Dickinson*, 1934 and 1973, and *The Autobiography of G. Lowes Dickinson*, edited by Dennis Proctor, 1973.)
15. Vanessa Bell and her two sons Julian Heward (1908-1937) and Quentin Claudian Stephen (b. 1910), and their nurse Mabel Selwood.
16. Frank Gunn of Itford Farm was farm bailiff for Mrs J. D. Hoper, owner of this and Asheham House.

Thursday 16 August

L. & G.L.D. played chess all the afternoon. I went to post at Southease; the church now surrounded by scaffolding poles, & old wood panels leaning against the wall; bricklayers sitting by the gate. Woman asked me to find her children pad[d]ling in river: they did not want to go home. L.S. arrived.[17] went into the hollow.

Friday 17 August

All these days have been very fine, hot, blue sky, rather a high wind. Same again today. L.S. wrote on the terrace in the morning. G.L.D. & L. played chess there in the afternoon. G.L.D. decided to go to Guildford, so we walked to Beddingham with him. L.'s foot better, but got worse with walking. Found no mushrooms; we suppose the rain brought them prematurely. No yeast, so had to eat Bakers bread, wh. is very dull & dry.

Saturday 18 August

Went into Lewes, with prisoner, saw Cinema; bought several things. Met K.M.—her train very late.[18] Bought 1 doz. Lily roots & some red leaved plants wh. have been put in the big bed.

Sunday 19 August

Sat in the hollow; & found the caterpillar, now becoming a Chrysalis, wh. I saw the other day. A horrid sight: head turning from side to side, tail paralysed; brown colour, purple spots just visible; like a snake in movement. No mushrooms. Walked over the down with L.S. B. & Mr Garnett for dinner.[19]

17. (Giles) Lytton Strachey (1880-1932), critic and biographer, a contemporary and friend of both Thoby Stephen and LW at Trinity College, Cambridge, and like the latter an Apostle. After her brother's death in 1906, Lytton became one of VW's close friends and in 1909 he briefly contemplated marrying her. (See *I QB*, 141.) He was now finishing the last of the four biographical essays—that on General Gordon—which were to make up his highly successful *Eminent Victorians*. See *Holroyd*.

18. Katherine Mansfield was the adopted name of the New Zealand-born writer Kathleen Mansfield Beauchamp (1888-1923). She had met the Woolfs probably towards the end of 1916; they had now undertaken to print and publish her story *Prelude*.

19. Bunny and his father Edward Garnett (1868-1937), writer and publisher's reader, and husband of Constance, the translator of the Russian classics. It was he who had in 1913 read and recommended Duckworth to publish VW's first book *The Voyage Out*.

Monday 20 August

To Firle after tea over the down. The thistledown has been blowing
(English Maryland. about these last few days. Shepherd says mushrooms
11d S. Kensington come for a fortnight & go for a fortnight. Very fine
Station)[20] still, always S.E. wind, rather high. Home by the
fields. A great deal of the corn has to be cut by
hand. Men still working & women too at 7.

Tuesday 21 August

L. to London for second conference. Very hot. L.S. went to Charleston
after tea. K.M. & I walked on M.'s walk. The thistledown beginning to
blow. Saw the Silver Queen over the down, going towards Brighton &
coming back again.[21] A great many aeroplanes passed over the house.
Most of the butterflies have red spots on their necks—some parasite.
Planted a red flower with bulb given by Mrs Wooler to Nelly—some sort
of lily.

Wednesday 22 August

L. up to London again to see man from the foreign office.[22] Very hot
& windy again. Thistledown blowing across the house & over the field
L. bought me 10 very thick. K.M. went after lunch, in the fly from
packets of cigarettes: the Ram, which took Lytton's bag also.[23] Two
importation stopped. mowing machines, with 3 horses each, cutting the
corn in the field across the road. Cutting round &
round: finished last patch about 5. Corn already cut & standing on the
fields across the river. Eating potatoes from the garden. There was a raid
today. Ramsgate.

Thursday 23 August

Glad to be alone. L.'s leg cured now. Lottie sick from eating plums at
Charleston. We walked along the top, finding a few mushrooms, & down
the next hollow, in hopes of some, but found none. Odd that they should
stick to Asheham. Mist & rain; but on the whole fine, wind very high.

20. A brand of cigarettes costing 11d for 20 probably recommended by Katherine
Mansfield who was living not far from South Kensington Station.
21. One of several Royal Naval Air Service submarine-spotting airships which from
1915 were stationed at Polegate, near Eastbourne.
22. LW went up to a League of Nations Committee meeting with G. L. Dickinson
and J. J. Mallon, and later met Alwyn Parker of the Foreign Office, presumably to
discuss the proposed Stockholm conference. (See above, 10 August 1917.)
23. The Ram was the public house in Firle; a fly a one-horse carriage.

Heather growing on the top, making it look purple: never seen it there before.

Friday 24 August

Wind still higher. Nelly went to Lewes to fetch book sent for review; almost blown off on bridge. We walked, startled hawk in the hollow, & found the feathers of a pigeon, he having carried away the bird.

Saturday 25 August

I went to post at Southease. L. gardened. Another windy day. Seeing the church surrounded by scaffolding, I went in, found floor up, pews taken away, ladders all about. A notice to say that restoration will cost £227. The church there in 966 A.D. Holes in the tower & roof visible.[24] Men at work carting corn in the field by the road.

Wood from the church so rotten that it left sawdust on the grass where it stood.

Sunday 26 August

We meant to have a picnic at Firle, but rain started, as we were ready, & so we went to post at Beddingham instead. Left my macintosh in the hedge, so it came down hard, & we were very wet. It rained hard & steadily the whole evening & was raining violently when we went to bed. This is the first bad day we have had; even so, the morning was fine. The high wind of the last few days has broken leaves off, although only a few of the trees have begun to turn. Swallows flying in great numbers very low & swift in the field. The wind has brought down some walnuts, but they are unripe; the wasps eat holes in the plums, so we shall have to pick them. My watch stopped.

Monday 27 August

We had meant to go to Eastbourne, to get my watch mended, among other things, but about 12 it not only blew very hard but rained. The field full of swallows, & leaves broken off in bunches, so that the trees already look thin. L. thinks that the swallows are driven into the hollow by the gale, in hopes that fly's may be out in the shelter. Swallows & leaves whirling about look much the same. L. took ms. to catch London train at Glynde:[25] then we walked by M.'s walk on to the down; got some blackberries: the bushes laden with them; & a few mushrooms. Such wind &

24. Of Saxon origin, the small flint-walled Norman church at Southease has a round tower, one of three in Sussex.
25. Probably VW's review of *Beyond* by John Galsworthy, which appeared in the *TLS*, 30 August 1917 (Kp C84).

rain however that we were wet through & had to come home. Lit wood fire after tea. We have had them after dinner, but not yet after tea. Rained steadily; water came through the garden door.

Tuesday 28 August

Another most appalling day. Leaves & swallows blown about in the field; garden dishevelled. Branches down across the road; corn cocks tumbled over; rain drenching. Servants had meant to go to Brighton, but gave up. Had forgotten to order meat, so had to walk to Firle. Wind behind us going. A tree down at corner by the pond, made a frightful noise as one went beneath them. But it stopped raining, & there was some blue sky over the downs. Early closing in Firle. Grocer doing stamps in lamplight. Telephone broken by gale. Home against the wind, but dry. German prisoners now working for Hoper:[26] work very well, if given tea at 4.30, wh. they insist upon, & will then work an extra hour. Impossible to carry corn in this weather. Gunn comes very seldom. Harvest wh. was good, now said to be ruined. Rain started again in the evening. Had to have a candle to end dinner with. Fires before dinner.

Wednesday 29 August

Another very bad day, though wind less furious. Swallows flying higher. Papers say storm has been all over England. Tremendous rain in the afternoon; which stopped, & we went to post at Southease, arguing about education, back over the hill; a fine evening—great sun appeared as we dined, & sunset for the first time since Saturday.

Thursday 30 August

Not actually raining, though dark so the servants went to Brighton. I went over the Down; L. cut the grass in the garden. Trees have suddenly turned brown & shrivelled on their exposed sides, though still green in shelter; as if dried up by very hot sun. No autumn tints. Blue butterflies ragged & washed out. L. was stung on the ankle by a wasp. He cut into their nest. Barbara & Nick Bagenal came over to tea & dinner, which we had to scratch up for them, servants being out.[27] Rain came on after dinner again; but wind much fallen.

26. Mr J. D. Hoper of Rugby, whose wife had inherited Asheham House and its surrounding farm lands, managed by their bailiff Mr Gunn from neighbouring Itford farm.
27. Nicholas Beauchamp Bagenal (1891-1974); King's College, Cambridge, 1910-13; in 1914 commissioned in the Suffolk Regiment and transferred to the Irish Guards in 1916. He was in love with Barbara Hiles, whom he had met through his sister-in-law who shared a home with her early in the war.

Friday 31 August

Last day of August a very beautiful one. Wind soft, & steadily grew finer & hotter so that we sat out on the terrace after tea. L. cut grass again, & I went in the water-meadows & so round onto the road, up the down, creeping behind old Bosanquet.[28] I saw a herd of cows on the top of the down driven by a soldier & a man on a large black horse. Very odd sight. The mushroom seems to be extinct. After dinner, it still being light & hot, we took the wasps nest, burning it thoroughly, though when we left it, wasps were swarming at the mouth. Great question about Mrs Wooler's chicken; offers it for 2/6. Eggs now gone up to 3/- the dozen. Sausages here come in.

Saturday 1 September

In spite of a perfect moonlit night, mist rain & wind, black all over the downs this morning. As bad as ever. However it blew so hard that it stopped raining in the afternoon. We went into the hollow, started a great hare, & then saw a man shooting. In fact they had shot at pigeons very near us. We went round & over the top. Seems now mid-autumn or even early winter from the look of things. Trees an ugly leaden colour outside, as if shrivelled, flowers beaten down & brown; butterflies scarcely flying. L. to Lewes to meet Mrs W[oolf]. & B. who came here about 7.[1] Lovely night again. A great white owl, looking like a sea gull, sat on the rail, & flew about. Mushrooms started on my patch. L. took wasps.

Sunday 2 September

Uncertain, windy weather, with showers in the morning; but the sun seemed to get the better steadily, & it was a fine afternoon. Round M.'s walk, in a high wind, with the visitors. Hawks out, but saw nothing else. A superb evening, hot on the terrace & light over the downs till past 9. A fine September predicted. According to the papers, in most parts every day in Aug. had rain—one of the worst on record; so we have been in luck. H.W. & M.A. went after tea.[2]

28. Sir Albert Bosanquet (1837-1932), K.C., was the tenant of Cobbe Place, Beddingham, which VW circumambulated.

1. Bella Sidney Lock, *née* Woolf (1877-1960), LW's eldest sister, a widow since the death of her first husband, the botanist R. H. Lock, in June 1916. She contributed to the children's magazine *Little Folks* and was the author of numerous books. In 1921 she married W. T. Southorn, later Sir Thomas Southorn, of the Colonial Service, with whom LW had shared a bungalow when he first went to Ceylon and was posted to Jaffna in January 1905.

2. LW's brother Herbert came for the day with their cousin Martin Abrahamson (1870-1962), an Anglo-Danish electrical engineer and company director; his mother was Mrs Woolf's sister.

Monday 3 September

Perfect day; completely blue without cloud or wind, as if settled for ever. Watched dog herding sheep. Rooks beginning to fly over the trees, both morning & evening, sometimes with starlings. Mrs W. & B. went after lunch. Took us to Lewes with them. Asked about watch; but can't get it done for 3 months. Boots gone up to 40/- but found an old 15/ pair in a small shop, wh. I bought; & then found a good pair in the cupboard at home. Back by train; L. bicycled. Made a straight line across fields from Glynde, a very good way. Met Nelly bringing back Co-op. box,[3] so walked with her. Evening so fine we went out again into the hollow. Saw a shining spot, which we could not find when we came up to it. Painted Lady [*Vanessa cardui*] seen near Glynde.

Tuesday 4 September

Woke to find the house in a mist. We have seen this on the meadows at night. It cleared, & was a perfect day, almost without wind. In the afternoon we began to pick our apples; I did the lower ones & L. the higher ones, on a farm ladder. In the middle, Clive & Mary H. appeared, so I had to stop. They stayed for tea & dinner, & walked back over the downs.

Wednesday 5 September

Another fine morning. I walked, & L. did the garden. I saw a clouded yellow [*Colias edusa*] on the top—a very deep yellow the first for a long time. Clouds brewed over the sea, & it began to rain at tea; then great thunder claps, & lightning. Difficult to distinguish thunder from guns. German prisoners walked across the field. They are now helping on this farm. Corn over the road still standing in shocks uncarted. Servants stayed at Charleston all night; say that there was gun fire as well as thunder.

Thursday 6 September

To the post at Southease. A fine day, but nothing particular to be noticed.

Friday 7 September

In to Lewes, by Glynde, & the new way across the fields, to the station. Shopped, & back expecting Pernel, but she never came.[4] A very hot,

---

3. Presumably the container for the groceries ordered from the Co-operative Stores.
4. (Joan) Pernel Strachey (1876-1951), fourth of Lytton's five sisters, was Tutor, Director of Studies and Lecturer in Modern Languages at, and Vice-Principal of, Newnham College, Cambridge.

steamy day. A snake, grass, about 2 feet twisted across the path in front of us.

Saturday 8 September

We went to get blackberries on the top. Found enough easily for a pudding. A cloud over the land all day, except late in the evening, when the sun came out beneath it in an odd way. Pernel came, then Philip M[orrell]. then Sydney W[aterlow]. as we were sitting down to dinner.

Sunday 9 September

An almost motionless day; no blue sky; almost like a winter day, save for the heat. Very quiet. Over to picnic at Firle in the afternoon. Nessa & 5 children came after we had done; sat outside the trees.[5] Walked home over the downs. Red sky over the sea. Woods almost as thin as winter, but very little colour in them.

Monday 10 September

To post at Southease, but my boots hurt, from being too big, so we sat down, & L. went on. A perfect rather misty but cloudless day, still & very hot. Odd to find no flowers in the hedges, all brown & dead, because of the storm. Often a sound like rain, which turns out to be leaves falling. German prisoners stacking corn at the back of the house. They whistle a great deal, much more complete tunes than our work men. A great brown jug for their tea.

Tuesday 11 September

Went over the downs by the farm; saw 2 clouded yellows by the warren, & another pair over towards Bishopstone. Heard guns & saw two airships maneuvring over the sea & valley. Found Lady's Tresses, & Field Gentian on the Downs. Very hot day, but cold in the evening, & so had fire. Swallows have quite left the field. Pernel left. L. found a walnut sprouting with leaves & planted it in the garden.

Wednesday 12 September

I bicycled to Charleston, getting there at 12.30 A long & rather dull bit of road between Glynde & Charleston—but going slowly it is easy to do

5. Julian and Quentin Bell and the three children of Desmond and Molly MacCarthy who were staying at Charleston.

it in under the hour. L. came after tea & we bicycled back the other way by Beanstalk lane, discovered a probable short cut. Gigantic sun; colder, & windier than before. Corn in field opposite carried about now.

Thursday 13 September

A windy day. I went onto the down, after going to Southease. They have taken a slice out of the church tower; you can see a wooden frame inside. Blew up a storm of rain, had a fire after tea; servants to Charleston, home in storm over the downs. Had tea in kitchen, & saw old man who is thatching the ricks raking apples off the tree into a bucket. L. called out "When you've done!" & he ran away.

Friday 14 September

Meant to go to Lewes, as it became fine, but my bicycle found punctured; very annoying; but it was hopeless to start, so Nelly went instead on Mrs Hammond's, & got us a lot of things.[6] Very hot & fine by degrees; seems to take a lot of time to get really fine. We went after mushrooms but found none— A most disappointing season. Cut up a great fungus like cheese.

Saturday 15 September

A perfect day for our treat. We went to Eastbourne. Sat in Devonshire park & watched tennis & heard band. Saw an aeroplane in field near Glynde. It looked like a toy. Children round it: man working propeller round. Had tea & ice; bought Kodak; home to Lewes, where we bought stuff &c. Lord Hugh Cecil got out of the train at Glynde, with a guardsman &c; very amusing to watch: he had 3 leather bags; dressed as flying officer; quite white haired.[7]

Sunday 16 September

An almost sunless, but fine day. Clouds too high for rain. Walked to Firle & had picnic. L. went on with Kodak to Charleston. I waited for him by the trees. After a time, Robin Mayor & Bobo M. came, to my

---

6. Probably Mrs Hammond of Itford Cottages near by; Hammond is a common Sussex name.
7. Lord Hugh Cecil (1869-1956), fifth and youngest son of the 3rd Marquess of Salisbury (and brother-in-law of VW's friend Lady Eleanor Cecil) was at this time Conservative MP for Oxford University. In 1915 he had joined the Royal Flying Corps and, in spite of his age, succeeded in gaining his pilot's wings on condition he never again undertook a solo flight.

surprise: at Talland (wh. they still have) for week end: had let it to Belgians.[8] L. came back; N[essa]. thought the Kodak wd. cause great jealousy, so kept it. Silver Queen over sea; a bar of red across the sea, like last Sunday. Will brought his ferrets & caught a rabbit for the servants.

Monday 17 September

Servants went in float, driven by Will, at 10:[9] Mrs Hammond came. Time changed at 3 to winter time. A windy changeable day. Telegram from MacCs' after lunch. Molly cant come; D. comes tomorrow. Went to post at Southease & back the usual way over the downs, talking about arctic regions. Rainy. Made chair cover after tea. A very dark evening, by new time.[10]

Tuesday 18 September[11]

A furious wet day; rain lashing across, sea mist when not pouring. Nevertheless we started for Lewes; but were driven back at the turning by the water mill. Spent afternoon indoors, a treat. Settled down after dinner to print photographs, deciding that D[esmond] wouldn't come; but he arrived at 8; had driven out in a fly; had to find some dinner for him.

Wednesday 19 September

Telegram to put off picnic. Day looked very bad, rained & blew all the afternoon. Walked with D. to Rodmell to ask about whiskey. Public House shut up; man came & cd. sell us none till 6. Stayed talking about

8. Robert ('Robin') John Grote Mayor (1869-1947), Fellow of King's College, Cambridge, and an Apostle, was an Assistant Secretary at the Board of Education. He had married in 1912 Beatrice ('Bobo') Meinertzhagen (1885-1971), one of the ten children of Daniel and Georgina Meinertzhagen and a niece of Beatrice Webb. The Mayors had taken over VW's tenancy of Little Talland House in Firle when she moved to Asheham.

9. A float was a low, broad and flat farm cart, used for carrying heavy articles such as milk churns.

10. Summer Time (daylight saving), whereby during the summer months the time was one hour in advance of Greenwich Mean Time, was introduced as a temporary war-time expedient in May 1916 (it is still in force). In 1917 the clocks reverted to GMT during the night of 16/17 September.

11. On the left-hand page, facing the entries for 17 and 18 September, VW has made a note:

> *Wed. 19:* have had 6 eggs from Mrs W.
> 3 „ „ Will.
> there are 2 over (Wed. A.M.)
>
> *Thu:* 6 eggs fr. Mrs Att:
> There are 5 at Thu. A.M.

the war "Whats it *for?*" & how soldiers wd. break the windows if they came home & found no beer. Met German prisoners on the road. D. said Guten Tag, & they all answered. Sentry said nothing. Real winter now.

Thursday 20 September

Another grey windy day, though not so much rain. Brilliant sun & blue sky for about 10 minutes in the afternoon. L. had to get whiskey in Rodmell. Picked apples, he on the table. Then to get milk at cottage, & round into hollow, where we found 3 mushrooms; & the spine & red legs of a bird, just devoured by a hawk—either pigeon or partridge. Very windy, but a starry night.

Friday 21 September

A fine day happily, though windy. L. went into Lewes to have his hair cut. I walked round M.'s walk with Desmond. Lay down a great deal in the sun, talking about society in the 70ties. Five Silver Queens over the sea round Newhaven looking for submarines D. says.

Saturday 22 September

Another very fair day, though well in autumn now. The rooks settling on the trees, & making a great noise in the early morning. A few walnuts ripe. Dahlia fully out in the bed. Trees now so thin that I can see the postman through them at the top of the hill. Clover in field opposite has been cut, & lies on the field. Still some corn standing across on the downs. Sat on the terrace after lunch: L. did garden. D. went to Glynde after tea; we sat over fire.

Sunday 23 September

Fine day. Picked apples in the afternoon, & stole straw & laid them on straw in the attics. Strolled out after tea. It becomes suddenly very cold. A more wintry sunset—very highly coloured. Too cold to stay out late. Desmond's story after dinner.

Monday 24 September

Desmond left at 9 in the fly. An absolutely perfect autumn day. Lewes half under mist, gradually lifting. No wind. To Lewes. I to Glynde, L. bicycling all the way in order to buy plants. I met Duncan at Glynde, going on his holidays. Had 2 pears. Great crowd for the London train. Apparently my letter to Nessa lost. Shopped in Lewes. Back to Glynde & bicycled home, through a herd of Alderneys; goat got in front & ran some way. Superb sunset. Men working very late carting the clover. A threshing machine at work behind the wood.

Tuesday 25 September

The day looked so fine that we planned a picnic at Telscombe. However it turned windy with a strange black haze over the sun—like a sea mist gone black, & only in parts, for it was very fine over Lewes. But it seemed too cold to picnic far away, so we went into the valley by the deserted farm. Saw a woman painting, & asked her to keep an eye on my bicycle. Went into the valley, up a little on the other side. Had tea there. Found a field of corn flowers & poppies, apparently sewn in rows. Picked a bunch, also some roots wh. L. has planted in the front garden.

Wednesday 26 September

A rather cold day, though fine. L. picked apples, having borrowed the shepherd's ladder. I went to post at Southease. Passed 2 troops of cadets, each headed by officer & chaplain. Home over the down—a stray horse running along the road the only other incident. Our sunflowers out now. A shooting party walking about, firing a good deal.

Thursday 27 September

A fine still day. Walked along the top, after getting a few apples in a butterfly net, & found the best clumps of mushrooms for a long time in the hollow. Still hazy, perfectly fine day. The Woolers picked apples; were given half.

Friday 28 September

Another very quiet day, which grew dark, though warm & still. Bicycled to Charleston. Roger there.[12] Fine border of flowers. Monk-brettia(?) is the name of the orange lily. Old man brought our flowers out.

12. Roger Eliot Fry (1866-1934), descended from generations of Quakers, gained first class honours in Natural Science at King's College, Cambridge, where he became an Apostle. He abandoned science for the study and practice of art, and became an established and respected figure in the museum and art world in England, France and America. He had married in 1896, but his wife developed a thickening of the skull and became gradually but inexorably insane, and in 1910 she was consigned to a mental home. In that year, a slight earlier acquaintance with Vanessa burgeoned into close friendship with her and Clive Bell, and they and their circle became enthusiastic supporters of Fry's efforts to introduce the work of the Post-Impressionists to London and, in 1913, to establish the Omega Workshops (see above, 7 January 1915, n 26). He fell in love with Vanessa and she, for a while, with him—a love she transmuted into lifelong friendship. VW's *Roger Fry. A Biography* was published in 1940. See also *Letters of Roger Fry*, 2 volumes, 1972, edited by Denys Sutton.

Saturday 29 September

L. came over at 3.30. Morning very lovely—seems settled into perfect weather now. Took a great many photographs. Aeroplanes over the house early, which may mean another raid. Nights bright moonlight. Home bicycling across the fields all the way—more than a mile shorter than the other way. Great red sun sinking about 6. L. says the rooks came & picked walnuts off the tree this morning—saw one flying with walnut in his beak. Has planted the Japanese anemones etc. in the front beds, on the terrace & in the back garden. We mean to abolish the large round bed.

Sunday 30 September

A perfect day. Up on the top, & found a handkerchief full of mushrooms. Met Nessa & Roger walking up to meet us. They heard guns over London & saw lights last night. Another raid. We heard nothing; save Mrs Hammond, who heard the guns very loud, as she went home. Clear moonlit nights. They went back after tea.

Monday 1 October

Bicycled in to Lewes—there & back. Passed a drunk man being driven into Lewes on his fruit cart by a policeman. Met another shouting held by 2 policemen in Lewes. Market presumably. Shopped. Met Roger. Anxious about raids. Another last night between 7 & 8: we listened but saw & heard nothing. The weather still perfectly fine warm without wind. Men came & fetched fallen trees, dragging them with horses.

Tuesday 2 October

Another fine day. Started the path in the walled garden this afternoon, & the flower bed by it. We make the path with cobbles from the wall, & work the old cement in. Great fun to do, & looks very nice from the drawing room already. Children came to tea. Looked about the house; we gave them 2 of L.'s heads of deer which they liked very much.[1] Walked a little way back, & onto the down for mushrooms, which have begun again. Had to lie down to escape Henry who ran over the top. Clouded after tea. Heard firing.

1. Julian and Quentin each carried home an antlered skull (trophies no doubt of LW's life in Ceylon) and hung them in their attic nursery; they may perhaps be rediscovered in *To The Lighthouse*, p. 176.

Wednesday 3 October

Not such a fine day. Wind rose, & grew cloudy. However, the raids will be stopped. Did the garden path all the afternoon. Planted some wall flowers, daisies, foxgloves. Into the hollow after tea, when almost dark. Had to send Will in for book to Lewes. Got windier. He only came back at 10; knocked, & could not make us hear (so he says).

Thursday 4 October

Our last day a thoroughly bad one from the point of view of weather. Wind & rain; completely black sky. L. had to go, walking there & back, to Lewes to order our car for tomorrow. I went round M.'s walk for the last time. Rain stopped, but wind so tremendous that Nessa & Duncan wouldn't be able to come as arranged. Mushroom season evidently setting in. Found several on the top. Had to lean against the wind coming down. Great fall of walnuts. Men throwing sticks to bring them down. Couldn't work at the path. A fine starry night however.

The Woolfs returned to Richmond on 5 October after three months at Asheham, and VW began a new book for her diary (see Appendix 1, III). The title-page is inscribed

Hogarth House
Paradise Road
Richmond
Oct. 1917

Monday 8 October

This attempt at a diary is begun on the impulse given by the discovery in a wooden box in my cupboard of an old volume, kept in 1915, & still able to make us laugh at Walter Lamb. This therefore will follow that plan—written after tea, written indiscreetly, & by the way I note here that L. has promised to add his page when he has something to say. His modesty is to be overcome. We planned today to get him an autumn outfit in clothes, & to stock me with paper & pens.[2] This is the happiest day that exists for me. It rained steadily of course. London seems unchanged, making me think of the change there used to be when one was a child. There was a man buying boots who had such a taste in boots that he knew different cuts & rows of nails; & was very cross when told his pair was "nice & strong". "I hate nice, strong boots" he growled. Evidently there

2. LW'S diary for 8 October: 'Went Regent St. &c wV to buy hat &c.'

is a taste in boots. We walked through Gough Sqre; Dr Johnson's house a fine, very well kept place, not so shabby as I expected.[3] A little square, folded in behind Chancery Lane, & given over to printing presses. This is the best part of London to look at—not I now think to live in. Carrying my manuscript to the Times I felt like a hack much in keeping.[4] We left it with a porter, & ran into Bruce Richmond, shining out a perfect gentleman in white gloves on the Ludgate Hill platform. He flourished his hat & disappeared.[5] Liz has a son; therefore our fears as to paternity are set at rest.[6]

Tuesday 9 October

We had a horrid shock. L. came in so unreasonably cheerful that I guessed a disaster. He has been called up. Though rather dashed for 20 minutes, my spirit mounted to a certainty that, save the nuisance, we have nothing to fear. But the nuisance—waiting a week, examination at 8.30 at Kingston—visits to Craig & Wright for certificates—is considerable.[7] It was piteous to see him shivering, physically shivering, so that we lit his gas fire, & only by degrees became more or less where we were in spirits; & still, if one could wake to find it untrue, it would be a mercy.

We took a proof of the first page of K.M.'s story, The Prelude.[8] It looks very nice, set solid in the new type. Masses of bookbinding equipment from Emma Vaughan arrived this morning—rather a testimony to her

3. Dr Johnson's house at 17 Gough Square, Fleet Street, where he lived from 1748-1759 and wrote his *Dictionary of the English Language*, is preserved as a museum.

4. Probably VW's review of *The Gambler and Other Stories* by Fyodor Dostoevsky, translated by Constance Garnett, which appeared in the *TLS*, 11 October 1917 (Kp C88).

5. Bruce Lyttelton Richmond (1871-1964), editor of *The Times Literary Supplement* from its inception in 1902 until his retirement in 1938. His wife was Elena, *née* Rathbone, for whom VW had in her youth a sentimental admiration.

6. Liz was a sister of the Woolf's cook Nelly Boxall; her husband Bert was a soldier on active service.

7. LW had previously been called up and was exempted from military service on 30 June 1916 on the strength of letters from Dr Maurice Wright, attesting that he suffered from an 'Inherited Nervous Tremor', and from Dr Maurice Craig (a specialist in psychological medicine who had earlier been consulted on VW's behalf) that the removal of LW's care might be highly detrimental to his wife's unstable condition. Both doctors now furnished further letters certifying that LW was not fit for military service.

8. Katherine Mansfield's long short story was the second undertaking of the Hogarth Press though in fact its third publication. It took nine months to produce.

fads, for it is all good, & I suppose she never bound a book.[9] But this is uncharitable considering. We had a short walk by the river. As it is a fine, fairly still evening, perhaps I shall have a raid to describe tomorrow. Trissie is staying her holiday with us.[10] I forget how many people rang us up this morning, Alix for one, who wants to start her work apparently; & we have a liver & bacon Clumber [spaniel] in view, living at Wimbledon, the property of a man taken for the army. The K. Shuttleworths advertise the birth of a boy with the statement "His Perfect Gift" a good title for an Academy picture, or a Mrs Ward novel, & rather a terrible testimony to the limelight now desired by the rich upon their sacrifices.[11]

Wednesday 10 October

No air raid; no further disturbance by our country's needs; in fact L. made out in his bath that he deserved some good fortune, & opening his letters found a cheque for £12 from a Swedish paper which never was born & yet pays its debts. And I had 4/ for myself. Late last night, I was told to have my Henry James done if possible on Friday, so that I had to make way with it this morning, & as I rather grudge time spent on articles, & yet cant help spending it if I have it, I am rather glad that this is now out of my power. And another article upon the country in Hardy & E. Brontë is suggested.[12] We walked down the river, through the park, & back to an early tea. At this moment L. is bringing the 17 Club into existence.[13] I am sitting over the fire, & we have the prospect of K.

9. Emma ('Toad') Vaughan (1874-1960), youngest child of VW's aunt Adeline and Henry Halford Vaughan. She studied music in Dresden, and was now engaged in relief work with German prisoners of war. In 1901 she and VW planned to learn bookbinding together; VW continued all her life to do a good deal of binding, seldom very proficiently. Some 40 early letters from VW to Emma are in MHP, Sussex.

10. Trissie Selwood, Mabel's sister, was Vanessa Bell's cook at Charleston, and was very friendly with VW's servants.

11. The birth of a posthumous son to Captain the Hon. Lawrence Kay-Shuttleworth was announced in *The Times* of 9 October 1917; the brother of Jack Hills, widower of VW's half-sister Stella, had married a Kay-Shuttleworth. Mary Augusta Ward (Mrs Humphry Ward, 1851-1920), granddaughter of Thomas Arnold of Rugby, an immensely energetic and philanthropic woman and an active opponent of Women's Suffrage, was best known as a prolific and successful novelist.

12. VW's review of *The Middle Years* by Henry James appeared in the *TLS*, 18 October 1917 (Kp C89). The other suggestion does not appear to have been pursued.

13. The 1917 Club, named after the February Revolution in Russia, was founded to provide a meeting place for people interested in peace and democracy; it soon attracted a membership of unpopular radical politicians and intellectuals. Its premises were in Gerrard Street, Soho.

Mansfield to dinner, when many delicate things fall to be discussed. We notice how backward the leaves are in falling & yellowing here compared with Asheham. It might still be August, save for the acorns scattered on the path—suggesting to us the mysterious dispensation which causes them to perish, or we should be a forest of oaks.

Thursday 11 October

The dinner last night went off: the delicate things were discussed. We could both wish that ones first impression of K.M. was not that she stinks like a—well civet cat that had taken to street walking. In truth, I'm a little shocked by her commonness at first sight; lines so hard & cheap. However, when this diminishes, she is so intelligent & inscrutable that she repays friendship. My saying—Chaste & the Unchaste—was exaggerated by Murry for reasons of his own; reasons that make him wish all of a sudden to break with Garsington.[14] We discussed Henry James, & K.M. was illuminating I thought. A munition worker called Leslie Moor came to fetch her—another of these females on the border land of propriety, & naturally inhabiting the underworld—rather vivacious, sallow skinned, without any attachment to one place rather than another.[15] Today poor L. had to go the round of Drs & committees, with a visit to Squire thrown in. His certifications are repeated. He weighs only 9.6. I bought my winter store of gloves, got a reference in the London Library, & met L. at Spikings for tea. Heaven blessed us by sending a quick train, & we came home, very glad to be home, over our fire, though we had to light it, & cook up our dinner, owing to the servants off day.

Sunday 14 October

That is an awful confession, & seems to show the signs of death already spreading in this book. I have excuses though. We were rung up & asked

14. John Middleton Murry (1889-1957) literary critic, editor and author, leading luminary in that world of literary journalism and promotion which VW called 'the Underworld'. He wrote criticism for *The Westminster Gazette* and the *TLS*, and founded and edited *Rhythm* (later *The Blue Review*) with Katherine Mansfield, with whom he was living (and was to marry in 1918). During the war he worked in the political intelligence department of the War Office. He and Katherine were regular guests of Philip and Ottoline Morrell at Garsington. See F. A. Lea, *The Life of John Middleton Murry*, 1959.

15. Ida Constance Baker (b. 1888), a fellow-pupil of Kathleen Mansfield Beauchamp at Queen's College, Harley Street, 1903-06, and thenceforward her devoted friend. Katherine Mansfield and Lesley Moore were names they adopted at school and retained. She came from a conventional middle-class family with Rhodesian connections; in 1916 she had taken a war job as a tool-setter in an aeroplane factory in Chiswick.

to dine with the Bells in Soho, & this, I regret to say, led to much argument; we put off going to Kingston; the night was wet, & L. didn't want —old arguments in short were brought out, with an edge to them.[16] So we went dolefully enough, found the place, behind the palace, dined with Roger, Nina Hamnet, Saxon & Barbara & a party such as might figure in a Wells novel: I enjoyed it though, & L. was a model of self-control.[17] Clive's remarks tended to prove that he is at the centre of everything, but not so aggressive as usual. Nessa has found her governess—sent, apparently by the hand of God.[18] Then on Saturday—what happened? Saturday was entirely given over to the military. We are safe again, &, so they say for ever. Our appearance smoothed every obstacle; & by walking across Kingston we got to the doctor about 12, & all was over by half past. I waited in a great square, surrounded by barrack buildings, & was reminded of a Cambridge college—soldiers crossing, coming out of staircases, & going into others; but gravel & no grass. A disagreeable impression of control & senseless determination. A great boarhound, emblem of military dignity I suppose, strolled across by himself. L. was a good deal insulted: the drs. referred to him as "the chap with senile tremor", through a curtain. Mercifully the impression slowly vanished as we went about Richmond. Herbert came to tea, bringing the dog, Tinker, a stout, active, bold brute, brown & white, with large luminous eyes, reminding me a little of Dominic Spring-Rice.[19] We have taken him

16. The old arguments concerned VW's thirst for social life and LW's anxiety lest she should over-strain or excite herself. His medical examination at Kingston Barracks had, because of the dinner party, to be postponed from 12 October until the following day.

17. The place was Gustave's Restaurant, 39 Greek Street, behind the Palace Theatre, Cambridge Circus. Nina Hamnett (1890-1956), briefly married in 1914 to Roald Kristian, Count de Bergen; painter, writer and bohemian, she had been employed by Roger Fry in the Omega Workshops. Saxon Sydney-Turner (1880-1962) was contemporary and close friends with Thoby Stephen, LW, and Lytton Strachey at Trinity College, Cambridge, where he took a double first in classics and was an Apostle. A life-long devotee of the opera, particularly of Wagner, he had accompanied VW and her brother Adrian to Bayreuth in 1909 (see *I QB*, 149-152). On leaving Cambridge he had entered the civil service and was now, and remained until his retirement, in the Treasury. He was in love with Barbara Hiles. His peculiar and eccentric character is described in *I LW*, 103-108 and 114-119. VW made him the subject of an essay (unpublished) entitled 'One of Our Great Men', MHP, Sussex, MH/A 13c.

18. Miss Eva Edwards went to Charleston on 22 October as governess to Julian and Quentin Bell. It was an arrangement, as it turned out, that pleased no one.

19. Dominic Spring-Rice (1889-1940), educated at Eton and King's College, Cambridge, whose connections qualified him for inclusion among the 'Hyde Park Gaters'—the social circle of the Stephens and Duckworths when they lived in Kensington.

for a walk, but directly he is loosed, he leaps walls, dashes into open doors, & behaves like a spirit in quest of something not to be found. We doubt rather if we can cope with him. Have I put down our Manx cat, also presented to us, one day this week?

L. is up at Hampstead. We are to have Alix & Lilian [Harris] to dinner.

Monday 15 October

The chief fact today I think is the development & discovery of Tinker's character—all in the right direction. He was taken a long walk by the river the avenue & the Park; his spirit is great, but almost under control. He fell into the river twice; jumped out again; circled madly with a black poodle, & investigated several garden gates, which seem to have a fascination for him. He is a human dog, aloof from other dogs. Alix & Lilian were much as usual last night, save that Lilian had a dark patch on the top of her head, & heard almost perfectly; the dark patch is a cup for catching sound. A more modest, amiable, & yet quietly well informed & resolute character does not exist. Her principles are invariably liberal, although her character is naturally conservative—rather a good mixture. Moreover, she has always depended on her brain, & thus discusses with great sense any question, so long as it isn't art, that comes up. Alix has the same air of level headed desperation, solid, capacious, but as low in tone as a coal cellar. However we found her very anxious to take on our work; & comes to learn tomorrow. Manx is sitting on L.'s knee; Tinker occasionally looks at him.

Tuesday 16 October

Its odd how fate crams money into our mouths when we've got enough, & starves us when we're empty. Here we've made 270 (I think) in Bah Lias, & this morning they write to say that Mitchells is paying 4/ in £. so that brings us another £120.[20] Two years ago we had awkward debts, & had to sell out to pay them. We both make big or fairly big cheques monthly by reviewing. We started printing in earnest after lunch, & Alix came punctually; was instructed, & left on her high stool while we took the air with Tinkler, who jumped from a parapet into a boat covered with tarpaulin, crashed through, & out again, unhurt though surprised. We came back to find Perera, wearing his slip & diamond initial in his tie as usual;[21] in fact, the poor little mahogany coloured wretch has no

20. These financial mysteries have not been elucidated.
21. E. W. Perera, a Colombo advocate, with D. B. Jayatilaka (1868-1944), Barrister and later Vice-Chairman of the Board of Ministers of Ceylon, were in England as Sinhalese delegates to press the British Government for an enquiry into the repressive measures taken against the population following a serious outbreak of

variety of subjects. The character of the Governor, & the sins of the Colonial Office, these are his topics; always the same stories, the same point of view, the same likeness to a caged monkey, suave on the surface, inscrutable beyond. He made me uncomfortable by producing an e[n]velope of lace—"a souvenir from Ceylon Mrs Woolf"—more correctly a bribe, but there was no choice but to take it. He being gone upstairs, Alix solemnly & slowly explained that she was bored, & also worried by her 2 hours composing, & wished to give it up. A sort of morbid scrutiny of values & of motives, joined with crass laziness, leads her to this decision; as I expect it will lead her to many more. She has a good brain, but not enough vitality to keep it working. The idea weighed upon her, & I assured her there was no need for it to weigh.

Wednesday 17 October

I went up to the show of pictures at Heal's this afternoon, L. having spent the morning at a Coop. conference.[22] First I stood at Mudies counter while a stout widow chose 10 novels; taking them from the hand of Mudies man, like a lapdog, only stipulating that she wanted no vulgarity, not much description, but plenty of incident.[23] Her companion recommended South Wind—much praised by the reviews—all clever conversation, Italy; "but I can't bear conversation—I like sensation" said the widow & gulped down another mass of sweet sensation warranted not about the war, nor about drunkards. "I must really reduce my subscription to 8 I think" she observed; & waddled off with her ten volumes to Woking, so I guessed.

Ottoline was not at her ease; closely buttoned up in black velvet, hat like a parasol, satin collar, pearls, tinted eyelids, & red gold hair. Needless

---

rioting in 1915. LW collaborated with them in preparing their case. (See *III LW*, 229.) A 'slip' was a sort of under-waistcoat, providing white edges to the neck opening of the waistcoat proper. VW's Duckworth half-brothers, who were sticklers for correctness, wore one during the day in town; so did Walter Lamb. Cf *Mrs Dalloway*, p. 21.

22. Following Lloyd George's refusal to meet representatives of the movement, a 'National Emergency' meeting of the Co-operative Union was being held at Central Hall, Westminster, to press for a voice in the Government's food policy during a time of scarcity and profiteering. VW went to *An Exhibition of Works Representative of the New Movement in Art*, organised by Roger Fry, at the Mansard Gallery at Heal & Son, 196 Tottenham Court Road, from 8 to 26 October 1917. See *Letters of Roger Fry*, edited Denys Sutton, 1972, Vol. II, p. 413, where the catalogue is reprinted.

23. Mudie's Select Library, 30 New Oxford Street, near the British Museum. Possibly VW had transferred her custom from Day's, to which she had subscribed in 1915. (See above, 11 January 1915, n 44). *South Wind* was by Norman Douglas (1917).

to say one saw nothing of the pictures. Aldous Huxley was there—infinitely long & lean, with one opaque white eye.[24] A nice youth. We walked up & down a gallery discussing his Aunt, Mrs Humphry Ward. The mystery of her character deepens; her charm & wit & character all marked as a woman, full of knowledge & humour—& then her novels. These are partly explained by Arnold, who brought them near bankruptcy 4 years ago, & she rescued the whole lot by driving her pen day & night.[25] We had tea with Roger. I was very much conscious of strain—Ott. languid, & taking refuge in her great ladyhood, which is always depressing. They both seemed to have their quarrel before their eyes.[26] I walked with her in the downpour to Oxford Street, she buying me crimson carnations, without cordiality.

Thursday 18 October

L. out until 5 at his conference: & the telephone rang constantly (so I thought, as I tried to pin Mrs Meynell down in a review).[27] A dull life without him! Even Tinkler's restless mind did not make up. One's right hand becomes quite cramped holding his chain. Let loose he is very random, but on the whole obedient.* I had my tea in the kitchen, & L. came as I finished it; we sit surrounded by kittens & dogs, who now verge upon a suspicious relationship of some sort. We now expect Ka.[28]

*This, I must say, applies to Tinker, not to L.

24. Aldous Leonard Huxley (1894-1963), writer, had as yet published but occasional poems and one small book of poetry. His white eye resulted from an attack of *keratitis punctata* in 1911, and rendered him unfit for military service; he was at this time a temporary master at Eton, having spent most of the previous twelve months at Garsington.

25. Aldous Huxley's mother Julia had been a sister of Mrs Humphry Ward, whose only son Arnold (1876-1951), after a brilliant early career leading to a seat in Parliament, had become a compulsive gambler and was in serious financial difficulties.

26. The circumstances of this painful quarrel are uncertain; it had occurred at the time (May 1911) when Roger Fry and Vanessa Bell fell in love. Until then he and Ottoline had been on very intimate terms, but afterwards he accused her of spreading word that he was in love with her, which she vehemently repudiated. His sensitivity on the subject was very likely due to his new-found love for Vanessa and her jealous teasing. Thenceforward relations between Ottoline and Roger remained polite but frigid. See *The Early Memoirs of Lady Ottoline Morrell* edited by Robert Gathorne-Hardy, 1963, pp. 212-13, and *Ottoline* by Sandra Robson Darroch, 1976, pp. 99-100 and 106-08.

27. VW's review of *Hearts of Controversy*, critical essays by Alice Meynell, appeared in the *TLS*, 25 October 1917 (Kp C90).

28. Katherine ('Ka') Laird Cox (1887-1938); Newnham College, Cambridge, 1906-10, where she gravitated into the circle of Rupert Brooke, with whom she had a

Friday 19 October

The sweetness of Ka's nature, so we thought, is triumphing over the bureaucracy which threatened to straitwaistcoat all her charm. Not but what office life isn't a pool past which one has to lead her. She complains of falling hair; but looked to me softer & rosier, & more of the smoothness of cream than for a long while. She spent the night, was down with her leather case in hand to catch an early train. I had a letter from Nessa, about servants, & so went up to Mrs Hunts this afternoon—a mysterious building, all glass compartments, leading to a space given up to the ironing & washing of pink & blue pinafores, or so it looked.[29] Not a parlourmaid to be had. With some skilful manipulation of trains, I reached the Aeolian Hall, paid my shilling & heard a very long & very lovely Schubert octet.[30] Coming out, I saw a grey, shockheaded woman without a hat—Alix; & we had tea at Spikings. She has a kind of independence & lack of concern for appearances which I admire. But as we walked up & down Dover Street she seemed on the verge of rolling up the usual veil of laughter & gossip & revealing her sepulchral despair—poor woman.

Where are you going now Alix?

I really dont know.

Well that sounds dismal! Dont you look forward to say eleven tomorrow morning?

I merely wish it didn't exist that's all!

So I left her, hatless, aimless, unattached, wandering in Piccadilly.

Saturday 20 October

Happily, or she might say unhappily for Alix she didn't presumably wander in Piccadilly all night, or the great bomb which ploughed up the pavement opposite Swan & Edgar's might have dug her grave.[31] We heard two soft distant but unmistakable shocks about 9.30; then a third which shook the window; then silence. It turns out that a Zeppelin came over, hovered unseen for an hour or two & left. We heard no more of it.

---

difficult emotional relationship. She first met VW in 1911, and proved a dependable friend during her illnesses. In 1915 she had organised Serbian Refugee Camps in Corsica, and was now a temporary Principal in the War Trade Statistical Department.

29. A Domestic Agency at 86 High Street, Marylebone.

30. The Æolian Hall, 136 New Bond Street; Schubert's Octet in F, op. 166.

31. In this raid the high-flying German airships failed to find their proper targets owing to ground mist; the 50 kg bomb which fell near Swan & Edgar's department store on Piccadilly Circus seems to have been dropped at random.

Going out for a walk, we ran into a smooth, sleek provincial looking man at the pillar box, our Walter—sent by Heaven for the baptism of this book I think. And he stuck to us for hours; walked with us, came back to tea, & would with encouragement, which flagged, have dined. His stories were all of Lord Canterbury, & Mrs Saxton Noble, & the R.A.:[32] each story throwing a gleam of light upon his own success, or tact, or prosperity. Not much gossip about the King however. He prefers the Queen, & mad Princess Victoria, who breaks into his room & announces that she means to live in his house. His complexion is that of a wax figure, his head is as smooth as an egg; he has the same cultivated taste in books, & style that he used to have, though no longer a writer, or indeed anything but a Secretary to the President, to whom he seems filial & parasitic.[33] To us his attitude is half friendly, half suspicious. He has cast in his lot with the orthodox, but can't make up his mind to lose the other world entirely.

Sunday 21 October

Lytton came to luncheon, & Goldie to dinner—so we must have talked for 6 or 7 hours. We walked down the river & through the Park. Lytton in good spirits, having finished a book of 100,000 words, though now pretending that it can't be published.[34] He means to leave London, & live "for ever" in the country. At this moment Saxon & Oliver are inspecting houses in Berkshire.[35] It seems a good thing that one's friends should try experiments. Poor old Goldie is evidently beyond that stage. If I were malicious I should say he had reached the stage of the complete conversationalist. A long story at dinner, very skillfully told; suited to keep the High Table amused; then facts with Leonard after dinner. One finds less power of detachment in the elderly. This war seems to possess him, to leave little over. In fact he looked shrunk & worn: infinitely good, charming, devoted, every ounce of vitality rightly applied—no time for experiments, not enough curiosity perhaps, though extreme kindliness & sympathy, which in the case of young men, becomes amorous. He has been

32. Henry Frederick Walpole Manners-Sutton, 5th Viscount Canterbury (1879-1918), had succeeded his father in 1914, inheriting vast estates in Norfolk. Mrs Saxton Noble, *née* Celia Brunel James (1871-1961), wife of the wealthy director of armaments firms, was a noted hostess and patroness of the arts.

33. The President of the Royal Academy was Sir Edward Poynter (1836-1918).

34. *Eminent Victorians*, to be published by Chatto & Windus on 9 May 1918.

35. Saxon Sydney-Turner and Oliver Strachey, among other friends, were subscribers to a scheme of renting and maintaining a country house to enable Lytton, who was still largely dependant upon his mother, to live and work in more congenial circumstances. (See *Holroyd*, p. 703.)

asked to go to Russia for The Manchester Guardian; but doubts if he will get a passport.[36]

Monday 22 October

The moon grows full, & the evening trains are packed with people leaving London.[37] We saw the hole in Piccadilly this afternoon. Traffic has been stopped, & the public slowly tramps past the place, which work-men are mending, though they look small in comparison with it. Swan & Edgar has every window covered with sacking or planks; you see shop women looking out from behind; not a glimpse of stuffs, but "business goes on as usual" so they say. Windows are broken according to no rule; some intact, some this side, some that. Our London Library stands whole, however, & we found our books, & came home in the tube, standing the whole way to Hammersmith, & have just come in. Bert is wounded, & Nellie has gone to Liz. She felt it her duty & also her right—which shows how the servant is bettering her state in this generation.

Tuesday 23 October

Another lapse in this book, I must confess; but, if I do it against my humour I shall begin to loathe it; so the one chance of life it has is to sub-mit to lapses uncomplainingly. I remember though that we walked, printed, & Margaret came to tea. How pale these elderly women get! The rough pale skin of toads, unfortunately: M. in particular easily loses the flash of her beauty. This time we were whelmed in the Coop. revolution; the characters of Mr King & Mr May, & possibilities.[38] I get an occasional swinge of the tail which reminds me of the extremely insignificant position I have in this important world. I get a little depressed, a little anxious to find fault—a question of not being in the right atmosphere. L. I suppose feels the same about Gordon Sqre. And then the minute care which the elderly & solicitous take of each other impresses me: "must be back or Lilian will be anxious" questions of fatigue or cold always cropping up—partly the unmarried state perhaps; partly the sense of being the centre of one's world, which Margaret very naturally has. But of course her niceness & valiancy always conquer me in spite of injured vanity.

36. He did not go.
37. Enemy bombing raids on London were normally carried out by moonlight.
38. In 1917 the Co-operative Congress, after vehement debates, reversed its traditional policy of neutrality in politics and decided to seek direct representation in national and local government. Henry John May (1867-1939) was the secretary of the Parliamentary Representation Committee then set up, and became the first Co-operative Parliamentary candidate. Mr King was possibly the Liberal MP Joseph King (1860-1943), 'a well-known radical gadfly' (Margaret Cole).

Wednesday 24 October

L. to some confounded meeting; but also to take our selected sample of paper to Mr Byles, whom he met coming out of the New Statesman office.[39] I did a little printing, & then up to Janet. With time one would naturally welcome wet & wind; already the worst chill of them is over, because one thinks of them as safety against the raid. So today I hardly grumbled, though it was heavy rain, cold, dark, inhuman, primeval weather. The Case ménage is extremely cheerful to step into; such a welcome, such anxiety about China tea or Indian, an egg, fresh bread & butter—clothes dried with a duster. Emphie spirited, discursive, inconsecutive as usual, about her day & her Ecko [a wireless set], & servants, & sugar & honey, all fresh & sensible, & evidently the fruit of experience, which has not embittered or aged her, though it has not given her much power of concentration. She went to write her notes, after tea (this is her great occupation) Janet & I talked, getting on well as usual. But I was packed off to wait 15 minutes at Finchley Road, lest I should miss my train; & travelled with a mother & three boys who made all the elderly gentlemen shy & yet cordial to watch their kisses & antics from behind their newspapers.

Thursday 25 October

Owing to the usual circumstances, I had to spend the day recumbent.[40] However this is much mitigated by printing, which I do from my bed on the sloping table. We took off a proof of 2 pages, on paper of the right size & liked the looks of it immensely. Our paper will be soft & yellow tinted. A melancholy letter from Ott. this morning, complaining of age & ugliness, the weariness of London & the sadness of not being wanted— all so true, I suppose, that we have accepted an invitation, on my part rather out of pity; though also a feeling of liking for her persists.[41] Saxon & Barbara dined with us; we are lending Asheham to the whole of that curious constellation—Nick & Saxon will revolve round Barbara; who

39. LW's meeting was as a member of the editorial board of the small monthly magazine *War and Peace* which propagated the ideas of Norman Angell as expounded in his book *The Great Illusion* (1910). The offices of the *New Statesman* were then in Great Queen Street, WC2; R. B. Byles was its manager from 1914 until his death in 1920. No doubt LW sought his technical advice in connection with the printing problems of the Hogarth Press. He then had tea with Mr Perera at the National Liberal Club.

40. VW invariably spent the first day of each of her monthly periods recumbent; it is difficult to say whether this was dictated by necessity, medical advice, or contemporary custom.

41. Lady Ottoline's letter, dated from Garsington on 22 October 1917, is among the three dozen from her to VW in MHP, Sussex.

twinkles rosily but modestly in the light of their admiration; very neat, nice, motherly. Saxon as usual when with her—gentle & giving off a sound as of a boiling, but not over boiling, kettle; speechless of course. As she has only simple direct things to say, L. & I were a little sleepy; but we have arranged that she is to take up printing when Nick goes back [to France]. I am going to Asheham on Monday with Saxon.

Friday 26 October

Either it is cold or wet or windy at night, so we sleep well, though the moon is now almost full. We are faced with the problem of providing for Tinker. His spirits make him an exacting guest. We went to find a home with the Vet. today, & discovered that a Vet. lives in part of the great red house at the back of us. We looked into a room, laid for tea, the table-cloth laid like a diamond across the table; a girl came; & I saw a black & white paved hall, evidently a fine house, now cut up into different bits. Nelly has just come back: the usual laughter begins again. We gave Lottie 5/ for doing so well.

Saturday 27 October

We were just setting off for Kingston Barracks this afternoon to get L.'s exemption card, when the telephone rang, & I heard Clive's now unfamiliar & apparently rather nervous voice asking whether he might dine with us. So the breach is to be repaired very rapidly.[42] We walked through the Park to Kingston,[43] failed to get the card, & then had tea in Kingston, ending by buying me a 15/ watch for my wrist—a round bright, serviceable turnip, which I look at constantly, & really find it a saver of time. We were back late; & Clive came & was I thought, very pleasant, easy garrulous; starting a great many hares & chasing them smartly, & letting off his little tributes to himself quite inoffensively. He is so brisk & well kept mentally that I like an evening of him. L. immensely good tempered & urbane into the bargain. We gossiped; spun swiftly from thing to thing—Characters, French books, the Mansfield intrigue, & so on.[44]

---

42. Maynard Keynes had taken Clive Bell to tea with VW at Hogarth House (his first visit) on 28 July 1917; they had gossiped about Katherine Mansfield. Clive was sure that VW had repeated this to Katherine who dined with the Woolfs next evening, and felt some resentment towards VW in consequence.
43. A walk of over three miles.
44. Clive Bell, as a pacifist, was at this time nominally a farm worker living at Garsington, where 'intrigue' was a staple commodity. This gossip may relate to the 'Quarrel with the Murrys', Chapter V of *Ottoline at Garsington. Memoirs of Lady Ottoline Morrell, 1915-1918*, edited by Robert Gathorne-Hardy, 1974; or to 27 October 1917, n 42, above.

He wears his chestnut suit; combs his hair back to hide the bald spot, but didn't hitch his trousers so much as usual—in short, he was at his best. Adrian has a drs. order not to work on the land any longer.[45]

Sunday 28 October

Still no raids, presumably the haze at evening keeps them off, though it is still, & the moon perfectly clear. The numbers who have gone out of London this week must feel a little foolish. A perfect cold October day; sun red through the leaves which are still hanging. In order to keep as much in L.'s company as I could, I determined to go to Staines with him. We walked from Shepperton through Laleham, & so to Staines by the river.[46] Flat very quiet country, or country just turning into town. Pink arm chairs were drawn up round a crowded but not luxurious tea table; a multiplicity of little plates, minute knives, people told to help themselves. Mr Lock, with some impediment was there, & soon Alice, Flora, Clara & Sylvia all appeared—malice suggested the whole of Kensington High Street poured into a room. The normality of it all impressed me. Nothing beautiful; nothing definite; most strange why nature has produced this type in such abundance. Then, the servant said "Mr Sturgeon"; Flora cried "I will go" dashed from the room; everyone said Oh! Ah! How Splendid!, as if on the stage, which indeed the whole scene might have been.[47] We went, after the 2nd act; Tinker dashed off; but was recovered, & so home, very cold, & Herbert looked in, & here we sit over the fire, & I wish it were this time next week.

On Monday 29 October, while LW was away, VW went with Saxon Sydney-Turner to Asheham; she left him there and went on to Charleston, returning to Hogarth House on Friday. There are two characteristic entries in the Asheham Diary(not repeated here).

Friday 2 November

It almost is "this time next week"; though not quite—in fact not nearly, since L. is giving a lecture at Birkenhead at this precise moment, &

---

45. As a conscientious objector to military service, Adrian Stephen had had to undertake farm work; he was six foot five inches tall and not robust, and the work strained his heart.

46. LW's mother and others of his family were now living at Staines.

47. LW's sister Bella was the widow of Richard Lock; Mr Lock 'with some impediment' was possibly her father-in-law; Flora and Clara were LW's other sisters, Alice and Sylvia his sisters-in-law.

will then I suppose travel all night across England before reaching me.[1]
I find it impossible to read after a railway journey; I cant open Dante or
think of him without a shudder—the cause being I think partly the enormous numbers of newspapers I've been reading in. Lottie brought me all
the Times's which have accumulated. I feel as if I'd moved about a great
deal; kept moving to keep myself warm. I mean Asheham & Charleston
were rather in the nature of distractions, so as not to think how strange &
solitary I was. Not solitary in the literal sense of course. First I spent 2
days with Saxon; much detail, rather heightened by his greater warmth of
intimacy. He is still surprised by his own sensations; takes them out, sees
how they fit in; very anxious to be sure of their quality. Of course the
quality is very high. The worst one can say is that his lack of virility tends
to prettify & belittle to some extent. But I daresay this is the effect of B's
not very marked or magnificent nature. And of course, too, he's exquisite
in his own way; so pure, wise, good, & sensitive. Most curiously unable
to cope with anything needing decision; his instinct is obviously always
to avoid risk by remaining motionless. When forced to order coal or a
cab his indecision is that of a spinster of 70. And yet intellectually he is
definite enough; definite, but meticulous. He's in love, & yet content
that B. should marry Nick.

There was the new governess, Miss Edwards at Charleston; a very
pretty, rather sharp, not very well bred or well educated young woman
who has I should imagine lived on the capital of her large eyes, flaxen
hair, straight dark eyebrows so much that she is a little out of it in an element where these attractions are discounted. There is no one to make eyes
at—save Bunny, who remains impervious. But she controls Julian; talks
French evidently rather more naturally than English. I meant to ask her
what she thinks in. Yesterday it rained all day, so I sat in; writing about
Aksakoff in the morning;[2] sitting in the Studio after luncheon. Duncan
painted a table, & Nessa copied a Giotto. I unpacked all my bits of gossip.
They are very large in effect, these painters; very little self-conscious; they
have smooth broad spaces in their minds where I am all prickles & pro-
montories. Nevertheless to my thinking few people have a more vigorous
grasp or a more direct pounce than Nessa. Two little boys with very
active minds keep her in exercise. I like the feeling that she gives of a whole
nature in use. In working order I mean; living practically, not an amateur,
as Duncan & Bunny both to some extent are of course. I suppose this is
the effect of children & of responsibility, but I always remember it in her.

1. LW went to Manchester on 29 October to lecture on International Government to
   a number of Co-operative Societies in Lancashire and Cheshire. He returned by
   the night train from Liverpool to Euston on 2 November. (See *III LW*, 111-14.)
2. VW's review of *A Russian Schoolboy* by Sergei Aksakoff appeared in the *TLS*,
   8 November 1917 (Kp C91).

A love of the actual fact, is strong in her. Julian came with his letter into my room this morning; & at once curled up on my bed, & went on reading a book with a picture of a Bird of Paradise in it. He told me he had read Gardiner's history perhaps 50 times.[3] He disliked Kings because they were so dull; but liked Newcastle. Irish history bored him because it was shapeless, as far as I could make out; he couldn't see that either side was in the right about the American war, which annoyed him; & he thought if we had given way about the taxes we should have got our way without their knowing it, as we have done with our other colonies. Quentin called him to lessons, or he would have gone on at length. I was a good deal impressed. Suddenly to find a child reasoning & inheriting these old puzzles gives one rather a shock. It seems a pity there can't be a new history for each new generation; & yet its queer to hand over the old things to the new brains. I daresay he'll do a lot of work one of these days; is it a sign of age that one's interested & inclined to see great virtue in the youngest generation?

But I was glad to come home, & feel my real life coming back again—I mean life here with L. Solitary is not quite the right word; one's personality seems to echo out across space, when he's not there to enclose all one's vibrations. This is not very intelligibly written; but the feeling itself is a strange one—as if marriage were a completing of the instrument, & the sound of one alone penetrates as if it were a violin robbed of its orchestra or piano. A dull wet night, so I shall sleep. The raid happened of course, with us away.

Saturday 3, Sunday 4, Monday 5 November

The raid didn't actually happen but with our nerves in the state they are (I should say Lottie's & Nelly's nerves) the dipping down of the electric lights was taken as a sign of warning: finally the lights went out, & standing on the kitchen stairs I was deluged with certain knowledge that the extinction of light is in future our warning. I looked out of the hall door, however, heard the usual patter & voices of suburbans coming home; & then, to bear out my assurance, the lights suddenly came on again. We went to bed & to sleep. I woke 5 minutes before 7, & lay listening, but heard nothing, & was about, at 8 o'clock to flatten out all my expectations when I heard L. at the door & there he was! With the softness of a mouse he had let himself in & breakfasted. We talked for as long as we could; things kept oozing out; sudden silences & spurts; divine contentment at being once more harmonious. L. travelled all night. The most pungent of his tales is to me the story of the arguing & enquiring &

3. *A Student's History of England from the Earliest Times to 1885*, 3 vols, 1890-91, by Samuel Rawson Gardiner (1829-1902); the battered volumes read by VW in the schoolroom at Hyde Park Gate had been passed down to her nephews.

experimenting. Mrs Ekhard who thrust herself into all sorts of subjects, with L., while he cut down her trees.[4] The palms of his hands are still black from the soot of Manchester bark. We walked by the river, & to bed rather early. L. having denied that he was at all tired, tumbled asleep & slept till he was called.

On Sunday I finished my Aksakoff, & writing has the advantage of making a weekday out of the Sabbath, in spite of the clamour & blare of military music & church bells which always takes place at about 11—a noise which the other people have no right to inflict. We went up the river & through the Park, for it was a lovely warm day; & passed our Walter again with a man who looked like a schoolmaster. No deer are to be seen in the lower park, where the cedars are. And Perera came to tea, & I shut him alone with L. having no wish for more yards of lace. I think, however, that L. is now menaced with a gold watch, owing to the success of the Ceylon business. The Daily News bursts out in three separate places in indignation.[5]

And today we've been to London, & just come back, & sit waiting for dinner. Expecting life & smartness at least I spent 8d upon a Magazine with Mrs Asquith's love letters, & they're as flat & feeble & vulgar & illiterate as a provincial Mrs Glyn might be; with something insolent about them, as though she condescended in scribbling—[6] We went to the London Library, as usual; coming out ran in to the hatless dusky figure, L.'s dame secretaire: Alix; on her way to grope for facts, which L.'s eye finds a good deal quicker.[7] We saw the hole in Piccadilly almost mended, though the glass is still broken. L. to Williams & Norgate about his book, which kept him so long that I had time to despise Mrs A. pretty thoroughly in Clifford's Inn tea rooms. The talk was heated; L. accused of low dealing in offering his book to Bell. (Margaret's doing).[8] Some arrangement may

4. Mrs Eckhard was Sydney Waterlow's mother-in-law; LW stayed with her in Manchester. See *III LW*, 112.
5. The Ceylon business: see above, 16 October 1917, n 21. *The Daily News*, the most radical newspaper of the time, had taken the matter up and held that there had been 'few more terrible indictments in the whole history of British Colonial administration'.
6. Emma Alice Margaret (Margot) Asquith, *née* Tennant (1864-1945), in 1894 married, as his second wife, H. H. Asquith, Liberal Prime Minister 1908-16. A woman of undisciplined intelligence, unrestrained candour, great vitality and feeling, she was, if potentially a political liability, a stimulating influence upon society. The Magazine has not been traced. Elinor Glyn (1894-1943) was a successful romantic novelist.
7. Alix Sargant-Florence was helping LW with research for a report which eventually became his book *Empire and Commerce in Africa*. (See below, December 1918, n 10.)
8. LW had been commissioned to write a book on the Co-operative movement for the Home University Library; it was to have been issued in November, but Williams & Norgate the publishers postponed it until the war should be over. Margaret

be come to; but the man an incompetent & stupid creature, who wont give way, & will have his rights. Hanging on a strap in the Tube was Malcolm Macnaghten; grey, spruce & prosperous looking.[9]

Tuesday 6 November

The melancholy fact is that Tinker, at the present moment, 5.30, is lost. He was let out in the garden, got into the next door house, & finding their garden door open, presumably escaped. This was discovered at lunch time. When we had done L. went off to look in the neighbourhood, but without success. We took the Bus to Kingston; visited for the last time let us hope in our lives, the Recruiting Office, & after waiting in the familiar room with the two wooden benches, the towel hanging up & the khaki coat, L. was summoned, & given his paper which states that he is "permanently & totally disabled." We suppose this might fetch £500 if sold. However, we were rather dashed by the loss of the spaniel whom we had come to like. We gave information at the Police Office. Their immense kindness & good sense much impressed us. After taking notes, ringing up Kew &c. the police sergeant said "Much obliged to you, Sir". Its melancholy to be asking about lost dogs again. After our experience with Tim even I find it hard to be altogether sanguine.[10]

Saturday 10 November

Another melancholy fact is that I've let all these days pass—two of them, Wednesday & Thursday because I was out late, the third Friday because I was too gloomy, & we were both too argumentative, to make writing possible. However, to deal with the dissipations first, though I dont admit they were the cause of the gloom. Nessa was up, & I had a Bloomsbury afternoon. First I took my watch to a man in Poland Street, who says it needs cleaning only, then I went to the Omega where in the semidark Roger was convoying three chattering Frenchwomen round the show, & giving the impression as usual that French manners & language have a peculiar relish for him. The pictures glimmered through the dusk; & I was chiefly impressed by the Gertlers; Vanessa, too, very good: Duncan, I thought, a little pretty or tending to be. Faith vacillated about,

---

Llewelyn Davies suggested (MHP, Sussex, letter to LW dated *11 H. Sqre Monday night*) that LW should get George Bell & Son to publish it at once as a 1/- book. It was finally published as *Co-operation and the Future of Industry* by Allen & Unwin in January 1919. See *III LW*, 166.

9. The Hon. Malcolm MacNaghten (1869-1955), Barrister, and an Apostle; he married in 1899 Antonia Mary ('Dodo') Booth, whose parents and VW's had been close friends.

10. VW had lost 'poor old Tim' on Sunday 22 April 1917. See *II VW Letters*, no. 829.

endeavouring to make me see her show of dresses, this being private view day.[11] We had tea in the sewing room—walking up & down munching dry cake, while Mabel stitched lining in a corner, & Roger wrote letters on his knee. Nessa came on top of this & we left, I buying an apricot coloured coat on my way. I had tea in Gordon Square, which always puzzles me under the new arrangement, there being no sitting room.[12] She is brooding some new educational scheme—6 boys, a tutor & a governess; has planned it all for next summer. Miss Edwards has taken to meeting soldiers on the downs, & her capacity won't last long. This was the prelude to a party [at 46 Gordon Square] on Thursday, to which I went, through the wet & the dirt, a very long expedition for 2 hours of life, though I enjoyed it. The usual people were there, the usual sensation of being in a familiar but stimulating atmosphere, in which all the people one's in the habit of thinking of, were there in the body. A great many mop headed young women in amber & emerald sitting on the floor. Molly, Vanessa & I represented mature matronhood. Oliver seemed to be the friendly & amorous Uncle. Ray one might call the grandmother; very commanding, immensely well nourished, & competent. I spent most of my time with Oliver, & as the clock struck 10 I got up and went—an example of virtue if ever there was one. And now we see how the gloom came about. L. was testy, dispiriting, & tepid. We slept. I woke to a sense of failure & hard treatment. This persisted, one wave breaking after another, all day long. We walked on the river bank in a cold wind, under a grey sky. Both agreed that life seen without illusion is a ghastly affair. Illusions wouldn't come back. However they returned about 8.30, in front of the fire, & were going merrily till bedtime, when some antics ended the day.

Today has been very cheerful, in spite of the worst assortment of elements to be had; bitter cold, stormy sky, rain. L. went to the Lost Dogs Home, but without success; we have put up notices, but hope runs low. I've been without letters for 2 days.

Sunday 11 November

Sunday, I see, is becoming for us much what it was to our fathers, the day on which social life becomes swept; & as it's by the nature of things a

11. Faith Marion Jane Henderson, *née* Bagenal (b. 1889), elder sister of Nicholas Bagenal (see above, 30 August 1917 n 27); Newnham College, Cambridge, 1908-1911; married in 1915 the economist Hubert Henderson. She was helping temporarily with the dressmaking activities of the Omega Workshops.

12. In 1916 the lease of the Clive Bells' house at 46 Gordon Square had been taken over by Maynard Keynes; several friends who had reason to live in London during the war were accommodated there, and Clive Bell retained a room for his own, and occasionally Vanessa's, use. For the latter's educational scheme, see *II VW Letters*, no. 926 fn.

dull solemn day, the plan isn't so bad. Still, I hardly see on what principle one can approve of our luncheon at the Webbs. L. has known them;

[*In LW's hand*] I rashly said that I would occasionally write a page here & now V. calls on me to redeem my word, & as it will take me from reading Joseph Chamberlain's speeches, I dont see why I shouldn't.[13] We went to the Webbs for luncheon & there too were Mr & Mrs Tawny.[14] I had met her but not him. Before they came, the Webbs told us that he was an idealist. Now that I've met him the only thing which I can add with certainty is that he is an idealist with black teeth. One of the worst Webb meals to which we have been. V. between Webb & Tawny & I between Mrs W. Mrs T. Mrs W. began to talk almost at once about the Reconstruction Committee which she is on.[15] She talked incessantly & every tenth word was "committee". She has apparently succeeded in inventing a committee for babies, a committee for lunatics, a committee for the sick, a committee for the disabled, & a committee for the dead; but the scheme or the Cosmos is not complete because she has so far failed to invent a Committee for the Able-bodied & unemployed. However she still has hopes. Meanwhile V. at one corner, & I at another sunk in silence, while Mrs T. vacuously asked W. about the case of a woman with a broken hip in an infirmary in a Union in Walthamstow. Immediately after luncheon we fled. Took a bus from Westminster to Hammersmith, very cold but refreshing after the discourse on committees.

& when we got back here we found the room full of people—Rosalind Toynbee Arnold T. & Ka.[16] I liked her, small, pale, with dark eyes, a

13. The speeches of Joseph Chamberlain (1836-1914), edited by C. W. Boyd, were published in 2 volumes in 1914.

14. Richard Henry Tawney (1880-1962) and his wife Annette Jeannie, *née* Beveridge (d. 1958). At his death considered the most distinguished economic historian of his generation, he had been invalided out of the army after being severely wounded in 1916 and had resumed his activities in the Workers' Educational Association (of which he was later to become president). She was acting as an Inspector of Factories at the Home Office.

15. The Ministry of Reconstruction was established in August 1917 (disbanded 1919) to consider and advise upon the problems arising from the war and its future termination. The Minister was the Rt. Hon. Christopher Addison, MP, and the fourteen members of the Reconstruction Committee included Mrs Webb. Its sub-committees surveyed almost every aspect of British life.

16. Arnold Joseph Toynbee (1889-1975), who was to become the great historian of world civilisations, was at this time working for a government department. He married in 1913 Rosalind (1890-1967) the daughter of Professor Gilbert Murray (see below, 28 October 1918, n 35): her mother was a daughter of the 9th Earl of Carlisle.

wisp of hair, still, & decided in her manner. I'm not sure that I did much like him. He seemed rather more commonplace & conventional than the young man one's used to. But we talked away briskly about art & literature; & I observed R.T. thinking, when spoken to—a good sign. As far as one can see, she is so trained in culture that she is almost a specialist; if one got to know her, I mean, one would find some carefully arranged theory netting in all her feelings about literature. For example, she doesn't like King Lear. But, or perhaps therefore, I thought her rather distinguished, more so, at any rate than the crop-heads of Blooms-bury. As we sat, with great rolls of fur, in the shadow, I cant verify my guess as to the crop-head in her case. It struck me now & then that her half-aristocratic parentage had produced a kind of old fashioned decorum in her. Her views upon the proper relation of cooks & governesses were certainly decorous. Something I think may be due to the difference be-tween Oxford & Cambridge. It's strange to think how much one's mind has been affected by this difference—even mine has, I suppose, though I was never there, & am by nature critical of them. But Arnold seemed to me not very easy to talk directly to.

[*Monday 12 November*]

Today we've been to London, as usually happens on Monday. We went to the Omega, & as we were looking round us, in came Roger, which embarrassed me a little, partly because of his own pictures, & also because I don't like talking of art in front of him. He was in process of painting a table though, & disappeared. Then we went to Gordon Sqre to fetch my umbrella, 2 pictures, & a hair binder, all left there, & who should open the door but Clive? He asked us in, & there was M.H. in one of the big armchairs, a piteous half moon of a woman, to my thinking. She seems so crushed & submissive always. I half smoked a gold-tipped cigarette, & listened to some Garsington gossip. K.M. has broken with Ott. in a letter which says "You shan't play the Countess to my cook any more" or words to that effect. We left however, & I went to Mudies, & got The Leading Note, in order to examine into R.T. more closely, & L. went on to meet Edgar for a mysterious interview;[17] & I came home with my book, which does not seem a very masterly performance after Turgenev, I suppose; but if you dont get your touches in the right place the method is apt to be sketchy & empty. L. is at the Suffrage; & I watch 3 fireballs glowing red hot.

17. *The Leading Note*, a romantic novel by Rosalind Murray, was published in 1910 and reissued in 1913. According to LW's diary, it was his brother Harold, not Edgar, whom he met for tea; after which he went to a League of Nations Society Executive Committee meeting.

Tuesday 13 November

I must again register my complaint that people wont write to me. I dont write to them, but how can one? And no book from the Times either, for which I'm glad though, as I want to get on with my novel.[18] The other day L. began his book, & has already done two chapters. He's like one of those mowing machines I used to watch from my window at Asheham; round & round they go, without haste without rest, until finally the little square of corn in the middle is cut, & all is done. We began our printing off this afternoon. Our first discovery was the important one that the springs aren't even, or the balls different in weight. We—or L.— put this more or less right, & we printed 300 copies of the first page, but we should be glad of another press, though the results are very good for the most part.[19] A very cold day. Indeed, I might have remarked the beginning of winter. No leaves to speak of left on the trees now; a sharp chill in the air. One's room after tea most emphatically a little centre of light in the midst of profound darkness. L. is making up a lecture he's giving at Hammersmith; I'm to preside over the Women's Guild.[20]

Wednesday 14 November

L. gave his lecture; I presided over my guild. It always puzzles me to know why the women come, unless they like sitting in a room not their own, gas & light free, other women on other chairs. They don't pay much attention apparently; save Mrs Langston no one has a word to offer. Tonight Mrs Allan—a rosy, bright eyed, shrewd, but not very enlightened woman spoke for an hour upon Congress.[21] It might have been a report; & had little more interest. When she'd done, & I'd done, no questions were asked, & she started off upon food—not the food of the country, but the individual dinner & tea provided at Torquay. Upon this subject she spoke fluently & even passionately for 15 minutes. The vices of outside traders & the virtues of self control were both illustrated at length. L.

18. This is the first reference to *Night and Day*. For LW's book, see above 3/5 November 1917, n 8.
19. They were printing *Prelude*.
20. LW was to lecture that evening to the Hammersmith Branch of the Union of Democratic Control, an organisation formed in September 1914 to unite and inform opposition to the war and to press for a negotiated peace. VW for the past year had presided over the monthly meetings of the Women's Co-operative Guild held at Hogarth House, for which it was her responsibility to provide speakers; these she found among her friends as well as from Guild headquarters. This office she carried out for four years.
21. The Annual Congress of the Guild; Mrs Allan was a speaker sent from headquarters. Mrs Langston appears to have been the most prominent and responsible member of the Richmond Branch.

was back about 10.30, after a more profitable evening at the U.D.C. where soldiers & an Indian were among the audience. Today the servants went to see Bert in hospital at Epsom; L. went to the Dogs Home, with no result; & finally we walked towards Kew, & noticed how the great chestnut trees [were] as black and bare as iron. A dozen men stand fishing in the quiet water beneath the lock—a cheerful sign of undiminished stability. We looked in, & spent half an hour, talking to the little printer, who has 2 machines & 1 press for sale. The difficulty is to decide; but probably we shall buy one, & leave the refinements of perfection for the present, which Riddell thinks necessary, but presumably can't provide. Besides, these machines are running & only cost £14 or £15.[22]

Again a day of no letters.

Thursday 15 November

Again a day of no letters, unless I can count my weekly reprimand in the Supt. for what I said or didn't say about Arnold's poems about nature.[23] This time I'm almost inclined to answer useless though it is, but I should like to protest against this flood of Oxford superiority. We printed off another page, very successfully, which took till tea time, & then we went round in the semi-darkness to the little printer, who will come round any moment now to see the room for the press. One little boy about the size of Julian works for him. Yesterday his cellar was flooded by the ladies bath next door. He is very precise in his language: perhaps the result of a semi-literary profession.

Monday 19 November

The little printer came round at the end of the last page, & stayed perhaps 1 hour—until Lottie had to ring the bell with meaning, but as I don't suppose he dines himself, the meaning may have been obscure. We have advanced £10, & for that bought the cutting press, & stipulated that the printing press shall be here by Jan. 14th. The difficulty about these people is their flow of language; personal history must be told at length: I believe

---

22. The printer was Mr McDermott (d. 1926), owner of a small independent business, The Prompt Press, in nearby Duke Street, Richmond, whose technical advice LW had sought. See *III LW*, 237-40. J. Riddell was on the staff of the St Bride Foundation Printing School.

23. VW's review of *A Literary Pilgrim in England* by Edward Thomas had appeared under the title 'Flumina Amem Silvasque' in the *TLS*, 11 October 1917 (Kp C87). In agreeing with the author that Matthew Arnold was 'the poet of the garden and the highly cultivated land' she wrote: 'if one takes a bird's eye view of Arnold's poetry, the background seems to consist of a moonlit lawn, with a sad but not passionate nightingale singing in a cedar tree of the sorrows of mankind'. This opinion was warmly rejected by several correspondents.

its a form of good manners. On Friday we went to a concert, walking out when the English piece came on into a disreputable side street clinging to the back of Bond St—reminds one rather of a Thackeray novel—a place for the footman of the great to gamble in.[24] Tea at Spikings, with some of the upper classes; who looked like pet dogs threatened with a cold bath. They were talking of the scarcity of motor cars. I bought a pair of stockings & then home.

The stockings were in preparation for Garsington. We came back from that adventure 2 hours ago. It's difficult to give the whole impression, save that it wasnt much unlike my imagination. People strewn about in a sealingwax coloured room: Aldous Huxley toying with great round disks of ivory & green marble—the draughts of Garsington: Brett in trousers;[25] Philip tremendously encased in the best leather; Ottoline, as usual, velvet & pearls; 2 pug dogs. Lytton semi-recumbent in a vast chair. Too many nick nacks for real beauty, too many scents, & silks, & a warm air which was a little heavy. Droves of people moved about from room to room— from drawing room to dining room, from dining room to Ottoline's room—all Sunday. At moments the sense of it seemed to flag; & the day certainly lasted very long by these means. Fredegond was admitted in the morning;[26] & then after tea I had perhaps an hour over a log fire with Ottoline. Going for a walk we ran into a motor full of speckled & not prepossessing young men—one I entirely forget, but he existed, as I counted 4. The most obvious was Evan Morgan, a little red absurdity, with a beak of a nose, no chin, & a general likeness to a very callow but student Bantam cock, who has run to legs & neck.[27] However he was evidently most carefully prepared to be a poet & an eccentricity, both by his conversation, which aimed at irresponsible brilliance, & lack of reticence, & by his clothes, which must have been copied from the usual

24. The concert, by the London Trio, was at the Æolian Hall in Bond Street. VW had tea alone at Spikings, as LW was meeting Perera and Jayatilaka at the National Liberal Club.

25. The Hon. Dorothy Eugénie Brett (1883-1977), daughter of 2nd Viscount Esher, studied at the Slade 1910-16, where her particular friends were Carrington and Mark Gertler (see below, 21 December 1917 and 7 June 1918). She was now a semi-permanent resident at Garsington.

26. Fredegond Shove, *née* Maitland (1889-1949), poet, daughter of VW's cousin Florence (Fisher) and the historian F. W. Maitland, her father's biographer; was at Newnham College, Cambridge, 1910-13; in 1915 she married Gerald Shove (1887-1947), economist, Fellow of King's College, Cambridge, and an Apostle, who as a conscientious objector had obtained work on Philip Morrell's farm.

27. The Hon. Evan Frederic Morgan (1893-1949), son and heir of 1st Viscount Tredegar, described by Aldous Huxley as 'poet, painter, musician, aristocrat and millionaire', was at this time unpaid private secretary to the Parliamentary Secretary of the Ministry of Labour, W. C. Bridgeman, MP.

Shelley picture. But he was as innocent as a chicken & so foolish that it didn't seem to matter. On the whole I liked Ottoline better than her friends have prepared one for liking her. Her vitality seemed to me a credit to her, & in private talk her vapours give way to some quite clear bursts of shrewdness. The horror of the Garsington situation is great of course; but to the outsider the obvious view is that O. & P. & Garsington house provide a good deal, which isn't accepted very graciously. However to deal blame rightly in such a situation is beyond the wit of a human being: they've brought themselves to such a pass of intrigue & general intricacy of relationship that they're hardly sane about each other. In such conditions I think Ott. deserves some credit for keeping her ship in full sail, as she certainly does. We were made immensely comfortable; a good deal of food; the talk had frequent bare patches, but then this particular carpet had been used fairly often. By talking severely to Philip, L. made him come up to Parliament today. He is a weak amiable long suffering man, who seems generally to be making the best of things, & seeing the best of people whom by nature he dislikes. We came home by Oxford (where I bought 2 writing books, & L. bought a pipe, & we had coffee, & saw the colleges) then to Reading, where we lunched; then to Ealing, where we changed to Richmond. On the top of our return, Alix appeared, & has just left; but I missed most of her, feeling it necessary to have a bath.

Thursday 22 November

I boasted so much about this book & the charm of filling it from a never exhausted fount at Garsington that I'm ashamed to miss days; & yet as I point out, the only chance it has is to wait one's mood. Ottoline keeps one by the way, devoted however to her "inner life"; which made me reflect that I haven't an inner life.[28] She read me a passage in my praise though, so the realities do come in sometimes. On Tuesday L. went to Williams & Norgate, who offer terms for a 2/6 book—which must be considered. Evidently they want him very much; & can't altogether conceal this in spite of their wish to drive a hard bargain. I rather think I finished taking down a page. Anyhow on Wednesday Barbara came to make a start, & the machine thereupon completely struck work, one of the rollers being cut, & jibbing, & as our stock of K's ran out, she could only set 4 lines.[29] This she did however, quickly & without fault, so that she promises well. She

28. 'When we were talking about keeping a journal, I said mine was filled with thoughts and struggles of my inner life. She opened her eyes wide in astonishment.' From *Ottoline at Garsington. Memoirs of Lady Ottoline Morrell, 1915-1918*, edited by Robert Gathorne-Hardy, 1974, p. 244.

29. Barbara Hiles had volunteered to replace Alix Sargant-Florence as apprentice in the Hogarth Press; she was to work three days a week, be given lunch and tea, her fares, and a share in the (minimal) profits.

bicycled from Wimbledon, her small crop head, bright cheeks, brilliant waistcoat give her a likeness to some vivacious bird; but I don't know that I think this very emphatic appearance particularly interesting. It always seems to say "Now all the decks are cleared for action" & action there is none.

I dined with Roger & met Clive.[30] We sat at the low square table covered with a bandanna, & eat out of dishes each holding a different bean or lettuce: delicious food for a change. We drank wine, & finished with soft white cheese, eaten with sugar. Then, taking a splendid flight above personalities, we discussed literature & aesthetics.

"D'you know, Clive, I've made out a little more about the thing which is essential to all art: you see, all art is representative. You say the word tree, & you see a tree. Very well. Now every word has an aura. Poetry combines the different aura's in a sequence—" That was something like it. I said one could, & certainly did, write with phrases, not only words; but that didn't help things on much. Roger asked me if I founded my writing upon texture or upon structure; I connected structure with plot, & therefore said "texture". Then we discussed the meaning of structure & texture in painting & in writing. Then we discussed Shakespeare, & Roger said Giotto excited him just as much. This went on till I made myself go precisely at 10. And we discussed also Chinese poetry; Clive said the whole thing was too distant to be comprehensible. Roger compared the poetry with the painting. I liked it all very much (the talk I mean). Much no doubt is perfectly vague, not to be taken seriously, but the atmosphere puts ideas into one's head, & instead of having to curtail them, or expatiate, one can speak them straight out & be understood—indeed disagreed with. Old Roger takes a gloomy view, not of our life, but of the world's future; but I think I detected the influence of Trotter & the herd, & so I distrusted him.[31] Still, stepping out into Charlotte Street, where the Bloomsbury murder took place a week or two ago, & seeing a crowd swarming in the road & hearing women abuse each other & at the noise others come running with delight—all this sordidity made me think him rather likely to be right.[32]

Today has been a perfectly warm, very still day, & we just had time after printing off a page to reach the river & see everything reflected per-

30. When in London, Roger Fry occupied a studio at 21 Fitzroy Street, a continuation northwards of Charlotte Street.

31. *Instincts of the Herd in Peace and War* (1916), a study of individual and social psychology by Wilfred Trotter, MD, FRCS, had been the basis of an article by LW in the *New Statesman*, 8 July 1916.

32. On 3 November 1917 the mutilated remains of a Belgian woman, wrapped in sacking, had been found in Regent Square, Bloomsbury; her murder and dismemberment had taken place in the basement of 101 Charlotte Street. Louis Voisin was convicted of the murder and was hanged on 2 March 1918.

fectly straightly in the water. The red roof of a house had its own little cloud of red in the river—lights lit on the bridge made long streaks of yellow—very peaceful, & as if the heart of winter.

Friday 23 November

L. went up to London with the rollers, & I meant to go to Kew. On the way it struck me that one ought to decide things definitely. One ought to make up one's mind. To begin then, I settled that if it was the 6d day at Kew I wouldn't hesitate but decide not to go in.[33] It was the 6d day; I turned without pausing & had therefore to walk back. Certainly this decision brings a feeling of peace, though I rather think I was wrong. It was a warm, windless day, the sky genuinely blue. I counted my lumps of sugar, 31: but Saxon came in, & took one; hadn't slept, & so was cutting his office. I meant to read Brooke's sermons, & couldn't;[34] & Saxon hadn't much to say. We discussed the jealousy of vanity & the jealousy of affection. He is immune from both. I have the one & not the other—perhaps from lack of cause. L. came in after seeing Squire, whose insignificance takes the lustre from reviewing rather. Then came Barbara, who wanted a bath; & Saxon followed her; & then Clive came in, & we chattered away—he & I in duet for the most part—till 10.30; when he went dressed like a Newmarket gent in an immensely thick coat. I find his sprightliness a rest. No hunt for subjects needed. He is after another before the first is disposed of. He abused Ott., but frankly. He discussed Lady Mary Montagu: his reviews—a publisher has offered him £40 for a book of them.[35] He has become rather a raconteur; but there is, I think, something intellectual about him; something of the Cambridge standard, perhaps, surviving. He's no fool, though his manners suggest overwhelming reasons for thinking him one now & then—this perpetual effort to shine, to be 'in the know'—this vanity. A long talk with M.H. on the telephone interrupted him. He has become a great writer of intimate letters. He makes a business of knowing everyone, or at any rate their affairs; but I like this.

[24 November]

Today Saturday the usual reasons have kept me recumbent; in the mitigated form which allows setting up & distributing. Barbara brought

---

33. Admission to the Royal Botanic Gardens at Kew was 6d on Tuesdays and Fridays, 1d on other days.
34. The Rev. Stopford Augustus Brooke (1832-1916), Divine and man of letters, published several volumes of sermons as well as works on English literature.
35. Lady Mary Wortley Montagu (1689-1762) spent a year at Constantinople when her husband was Ambassador to the Porte in 1717-18; her *Letters from the East* were published posthumously. Chatto & Windus published Clive Bell's *Potboilers* in May 1918.

the new rollers. She lunched & stayed to tea, & has indeed only gone a short time, which wont, I hope become a habit.

Monday 26 November

I dont like Sunday; the best thing is to make it a work day, & to unravel Brooke's mind to the sound of church bells was suitable enough. Such a wind in the night, by the way, that the milkman reported much damage down the road this morning, & raised our hopes, which were dashed on going out to see nothing smashed—not a stain of blood, or even the remnant of a hat. It was fine & wet by turns, with a high cold wind continuously. We went to Kew, & saw a blazing bush, as red as cherry blossom, but more intense—frostily red—also gulls rising & falling for pieces of meat, their crowd waved aside suddenly by three very elegant light grey cranes. We also went into the orchid house where these sinister reptiles live in a tropical heat, so that they come out in all their spotted & streaked flesh even now in the cold. They always make me anxious to bring them into a novel. L. went on to Hampstead, & I back here; where I had tea in the kitchen with the Manx cat. L. saw Margaret & discussed labour I suppose. & his book. I wish my range extended so far.

Today I went into London with my ms: & Leonard went to Harrisons.[36] (which entry was broken off somehow—but my recollection is that L. found Desmond at the L.L.: together they look up the word f—— in the slang dictionary, & were saddened & surprised to see how the thumb marks of members were thick on the page. My afternoon was by comparison chaste; though I'm hardly proud of the fact that I completely lost my way in seeking Printing House Square, & got into a maze of little half lit, very busy & professional looking streets which I should like to investigate. The profession of journalism has its heart here; carts were standing lengthwise for bales to be dumped into. A kind man in uniform, something at a warehouse he told me, took me to the Times at last; though I (still managed to miss my way, I think it must have been, for I remember walking rapidly in the wrong direction, which got darker & darker until I became suspicious & went back again—but this is a week old).

Monday 3 December

Its impossible to remember a week at a stretch, which I must confess would be my task if I were to pretend to be accurate. One day I went to

36. VW's review of *Life and Letters of Stopford Brooke* by L. P. Jacks appeared in the *TLS*, 29 November 1917 (not listed in Kp). LW went to the dentist, probably Edward Harrison, 17 Welbeck Street.

the dentist; & we had Barbara here for 3 days, with disastrous results, for when we looked at her work, it was so full of faults we had to take it down. I should have expected, not much intelligence, but the quickness & accuracy of a good needlewoman. This was annoying. On Saturday L. gave a lecture at Hampstead.[1] Strange what a stamp Hampstead sets even on a casual gathering of 30 people; such clean, decorous, uncompromising & high minded old ladies & old gentlemen; & the young wearing brown clothes, & thinking seriously, the women dowdy, the men narrow shouldered; bright fire & lights & books surrounding us, & everyone of course agreeing beforehand to what was said. Old Dr Clark indeed could quote clauses in Treaties by their numbers;[2] & Hobson was shrewd, judicious & kindly; Janet came in looking very well. But we had to race off in the Tube to Leicester Sqre to dine with Barbara Saxon & a young woman called G.[3] Then on to Figaro at the Old Vic. It's perfectly lovely; breaking from one beauty into another, & so romantic as well as witty— the perfection of music, & vindication of opera.

On Sunday we heard of Cecil's death, & Philip's wounds.[4]

We walked along the river in the afternoon, when L. came back from Staines, & came to an old hollow elm tree, in the sawdust of which someone so we guessed, had stuck a match. The wind was blowing in, & soon the flames were running high. A crowd stopped. The first old gentleman was so positive that I believed him; he said it was a usual process, done to get rid of an old tree; nothing to marvel at; no question of accident or malice; & so he marched on with obvious contentment. The second old gentleman admitted doubts, finally swung round to our view that no one would burn a tree down on the public path on a Sunday too. Meanwhile the tree burnt rather beautifully; we called at the police office & told them, in case the fire might run along by means of bushes to other trees. Leonard's cold very bad—a horrid nuisance.

Today he stayed in & set up 21 lines. I went to Harrison, to Mudies, to the Times, with an article on Mrs Drew, & am just come in.[5] Frostily cold night; stars polished to their brightest: so much brighter than the streets are. I lost my way again, & as no one knows where Printing House Sqre is, one has full scope for wandering in. I got the 2nd vol. of Ld Morley's memories, a real solid book, I think, like the books father used to buy,

1. To the Hampstead Branch of the UDC (see above, 13 November 1917, n 20).
2. Dr Gavin Brown Clark (1846-1930), teetotaller, pacifist, internationalist, and champion of labour and agricultural reforms, had been MP for Caithness, 1885-1900. He lived in Hampstead.
3. Georgina Bagenal, younger sister of Faith Henderson and Nicholas Bagenal.
4. For an account of the circumstances, see *III LW*, 181.
5. VW's review of *Some Hawarden Letters, 1878-1913*, appeared in the *TLS*, 6 December 1917 (Kp C92). The letters are to Mary (1847-1927), Mr Gladstone's third daughter and his secretary, who married the Rev. Harry Drew in 1886.

looking like them too, an ugly red.[6] One night Walter Lamb dropped in, as we sat over the fire; & his proud crest is a little dashed I think by my overpowering snobbery.

Wednesday 5 December

Our apprentice weighs rather heavily upon us. For one thing, though I'm always ashamed in her presence to feel this, her presence is rather in the way of our complete comfort. It may be her youth; something highly polished so as to reflect without depth about her— On the other hand, she's nice, considerate; one can be open with her. The real drawback is her work. Today has been spent by L. in the futile misery of trying to print from one of her pages which wont lock up.[7] As the other page had to be entirely taken down & re-set, her work amounts to *nil*; less than nil, considering L.'s time wasted. A bitter cold day too. Our only outing after dark to the printers to borrow inverted comma's. Yesterday L. saw Philip at Fishmonger's Hall.[8] I set up in one room, Barbara in the other. These days indoors don't provide much in the way of incident, & pass with the swiftest rush, so that at 9 o'clock, the present hour, one seems only starting on the days work—perhaps the result of passing without question straight from one occupation to another. L. reading Life of Dilke; worried by a flea up his back; I'm past the middle of Purgatorio, but find it stiff, the meaning more than the language, I think. We got Hardy's new poems, but lent them to Philip.[9]

Thursday 6 December

When I wrote that we were only at the beginning of our days work, last night, I spoke more truly than I knew. Nothing was further from our minds than air raids; a bitter night, no moon up till eleven. At 5 however, I was wakened by L. to a most instant sense of guns: as if one's faculties

6. John Morley (1838-1923), 1st Viscount Morley, statesman and man of letters, had been a firm friend of Leslie Stephen. His *Recollections* were published in two volumes in 1917.

7. Type for printing was set letter by letter and line by line into a chase, or iron frame, which when the page was complete had to be locked tight before being inked and printed off.

8. The splendid Hall at London Bridge of one of the richest and oldest of the City Livery Companies was in use as a Military Hospital.

9. A two-volume *Life* of the statesman Sir Charles Wentworth Dilke, Bt (1842-1911), by Stephen Gwynne and Gertrude Tuckwell was published in 1917. VW possessed her father's copy of Charles Eliot Norton's translation of Dante's *Purgatorio* (1891: *Holleyman*, VS I, p. 60); as she did not seriously study Italian until later, it is possible she was reading a translation. *Moments of Vision, and Miscellaneous Verses* by Thomas Hardy appeared in 1917.

jumped up fully dressed. We took clothes, quilts, a watch & a torch, the guns sounding nearer as we went down stairs to sit with the servants on the ancient black horse hair chest wrapped in quilts in the kitchen passage. Lottie having said she felt bad, passed on to a general rattle of jokes & comments which almost silenced the guns. They fired very quickly, apparently towards Barnes. Slowly the sounds got more distant, & finally ceased; we unwrapped ourselves & went back to bed. In ten minutes there could be no question of staying there: guns apparently at Kew. Up we jumped, more hastily this time, since I remember leaving my watch, & trailing cloak & stockings behind me. Servants apparently calm & even jocose. In fact one talks through the noise, rather bored by having to talk at 5 A.M. than anything else. Guns at one point so loud that the whistle of the shell going up followed the explosion. One window did, I think, rattle. Then silence. Cocoa was brewed for us, & off we went again. Having trained one's ears to listen one can't get them not to for a time; & as it was after 6, carts were rolling out of stables, motor cars throbbing, & then prolonged ghostly whistlings which meant, I suppose, Belgian work people recalled to the munitions factory. At last in the distance I heard bugles; L. was by this time asleep, but the dutiful boy scouts came down our road & wakened him carefully; it struck me how sentimental the suggestion of the sound was, & how thousands of old ladies were offering up their thanksgivings at the sound, & connecting him (a boy scout with small angel wings) with some joyful vision— And then I went to sleep: but the servants sat up with their heads out of the window in the bitter cold—frost white on the roofs—until the bugle sounded, when they went back to the kitchen and sat there till breakfast. The logic of the proceeding escapes me.

Today we have printed, & discussed the raid, which, according to the Star I bought was the work of 25 Gothas, attacking in 5 squadrons & 2 were brought down. A perfectly still & fine winter's day, so about 5.30-tomorrow morning perhaps—

Friday 7 December

But there was no raid; & as the moon wanes, no doubt we are free for a month. Happily no apprentice today, which gives a sense of holiday. We have had to make it rather clear to Barbara that this job may not be followed by another. She refuses payment for last week. So there's no fault to find with her. No one could be nicer; & yet she has the soul of the lake, not of the sea. Or is one too romantic & exacting in what one expects? Anyhow, nothing is more fascinating than a live person; always changing, resisting & yeilding against one's forecast; this is true even of Barbara, not the most variable or gifted of her kind. Nessa was up about a governess (Mrs Brereton suggested in place of the faultfinding & man-hunting Miss E.)[10] so I ended my afternoon in one of the great soft chairs at Gordon Square. I like the sense of space & deep large pattern one gets there. I sat alone for 20 minutes, reading a book on Children & Sex. When Nessa came we had tea & it was discovered that Clive & Mary were in the house; & Norton came in, the same party as usual.[11] As usual to my liking; so much alive, so full of information of the latest kind; real interest in every sort of art; & in people too. I rather expect L. to disagree with all this. I judge by the amount of animation of brain produced in myself, & sense of thoughts all liberated. Not that M.H. opens her lips, but she has an air of mute sympathy. I like Norton too—all that brain hoarded in his head for the most exalted ends, which makes his criticism always impartial. Clive starts his topics—lavishing admiration & notice upon Nessa, which doesn't make me jealous as once it did, when the swing of that pendulum carried so much of my fortune with it: at any rate of my comfort. Maynard says that Bonar Law has dished the Government; the country entirely with Lansdowne, & the Government unable to stick to its own declarations. This was from Lord Reading.[12] It sometimes occurs to me that there's not a single secret in politics; everything is to be guessed from the newspapers. Nessa had to go round to Rogers, & I walked with her, buying sausages & cheese for a supper party on the way. Roger is becoming one of the successes of the day as a painter of perfectly literal & very unpleasant portraits.

Today (Saturday) we walked to Twickenham, where Leonard took train for Staines. I found Marny when I got back.[13] Its 6.30 & she has

10. The suggestion came from Roger Fry; Mrs Brereton had looked after his wife before she was confined to an asylum. Estranged from her clergyman husband, she and her daughter Anne arrived at Charleston on 11 January 1918.

11. Henry (Harry) Tertius James Norton (1886-1937), mathematician and Fellow of Trinity College, Cambridge, and an Apostle. Vanessa had been the object of his unrequited love. He had rooms at 46 Gordon Square.

12. Andrew Bonar Law (1858-1923), Unionist MP of Canadian origin, Chancellor of the Exchequer and leader of the House of Commons in Lloyd George's Coalition Government; he had imposed his own policy of financing the war upon his colleagues—measures which in fact proved remarkably effective. Lord Lansdowne, 5th Marquess (1845-1927), leader of the Conservative party in the House of Lords, was author of the so-called 'Lansdowne Letter' published in *The Daily Telegraph* of 29 November 1917 advocating a statement of war aims as a stimulus towards a negotiated peace, for which he was violently accused of disloyalty to the Allied cause. Rufus Isaacs, Lord Reading (1860-1935), was at this time British high commissioner for finance in the United States and Canada; Maynard Keynes as a Treasury official had just accompanied him to America and Paris.

13. Margaret ('Marny') Vaughan (1862-1929), second daughter of VW's aunt Adeline and Henry Halford Vaughan, sister of 'Toad' (see above, 9 October 1917, n 9). She did philanthropic work among the London poor. VW re-wrote this account of her visit for Vanessa Bell (see *II VW Letters*, no. 894).

just gone; so that if I don't cover the next 10 pages with family gossip & detail of all sorts its not for want of it. Let me put a little of it down, if I can remember—but it goes so fast, & turns to ashes without the atmosphere. But Florence Bishop, married to a naval Dr lives in a flat in Earls Court—gives you Tiptree jam for tea, & looks like a picture, & is very poor, owing to old Bishop's failings; but her husband is an elderly man, & now takes charge of wounded soldiers in trains.[14] And we haven't had butter for a long time, & sometimes we can't even get the nice kind of margarine, but I wont deal at Barkers, not after the evidence at that fire.[15] Wright's Coal shed burnt down behind us the other night—all that coal wasted, & once last winter we'd run out. It was a Saturday too, & I went from shop to shop begging even a scuttlefull, & who should I meet at Knightsbridge but Kitty Maxse? & she said O I'll give you coal—why I've got 2 cellars full: & sure enough that very afternoon up she drove in a taxi with a sack full, & that saw us through, but I've not seen her since that day, so distinguished looking, & not a year older, though she must be 50.[16] Well, I'm 55; & Toad 43—but one forgets peoples' ages, & I'm sure I don't feel old; & you look like 25—And Nessa as lovely as ever I suppose! (here followed the whole history of Nessa, Clive, Duncan, Adrian & ourselves).

Dear me, how we all move about—partly owing to the war to be sure; though I do see some of my old friends still, like Miss Harris, who paints, you know, & very well too, but she wont show anything because she only considers herself an amateur, & she's very busy now with war work. And Hilda Lightbody, I see her; though she's making papier maché splints all day—yes, a widow she is, her husband having been a great invalid[17]—And I sometimes see Adeline, who lives with Hervey, at Hastings for the winter, not having meant to stay there, but they went for a change & there wasn't any reason why they shouldn't stay—near the sea, of course; & Millicent not very far off.[18] Millicent's boy died you

14. The Bishops were erstwhile family friends of the Vaughans and Stephens; Florence's married name was Burke.

15. During the night of 2/3 November 1912 fire had broken out on an upper floor of John Barker's store in Kensington where twenty female servants slept; five deaths resulted. At the inquest it was revealed that the recommendations of the London County Council fire inspectorate made a year previously had not been carried out owing to the expense involved.

16. Katherine (Kitty) Maxse, *née* Lushington (1867-1922), whose parents and VW's had been close friends. She had married in 1890 Leopold Maxse, political writer and owner-editor of *The National Review*. VW later wrote of her that she had 'served as a foster mother in the ways of the world' and to some extent used her as the model for Mrs Dalloway.

17. Miss Harris and Hilda Lightbody have not been identified.

18. Two of VW's and Marny's eleven Fisher cousins. Adeline (1870-1951) was married to the composer Ralph Vaughan Williams; though disabled by arthritis,

know, & Virginia milks cows at Lord Rayleigh's place in Essex. She prefers horses, but she couldn't get horses, & she's very fond of cows. Yes
Millicent still lives at Hastings, though she doesn't like it, but Vere does,
because of the sea & they know a great many people, & Millicent got up a
series of dances for young people last winter, though she didn't feel like
dancing I'm sure, & she keeps the musical Festival going, though she
won't do any war work; & Augusta always loved Kent, & now theyve got
a house in Kent, & a little garden, & Bob works for a neighbour sometimes, & so they get along you know—all the children out in the world
now.[19] O its wicked how they grow up—Halford quite a big boy—with a
poetic side, but very practical I'm glad to say, & Janet very like Madge;[20] &
I wish Madge *would* write. Perhaps she'd be happier then, though I don't
think Madge could ever be really happy, but its a wonderful piece of work,
& I'm sure Will owes her a great deal. I dont think I've gossiped so much
for years. And Cousin Mia dead, & Aunt Mary killed—yes. That was
extremely sad, but better than a lingering illness I daresay! And Herbert
in all the papers; but Lettice doesn't like London at all, but Herbert does,
& she goes back to Sheffield for change of air[21]— & when the raids come,
we go & sit with the Wales' on the ground floor.[22] But they ought to tell
one about the Bugles. Why, when they first blew, I thought it might be

she devoted herself, after their mother's death in 1916, to the care of her brilliant
but unstable and handicapped brother Hervey. Millicent Isham, *née* Vaughan
(1866-1961), one of Marny's younger sisters, had married in 1895 Vere Isham, who
succeeded his father as 11th Baronet in 1903. Their elder son John Vere, Lieutenant
in the Dragoon Guards, died on active service in 1916; their only daughter
Virginia (b. 1898) was working as a land girl at Terling Place, near Witham, Essex.

19. The marriage of Marny's eldest sister Augusta to Robert Croft had not been
very gratifying to her relations; he failed as a farmer, and became to some extent
dependent upon his brother-in-law Sir Vere Isham. There were four children.

20. Margaret (Madge) Vaughan, *née* Symonds (1869-1925), third daughter of the
writer J. Addington Symonds, in 1898 married Marny's brother W. W. Vaughan
(see above, 9 January 1915, n 35); Janet (b. 1899) and Halford (b. 1901) were their
two elder children.

21. Maria ('Mia') MacNamara, *née* Bayley, was a first cousin of the mothers of VW and
Marny and of their aunt Mary Fisher (see above, 12 January 1915, n 46), who had
been knocked down and fatally injured by a motor car opposite Chelsea Town
Hall on 24 August 1916, aged 75. Her eldest son Herbert Albert Laurens Fisher
(1865-1940), the historian, became Vice-Chancellor of Sheffield University in
1914, but at the end of 1916 was appointed President of the Board of Education by
Lloyd George, a position he held until the fall of the coalition government in
October 1922. In 1899 he had married Lettice, eldest daughter of Sir Courtney
Ilbert, Clerk of the House of Commons.

22. Margaret and Emma Vaughan lived together in a flat, 9 Kensington Square
Mansions, Young Street; no. 1 was inhabited by the Rev. F. H. Wales.

the Germans themselves, & I went out onto the landing & met a lady, though it was 2, dressed for going out, & she told me—&c &c— —

Sunday, Monday, Tuesday, & Wednesday;
Wednesday being the 12th of December

A melancholy record— The truth is, when we're not printing & therefore don't have Barbara here, we do jobs in London, & get back late & I'm disinclined to get out pen & ink. On Sunday Lytton came to tea. I was alone, for L. went to Margaret. I enjoyed it very much. He is one of the most supple of our friends; I don't mean passionate or masterful or original, but the person whose mind seems softest to impressions, least starched by any formality or impediment. There is his great gift of expression of course, never (to me) at its best in writing; but making him in some respects the most sympathetic & understanding friend to talk to. Moreover, he has become, or now shows it more fully, curiously gentle, sweet tempered, considerate; & if one adds his peculiar flavour of mind, his wit & infinite intelligence—not brain but intelligence—he is a figure not to be replaced by any other combination. Intimacy seems to me possible with him as with scarcely any one; for, besides tastes in common, I like & think I understand his feelings—even in their more capricious developments; for example in the matter of Carrington.[23] He spoke of her, by the way, with a candour not flattering, though not at all malicious.

"That woman will dog me"—he remarked. "She won't let me write, I daresay."

"Ottoline was saying you would end by marrying her."

"God! the mere notion is enough— One thing I know—I'll never marry anyone—"

"But if she's in love with you?"

"Well, then she must take her chance."

"I believe I'm sometimes jealous—"

"Of her? thats inconceivable—"

"You like me better, dont you?"

He said he did; we laughed; remarked on our wish for an intimate

23. Dora de Houghton Carrington (1893-1932), known as Carrington, fellow-pupil at the Slade of Barbara Hiles, Brett, and Mark Gertler, who was in love with her. At the end of 1915 she had fallen in love with Lytton Strachey, the beginning of a lifelong devotion which was now about to assume a domestic form at the Mill House, Tidmarsh, rented by a consortium of Lytton's friends ostensibly for joint use but in effect to be a home created by Carrington for his comfort. (See *Carrington, Letters & Extracts from her Diaries*, edited by David Garnett, 1970; also *Holroyd*.)

correspondent; but how to overcome the difficulties? Should we attempt it? Perhaps.

He brought us his Gordon. Next day he was to take the book to Chatto & Windus.[24]

Monday [10 December]

Today was a string of meetings for L. Out to lunch, to Philip, to another meeting & not back till 8.30; I pacing the room in some anxiety till I heard him. My afternoon was very nearly normal; to Mudies, tea in an A.B.C. reading a life of Gaudier Brzeska;[25] home again; wet soft vaporous day.

Tuesday [11 December]

The infliction of our apprentice. Things on the whole went better; & L. & I slipped out for half an hour before tea, into the brownish red light of the wintry afternoon. The green gives a very good sample of the sky & bare trees, one or two old rooks nests in the upper twigs. Back to tea; & Perera came for private talk. I own that I sounded the very depths of boredom with Barbara. She gives out facts precisely as she received them —minute facts about governesses & houses. And no doubt of her own adequacy crosses her mind; all so nice, honest, sensible, how can there be a flaw? Indeed, one figures her nature as a flawless marble, impervious, unatmospheric. And the time passed; she missed her train; waited on for another—waited until 6.10; & we were to dine at 7—& my evening fretted away without sensation, save of one standing under the drip of a water spout. My excuse for such extravagance is that I had to go in to the Guild today. No speaker came, & we were clearing the table at 9 after a lot of letter reading & intermittent discussion when a private omen came true. The speaker arrived. A Mrs Moore from Kensal Rise: middle class; dressed in velvet; vulgar, fluent. Spoke on propaganda for 20 minutes; more words than brain, & indeed she couldn't explain her sayings to the satisfaction of Mrs Langston, & was perturbed when I showed how much I knew. But I admired the way in which she got her steam up when we were all anxious to go. The women said it was a splendid speech; sentences that melt into each other impress them.

24. 'The End of General Gordon' was the last of the four studies comprising *Eminent Victorians*.
25. *Gaudier-Brzeska. A Memoir*, by Ezra Pound, published by John Lane in 1917, commemorated the French sculptor Henri Gaudier-Brzeska (1891-1915) who, after living in London for several years, joined the French army and was killed in June 1915. An A.B.C. was one of the chain of popular tea-rooms of the Aerated Bread Company.

Wednesday [12 December]

This morning ruined by the tears & plaints of Lottie, who thinks her work too hard, & finally demanded higher wages, which she could easily get, & so could Nell. I lost my temper, & told her to get them then. Up came Nelly in a conciliatory mood regretting Lottie's outburst; though pointing out the hardships of our printing-room, so untidy—work endless; had meant to ask a rise in February—everyone's wages raised— Of course we had to pay extra for food, but then we'd got to— We were very amicable; no difficulty about money; but L.'s taunts seemed to me unpleasant—I charged her to find out the truth—if there is such a thing in the midst of that bluster— At last she went. Walked by the river having done a little printing.

Thursday 13 December

By careful arrangement I limited the reconciliation scene with Lottie to 15 minutes at eleven sharp. She sobbed; repented; took back everything she'd said; told me how her temper had led to constant rows at "Frys" as they call it; all a fabrication about over work, & the more people we had & the more mess we made the better she liked it. She begged me not to tell anyone; she kissed me & went off, like a chastened child, leaving me with a mixture of pity & (I suppose) self complacency. The poor have no chance; no manners or self control to protect themselves with; we have a monopoly of all the generous feelings—(I daresay this isn't quite true; but there's some meaning [in] it. Poverty degrades, as Gissing said). Barbara had a cold & didn't come, to my relief certainly. But that's inaccurate; she came after luncheon, & brought a letter from Nessa who invites her to be governess there for a month, pending Mrs Brereton. Barbara was so sensible, & matter of fact that I repented & certainly she treats us with the strictest honesty, making a serious undertaking of the printing (here the light went out) which is creditable, & one could depend upon her, I fancy, to keep the exact letter of her promise. She went off directly after tea to conduct one of those curious gatherings of Nick, Oliver, & Saxon & Carrington about their house in the country. The work of furnishing has fallen of course upon Carrington; but Barbara is a good second & keeps the accounts, which will end, I assured her, by absorbing all her money on things she'll never be paid for.

Friday 14 December

Today we went to see Philip at Fishmongers Hall. Rather a strange place a few feet from London Bridge. A pompous hall, with a porter, a gigantic fire for that porter, a German gun; & within banisters draped with crimson folds of stuff, as if for a royal visit; Nelson's flag in a glass case;

Dick Whittington in plaster standing in an alcove; a branching staircase taking one to a great gallery now divided into cubicles. Two or three nurses sat sewing outside. We found Philip up; his chair by the open window, looking into the street, which was noisy, & just catching sight of the river. I saw a notice warning patients not to throw cigarette ends out, or they might catch inflammable bales upon the wharf. To me, Philip looked well; though there was that absentmindedness which one sees in Nick. I suppose to Philip these days pass in a dream from which he finds himself detached. I can imagine that he is puzzled why he doesn't feel more. He still talks of "we" & "our" things. I thought he must look to going back again with something like hope. But he talked very easily & cheerfully—about horses & books & so on— Another man—a great burly cavalry officer was reading his book in a far corner; unused to reading books, I should think. Nurses seemed very kindly. A feeling of the uselessness of it all, breaking these people & mending them again, was in the air, I thought. We asked Philip to Asheham, when he can move.

Home to find Sidney [Waterlow] already in the chair by the fire. He was in very good feather, & rolled out the word "I" with a sort of tremor of pride; he has indeed negotiated treaties in Paris since we met.[26] Being self conscious & diffident his triumphs give him enormous pleasure; there is the same tremor of half incredulous self approbation in his tone when he talks of his children. I laughed at him about our quarrel. He had thought it all over, so he said—as if it mattered; & was highly pleased by the removal of the cloud. Saxon came, very late, to dinner. I gave it him, & he told me how selfish Alix was—can't pack her own boxes; waits for Carrington. Saxon attributes this to love; I believe its in imitation of the beloved. She has picked it up from James, sees it in him & thinks it stands for the consciousness of superiority, I believe.[27] Sydney stayed the night; & Saxon stayed till eleven; & he only spoke 3 times; & then rather pedantically, in his old way, which he has rather dropped lately.

Saturday 15 December

A cold but sunny day. It seems long since we had a day to ourselves. No printing done. We took a walk in the old style through the Park, down the avenue & back by the river, which was flooding up fast, & cut

26. Sydney Waterlow had returned to the Foreign Office on a temporary basis, and was to be re-established in 1920. He now had a daughter and a son.

27. James Beaumont Strachey (1887-1967), the youngest of the ten children of Sir Richard and Lady Strachey. He followed his brother Lytton to Trinity College, Cambridge, and became an Apostle. On coming down in 1909 he became secretary to his cousin St Loe Strachey, editor of *The Spectator*, but was dismissed in 1915 for his pacifist views; in 1916 he was awarded 'non-combatant' status by the Tribunal.

us off, making us creep along a railing so as to reach dry land. The streets remind me of Cambridge streets. People walk down the middle. This is partly because of the queues waiting to buy at Liptons.[28] One has some difficulty in keeping on the pavement, & the motor buses are always grazing people's sides. Home & a large tea by ourselves. Masses of papers. Perera, of course, to consult one more; & he is still sitting with L. in his room.

Monday 17 December

Monday, as I think I've noted before, is our marketing day—but I'm forgetting Molly MacCarthy & Walter Lamb last night—The thing arose in this way. Wat offered us the loan of his Norfolk maps. Thinking it a little cool to borrow without invitation, we asked him to bring them. We then found ourselves faced with the unbearable prospect of unmitigated Walter. But who to get at the last moment? The Strachey household denuded owing to Tidmarsh; Squire engaged; at last the idea of Molly came to me, & Heaven granted this favour. I'm not sure that her deafness doesn't lend her a kind of piquancy (like a stammer); she ——

On Thursday 20 December the Woolfs went to Asheham for Christmas. VW made one entry in her Asheham Diary, a summary report on food supplies, weather, and visitors, which is recapitulated in the next entry, written on her return to Hogarth House.

[Thursday 3 January 1918]

I forget who it was that came in at this moment; & I have excuse for forgetting, since it is now Thursday, 3rd Jan. 1918. & we're just back from Asheham. I remember though that the last days were full of people. Walter & Molly as I began to relate— She has sent her novel to Chatto & Windus, & calls it The Band on the Pier, or Ring Fence. The last dull I think.[29] W.L. spruce & a little suspicious when the Royal Family appeared, as it did; wouldn't shoot at those rabbits again for my diversion. And then I can remember that we had Ka; who contemplates resignation; & then, the night after, Bob[1]; with his pockets bulging with Georgian poetry, his talk all of books & prices asked for printing, & number of copies sold, in the midst of which Nelly burst in to say that the Take Cover had sounded. So we had our dinner partly in the cellar; Bob. talking at such a rate that it was necessary to listen at the window for the guns, loud enough though

28. A chain grocery store.
29. Mary MacCarthy's first book, *A Pier and a Band. A Novel of the Nineties*, was published by Chatto & Windus in 1918.
 1. Robert Calverley (Bob) Trevelyan (1872-1951), poet and classical scholar, brother of the historian G. M. Trevelyan; Trinity College, Cambridge, and an Apostle; in the 1890's he had shared a house with Roger Fry.

they were. I remember him attached to a large plate of suet pudding in the basement, & L. sitting on a wooden box in the coal hole reading the paper & finding one of my red pens there. All clear sounded about 10: a bad raid, though, & Barbara & Saxon suffered more than we did at Hampstead.

After that—the very next night—we went to the 17 Club dinner; a great deal of eating by some 200 people at long tables.[2] Waiters thudding swing doors imitated guns so successfully that various officials came round & warned one of a raid. Jos.[Wedgwood] made a speech. I noticed poor Marjorie listening with her eyes on her lap. She came up from Darlington, & was dressed, poor creature, in muslin picked out with red roses & cut low; though every one else was more or less in working clothes, & fur capes. I was caught in the net of Sylvia Whitham, who cross examined me about her husbands novels; & in despair of revealing my true opinion I pretended never to have read Wolfgang[3]— Most suitably, of all our friends shes the one to have a bomb dropped next door, & to receive it without surprise. And she's taking to literature, & begins by translating Flaubert —a remarkable instance of a person without gift of any kind, always pushing along in the wake of other more advanced people.

Next day we went to Asheham, & the journey was the worst in our record—5 hours; spent mostly outside Clapham Junction; fog, bitter cold; every move stopping short in a minute or two. Motored out, I remember, & found the roads under snow; but very pleasant coming into the drawing room, save that we were without milk.

One of the coldest & finest of Christmases. Rather to our relief, we spent it alone, Ray falling ill, Ka coming for week end, & Nessa's children. There was the usual visit from Maynard & Clive; my usual failure to get to Charleston corresponding to Nessa's failure to get to Asheham. I spent a night there, & enjoyed [?] myself, through the rather obtuse barrier of poor Bunny, who took to his bed at one point, without sympathy from Nessa, who had often put him to bed, she said, for no perceivable cause. Duncan came back from London, with gossip for us; chiefly about Alix & a party at the play, who broke the partition dropped cigarettes, & had to be asked to leave.[4] But what I like most about Asheham is that I read books there; so divine it is, coming in from a walk to have tea by the fire & then read & read—say Othello—say anything. It doesn't seem to matter what. But one's faculties are so oddly clarified that the page de-

2. The 1917 Club dinner followed the first general meeting on Wednesday 19 December 1917. LW put the number of diners at about 120.

3. Sylvia Milman (see above, 21 January 1915, n 72), had married in 1916 the writer John Mills Whitham; his lugubrious novel *Wolfgang* was published early in 1917. They collaborated in translations from the French.

4. This may refer to a party given after Christmas at 46 Gordon Square at which Marjorie Strachey produced her version of Arthur Schnitzler's comedy *Reigen* (*The Roundelay* or *La Ronde*).

taches itself in its true meaning & lies as if illumined, before one's eyes; seen whole & truly not in jerks & spasms as so often in London. And then the trees, spare & leafless; the brown of the plough, &, yesterday, downs mountainous through a mist, which isn't palpable, for only dead detail vanishes & the live grows larger & larger, & fires can be seen burning through. Solitary sportsmen beat up duck & snipe on the marshes. Windows were almost always frozen in the morning, & each blade rough with frost. Partridges would come & sit in the field, lifeless little lumps they looked, half stiff with cold perhaps.

The diary habit has come to life at Charleston. Bunny sat up late on the Old Year's night writing, & Duncan came back with a ledger, bought in Lambs Conduit Street. The sad thing is that we daren't trust each other to read our books; they lie, like vast consciences, in our most secret drawers. Clive, by the way, enlivened Christmas by a small book of verse—the prose fantastically foppish, the verse very pretty & light, to my mind (by wh. I mean not altogether to L.'s mind). He can do his little Owl very efficiently—Anyhow, I prefer it to the last Georgian effort—bound in blue this year, & housing that ridiculous Squire.[5]

So we come to an end of the year, & any attempt to sum it up is beyond me, or even to cast a final glance at the evening paper, with news from Russia, which has just come in and drawn L. to remark

"A very interesting state of things—"

"And what's going to happen?"

"No human being can foretell that."[6]

The End

5. *Ad Familiares*, a booklet of 28 pages in paper cover, printed at The Pelican Press, October 1917, contained thirteen poems among which one, dated 1909, is addressed 'To V.S. with a book'; they were reprinted, with four additional poems, by the Hogarth Press in December 1921. The expression 'do his little owl', used fairly often by VW, appears to mean show off, perform. *Georgian Poetry 1916-1917*, the third of the series edited by Edward Marsh, was published by The Poetry Bookshop in November 1917.

6. The *Star* of Thursday 3 January carried a banner headline 'Return to Brest-Litovsk'. On assuming power in November 1917, the Soviet Russian Government had taken immediate steps to open negotiations for a 'just and democratic peace, without annexations or indemnities', and on 3 December their preliminary contacts with the Central Powers at Brest-Litovsk resulted in a truce followed by an armistice from 15 December to 14 January. Formal negotiations were opened on 22 December; on 28 December the Russians suspended the conference on the pretext of securing the inclusion of the Entente powers, in the hope and expectation that workers' risings throughout Europe would strengthen their bargaining position; but in this they were disappointed. They returned to Brest-Litovsk on 9 January, and ultimately signed a humiliating peace treaty on 3 March 1918.

1918

1918

Having recalled the last two weeks of December 1917 in the long entry written on 3 January 1918 at the end of Diary III, VW now begins a new book (Diary IV) for 1918, which lasts her until July. The opening page is inscribed:

> Hogarth House
> Paradise Road
> Richmond
> January: 1918

Friday 4 January

There's no reason after all why one should expect special events for the first page of a new book; still one does: & so I may count three facts of different importance; our first use of the 17 Club; talk of peace; & the breaking of my tortoiseshell spectacles. This talk of peace (after all the most important of the three) comes to the surface with a kind of tremor of hope once in 3 months; then subsides; then swells again. What it now amounts to, one doesn't even like to guess, having a sort of superstition about guessing; at any rate, one can't help feeling something moving; one may wake to find the covered murmur proclaimed in every newspaper.[7] The 17 Club is a success, on the basis of one tea. We met Alix, settled in, already an habitué by the fire; together with a knot of very youthful revolutionaries, one officer, & two sallow democratic officials. The rooms are light, bear traces of Omega, & are less formal than usual. Before this, I did my usual round; Partridge & Coopers; walk through Lincolns Inn Fields to Mudies; L. passing his afternoon in Committees.[8] Margaret has just rung up to consult him on certain peace maneuvres in which she figures. Talk with Alix about possible books she might write: "One's wretched without work"—"Oh, perfectly wretched" she echoed, with a glance in the direction of James, I suppose. "No hope of writing well: I see things as they are."

7. Possibly an echo from the prologue to *King Henry V*, act IV:
   > 'Now entertain conjecture of a time
   > When creeping murmur and the poring dark
   > Fills the wide vessel of the universe.'
8. Partridge and Cooper, a large firm of stationers with premises at the corner of Fleet Street and Chancery Lane. The book in which this and other diaries was written was probably bought from them. LW's diary records that he went to an editorial committee meeting of *War and Peace*, which he was to edit that month. (See above, 24 October 1917, n 39, and below, 18 January 1918, n 33.)

Saturday 5 January

We went to Hampton Court, for the first time since we skated there, so I believe.[9] We walked across Bushey Park, & a troop of horses took the opportunity to run from one side to the other. The gilt statue was surrounded by ice, & the ice had an inch of water on it; I broke through with my umbrella.[10]. The beds at Hampton Court are uniformly brown, save for one yellow & one pink flower, primula's I think. There were sacks at intervals, which L. thought might be laid down for the gymnastic exercises of Mrs Creighton.[11] We looked in at her windows. As usual we saw nothing but those great vellum folios, containing Italian History, so I suppose. We walked along a raised bank beneath trees to the river; & sat on one of the semi-circle of empty wooden seats. It was cold, but still. Then we took a tram to Kingston & had tea at Atkinsons, where one may have no more than a single bun. Everything is skimped now. Most of the butchers shops are shut; the only open shop was besieged. You can't buy chocolates, or toffee; flowers cost so much that I have to pick leaves, instead. We have cards for most foods. The only abundant shop windows are the drapers. Other shops parade tins, or cardboard boxes, doubtless empty. (This is an attempt at the concise, historic style.) Suddenly one has come to notice the war everywhere. I suppose there must be some undisturbed pockets of luxury somewhere still—up in Northumbrian or Cornish farm houses perhaps; but the general table is pretty bare. Papers, however, flourish, & by spending 6d we are supplied with enough to light a weeks fires. A man called Richardson works out a highly complex mathematical method of voting in the trenches.[12]

Sunday 6 January

An infernal wet day. I left L. at the station, he having to go to Hampstead to answer a list of questions for Margaret. Home to tea alone. Alix & Fredegond for supper. The talk, after flaunting round Clive, Barbara, Garsington &c. settled upon conscience: social duties, & Tolstoy.

9. LW's diary records that he and VW skated at Hampton Court on 8 and 9 February 1917.
10. On the approach to Hampton Court Palace in Bushey Park—which is also Crown property—is a large circular fish basin, from the centre of which arises an ornamental fountain surmounted by a gilt-bronze statue of Diana dating from the time of Charles II.
11. Louise Creighton (1850-1936), widow of Mandell Creighton, Bishop of London, after whose death in 1901 she was granted a grace-and-favour residence in Hampton Court Palace. She was a prolific writer on historical subjects. The Creightons were acquaintances of VW's parents.
12. L. F. Richardson (1881-1953), a Cambridge contemporary of LW's. See MHP, Sussex.

Gerald [Shove] read Tolstoy the other day, & determined to give up tobacco, but now argues that Tolstoy's commands were for men of looser life than he, so that he may smoke cigarettes. He thinks seriously of starting a nursery garden after the war, & threatens to give up their capital.

"What's the use of that? L. demanded. Thats the worst of all things to do. We dont want people to live on 30/ a week."

"Psychologically it may be necessary if one is to abolish capitalism" I remarked.

"I dont agree." said Alix. "Besides who would he give his capital to?"

"In the ideal state everyone would have £300 a year" L. went on.

"Please tell me some reason that I can remember to take back to Gerald" Fredegond pleaded.

I forget now what the reason was.

"He's got an awful conscience, she continued. He ate a large Christmas dinner, & then he & his brother sent out for preserved fruit & when they had finished them they were miserable. "We've behaved like pigs! We're brutes!" they cried. They were both miserable." L. gave us a great many reasons why we should keep what we have, & do good work for nothing; I still feel, however, that my fire is too large for one person. I'm one of those who are hampered by the psychological hindrance of owning capital. Alix represented some sturdy & hardheaded economy, derived from Strachey's. After this long argument, it was time for them to go.

Monday 7 January

To London today, L. with my Jack's article to the Times, I to Spiller about my spectacles; & I must get a new pair at a cost of £2.2.[13] After that we met at the London Library, & then to tea at the Club; where Alix almost plays hostess; & the woman still smokes her pipe in the corner. Lytton came in, & I finished my tea with him. He is bargaining with Chatto & Windus about his book.

"When I'm asked if I like Tidmarsh, I say the country suits me", he said, rather cryptically.

His mild benignancy with the young ladies— Fredegond, Faith & Alix, very noticeable. I told him he wrote too much after the pattern of Macaulay.

"I see you didn't really like Gordon" he said.

He was quite unmoved, contented, almost sleek. People going in & out all the time make it difficult to talk. Chief topic the approach of peace; save that the evening papers throw doubts upon it.

13. VW's review of *Philosophy in Fiction* by L. P. Jacks appeared in the *TLS*, 10 January 1918 (Kp C97). George Spiller Ltd of Wigmore Street were opticians and spectacle makers.

Tuesday 8 January

As a sign of the times we live in, I note that Fredegond who wants to spend some months in London is advised by her practical friends to live in a hotel. They say that she would have difficulty in getting food, even if she found a servant, or a room to live in. Consequently, she is taking rooms at the Thackeray Hotel.[14]

Some fragments came to mind today which, having nothing to record, I may as well put down. How I went to a Registry Office for Nessa; & noticed that the woman had 6 or 7 pens on her table, tried one after another, found all save one unusable; nibs stuck to the holder with crusts of ink. One night last summer getting down from a bus, I saw a fish bag left on the seat, & gave it to the woman in front of me. She thanked me & said, with half a smirk, "That comes of me not being used to carrying a bag". The bag was evidently the mark of a lower social scale. There were of course other fragments, which at hint of needing them dissolve in my mind. Its odd, considering their triviality, how these little scenes come up again & again at odd moments: are thought of, re-enacted, & disappear. Odd too how one thinks by help of pictures of surroundings. Yesterday I couldn't remember whether I'd left a book in my room. And then I saw myself moving my spectacles, & remembered that I moved my spectacles in order to put the book down: sure enough there it was. I'd give a good deal to know something of psychology. That was one of the books I suggested that Alix should write: but "whats the good if one can't do it *really* well?" To the Printers [McDermott] today, & find him calmly asserting that he really can't send the Press on the 14th. Can't find anyone to move it. This is cool as he took our £10 on the understanding we should have the press without fail. However, these chilly half animate overworked little creatures can't be taken seriously. They don't attach the same meaning to promises, even written & stamped promises, that we do. People badgering him with small jobs, he said, & hasn't even the time to claim his money. For the first time for weeks or months I spent a whole afternoon shopping. Coppers accumulate in my purse, parcels hang from every finger; shop people cross; shops crowded: in fact a most disagreeable duty, when done in a mass.

Wednesday 9 January

The 17 Club is something of a lure; certainly promises better conditions for tea than a shop. So, having gone for my spectacles, I went to Gerrard Street. Found Fredegond & Faith there, also a large semi-circle of

14. The Thackeray was a temperance hotel facing the British Museum in Great Russell Street.

Cambridge youths; including a young man with a flop of hair who had written a play, which he had with him; the pipe-smoking girl, & one or two others.[15] I was amused at the repetition of certain old scenes from my own past—the obvious excitement, & sense of being the latest & best (though not outwardly the most lovely) of God's works, of having things to say for the first time in history; there was all this; & the young men so wonderful in the eyes of the young women, & young women so desirable in the eyes of the young men, though this was not perceptible to me sitting elderly upon my sofa— This sort of talk—

"Ah, but have you read his play? & do you approve?"

"Most decidedly I do."

"And you like the handling."

"Oh immensely!"

Then a second, less favoured young woman, leans forward & says, "But may I see it?"

"Certainly" says the youth, & produces it from a despatch box, to the girl's delight.

"I represent the public. Edith's so unconventional."

However, then I was summoned to have my tea at the far end of the room; & Lytton came in, carrying Lord Morley, whom he's reviewing for L.[16] We tried still to overhear young Cambridge, & L[ytton]. finally decamped, on my daring him, to that party, now grown even larger by the addition of several young men with large foreheads, hair combed back, in hiding from the police.

I then had some private talk with Faith. According to her Nick is getting a great deal of pain from the Saxon Barbara Nick combination. His claims are disregarded; Barbara prefers Saxon; & seems to be ashamed of the unintellectuality of Nick. She wont take him to see her Bloomsbury friends. Bloomsbury, I think, will have one more corpse to its credit; for poor B.'s attainments aren't such as to give her a very secure footing there; & to my thinking a marriage with Nick offers more solid value than a cold blooded & only semi-real attachment with Saxon. I explained my view, with which both Faith & Fredegond agreed. I promised kindness; in case kindness persuades Barbara that there's more in N. than she sees. Her snobbishness is irritating though natural. In the street my grey

15. From VW's letter of 17 January to Vanessa Bell (*II VW Letters*, No. 903), the young man can be identified as Lancelot Hogben (1895-1975), late of Trinity College, Cambridge, subsequently the eminent social biologist and author of *Mathematics for the Million* (1936). He was a conscientious objector to military service, and had been sent to prison for upholding his principles.

16. Lytton Strachey's review of the two-volume *Recollections* (1917) of John Viscount Morley appeared in the February 1918 issue of *War and Peace* of which LW was temporarily acting as editor. It is reprinted in his *Characters & Commentaries* (1933).

knickers came off. So it happened once to Emmy Fisher, & she wrapped a starving dog in them.[17] Fredegond walked with me to Charing Cross. I feel like her in some fundamental way.

Thursday 10 January

Our pipes burst yesterday in the sudden thaw. From sharp frost we changed in an hour or two to mildness. L[ottie]. & N[elly]. dealt with this sensibly, but we are without baths. Set up in the afternoon, then to the printers. L. did not lose his temper; little MacDermott asserts that there was a verbal understanding that he need only deliver the press if his was put up. So mild, pertinacious, & muddle headed that we made no impression. The truth is he takes us for amateurs, who needn't be treated seriously. We are to think things over.

Friday 11 January

Another sedentary day, which must however be entered for the sake of recording that the Lords have passed the Suffrage Bill.[18] I dont feel much more important—perhaps slightly so. Its like a knighthood; might be useful to impress people one despises. But there are other aspects of it naturally. L. to lunch with Ka & a Serbian; I set up, & now find it easily possible to finish a page in an afternoon. L. back, & we took a round by the river, & so home to tea, a great many books. (Life of Keats at last).[19]

Saturday 12 January

Now that printing has set in (we're at page 18) there isn't much to write down, though the day seems as well filled as a picture puzzle with succeeding events. We are still without baths, & this lends some severity to other restrictions which we have to suffer. Today, we can only get one small joint of beef, which is to last a week. There is no fat to be had; no margarine, no nutter.[20] We are reduced to 1 lb of butter a week; eggs are 5d each, a chicken anything from 10/ to 15/. Mrs Langston made Sunday dinner last week off sausages & bread & dripping—"Never had such a Sunday dinner for 5 & 20 years."

After printing we allow ourselves a short walk, & saw a vision of

---

17. Emmeline Morris, *née* Fisher (1868-1941), was the fourth of VW's eleven Fisher cousins; the girls of that family had a reputation with the Stephens for being almost idiotically fond of animals.

18. The Representation of the People Act (1918) gave women over thirty the right to vote.

19. Sir Sidney Colvin's *John Keats, His Life and Poetry, His Friends, Critics, and After Fame* had been published in November 1917.

20. A butter substitute made from nuts.

Tinker,—all but the nose accurate; but each dog has an unmistakable impression. The hope of peace all broken up again; policies once more a running in every direction, so far as one can tell.

Monday 14 January

We had Saxon to dinner on Saturday. He was at his lowest ebb. It was impossible to talk to him, but I guessed that he grieves over the inevitable frailty of mankind: his dream of love & friendship triumphing over jealousy has, I expect, been shattered by the latest developments: & he finds himself in a position odious to so scrupulous & sensitive a man as he is. Still, the effects aren't enlivening for his friends. Even his gestures are weariful. He has been nowhere seen no one. I remember this fragment:
"Have you seen anyone Saxon?"
"I've finished the third volume of the Anthology."[21]
He brought me two books of selections from Italian literature. He wrote my name in them with extreme dexterity & neatness. Played chess with Leonard, was beaten which didn't add to his spirits, & left burdened with the mysteries of this unintelligible world.

On Sunday, Clive came to tea; he hadn't long settled in when the Shoves arrived; & we spent an hour or two in gossip. When one sees Clive fairly often, his devices for keeping up to the mark in the way of success & brilliance become rather obvious. We were all talking of the 17 Club: upon which he rapped out "I was among the haughty people who wouldn't join when they were asked, now of course I find its the thing to do, & I've had to climb down" the truth being that he wished to join & was blackballed by L. & others. Such would be the truth of many of his stories I daresay, if one knew. But one doesn't know; the results are quite agreeable, however produced. And as I persuaded him to lend me his typewriter for Asheham, I've no reason to be censorious. His habits are like those of some faded beauty; a touch of rouge, a lock of yellow hair, lips crimsoned. We talked chiefly about the hypnotism exerted by Bloomsbury over the younger generation. Some merriment over Clive's picture of "the complete schoolmaster" at Tidmarsh. F. and G. had gone there, & after tea master & pupil withdrew, but in she [Carrington] came to fetch a volume of Lord Macaulay; & later she asked to be enlightened about some anecdote of Rousseau. "That you'll know when you're older, my dear" said Lytton paternally. She took F. aside & confided to her some difficulty about Barbara & Nick. "Nick, she said, is reading hard", as though there might be hope for him in that. They're all "reading hard". Saxon asked Maynard the other day whether he thought Petronius suitable

21. The Greek Anthology was a collection of some 6000 short elegiac poems, epigrams, etc., by more than three hundred writers from about 700 B.C. to A.D. 1000.

reading for a young lady, who liked Apuleius.[22] But the young ladies dont like Apuleius—when they're alone. Its matter for a comedy. Indeed I see the plots of many comedies brewing just now among our friends. There's the comedy of Alix & Bunny; of James & Anonyma; & the tragi-comedy of the two cockatoos. After Clive went, F. & G. stayed to dinner, & were more at their ease. F. told us of A.'s wedding night; undertaken by her from a dutiful wish to gain experience, though the experience included so much autobiography on B.'s part, & I've no doubt, eulogies of his father, & peans of the lesser literary lights of the day, that I think she bought it dear. But "on the whole I'm feeling better: partly owing to Bunny". F. has a great turn for mimicry. She mimicked Karin breaking in late at night & asking "Have you a bite for Carry?" & proceeding to ransack their larder. Karin slapping her thigh & exclaiming "*We*'ll have a jaunt; *we*'ll crack a joke"; & also Karin bursting into tears one night from a sense that Maynard &c didn't want to see her. In fact the dominion that "Bloomsbury" exercises over the sane & the insane alike seems to be sufficient to turn the brains of the most robust. Happily, I'm "Bloomsbury" myself, & thus immune; but I'm not altogether ignorant of what they mean. & its a hypnotism very difficult to shake off, because there's some foundation for it. Oddly, though, Maynard seems to be the chief fount of the magic spirit. Talk about capital with Gerald: he says he means to part with his, but I guess that he always has some scruple to play with as an intellectual exercise.

Friday 18 January

Another skip, partly due to my writing a long letter to Nessa, which drained up some of the things I should have said here.[23] But I like this better than letter writing. Perhaps one should write novels for the 2 of us only. I can remember various doings however: Toynbees & Kot. to dinner on Tuesday [15 January];[24] & that afternoon Lady Strachey read to us—to me for the most part, as L. was late. She read Ben Jonson's masques. They are short, & in between she broke off to talk a little, so that it was lighter than before, & I enjoyed it. She told me how she used to read everything at her school; & can remember the books because

22. If the young lady liked the works of Apuleius, author of *The Golden Ass*, she would surely have liked those of Petronius, who wrote the *Satyricon*, for they have much in common. In some circles however she would not have been thought a lady for liking either.
23. See *II VW Letters*, no. 903.
24. Arnold and Rosalind Toynbee (see above, 11 November 1917, n 16); and Samuel Solomonovitch Koteliansky (1882-1955), an Ukrainian jew who came to England on a research grant from Kiev University in about 1910 and never returned to Russia. He was a familiar of Katherine Mansfield and her circle.

places are associated with them. At the age of 18 her father gave her leave
to read Tom Jones (I think) on condition she never said she'd read it.[25]
Told us that Lytton's failure to get a fellowship had been one of the dis-
appointments of her life "one of the many". "Well, this next book won't
be a disappointment", I said. But she thought the Arnolds would object.[26]
Her pride in Lytton & desire to see him a noted literary character very
evident. I presumed on this that she was well disposed about Tidmarsh:
but as she froze up, & pretended not to know where it was, I suppose
there's a family row— Indeed, its easy to see that when fronted by the
present she's not at her best; conventional, very nervous, thinks they're
ruined; once get her to the past she has no impediments of the sort, & told
stories of beautiful dead Pattles & Dalrymples with the greatest animation: how old Pattle shot out of his tank, & thereby killed his wife, who
thought him come to life again: how the sailors drank him dry on the
voyage to England; how "Dal" was charming; though not a good man to
marry; how Dr Jackson was so handsome & kind[27]—in fact she seems
to divide her life into the part of the exciting romantic illuminated play; &
the rest of it is merely trudging along the prosaic streets, with nothing to
look forward to. Her eyes collapsed; her teeth gone; deaf; but talk of the
past or of literature—& it all lights up again. Literature too must be of
the past though. She read us a poem called The Old Way, of a swashing,
patriotic kind, & exclaimed how fine it was, & how, as long as we had
Hopwood for a poet we needn't complain.[28]. Her patriotism has survived
everything else. Patriotism & family feeling, & sights she saw long ago—
as for example "You don't remember I suppose meeting me once on a Bus,
when you were 10 or 11? You & Vanessa were with your mother." She
has the family gift of fantasy. She ran out to get two little lozenge boxes
which she has covered in scraps of coloured paper, preserved from the
catalogues of drapers shops. She mayn't read much, or write, & plays

25. Henry Fielding's novel, published 1749, would hardly have been considered
    suitable reading for young ladies in the 1850's.
26. Dr Thomas Arnold was the third of the four subjects in Lytton Strachey's
    Eminent Victorians; the Arnolds, in the person of his granddaughter Mrs Humphry
    Ward, *did* object (see below, 12 July 1918, n 12).
27. 'Old Pattle' was the father of seven adult daughters, the fourth of whom married
    Dr Jackson and was VW's grandmother; the youngest married John Warrender
    Dalrymple, 7th Bt. (See Family Tree; also, for Pattle family history, *Julia
    Margaret Cameron*, 1973, by Brian Hill, who examines the various improbable
    stories concerning old Pattle's corpse.)
28. 'The Old Way' by Captain Ronald A. Hopwood, RN (1868-1949), first appeared
    in *The Times* on 16 September 1916; it was reprinted in *The Old Way and other
    Poems* published by John Murray the same year. Hopwood's sea poems were re-
    issued in 1951 with a foreword by Alfred Noyes who wrote that they 'speak of
    something which may be called, quite simply, the soul of England'.

patience by herself—I suppose she ruminates over her past. According to her it was a splendid time to live in. For one thing, she remembers India before the Mutiny. "Splendid men they were, the Company servants. Your Prinsep relations among the finest. Fancy my horror when I went to see the Delhi pictures the other day, & found they'd called the Prinsep Pier the Princes Pier!" But talk of womens votes doesn't move her much.[29]

From this ancient world we came back to one younger, as far as years go, than our own. But the Toynbees aren't spiritually very young: though surprisingly of our way of thinking (which one takes to be young & advanced still!) as to politics. I rashly took this for granted; & Arnold outdid me in anti-nationalism, anti-patriotism, & anti-militarism. At intervals Kot delivered a formal address upon Russia in broken English. There's a good deal to be said for Kot. He has some likeness to the Russians of literature. He will begin to explain his soul without preface. He explained Katherine [Mansfield]'s soul, not at all to her credit. Her lies & poses have proved too much for him, nor does he find more than a slight gift for writing in her. I dont know that this last pleases me however, though it sounds as if I wrote it down for that reason. He is individual in his view of politics, thinks Russia too little civilised to profit by revolution, but here in England its bound to come with immense benefit because we've carpets & gas in our poorest houses. Russia scarcely interests him; he never means to go back; prophesies civil war in the spring, & no advantage won by it. In 1905 they were burning houses & stabbing nobles too. Rosalind has merit to look at certainly. I like her better than Arnold, who improves though, & is evidently harmless, & much in his element when discussing Oxford. He hadn't much good to say of it; they were both sick of it, & will never go back, nor does he think that young men will ever be found to live there again, save as undergraduates. He knew the aristocratic heroes who are now all killed & celebrated—Grenfells, Lister, Shaw Steuart, Asquith, & loathed them;[30] for one reason they must have thought him a pale blooded little animal. But he described their rows & their insolence & their quick snapping brains, always winning scholarships, & bullying & bringing bath chairs

29. The third of the seven daughters of VW's great-grandfather James Pattle had married H. Thoby Prinsep, many of whose family had been officials of the East India Company and, after the Mutiny of 1858, of the Indian Civil Service. It is not clear what Lady Strachey (or VW reporting her) meant by the 'Delhi pictures'; Prinsep's Ghat (or pier) was in Calcutta and was used for regal and ceremonial landings. Lady Strachey was a pioneer advocate of women's suffrage.

30. The Hon. Julian and the Hon. Gerald Grenfell, sons of Lord Desborough, both killed in action 1915; the Hon. Charles Alfred Lister, Lord Ribblesdale's son, killed in action 1915; Patrick Shaw Stewart, killed in action 1917; and Raymond Asquith, son of H. H. Asquith, Prime Minister 1908-16, killed in action 1916.

full of rats into Chapel—& admitting no one to their set, so that in the end they were almost abolished by the Colonials, who hated them back. It reads much like a Mrs Ward novel.

Wednesday, 16th, I went to the Library, where I met L. who had been on his deputation to the Colonial Office, which was ill-treated by the Secretary;[31] & then to the Club, where we met Alix of course & Fredegond. These two were making painful efforts to set up house together; but neither could do anything decisive, though it was clear that Alix wished to come to terms, as much as she can wish anything. She had been down to Sidmouth, where her Aunt lies paralysed & doomed soon to die. Her eyelid just quivers, & one side of her lip moves; but in medical opinion she neither thinks nor feels. This had not made Alix either gloomier or less gloomy, though I believe she feels it beneath her gentlemanly good sense. As I left, F. beckoned & begged me to decide for her whether she should tell Alix how Gerald wished F. not to share with her, or prevaricate. I always say that people with short hair must be told the truth. I hear this (Saturday) morning that they have an offer of Amber's house, which they should take, I think, in spite of Gerald.[32]

On Thursday & Friday & Saturday we worked away at printing, so as to have 8 pages set up to print at McDermotts. Unvarying cold & gloom, which turns now to rain, now to snow. This is the Hell of the year. We seem to mark time in the mud. Wright dined with us on Thursday night— a kindly plausible but long winded man, leaning on L. for support at every point, & giving up his views when they conflicted. They went to see Rowntree together. I have my speculations, but can't go into them now.[33]

Monday 21 January

We had Nick to 'look at' on Saturday night; Barbara came too. He's nothing very much to look at, certainly; yet so unpretending that what he has to show is satisfactory. Besides he has a pleasant Irish voice, & a quiet

31. On 16 January the Parliamentary Under-Secretary to the Colonial Office rejected the demand of the deputation of which LW was spokesman. It had asked for an enquiry into the methods used in suppressing communal riots in Ceylon in 1915.

32. Amber Blanco White, née Reeves (b. 1887); a brilliant student of Newnham College, 1905-08, and an active member of the Cambridge Fabian Society. After an affair with H. G. Wells, she had married in 1909; she now had three children and was working in the Ministry of Munitions. Her house was at 44 Downshire Hill, Hampstead.

33. Harold Wright (1883-1934), liberal politico-literary journalist; Pembroke College 1908-13, President of the Cambridge Union, editor of *Granta*; editor of the monthly *War and Peace* (see above, 24 October 1917, n 39). This was financed by Arnold Rowntree (1872-1951), at this time Liberal MP for York and director of the Westminster Press, which also published *The Nation* and other Liberal papers.

very simple manner which make him very tolerable in the house. I rather think that Barbara watched to see what we made of him. He talked his own shop for the most part. Lewis guns, & their mechanism. There are food riots & strikes at Woolwich, & the guards have notice to march there at any moment, & fire on the people, which their own Woolwich regiments would refuse to do.[34] He takes things a little seriously. Next morning we had a long discourse about Irish character. He admires Synge: says that he's heard his own men talk exactly as Synge makes them talk.[35] They lie on the ground talking, & wont play games. They are deeply religious (the root of all evil in Ireland, he says) & die looking happy if the priest is with them, not otherwise. Their mothers constantly write to know if a son has had a grand funeral, if he has a cross over him; this is their great source of comfort. I suppose the soft, serious, rather plaintive disposition at which one guesses in Nick is Irish; & on top, but not at all offensive, there are signs of his deep admiration for the great Bloomsbury group, & culture, & problems. For instance, he deplores the gulf between what he calls the Quaker view, & the artists view; & he says the Quaker view will prevail with the young after the war. He quotes books seriously. However he went off to Hampstead; & L. went, Heaven knows what made him unless it was chess, to Gipsy Hill to lunch with the Waterlows. Lytton came to tea; stayed to dinner, & about 10 o'clock we both had that feeling of parched lips & used up vivacity which comes from hours of talk. But Lytton was most easy & agreeable. Among other things he gave us an amazing account of the British Sex Society which meets at Hampstead. The sound would suggest a third variety of human being, & it seems that the audience had that appearance. Notwithstanding, they were surprisingly frank; & 50 people of both sexes & various ages discussed without shame such questions as the deformity of Dean Swift's penis: whether cats use the w.c.; self abuse; incest—Incest between parent & child when they are both unconscious of it, was their main theme, derived from Freud.[36] I think of becoming a member. It's unfortunate that civilisation always lights up the dwarfs, cripples, & sexless people first. And Hampstead alone provides them. Lytton at different points exclaimed

---

34. There had been disorders in East London when shortages of margarine led housewives to besiege the local Food Offices. Rationing of staple foods was introduced by the Food Controller, Lord Rhondda, on 25 February; sugar was already rationed.

35. John Millington Synge (1871-1909), Irish poet and dramatist.

36. The ideas and writings of Sigmund Freud were becoming known in England before the war. LW had read *The Interpretation of Dreams* and reviewed *The Psychopathology of Everyday Life* in 1914. The 'British Sex Society' was no doubt the British Society for the Study of Sex Psychology which was founded in July 1914 and included among its members Edward Carpenter, Montague Summers and Laurence Housman.

Penis: his contribution to the openness of the debate. We also discussed the future of the world; how we should like professions to exist no longer; Keats, old age, politics, Bloomsbury hypnotism—a great many subjects. L. beat Sydney by his craft. They are leaving Gipsy Hill.

Today, Monday, I went to Harrison's to have a broken tooth mended; L. to Staines— Philip is back with his wound once more broken out, owing to lack of care at Fowey.

Here I was interrupted on the verge of a description of London at the meeting of sun set & moon rise. I drove on top of a Bus from Oxford St. to Victoria station, & observed how the passengers were watching the spectacle: the same sense of interest & mute attention shown as in the dress circle before some pageant. A Spring night; blue sky with a smoke mist over the houses. The shops were still lit; but not the lamps, so that there were bars of light all down the streets; & in Bond Street I was at a loss to account for a great chandelier of light at the end of the street; but it proved to be several shop windows jutting out into the road, with lights on different tiers. Then at Hyde Park Corner the search light rays out, across the blue; part of a pageant on a stage where all has been wonderfully muted down. The gentleness of the scene was what impressed me; a twilight view of London. Houses very large & looking stately. Now & then someone, as the moon came into view, remarked upon the chance for an air raid. We escaped though, a cloud rising towards night.

Wednesday 23 January

I see I've forgotten yesterday; but it was uneventful. L. went up to a meeting, Barbara was left in control of the Press, & I took a walk by myself. I went along the river to Marble Hill.[37] I must retract what I said about the Hell of the year. We have glimpses of Heaven. So mild that the landing window is open, & I sat by the river watching a boat launched, & half expected to see buds on the willows. River very high, swift & yellow, testifying to the floods higher up. They say its been raining heavily; I daresay it has, but such is the civilisation of life in London that I really dont know. What with fires, electric light, underground railways & umbrellas, how can one take notice of the weather. But we look out about bed time & notice the moon. Very clear cut & polished & almost full till 9 or so, & then, much as if God did turn over in his sleep & press a button, down comes a curtain of cloud, & we yawn & sleep sound. Last night, after giving B. her tea, which wastes the chief delight of the day, though poor woman she can't be better behaved, & if she were gifted no doubt one would hate her actively, we dined early & had the Guild. Mr Adams

37. Marble Hill House (built by George II about 1725 for the Countess of Suffolk) and Park, on the opposite bank of the Thames up river from Richmond; it was bought for the public in 1903 to preserve the view from Richmond Hill.

[unidentified] spoke. The level is certainly not a high one. Even when they know their subject, as he did, they dont know it in such a way as to to make it plain to the uneducated. I doubt whether more than 3 people in the room knew that he was talking of the Co-ops. & politics. He began in the middle. He read bald phrases from Congress resolutions. He could just pronounce such a word as "autonomous", but I don't suppose anyone understood it. As usual, L. & I were the only people to speak, save Mrs Langston; as usual it was only when talk drifted near food that one of the women broke silence. She wanted a bread shop. They all got bread late in the day: for a time they all spoke at once—stories of their own ill treatment & of their neighbours. Oddly phlegmatic these women for the most part; with a passive sort of pleasure in sitting there & watching like so many pale grey sea anemones stuck to their rocks. Still, the children, the housework—excuses enough if one troubled to look.

Talking of sea anemones reminds me that we're in treaty with D. H. Lawrence for his house at Zennor. Its very distant & improbable at present though sufficiently tempting to make me think of that sea & those cliffs several times a day.[38]

Today, Wednesday, B. didn't come, & we printed. L. did the most of it; & I made two little excursions into Richmond, one to discover the right way of spelling Mynah; the other to buy a new battery, price 1/3. Two of mine have perished during the lifetime of L's. methusaleh: the wicked old wretch still burns like a spark from a star. I think its wise to have mine in readiness for the raid, though three tradespeople of Richmond know for a certain that there will never be another. The bakers windows now provide almost nothing but little plates of dull biscuits; sections of plain cake; & little buns without any plums. If you see a plum, it is invariably a decoy plum; there are no others. This transformation scene has been stealing on imperceptibly; last year were we still allowed iced cakes? Its unthinkable!

Thursday 24 January

The last day of being 35. One trembles to write the years that come after it: all tinged with the shadow of 40. Another spring day; I do without a fire in the morning. The only drawback is the loss of a fire, & that sense of being in a cave of comfort, with wet & dark outside. Outside its a pale grey. I went to the [London] Library to get a handful of stories

38. In October 1917 the Lawrences had been ordered by the army to leave Cornwall where they had been living for eighteen months in a small cottage at Tregerthen, near Zennor, rented from a Captain Short for £5 per annum. The suggestion that the Woolfs should take over their tenancy—and that of the two adjacent cottages —came from Koteliansky. Nothing came of the matter at this time but it was revived a year later when the Woolfs had to leave Asheham. (See below, 22 March 1919 *et seq.*)

on the supernatural; met Sir Henry Newbolt, a slim greyheaded weasel, but we didn't know each other;[39] then I beat up & down Charing Cross Rd. asking for Keats' Letters, but they were not to be had anywhere. So to the Club, where I found Lytton by himself, & not feeling inclined for talk we read our papers near together. Fredegond came in; but after laughing a little at her telephone message, I went. She & Alix & Carrington getting together decided that I criticised them, wouldn't stand it, rang me up, demanded a retraction, which I would only give if they put their complaints in writing: I'm afraid they wont do this. They say I depress them, & the only explanation is that I'm a Saddhist. This is the first turn of the worm. Barbara, however, lets all criticism run off her without a trace. L. printed 4 pages off at the printers today, & only got back at 6; an unsatisfactory job, owing to the incompetence of the printer.

Friday 25 January

My Birthday. L. slid a fine cow's horn knife into my hand this morning. Nelly has knitted me a pair of red socks which tie round the ankle, & thus just suit my state in the morning. Another event kept me recumbent. Barbara came, & together we "dissed" 4 pages,[40] & L. printed off the second 4 at the printers—altogether a fine days work. At this rate Katherine's story will be done in 5 weeks. We rather think of doing a little book of woodcuts, either after this book or at the same time, on our small press. Our dinner tonight was a sacrifice to duty on a fine scale; never were we more ready for an evening alone; books to read; a sense of a great deal of talk already discharged this week; but rather before 7.30 came Clara [Woolf] & the Whithams, whom we had asked with a view to killing each other off without more waste than was inevitable. Whitham's elaborately literary get up is a fair index of his mind. He is what the self-taught working man thinks genius should be; & yet so unassuming & homely that its more amusing than repulsive. His passion for writing is the passion of the amateur—or rather of the person who's got it up from a text book. Seeing Cannan's new novel he said "Ah, Cannan, yes—he's very weak in construction isn't he?"[41] And so with all

---

39. Sir Henry Newbolt (1862-1938), barrister, poet and man of letters, served in the Admiralty and Foreign Office and became Controller of Wireless and Cables during the war. His wife was a Duckworth, and VW must have been acquainted with him since Hyde Park Gate days.

40. i.e.: dismantled the formes already printed, and distributed each letter of the type into its proper box so that it could be re-used.

41. Gilbert Cannan (1884-1955), prolific novelist and dramatist, was a friend of D. H. Lawrence, Middleton Murry and Mark Gertler; his novel *Mendel* (1916) is a barely disguised portrait of the latter. Presumably his *new* novel would have been *The Stucco House*, 1917.

the rest. He told me his books had a way of "screaming", & with great enthusiasm, after asking the fate of my fiction which is a point of honour in professional circles, he ran over all the novels he's got ready or half ready, or only in want of "phrasing"—which process he applies at the end. He begins with a synopsis, which takes him 3 months: but I didn't listen to the whole story. They withdraw soon to Devonshire, where directly the war ends (but even the war hasn't prevented him from adding a new book to the list) he is going to work hard. Writing all the morning, reading & walking the rest of the day. And so we may hope for some 20 Whithams during the next five years or so. When he had told us all this, he went on about spiritualism: their landlord being a fat pale solicitor of 50, who lies on a sofa all day down in Devonshire communing with spirits, & feeding upon bread & margarine. Whitham had dabbled in mysticism, & had made tables walz & heard phantom raps & believed it all, but was too much afraid of the results upon his character to go in for it seriously. I thought this showed weakness, and I expect he hasn't a good head on his shoulders, as his talk of novel writing makes one perceive. Sylvia sat marking time, & much pleased with the good impression she thought him to make; & in her precise way acknowledged the most revolutionary principles so that they seemed the gossip of a good housekeeper about the price of bacon. Clara's silence shows I think her subservient position in the family; a person who can never make herself felt— unhappy & comfortless always, I expect. She stayed the night.

Today (Saturday) we went to Kew. Snowdrops, dwarf cyclamen, some miniature rhododendrons out; also the points of some squills or crocuses coming through the grass & dead leaves.

Sunday 27 January

As we were going out we ran flap/slap into Desmond bearing round the corner in an impetuous way. This knocked the bottom from our hope of a solitary evening, but as mercifully as possible. We took a turn in the Old Deer Park. He seemed depressed; lines drawn upon his forehead; he sighs oh dear! oh dear! at intervals, thinking about the war or private difficulties, I suppose. Indeed I thought it unpleasant how one has to steer past certain questions with him: when's your book coming out, has Molly's novel been taken, are you writing &c—I divine that the answers depress him acutely in the early morning. We gave him tea, & discussed the development of psychology since Shakespeare's day. L. denied this; I asserted it. Desmond thought Othello & Desdemona very simple; but thought we were tolerably represented in fiction. I find myself altogether unmentioned there. Question whether one should write quick events in short scenes, whether fiction should be like life: whether Thackeray has profundity. Desmond has read some of the Newcomes lately: finds no depth, but a charming rippling conventional picturesqueness.[42] So on to Bob [Trevelyan]'s poetry: "a good commonplace poet", said Desmond— not the kind to bring up discoveries from his own entrails; looks upon the everyday world & finds the right phrase: classical—& therefore enduring — But I don't follow this. He brought Enid Bagnold in his pocket, & now, I'm sure thinks he's reviewed her himself. I'm not going to, after a glance at her mind. She led him to describe a Roumanian Prince, whose voice, he said, was the loveliest in London.[43] He rang him up (to account for not coming punctually for dinner) & I listened, & heard a soft hesitating voice stumbling over long words, rather romantic down the telephone. He went off at last, having wrought himself into a state of contentment & garrulity, so that he would have stayed & given the 4th Act of the Irenaid had he been able, & would have been able, had we pressed.[44]

Monday 28 January

On Monday I went to have my tooth finished, winding up for tea at the Club, which becomes as Goldie said, "quite a family party." You come in to find half a dozen pairs of legs radiating from chairs towards the fire. You hear, or I heard, "its a case of revolution or evolution" & then, if you've heard enough, you seek the Manchester Guardian, evade Sylvia Whitham, & hide yourself for precisely 10 seconds. Fredegond, with apologies breaks through the barrier. "But they're so fearfully dull, & I must talk something that isn't politics." That something, so far as I remember (its Saturday now) was Ottoline, Alix, poetry, love, until Bob, who had been jerking his head towards us could stand it no longer, but towered over us, flapping an elongated proof sheet, & wishing to know if we were talking secrets. "No such luck" I said, so he settled down, with his usual bagman's assortment of literary gossip. First he said how Clive proposes to buy up The Egoist & start a Bloomsbury review; & then

42. W. M. Thackeray's *Memoirs of a Most Respectable Family*, published in serial form in 1854-55.
43. Enid Bagnold (b. 1889), the writer, was a VAD nurse for a while during the war; her first book, *Diary Without Dates*, based on her experiences, was published early in 1918. Desmond MacCarthy, who was much taken with her, hoped to persuade VW to review it for the *TLS*, a suggestion she successfully resisted. (See also *II VW Letters*, no. 905.) His own review, entitled 'A Trip to Tartary', appeared in *The Nation* on 16 February 1918. The Roumanian Prince was Antoine Bibesco (1879-1951), rich, cultivated, a writer and a friend of Proust, who had acted as Counsellor at the Roumanian Legation in London. Enid Bagnold was in love with him.
44. The 'Ireniad' appears to have been a long saga by Desmond MacCarthy of his pursuit and subsequent evasion of Irene Noel, the daughter and heiress of Frank Noel of Achmetaga (whom the Stephens had visited on their journey to Greece in 1906). In 1915 she married Philip Baker, who added her patronymic to his own.

what did we think of Waley, & so on & so on, censorious, scandal loving, but innocent & indefatigable as ever.[45] Home I went, & there was a raid of course. The night made it inevitable. From 8 to 1.15 we roamed about, between coal hole kitchen bedroom & drawing room. I dont know how much is fear, how much boredom; but the result is uncomfortable, most of all, I believe, because one must talk bold & jocular small talk for 4 hours with the servants to ward off hysteria. Next morning,

Tuesday 29 January

the after effects of the raid were swept aside by Barbara.

"Virginia, I shan't come on Friday because I'm going to be married."

"You're going to marry—?"

"Yes, Nick."

"And Saxon?"

"Saxon doesn't mind. Nothing's to be changed. We're all agreed."

These are the terms. I dont myself think that she wishes to be married; but has convinced herself that she should. Moreover, the horror of Nick's return in a month keeps her graver than otherwise. She showed no wish to be congratulated or in any way fussed over. She stayed & printed as usual. And, expecting a raid, we asked her to sleep. This time it began at 9.10: the warning at least. It was far louder this time. An aeroplane went over the house about 11.30. Soon after, the guns were so near that I didn't like to fetch a pair of shoes left in the bedroom. We had arranged mattresses in the kitchen & after the first noise slackened we lay all together, L. on the kitchen table, like a picture of slum life. One thud came very near; but in an hour we had the bugles, & went up to bed. The thud, wh. L. distinguished from the rest, came from the explosion of bombs at Kew. Nine people, I think killed. Servants became plaintive, & Lottie began talking of the effect upon her head; they hint that we ought to leave London.

45. *The Egoist*, originally a fortnightly then a monthly successor to *The New Free-woman*, was from 1915 edited and almost entirely financed by Miss Harriet Weaver (see below, 10 April 1918, n 15). Through the agency of Ezra Pound, she had printed James Joyce's 'Portrait of the Artist as a Young Man' in instalments in the paper. By this time (1918) however, she was more concerned to publish books (particularly Joyce's) and T. S. Eliot, who had become her assistant editor in June 1917, was seeking means of continuing the periodical under new management. Clive did not buy it, other schemes came to nothing, and it finally ceased publication in December 1919. Arthur David Waley (1889-1966), born Schloss, had with the rest of his family changed his surname early in the war owing to the rabid anti-German feeling in England. After leaving King's College, Cambridge, he was from 1913 to 1929 in the Oriental sub-department of the Department of Prints and Drawings in the British Museum. In 1918 he published his first translations from the Chinese.

Wednesday 30 January

Up to a concert & tea with Ottoline. She is perched in the smallest bedroom of a Bloomsbury hotel, moulting, depressed, untidy, over-dressed. Not much talk of interest to me, though friendly & not so overpowering in certain directions as usual.

Thursday 31 January

A deep fog all day. We both set type. Dipping out to buy a bun for tea was as much of that air as we wanted. I remembered how glad we were, first of the fog, second of being alone, for Barbara slept at Hampstead.

Friday 1 February

A day of fog in patches. Last night the worst fog they say for 30 years, & old gents. who escaped the raid walked in numbers over the edge of platforms & were crushed.[1] A cook stepped into the Thames; people walked by rapping our railings to keep the road. L. went to London & coming home at 10.30, reported a starry night & clear afternoon, the fog deep once more when night fell here.

Saturday 2 February

The first walk we've had for ever so long. Damp, mild vaporous day. Funeral bells tolling as we went out, & màrriage as we came in. The streets lined with people waiting their meat. Aeroplanes droning invisible. Our usual evening, alone happily, knee deep in papers.

Sunday 3 February

Sunday has become as it used to be in Hyde Pk. Gate the social day. The sociability began early for L. at least, Riddell the printer [unidentified] coming, as we hoped to offer a press, but as we discovered only to say that presses aren't to be had. A female friend was with him. I listened behind the bathroom door. We found Goldie when we came in from our walk; & then Pippa came; curiously untidy, as all Strachey women become at the least provocation.[2] Without a certain degree of good looks it isn't worth being vain—thats their reasoning, I always suppose. The talk was hampered by the suspicion that she was a jingo: & secondly an

1. *The Times* of 1 February does indeed report several such accidents (one fatal).
2. Rather a case of the pot calling the kettles black. Philippa ('Pippa') Strachey (1872-1968) was the third of Lytton's five sisters, and an inconspicuous but indefatigable force at the centre of the constitutional women's movement. The first great women's suffrage procession through London in 1907 had been organised by her for the London Society of Women's Suffrage—which since the outbreak of war had become the National Society for Women's Service, of which she remained Secretary until 1951.

older fashioned type then we're used to. She has the disconcerting though worthy habit of remaining quite silent when she disagrees. She disagreed with me when I said I thought cooperative housekeeping (implying beds) was an improvement on the old style. Goldie shot his direct, well pointed arrows; my only criticism in his case is the feeling which his method produces of being a method. They dig for views too cleverly, these elderly Dons—Still—still— Pippa has faded curiously; looks older, & more worn. She spoke of old days of parties, H. B. Smith, George Duckworth, Jack Hills & Christmases at Corby.[3] She thinks that still the way to live; those people so "civilised" compared with our cropheads. But now she has no time for society; does suffrage, which will turn now into a campaign for equality, by day & night. "Mercifully, she said, there are people like you who keep out of it. Its most important that there should be people like you. That is so long as you've got or earned economic independence. Thats essential. No, I'm not clever. I've always cared more for people than for ideas—& now I must go. I've got work to do. I mustn't be lured into sloth here." So she went. It struck me that age consists not in having a different point of view, but in having the same point of view, faded. Goldie shows this too. An evening alone.

Monday 4 February

Up to the Times with a Coleridge article; & once more I lost myself, owing partly to the multiplicity of Water Lanes.[4] Met L. at the Club, where people for once had agreed to silence, & solitary reading of books, so we were left to ourselves. We have started a bottle of saccharine, & so save our sugar.

Tuesday 5 February

Karin came to give her lecture. She arrived at tea time. I can't help being reminded by her of one of our lost dogs—Tinker most of all. She fairly races round a room, snuffs the corners of the chairs & tables, wags

3. Sir Henry Babington Smith (1863-1923), CH, Eton and Trinity College, Cambridge, an Apostle, civil servant and financier. George Herbert Duckworth (1868-1934), VW's elder half-brother, Eton and Trinity, and a family authority on manners and society; he had married in 1904 Lady Margaret Herbert, became secretary to the Royal Commission on Historical Monuments but during the war transferred to the Ministry of Munitions. John Waller Hills (1867-1938), Eton and Balliol College, Oxford, solicitor; in 1897 he married VW's half-sister Stella Duckworth, who died three months later; from 1906 he had been Unionist MP for Durham City. His parents' home was Corby Castle, Cumberland.

4. VW's review of *The Table Talk and Omniana of Samuel Taylor Coleridge*, with a note on Coleridge by Coventry Patmore, appeared in the *TLS* on 7 February 1918 (Kp C101). There were several Water Lanes, but only one near Printing House Square; it is now Blackfriars Lane.

her tail as hard as she can, & snatches at any scrap of talk as if she were sharp set; & she eats a great deal of food too, like a dog. This extreme energy may be connected with deafness. She has become a Bolshevik. She has offered her services to the Labour party, & hopes they'll send her up & down England, organising constituencies, since she's tired of reading & writing—never did much like it, & now scents a scrimmage & wants to be in the thick of it. Socialism is nibbling at our friends in a curious way. She & Adrian have scruples about the size of their income, & wish to earn money, partly because half their income depends on Mrs B.[5] She gave her paper on League of Nations well, though speaking too quick. The difference that education makes is very marked though. I think they took her points. I was surprised to hear that she was much relieved when it was done. She stayed the night, & the next morning, which with a fitness of simile now to be explained, costs me a tooth to lose. Moreover, she sits over the fire, & I have to shout. But I see that Adrian must find her energy, her not fastidious or critical but generous & warm blooded mind, her honesty & stability a great standby—

LW notes that on Wednesday afternoon (6 February) he went with VW to see Dr Craig, who said that her weight was too low for safety; she then had a tooth extracted by Harrison under gas; next day they dined with Maynard Keynes at Gordon Square to meet Elizabeth Asquith who did not come; Molly MacCarthy and Duncan Grant did. On Friday VW had influenza and Dr Fergusson was sent for. They went to Asheham on 19 February until 1 March; there are no entries in the Asheham Diary for this period.

Saturday 2 March

What is the use of finishing a sentence left unfinished a month ago? Here we are; evening; I came back from Asheham, or rather Charleston, an hour ago. After Karin went that Wednesday, rather a monotonous time began for me. Influenza began on the Friday; I was kept in bed 8 days; on the next Tuesday [19 February] we went to Asheham. My chief complaint is that I was divorced from my pen; a whole current of life cut off— Secondly I saw no one; for 5 days I wasn't in a state for reading; but I did finally read Morley & other books; but reading when done to kill time has a kind of drudgy look in it. I was asked to write a book in a series—Makers of the 19th Century;[1] but after deliberation refused, nor

5. Mrs Berenson, *née* Mary Pearsall Smith, Karin's mother; she had left her first husband Frank Costelloe several years before his death in 1899 enabled her to marry Bernhard Berenson.

1. A series of biographical studies edited by the historian (Arthur Frederic) Basil Williams (1867-1950) and published under the title 'Makers of the Nineteenth Century' by Constable between 1915 and 1928.

did it at any moment seem possible. But I write this down partly to give an official look to this diary, & partly because it marks a middle aged condition. Undoubtedly the country develops the spiritual side of life. One day I sat in the garden reading Shakespeare; I remember the ecstasy: every other day at least we had to walk to Southease for milk; we were only allowed one quart a day—7d a quart. The garden shows great promise. L. dug up the large bed, & transferred plants from the round middle bed to our path bed. The buds visible on the trees; sheep in the hurdles on the side of the down. For 9 of our 10 days we saw no one; my letters even failed fairly completely; but the days melted into each other like snowballs roasting in the sun. On Thursday [28 February] Nessa came for the night, & I went back with her to Charleston for Friday night, L. taking the servants up to town. Henry Moss had just arrived.[2] We all met for dinner, for to my relief N. & I had tea alone in the drawing room. Moss & Mrs Brereton give off a fairly strong atmosphere of the paid & paying guest kind which is not pleasant. Mrs B. an elderly upright firm unflinching woman, whose integrity has been her chief capital in life. She reminded me strongly of Nurse Reid: she has the professional competence & composure.[3] Moss one might meet—practically anywhere. He is a pale insignificant young man, either very shy or very much out of his element. We carried on as best we could, entirely unhelped by him, & though Mrs B. spoke from a sense of duty, she allowed nothing to blossom in her presence, but dealt with each remark literally & sensibly. Ann, the daughter, is much more charming than one might expect— though no doubt marriage trials & poverty have flattened out Mrs B's charm prematurely. She calls H. Moss her "adopted son", which sanctions their withdrawal after dinner to his bed sitting room, where they are supposed to make up stories for the Saturday Westminster.[4] On Saturday morning Nessa, Duncan & I sat in the studio & gossiped. Part of the time we discussed art. This is what I like doing best with them. They say that there's no one worth considering as a painter in England today—no one like K.M. or Forster even with whom its worth discussing one's business.[5]

2. A protégé of Mrs Brereton, Henry Moss came to Charleston as tutor to Julian Bell and Ann Brereton. The arrangement did not last very long.

3. One of VW's attendants after her suicide attempt in 1913; she accompanied her from Dalingridge Place to Asheham in November and finally left in February 1914.

4. The Saturday *Westminster Gazette*, founded 1912, price 2d, carried editorial matter on current affairs, and a large selection of book reviews, poems, stories, literary competitions, etc. Mrs Brereton was also supposed to have been writing a novel based on the life and characters she encountered at Charleston.

5. Edward Morgan Forster (1879-1970), King's College, Cambridge, 1897-1902, and an Apostle. Living for the most part with his mother at Weybridge in Surrey, he was a rather elusive familiar in Bloomsbury. He had travelled in Italy and

In France this is reversed. Nessa showed me Saxon's letters. He has made her his confidante. He has been very unhappy; & made out his moments of exaltation & depression with his usual minuteness. In one he said that it was curious no longer to care for anything, death being as desirable as life. And then details about his health. We discussed also the peril of society, which has to some extent washed off poor old Desmond's bloom, & would submerge Maynard, if he were an artist. I left at 1.15, walking in a high wind with 2 parcels slung across my shoulders, to Glynde; through the park. Back here for tea, & met L. buying the Hanwell Gazette.[6] I found a letter from Saxon—a little cold, I can't help thinking, at least showing one, after his letters to Nessa, that in this crisis I'm *not* his confidante. Its queer how one chooses one figure each time one's in a state for reasons not perceptible to the figure herself. Last winter I was to hear everything.

Sunday 3 March[7]

A vile windy day. Sent off my Conrad article, at last[8]—& printed a few labels for Bunny, but we stayed in, & were very happy.

Monday 4 March

L. took 4 pages to the printer today to print off. I being useless for this purpose went off to get into touch with London again, which I did at the three usual points—Mudie's, London Library & Seventeen Club. London, from a spectacular point of view was at its worst; like a middle aged charwoman with hair scrubbed off a bleak forehead. In St James' Square a village of houses has been built to shelter some ministry, I suppose; & it was strange to see how holes have been cut in the walls & the roofs to allow the trees to stand undamaged.[9] Some of the clerks will have a tree trunk to wipe their pens upon. I found a silent group at the Club, all men, & unknown to me, with the exception of Alix who sat still as a statue

---

Greece, and spent six months in India (1912/13). From 1915 until the war was ended he held a post in the Red Cross in Alexandria. All his novels except *A Passage to India* (1924) and *Maurice* (published posthumously in 1971) had been published by 1910.

6. The *Hanwell Gazette & Brentford Observer*, a conservative, patriotic weekly published in Ealing, price 1½d.

7. VW has wrongly dated this entry *4th March*.

8. VW's article 'Mr Conrad's Crisis', a critical retrospective on Joseph Conrad's *Nostromo: A Tale of the Seaboard* (1904), appeared in the *TLS* of 14 March 1918 (Kp C102). The honeypot labels were printed from a wood block by Carrington.

9. This was a picturesque temporary structure resembling a country inn (and known as the Washington Inn), used by American and Overseas officers. It stood until 1921.

reading one of Berty Russell's books.[10] I interrupted though this is against my principles, & we had tea together. Her chief piece of news was that she & Saxon are going to set up together in Faith's house after Easter, for the duration of the war & 6 months beyond it. I fancy that they see something a little comic in this combination of the hopelessly enamoured, & indeed one can't help smiling rather at the thought of silences in which each will be thinking of someone else; & one fancies their common bond leading to a great deal of sympathetic collaboration, but the plan is evidently a good one. It recommended itself first to Mrs Bridgeman, the housekeeper, who thought two such quiet people should live together.[11] I did my best, this time, to keep low in tone, serious, & as far as possible sympathetic. Alix's feeling had been, she said, that I 'floated', & didn't mind how my prosperity reminded both her & Fredegond of all the things they lacked. But why should F. lack anything? I left her sitting there, as I believe she always sits, till they turn out the lights, or James comes to take her to dinner. What will she be at 45?

Home to find the two darkies [Perera and Jayatilaka] here. L. spent 3 hours or so printing, but did it in the end.

Tuesday 5 March

Another bitter day. L. up to a meeting at the 17 Club. I spent the afternoon "dissing", ran out into the High Street, and was inveigled into the penny Bazaar, where the simplicity of shopping tempts one to spend. The Guild meets tonight for Nick to address it.

Wednesday 6 March

Again one has to wonder why the women come—what inducement there is in such a passive employment as sitting silent, half asleep, in a chair for an hour. Nick was in the right style for them too; simple,

---

10. The Hon. Bertrand Arthur William Russell (1872-1970), philosopher and logician, Fellow of Trinity College, Cambridge, and an Apostle. His books to this date included *Principia Mathematica* (with A. N. Whitehead), 1910; *Problems of Philosophy*, 1911; and *Principles of Social Reconstruction* (in America: *Why Men Fight*), 1917. A passionate and intellectual pacifist, he was deprived of his lectureship at Cambridge, and since 1916 had devoted his energies to the No Conscription Fellowship; an article he wrote for its weekly paper *The Tribunal* had been judged seditious in February 1918 and he had been sentenced to six months' imprisonment—a sentence changed on his appeal, heard on 1 May, to confinement as a first-class misdemeanant in Brixton Prison from May until September.

11. It was not with Saxon, but with James Strachey, that Alix was to share the Henderson's house in Downshire Hill, Hampstead, for some months; Mrs Bridgeman, Faith's housekeeper, remained in the house.

detailed, casual, much at his ease. He spoke for an hour. The thing that remains in my mind of the lecture is the waiting for trains, & the marching out "with moon & stars looking very cynical" he said, along perfectly straight roads lined with poplars. His matter of fact way of speaking, as if necessity must be borne—however outrageous to his sense of decency & common sense also struck me. He seemed in good spirits; proud of Barbara; telling us of her conquests, which he believes in implicitly; talking more than usual, & telling me how after the war they'd like to live in the country & make good furniture after designs by Carrington. He's a human being of very good nature without special gifts to bend him this way or that; the same is true of her, I think. Its a rare production in our particular circle. L. to a meeting; we now have a mania for gambling over Demon patience.[12] I lost 4/ over this in a week. Impudent letter came from Williams, about L.'s book. He is showing, or means to show, the doubtful passage to co-operators, & therefore can't start printing yet. L. now threatens to 'put the matter in the hands of his lawyers'!

Thursday 7 March

In these 2 days I've 'dissed' 4 pages, in the hope that we may finish 8 pages of the story before we go away again. The raids seem so distant now that this precaution seems excessive. The servants still sleep in the kitchen however, as a shadow of moon remains. Philip came after lunch, & he & L. walked to Kew. I met them on the towing path. He is obviously very wretched; has no future wishes evidently, save to get out to France. He brought some of Cecil's poems, which we have offered to print at once, in a small book, in our old type— As giving him occupation it would be a good thing to do.[13] & he offers to come & help. The more one sees of the effects on young men who should be happy the more one detests the whole thing. Philip takes more interest in the military side of it than Nick, I think. He has refused an offer to work in London. A bitter day, & our coal finished tomorrow. The last raid dropped a bomb on the coal merchants.

Friday 8 March

From yesterday's writing it looks as if the raids were casting their shadow before me, & were sent expressly by God to rebuke my arrogance. However this may be, we played our patience; I lost my $3\frac{3}{4}$, and so to bed,

12. A solo card game played in competition with one or more players. For LW's book, see above, 3 November 1917, n 8.
13. *Poems* by C. N. Sidney Woolf, privately printed at the Hogarth Press, Richmond, was briefly noted in the *TLS* of 23 January 1919. It was the second publication of the Hogarth Press.

the only thought in our minds being, I think, something to do with patience or printing. I'd taken my third & final roll in bed, when there was an explosion. For half a minute a raid seemed so improbable that we made out it was one of the inexplicable outbursts of motor omnibuses. However, next minute the guns went off all round us & we heard the whistles. There was no denying it. So we got our things together & went to the kitchen. This was at 11.30. Looking out we could only see stars yellowish in some sort of mist; no moon; but a still night. As we lay down on our mattresses there was a great though distant explosion; & after that the guns set in very thick & fast to north & south, never, but once, so near us as Barnes. At 12.45 we had cocoa & went to bed. The bugles sounded at 1.35—two hours from start to finish.

I shall never forget the ecstasy with which L. burst into my room at breakfast. The wretch Williams has caved in. He agrees to cancel the contract. L. was as triumphant as a fighting beast who has driven his enemy to skulk into the bushes. I think he has reason to be. For one thing it looked as though he could still worry & impede for some months to come; & L. might have been forced to arbitrate. As it is, the way is open, & instead of dealing with a surly unwilling spiteful mangy exasperating cur, he can make his own terms—which he's doing this afternoon with Allen & Unwin. Going up in the lift at Holborn the other day I stood next a boy of 14 or so, whose head only was visible among the crowd. I noticed that it was an extremely interesting, sensitive, clever, observant head; rather sharp, but independent looking. One couldn't tell from his cap whether he was well off or not. I came to the conclusion that he was the son of an officer with whom he stood. When we got into the street I looked at once at his legs. His trousers had holes in them. From that one could judge what a wretched affair his life will be. I began setting up Cecil's poems this afternoon. They're not good; they show the Woolf tendency to denunciation, without the vigour of my particular Woolf. I had all sorts of accidents & only finished one.

Saturday 9 March

L. found Unwin very ready to consider the Co-operation book, &, what is more, unqualified in his abuse of Williams, who could, he says, be sued for the damage he's done to the book's prospects.[14] He proposes to issue 2 editions—one paper, one cloth, at once; after, that is, reading the book which he means to do directly. I daresay Williams will still try to keep his paw upon the manuscript.

We went to a meeting called a 'Suffrage Rally' in Kingsway this

14. Stanley Unwin (1884-1946) was the chairman of the publishing house of George Allen & Unwin Ltd.

afternoon.[15] It was a very fine afternoon & through a glass door one could see the day light—a difficult light for speakers to speak down. So prosaic, reasonable, & unconcentrated. The hall was fairly well filled; the audience almost wholly women, as the speakers were too. The pure essence of either sex is a little disheartening. Moreover, whether its a meeting of men or of women, one can't help wondering why they do it. I get one satisfactory thrill from the sense of multitude; then become disillusioned, finally bored & unable to listen to a word. In truth this meeting seemed to beat the waves in vain. The vote being won, only great eloquence could celebrate the triumph. None were eloquent; & yet they had to beat up a froth. The one who impressed us most was the Russian speaker, who had imagination, & seemed to feel what she said. But at best large indisputable platitudes, finely dressed & balanced, are the only things that can be put into speeches. I watched Mrs Pethick Lawrence rising & falling on her toes, as if half her legs were made of rubber, throwing out her arms, opening her hands, & thought very badly of this form of art.

We had tea at the 17 Club. One room was crowded, & silent; at the end of the other Aldous Huxley & a young woman in grey velvet held what should have been a private conversation. A. has a deliberate & rather dandified way of speaking. All we learned & virtuous people bent over our reforming papers in dead silence; an occasional sentence of the muffled dialogue came out plain from the other end of the room now & then. They were discussing Evan Morgan & his affairs of the heart I think.

We went on to the London Library; & as we walked down the steep street someone came ambling & crouching up to us—Bob. T.—laden with an infinitely shabby baggy portmanteau—full of books, I think. So we went on together; & first he confided in L. & then in me— At least he has the air of making a confidence, or asking for one. He wanted to know whether he could add my name to the list of devout Jacobeans.[16] Percy Lubbock & Logan Smith play this very characteristic game, of exquisite interest of course to Bob. They've counted 20, & Bob was

15. A rally of women Suffragists and supporters was held at the Kingsway Hall to celebrate the recent granting of the franchise to women; well-known women from Britain and from Allied and neutral countries gave five-minute speeches of congratulation. Mrs Emmeline Pethick-Lawrence, *née* Pethick (1867-1954) had joined the Pankhursts' Women's Social and Political Union in 1906, but in 1912 left it for the United Suffragists. With her husband F. W. Pethick-Lawrence she edited *Votes for Women* from 1907 to 1914; she had frequently been imprisoned for her activities and had gone on hunger-strike.

16. i.e., admirers of Henry James. Percy Lubbock (1879-1965), historian and biographer, educated at Eton and King's College, Cambridge; and Logan Pearsall Smith (1865-1946), born in New Jersey, educated at Harvard and Oxford, naturalised in 1913; they were both fastidious men of letters.

seriously exerting himself to find a 21st. But I refused—with some vehemence at first, thinking I was to be asked to subscribe to a memorial. Nothing so substantial; only an elderly cultivated game.

Monday 11 March

I spent 7/ on books this afternoon; a fact to be recorded, since its the only mention of buying books this year, or last, perhaps. As a matter of fact I've accumulated 12/ as Times money; add 5/ for a birthday present, & I have 17/—an unparalleled gain. First, however, I beat the town for chocolate or sweets. In the whole of the stores, not one ounce of choc. to be had; but some simple square drops, such as one used to buy in a bag for a penny. Half a crown will now buy a pound of them. Half a crown in old days would have bought a coal-scuttle full. Then I went on the top of a bus, for the day was of the quality of June, only fresher, & sadder too, to Nutt's shop to get a Leopardi;[17] then to Mudies where I bought Mill on Liberty; then to the Charing Cross Road where I bought the Happy Hypocrite, by Max Beerbohm; & Exiles of the Snow, by Lancelot Hogben.[18] In this way I laid out 7/. But I was amused to find that the lust after books revives with the least encouragement. I want a copy of Congreve. I could have had one containing all the plays I shall ever read for 2/6 I daresay; but this demon suggested that I might enquire for the Baskerville in two volumes.[19] The bookseller shared my lust which increased it; in short I told him to make enquiries. He would not commit himself to name any probable price, from which I judge that he is calculating on the lust to possess it when I see it. And, after all, nothing gives back more for one's money than a beautiful book—obviously I'm slipping. I sauntered round his shelves, as I had done in most of the shops. He is careful, select, bookish; no bargains but the type of book one might like to buy. These bookshops have an air of the 18th century. People drop in & gossip about literature with the shopkeeper who, in this case, knew as much about books as they did. I overheard a long conversation with a parson, who had discovered a shop in Paddington full of Elzevirs.[20] He

17. David Nutt, bookseller, was at 212 Shaftesbury Avenue, WC2. Giacomo Leopardi (1798-1837), the Italian poet and scholar.

18. *The Happy Hypocrite* by Max Beerbohm (1872-1956), critic, essayist, novelist and caricaturist, was published in 1897. *Exiles of the Snow and other Poems* was published in 1918.

19. Among the books at Monks House after LW's death were two (out of three) volumes of Congreve's works published by the Baskerville Press, Birmingham, in 1761. (Information from Mr G. Holleyman.)

20. Elzevir or Elsevier was a Netherlandish family of printers and publishers, active until 1712, whose name became identified with their series of literary classics issued in small duodecimo—books which became much prized by collectors.

denounced the government, particularly for its waste of paper. They should abolish all newspapers, & stick a sheet in the p. office, if there happened to be any news.

So to the Club, where I found L. Fredegond, Gerald [Shove], Goldie, Brailsford, & Alix.[21] The poet Hogben was also there. I laid his little book on the arm of my chair. Gossip of the usual kind. Poor Hogben's book is precisely the dreary imitative stuff one might have expected; or even worse than one might have expected—what Lytton would call "illiterate"; under the influence of Swinburne, incredibly ungifted, & weakly rebellious.

Home. L. to a L. of N. meeting.

Tuesday 12 March

This page should be wholly devoted to praise of the weather. One curious effect of spring in the suburbs is that it produces an astonishing amount of male & female singing in the evening. We sit with open windows, & a lady warbles out notes in apparent ecstasy. She may be forgiven though, considering— Here are some facts. I sat by choice on a seat in the shade at Kew; I saw two Heath butterflies; willows, crocuses, squills all in bud & blossom. Black clothes look like dusty palls. As for fur, it makes one laugh. We met at Kew.

I may say that I'm "rejected by the Times". To rub this sore point sorer, L. has 2 books from the Nation. Its the second week of my rejection; & it has the result of making me write my novel at an astonishing rate. If I continue dismissed, I shall finish within a month or two. It becomes very absorbing. We both notice that lately we've written at a terrific pace: L. 40,000 words & as yet hasn't touched the book itself; I'm well past 100,000—

Thursday 14 March[22]

If I'd written this diary last night which I was too excited to do, I should have left a row of question marks at the end. What excited me was the evening paper. After printing all the afternoon I went out later, bought a Star, looked at it casually under the public House lamp, & read that the

---

21. Henry Noel Brailsford (1873-1958), the influential socialist and journalist, was associated with Lowes Dickinson and others in the Union of Democratic Control who were working for a negotiated peace and a permanent international organisation for its maintenance.

22. VW was evidently so excited that she wrote the date wrong: this and the next entry are dated *March 7th* and *March 8th*—the week before.

Prime Minister needed our prayers.[23] We were faced with momentous decisions. We Britons must cling together. In a week or even a few days facts must be faced which would change the British Empire for ever. We evolved from this an offer of peace to France: but it appears to be only L.G.'s way of whipping up his gallery. Anyhow, I was whipped. Gerald who was to have dined, rang up to say that a raid was expected, & he must "stand by".[24] The night was cloudy, & we weren't much alarmed, partly because the warning came from official sources.

My dismissal is revoked. A large book on Pepys arrived, which I spent the evening reading, & now another on Swinburne awaits me at the Railway station.[25] I'm divided whether one likes to have books, or to write fiction without interruption. But I may make a few shillings to pay for my Baskerville.

Friday 15 March

Happily the weather is turned cloudy; spring blotted out, but one must sacrifice spring to the war. Philip came & we printed—I making rather a mess of the poems, to my annoyance. Philip talked about Blimey who is a shepherd near the Quantocks.

Monday 18 March

I wrote the date, & then something interrupted me—a letter I think, to Lytton giving reasons for *not* reviewing his book.[26] Today is Wednesday, & this the first moment I've had for writing after tea. On Saturday the chatter began. Lytton & Carrington came to tea—she apple red & firm in the cheeks, bright green & yellow in the body, & immensely firm & large all over. The talk has run off my mind, so that I don't suppose there was anything said of great importance. They'd been at Barbara's party till 5 the next morning. Fredegond & Nessa kept it off the rocks by giving

23. David Lloyd George (1863-1945), after resigning from and precipitating the resignation of H. H. Asquith's Liberal government in December 1916, himself became Prime Minister of the coalition government which continued in office until 1922. On Monday 13 March he had addressed the National Free Church (hence the request for prayers); he was indeed doing no more than 'whip up his gallery'.

24. Gerald de l'Etang Duckworth (1870-1937) was the younger of VW's half-brothers; after Eton and Cambridge he set up his own publishing house in 1898. He had published VW's first novel, *The Voyage Out*, in 1915.

25. VW's review of *The Letters of Algernon Charles Swinburne*, with some Personal Recollections by Thomas Hake and Arthur Compton Rickett, appeared in the *TLS*, 21 March 1918 (Kp C103); that of *Occasional Papers Read by Members at Meetings of the Samuel Pepys Club*, vol. I, edited by H. B. Wheatley, on 4 April 1918 (Kp C104).

26. See *II VW Letters*, no. 914, wrongly dated 15 instead of 18 March 1918.

an imitation of Ottoline. Nick & Saxon both gloomy in the background. Carrington going out of the room for a second, Lytton explained that he would like to stay with us without her, could it be managed. He asked me to review his book. I agreed without thinking. On second thoughts I dont much want to write under surveillance, or to ask B[ruce]. R[ichmond]. for what he must know to be the book of a friend. On Sunday the burden of visitors was oppressive. The list speaks for itself. Gerald [Duckworth] & Saxon lunch: Saxon tea; Barbara, Nick, Middleton Mur[r]y dinner. Gerald's likeness to a pampered overfed pug dog has much increased. His hair is white. There is hardly a gleam of life, let alone intelligence in his eye. The feebleness of his hold on life save through the stomach must be fearful. He has no opinions, but merely a seaweeds drift in the prevailing current. His commercial view of every possible subject depressed me, especially when I thought of my novel destined to be pawed & snored over by him. But the odd thing was that he had nothing to say.[27] This took till 3, perhaps; Saxon at his least urbane & most insignificant. Its melancholy that misfortune should be unbecoming, but I'm afraid in his case it is. His complexion suffers; his mind seems frost bitten. He was beaten at chess, & went, as if not wishing to meet N. & B. Nick was the only cheerful one of us. Poor Murry snarled & scowled with the misery of his lot. He works all day, & writes when he comes home. Worst of all, K.M. has been very ill with haemorrhage from the lungs, out in France, & has to be brought home, wh. is difficult, in order to see how bad she is. But I thought him very much more of a person & a brain than I had thought him before. I think this was partly due to the contrast with Nick. The difference between a good mind & a mediocre one is very sharp— Not that M. is as easy, or as agreeable. But he works his brains, always has worked them, & thus cuts his way through a different atmosphere. I had a good deal of talk about books with him, such as one couldn't have with Nick—though he's read Jane Austen, & can keep his end up by natural good sense & taste. B. was almost blotted out; scarcely spoke, I think. They went first; we said goodbye, the modern method of covering all obviously emotional crises with a varnish of prose & common sense makes such partings almost ostentatiously matter of fact. Murry stayed on, for a time, discussing French writers & Thomas Hardy. He will never write another novel, he says. Poetry is a short cut & "life seems to me now very precarious."

On Monday [18 March] I stayed here & did my compositors work. L. to London.

On Tuesday we had tea at the Club, meeting all the usual people, save that Bryn's a rarity, went to a general meeting, where L. was elected 5th

27. LW's comment on this lunch in his diary was 'Very difficult. G. almost speechless. S. quite.'

on the committee; & then on to dine with Ka. Arnold Forster the other guest.[28] Much to my surprise the first person to come in afterwards was Hilton Young.[29] I dont think I've said 6 words to him since 1908—when we had that interview. I've always guessed that dark dealings on the part of O.H. intervened; at anyrate we broke completely. This knowledge made me at least uncomfortable. But we are elderly now. He a perfect type of naval officer, cleanshaven, shorn, red faced, all blue cloth & gold braid with a ribbon on his breast. His dark enigmatic ways (the Sphinx without a Secret) are swept away; & yet I liked him—thought him kind & trusty & a little romantic—I'm afraid no longer romantic about me. But how even begin to guess another's feelings? I found myself pitying him for the very first time. I suppose he's more than 40, & after all, he wished for something which he's done without. We talked hard indeed. He find[s] no romance in the navy after four years. We wondered about our vision of England. Not knowing his degree of pugnacity, talk was difficult save on general subjects. The Shoves came, & a brisk friend of Ka's out of an office I think, as we left. Little W.A.F. very humble, very small, very innocent, as he used to be.

Wednesday 20 March

We printed—but just missed getting it done.

On Thursday 21 March the Woolfs went to Asheham, and VW reopened her Asheham Diary to recall that they had come there for ten days in February after her influenza. Now, on their Easter visit, her usual observations of local weather, natural phenomena, prices and their own movements are recorded: on 24 March Duncan Grant came to lunch, and LW returned with him to

28. Brynhild Popham, *née* Olivier (1887-1935), second of the four daughters of the Fabian socialist and civil servant Sir Sydney Olivier, all of whom had formed part of the group of friends called by VW the 'neo-pagans'. William Edward Arnold-Forster (1885-1951) had studied painting at the Slade 1904-08, but was now a Lieutenant-Commander in the Royal Naval Reserve and working in the Restriction of Enemy Supplies Department. He was a second cousin of Aldous Huxley.

29. Edward Hilton Young (1879-1960), third son of Sir George Young, Bt; educated at Eton and Trinity College, Cambridge, called to the Bar in 1904. His family and VW's had been long acquainted and after the young Stephens moved to Bloomsbury in 1904 he was frequently in their society. In 1909 (not 1908 as she recalls) he proposed to VW. Olive Heseltine, *née* Ilbert (1877-1950), one of whose sisters had married VW's cousin H. A. L. Fisher and another Hilton's eldest brother George, was suspected of manoeuvres to prevent such a match. Hilton Young was at this time Liberal MP for Norwich and was serving as a lieutenant in the RNVR; he had been awarded the DSC for action in Flanders in 1917; in 1935 he was created 1st Baron Kennet of the Dene. It was Desmond MacCarthy who had dubbed him 'the sphinx without a secret'.

*Charleston; the war news on 25 March was very bad, but better next day;
Lytton Strachey came to stay on 28 March, but Barbara Bagenal failed to
arrive; Lytton was sick and stayed in bed all day on 30 March; on 2 April
James Strachey and Noel Olivier came; the following day Lytton removed to
Charleston. On 5 April the Woolfs returned to Richmond, leaving James and
Noel to stay on at Asheham, and VW reverts to Diary IV.*

Friday 5 April

I think that Wednesday was broken off short, as they always tend to be
on the verge of a move, & so far as I remember it snowed hailed thundered
people. Off we went to Asheham on Thursday, in such a burst of summer
heat that people in the Tube pulled blinds down, & the uproar & potency
(what word will express the stir of life still cased in a soft velvet sheath?)
of Richmond worshipping a Tank was like the hum of bees round some
first blossom.[1] We had the bee & the blossom in no metaphorical sense at
Asheham. Once more my memory is most centred upon an afternoon
reading in the garden. I happened to read Wordsworth; the poem which
ends "what man has made of man".[2] The daffodils were out & the guns I
suppose could be heard from the downs. Even to me, who have no
immediate stake, & repudiate the importance of what is being done, there
was an odd pallor in those particular days of sunshine. There's always a
sadness in spring of course— Our visitors broke in upon the moods which
weave so thick a texture into life alone at Asheham. First Lytton. Then we
waited, with eyes upon the avenue, for the appearance of Barbara. She
never came though, & upon Sunday I had a letter telling the almost
incredible story of her repeated attempts to get into a train; how for three
days she went to Victoria; & sometimes was kept outside the barrier;
sometimes was stuck opposite the gap between the carriages; never got
in, & finally spent Easter alone in her studio, expecting, so we are told, to
find herself in some 9 months short of a fortnight, the mother of a child.
Lytton was with us one day less than a week. Our chief exercise was along
the road to Beddingham. We had short, & to me, very intimate talks;
intimate in the sense that he will understand from the sight of the tail what
the whole body of the thought is in one's mind. These thoughts were for
the most part about books; but books include a good deal of life. I suspect
that he is now inclined to question whether Eminent Victorians, 4 in
number, & requiring 4 years for their production, are quite enough to
show for his age, & pretensions. At anyrate he was evidently & rather

1. In November 1917 the comparative novelty of the military tank was enlisted in a
   campaign to increase the sale of War Bonds and Savings Certificates by the in-
   auguration of peripatetic 'Tank Banks', from which they could be purchased by
   members of the public. 'Tank Week' in Richmond, Surrey was 18-23 March 1918.
2. From 'Lines written in Early Spring, 1798', which begins: 'I heard a thousand
   blended notes . . .'.

painfully anxious about our opinion of their merits, & came back so often though so tactfully to the question of my review that I hesitate. I suppose the contrast (& to me there is a contrast) between his achievements & L.'s achievements made itself felt to him. Then he was sick one morning "green sickness", Lottie described it with her usual passion & enthusiasm for painting all colours at their brightest. His ebb of health is very low; & certainly health does make one careful, perhaps a little peevish, spiritually. I remarked, whether the result of bad health or not, a distinct increase in his family pride; it has now reached almost a religious pitch; a bad sign. Like patriotism it means that certain feelings are to grow large & lusty under shelter. For instance, James must be exalted as a man of "iron will", superb administrator &c: but the light is shed on each one of the family; & even upon cousins, like Mary H. I rather resent it. Then James & Noel came.[3] Our patience wore rather thin. Visitors do tend to chafe one, though impeccable as friends. I'm always glad at the end of a visit to find one's liking unmodified, as it was in all three cases,—yet I'm puzzled to account for the sense of strain & discomfort which the people one likes most manage to produce. L. & I discussed this. He says that with people in the house his hours of positive pleasure are reduced to one; he has I forget how many hours of negative pleasure; & a respectable margin of the acutely unpleasant. Are we growing old? Are our habits setting in like the Trade Winds? But this time the food difficulties certainly increased one's discomfort. One day we came back from a long walk to find the third of a loaf of bread on the table. No more to be had in the house. This was due to bad management on Nelly's part, but then at Asheham it's very easy to manage badly & needs considerable thought, cycling & carrying to manage even tolerably. At one point the servants wrought themselves into the usual row. The relief of being back in comparative plenty & anyhow next door to shops is quite recognisable. We came up on Friday, went straight to lunch at Clifford's Inn, dived into Partridge & Cooper, & then I came home and L. went to see Bonwick.[4]

The result of seeing Bonwick is what I foretold (see page [109]). They have offered him the editorship of the new Review, & indeed make his acceptance a condition of starting it, which they propose to do at once. Some arrangements must be come to with Wright, but they will solve themselves I suspect. L. has 10 days in which to decide. There's the

3. James Strachey and Noel Olivier (1892-1969), the youngest of the four Olivier sisters; educated at Bedales and the London School of Medicine for Women, she qualified as a doctor in 1917. Rupert Brooke, Adrian Stephen and James Strachey all fell in love with her.

4. Alfred James Bonwick (1883-1949) was at this time business manager to Arnold Rowntree; the question of their financing a paper, *The International Review*, proposed by LW as an extension of and improvement on *War and Peace*, was under discussion.

question of staff, of salary & so on. If he accepts, he will be able to give up feeding the omnivorous & callous throated Eagle with reviews.[5] Considering the merits of that cheap & thin blooded creature, (I speak of his journalism) & his methods of running the paper, his lack of power judgment & competence, I shall consider L. wise to take the other job merely as a means of escape. But in itself too it might be not a means but an end. Thus we had rather a sanguine happy sort of return, considering how disappointing returns generally are.

Saturday 6 April

This morning I had a letter from Barbara telling me that Nick was dangerously wounded on the 30th. The wound is in the back & kidneys, & they have operated. The last news said he was well through the operation. They have heard no more. If he recovers, perhaps he won't be sent out again—but who knows? At least she has had the blow soon, & if it were me, I should think that a blessing in itself. But the state of waiting for telegrams & letters, without any certainty when they'll come, & this baby in prospect, must be as fair a combination of torture as human beings can invent for each other. However, Saxon is moving house; she helps him; his voice on the telephone sounded as if pleasure of some sort had not entirely deserted him.[6] But when a crisis happens, scarcely anyone meets it naturally; either they're too composed & prosaic, or the other extreme. Saxon has a curious cul de sac of his own.

Rain all day till this moment, when it has turned brilliant. Plum in blossom in the garden, & flowers very healthy looking. To turn over books in Hiskoke's. I bought Collins' poems & Colley Cibber's Autobiography—1/ both together.[7] L. to Staines. Flora's husband has just gone abroad.[8]

Sunday 7 April

We are just back from tea with Barbara & Saxon in the Studio. Nick is already moved to another hospital & has written himself, so at least he must be in no immediate danger. Indeed they think he may be home any day now. We had tea; Saxon in his brown woollen vest, stepping fantasti-

5. i.e., J. C. Squire, literary editor of the *New Statesman*, whose pseudonym was 'Solomon Eagle'.
6. He moved to rooms at 37 Great Ormond Street, Bloomsbury.
7. Hiscoke & Son were booksellers at 22 Hill Street, Richmond. William Collins' *Odes* were first published in 1747, the *Apology for the Life of Mr Colley Cibber, Comedian*, in 1740; vol. I of the 1826 edition of the latter was among the Woolfs' books at LW's death (see *Holleyman*, VS I, p. 43).
8. Flora Woolf had married George Sturgeon (see above, 28 October 1917); he served as an officer throughout the war, and was posted to Damascus in 1918.

cally about the room to lay the table; Barbara so evidently nervous that I suppose the child must be a fact—but that 4 days waiting for news can try anyone's nerves. The couple in the interior were almost too perfect an illustration of the post impressionist spirit for my taste. Even the black & white cat seemed decorated by the Omega. White wash in which the hairs of the brush remain, a striped pole, Burnet for the covers, china dogs for the mantelpiece, check cottons wherever you looked, & to the censorious eye one or two uncertainties of taste or reversions to an earlier stage, as for example a bead necklace hanging on a nail.[9] However I came back to think my own room very ugly. The talk was sober, adequate, but not profuse. I don't think Saxon (who had just washed his head) had anything to say; & his demeanour is a little tart & gritty at the moment. He reminded me of a hen who has laid an egg—but only one. We did not like Hampstead. The vulgarity of Richmond is always a relief afterwards.

Monday 8 April

There is an awkward moment between coming back from London & dinner which is the salvation of this book. For some reason one can't settle to read, & yet writing seems the proper channel for the unsettled irritable condition one is generally in. Perhaps this condition is intensified by tea at the 17 Club, particularly if one happens to meet Roger in the Charing Cross Road, in his wideawake hat with four or five yellow French books under his arm. He is the centre of a whirlwind to me. Under this influence I was blown straight into a book shop, persuaded to lay out 3/7 on a French novel, Et Cie, by a Jew, made to fix a day for coming to Durbins, invited to a play & fairly overwhelmed—made to bristle all over with ideas, questions, possibilities which couldn't develope in the Charing Cross Rd. Of course he was in a hurry to keep an appointment at the Burlington, & to produce one or two plays somewhere else—ill too, so he said, but somewhat relieved in his mind by reading Fabre, who makes him see that after all our war, hideous though it is—but here we parted.[10]

9. Barbara Bagenal lived in a studio at 21A Heath Street, Hampstead. B. Burnet & Co., 'Art Furnishers & Upholsterers' of 22 Garrick Street, WC2, had a reputation for their bold and colourful fabrics, and did a considerable trade with the theatre.

10. *Et Cie* (1918) by Jean-Richard Bloch (1884-1947). Durbins was the house near Guildford designed for himself by Roger Fry in 1909. Israel Zangwill's play *Too Much Money* opened at the Ambassadors Theatre on 9 April with Lillah MacCarthy in the lead and scenery and furniture for the first act designed by the Omega Workshops. Roger Fry was joint editor from 1913 to 1919 of the art-historical journal *The Burlington Magazine*; its editorial offices were in Old Burlington Street. He had been translating the *Lysistrata* of Aristophanes, and the idea of staging it was in his mind. Henri Fabre (1823-1915), the French naturalist, was the author of *Souvenirs Entomologiques* published between 1879 and 1910 and collected in a 10-volume definitive edition in 1914-24.

I ran in to a kind of backwater of Roger at the 17 Club: Goldie, & Miss Dudley at least. Mrs Manus & Langdon Davies & L. can't be included under that heading.[11] We sat in the groundfloor room; & poor old Goldie wrinkled his forehead & flung himself lightly & ardently into one question after another in his usual way—the way of a bachelor who lives by plying his mind & moving by that means from person to person, having no settled abode. A sort of gipsy or vagrant. He mourned all the deaths of the young men—Eric Whitehead the last to be killed.[12] Said that he would fight if young enough; as it is he sits on committees. I left them to conduct another committee, & went to Poland St. to get my watch. On the way I walked through a narrow street lined on both sides with barrows, where stockings & ironmongery & candles & fish were being sold.[13] A barrel organ played in the middle. I bought 6 bundles of coloured tapers. The stir & colour & cheapness pleased me to the depths of my heart. But I couldn't pay 5/6 for my watch, owing to the seductive magic of Roger in the Charing X Road, & so had to leave it, ticking away like a young watch. Home by Victoria. A sunny evening, swarming with people.

Tuesday 9 April

This is most curious weather; also most unpleasant. Rain descends at intervals from a dark grey sky; even when it isn't raining the sky is still grey. Its warm, damp, & the young leaves have a lurid look in the winter atmosphere; the green is as if seen at night by electric lights. We quarrelled yesterday, about my jug of cream; & L. was unreasonable, & I was generous. The quarrel ended at 4.25 sharp. At 4.30 Miss Mattaei arrived.[14] I remember her at Newnham. She has left, we understand, "under a cloud". It is easy to see from her limp, apologetic attitude that the cloud

11. Goldsworthy Lowes Dickinson had been an intimate friend of Roger Fry's since they were at Cambridge in the 'eighties. Helen Dudley, an American who had studied under Gilbert Murray at Oxford, returned to England from Chicago in August 1914 in response to Bertrand Russell's proposal that they should live together—a proposal he withdrew on her arrival. She sat to Roger Fry in 1916, and her portrait by Vanessa Bell is in the Tate Gallery (no. T.1123). Bernard Noel Langdon-Davies (1872-1952) was a socialist, publisher, lecturer on international affairs, and chairman of the Council for Civil Liberties; Mrs Marjorie Manus was his assistant there, and also worked with him at the Labour Publishing Company.

12. He was the younger son of Alfred North Whitehead, the Cambridge philosopher and mathematician.

13. i.e., Berwick Street Market, Soho.

14. Louise Ernestine Matthaei (1880-1969), classical scholar and later Fellow and Director of Studies at Newnham College, Cambridge, 1909-16. In 1931 she was to marry her sister's widower, Sir Albert Howard. The 'cloud' was her German origin.

has sapped her powers of resistance. We skirted round the war, but she edged away from it, & it seemed altogether odious that anyone should be afraid to declare her opinions—as if a dog used to excessive beating, dreaded even the raising of a hand. She & L. discussed their business, which has to do with W[ar]. & P[eace]. & may result in an offer to her of a place on the staff. She has to earn her living. "I must tell you one thing, she said, when the talk was over, my father was a German. I find it makes a good deal of difference—it is a distinct hindrance commercially." L. agreed that it was. She is a lanky gawky unattractive woman, about 35, with a complexion that blotches red & shiny suddenly; dressed in her best, which was inconceivably stiff & ugly. But she has a quick mind, & is an enthusiast; said she loved writing.

Wednesday 10 April

A very wet dark day. Printed. I set up one page in 1 hour & 15 minutes—my record. At this rate, the book might be done in a month. I had a letter from Miss Harriet Weaver yesterday asking whether we would consider printing Joyce's new novel, which no other printer will do, owing presumably to its sentiments. They must be very warm, considering the success he had with his last. She is to come here, though we can hardly tackle a book.[15] I like this dipping into the great bran pie. By the way, I'm rejected by The Times once more; & thus reel off my book at a great pace, & I suppose books will flood in all in a heap one of these days. To the printer, who has almost set up his new machine, but without power & without a compositor we are still far from getting our rights.

Thursday 11 April

To the 17 Club this afternoon. But one must describe the weather. Imagine living inside a yellow balloon, the ceiling of which floats up & down, with an atmosphere inside of exhausted air. Such is our situation. When the ceiling sinks nearly to the top of our heads we have to turn on the electric light; as we did at luncheon. Occasionally rain falls, but brings no relief. Going to London all the lights in the train were on. I went to the Omega, got my pictures & ran into Roger, carrying a roll of manu-

15. Harriet Shaw Weaver (1876-1961), a woman of independent means and opinions, the virtual owner of the periodical *The Egoist* (see above, 28 January 1918, n 45), had with great difficulty (owing to printers' liability for prosecution under the laws of obscene libel) published James Joyce's *Portrait of the Artist as a Young Man* in instalments, and finally in book form in 1917. Now she was anxious to arrange for the publication of *Ulysses*, the first episode of which her printers had set up but refused to print. T. S. Eliot had suggested to her that the Woolfs might be able to print it on their private press.

script, which was, he said, his translation of the Lysistrata. This he has done, on a moderate knowledge of Greek, & wishes to have acted, but doubts how far one can go. I carried the pictures all the way to Gerrard Street,[16] stopping at Poland Street to pay 5/6 & get my old gold watch, whose distinction & dignity are very marked after 6 months of Ingersoll. At the Club I found—need I repeat that old scene once more? I think the change from toast to roll & honey interested me more than the fragments of Scurr Cousins & Marshall, or than the pale constrained solemnity of poor Alix. Having robbed her of a fortnight with James I felt rather guilty.[17] L. came in from the Natives meeting. He is going up again to a farewell party to Bertie at Mrs Hamilton's.[18] Last night he went, for less than 30 minutes, to a Labour Party meeting.

Saturday 13 April

L.'s farewell party was freely sprinkled with our non conforming friends. I don't know why their virtues in combination are so depressing. There was Dora & Adrian & Karin (she announces that she is with child) & Burns & Alix & so on.[19] Bertie broken down, & safe to be imprisoned either for his article or for his conscience. The new bill rakes in all the elder generations.[20] All their consciences are now being racked; but so far they seem inclined to stop short of prison.

Friday was a pleasant day; the sun out, & the blossom & leaves of a natural colour. We spent the afternoon printing. It was the first evening we had alone for a long time. Sunk deep in our chairs we were interrupted in our books by Walter Lamb. Upon review of the conversation we

16. To the 1917 Club; it is not known what pictures she got from the Omega Workshops.
17. Presumably members of the 1917 Club; Scurr was probably John Scurr (1876-1932), a strong anti-imperialist who was to become Labour MP for Stepney. VW's feeling of guilt in regard to Alix derived from her having let James Strachey and Noel Olivier stay on at Asheham after she and LW returned to Richmond on 5 April.
18. LW went to a meeting of the Anti-Slavery Society in Vauxhall Bridge Road, and in the evening to York Buildings, Adelphi, the home of Mary Agnes Hamilton, née Adamson (1882-1966), Newnham College, Cambridge 1901-04, writer and socialist and founder member of the 1917 Club. Bertrand Russell (see above, 4 March 1918, n 10) did not expect his appeal against imprisonment to succeed.
19. Dora Sanger, née Pease (1865-1955), the wife of C. P. Sanger (see below, 7 June 1918, n 4) was a high-minded and actively philanthropic woman whom VW found unsympathetic. She suffered from severe arthritis. Cecil Delisle Burns (1878-1943), socialist and social philosopher, was at this time working in the Ministry of Reconstruction.
20. The Manpower Act of April 1918 enabled the government to conscript men up to the age of fifty, and brought Irishmen for the first time within its scope.

agreed that he was slightly above his usual level. He told long stories of his walk in a snowstorm, with every detail given a prominence more interesting to him than to us; the wildest romance would be flattened, however, by that voice. Lord Canterbury is again to the fore. He is a Persian scholar & has given W. the Arabian Nights. He lives in a house which is not fashionable enough to do him justice. He has an Italian footman who secures meat from a friend in any quantity. A small loin of lamb was left at W.'s door the other morning. He expects to fall again before the temptation. He has given up reading, finding no time for it; but examines boys in the Classics. Told us stories about J. J. Thompson, whose mother keeps a small shop where Watty used to buy sweets as a boy.[21] So we slipped on; W. sitting between us, L. yawning without concealment, I yawning with an attempt at concealment. The Academy is storing its precious pictures, only 18 in number, in some Tube. They are told to expect immense bombs at the end of the month, which will dig 20 feet deep, & then explode.[22]

Today Saturday we printed, & finished 6 pages. As we only began on Tuesday we have done a record. A cold dismal day, & very bad news in the newspapers.[23] Stout red-faced elderly men are visibly perturbed. And Ireland has Conscription. If one didn't feel that politics are an elaborate game got up to keep a pack of men trained for that sport in condition, one might be dismal; one sometimes is dismal; sometimes I try to worry out what some of the phrases we're ruled by mean. I doubt whether most people even do that. Liberty, for instance.

Last night Desmond rang us up. I'm afraid our friends' motives won't stand scrutiny. His book comes out on Monday; he, though forgetting everything, yet remembers a vague joking promise of mine, uttered at least a year ago, to review it in the Times. He is sending me a copy.[24] He wants to stay here. I'm now debating how to deal with these damned authors—

21. Sir Joseph John Thomson (1856-1940), OM, FRS, Cavendish Professor of Physics at the University of Cambridge and shortly to become Master of Trinity College. He was at school at Owens College, Manchester, as was Walter Lamb's father, who became Professor of Mathematics there and at Manchester University; hence Manchester was Walter's home town.

22. In April 1918 twenty of the Royal Academy's most important works of art were deposited under the care of the authorities of the National Portrait Gallery in a specially constructed chamber in the underground railway beneath the General Post Office; a further twelve works were added in May.

23. *The Times* leader for 13 April was headed 'Our Backs to the Wall'; and the Commander-in-Chief's Order to the Army 'Fight it Out' was printed.

24. Desmond MacCarthy's *Remnants* was reviewed in the *TLS* on 2 May 1918; but not by VW. It consists of a number of articles on various subjects reprinted from the *New Statesman*, *The New Witness*, *The Eye Witness* and *The Speaker*.

Thursday 18 April

There is a grave defect in the scheme of this book which decrees that it must be written after tea. When people come to tea I cant say to them, "Now wait a minute while I write an account of you". They go, & its too late to begin. And thus, at the very time that I'm brewing thoughts & descriptions meant for this page I have the heartbreaking sensation that the page isn't there; they're spilt upon the floor. Indeed its difficult to mop them up again. And at this moment the mere length of my list of unrecorded visitors frights me from beginning. Judge Wadhams, Hamilton Holt, Harriet Weaver, Ka, Roger, Nessa, Maynard, Shepherd, Goldie, not to mention the Guild & Alix & Bryn & Noel, (who may be called the 17 Club:) all these have accumulated since Sunday; & each deserves something to mark their place, & I did mark it at the time. But how recover the impression of Wadhams & Holt?[25] It was a tremendously successful visit [on *Sunday 14 April*]. We had prepared ourselves most accurately. They made speeches & looked at the pictures & complimented L. all according to forecast. They were impressive to me in the first place for their vivacity which combined with their large well nourished bodies made them appear powerful; next because they treated me with respect; & then because they were simply & intensely in love with the League of Nations. Judge Wadhams had "spotted" every minister in America. They were in touch with every group of people in the world, as far as I could gather, with an army of stenographers who send out pamphlets with the personal touch wherever a pamphlet can lodge. Compared with this our record is tame. "We put you right on the top, Mr Woolf, of the constructive thinkers of the war—I can see your place on my shelves at this moment— . . . Pardon me, you have used the word "social" more than once. I dont rightly understand what you mean by it. . . ." We both explained for 10 minutes. "No; I don't understand." "Well we must proceed to the Sidney Webbs; but we've done no more than scratch your surface Mr Woolf, & we must try to do more next time— With thanks to you, Mrs Woolf, for letting us see your home—" & off they went. But almost instantly Harriet Weaver appeared. Here our predictions

25. Frederick Eugene Wadhams (1848-1926), a lawyer from Albany, N.Y., and Hamilton Holt (1872-1951), later President of Rollins College, were in England as members of an American organisation called 'The League to Enforce Peace'. Their visit to the Woolfs was no doubt an outcome of *International Government*. *Two Reports by L. S. Woolf prepared for the Fabian Research Department*, first published in 1915 as supplements to the *New Statesman* and issued in book form in 1916 (see above, 18 January 1915, n 63). The American edition (1916) carried an introduction by George Bernard Shaw which refers to LW turning cheerfully 'from *belles lettres* to the production of the present volume on terms which would certainly have been rejected with emphasis by a dock labourer'.

were entirely at fault. I did my best to make her reveal herself, in spite of her appearance, all that the Editress of the Egoist ought to be, but she remained inalterably modest judicious & decorous. Her neat mauve suit fitted both soul & body; her grey gloves laid straight by her plate symbolised domestic rectitude; her table manners were those of a well bred hen. We could get no talk to go. Possibly the poor woman was impeded by her sense that what she had in the brownpaper parcel was quite out of keeping with her own contents. But then how did she ever come in contact with Joyce & the rest? Why does their filth seek exit from her mouth? Heaven knows.[26] She is incompetent from the business point of view & was uncertain what arrangements to make. We both looked at the MS. which seems to be an attempt to push the bounds of expression further on, but still all in the same direction. And so she went. And Ka came & was made to drink castor oil out of an egg cup, & lay on a sofa, & was nearly sick, & had a disturbed night & was better next morning.

Then I went to Guildford. I don't see how to put 3 or 4 hours of Roger's conversation into the rest of this page; (& I must stop & read Viola Meynell[27]) it was about all manner of things; on growing old; on loneliness; on religion; on morality; on Nessa; on Duncan; on French literature; on education; on Jews; on marriage; & on the Lysistrata. Occasionally he read a quotation from a book by Proust; (whose name I've forgotten[28]), & then from his translation [of the *Lysistrata*]; & we woke next morning to find the hills covered in snow, & came up in a bitter wind & rain to the Omega; so to Gordon Sqre; where first the new Delacroix & then the Cézanne were produced.[29] There are 6 apples in the Cézanne picture. What can 6 apples *not* be? I began to wonder. Theres their relationship to each other, & their colour, & their solidity. To Roger & Nessa, moreover, it was a far more intricate question than this. It was a question of pure paint or mixed; if pure which colour: emerald or veridian;

26. See *Dear Miss Weaver* by Jane Lidderdale and Mary Nicholson, 1970.
27. VW's review of *Second Marriage* by Viola Meynell appeared in the *TLS*, 25 April 1918 (Kp C105).
28. Marcel Proust's *Du Côté de chez Swann* had been published in Paris in November 1913, and was reviewed appreciatively and at length in the *TLS* of 4 November that year. Even so, Roger Fry was one of the earlier enthusiasts for Proust's novel in England.
29. The important collection of paintings and drawings by his contemporaries made by Edgar Degas (1834-1917) was auctioned at the Galérie Georges Petit in Paris on 26 and 27 March 1918. Maynard Keynes was instrumental in procuring an Exchequer grant of £20,000 to spend on behalf of the National Gallery, and he and the Director attended the sale. The poor military situation depressed prices, and Keynes was able to buy for himself two drawings, and two paintings— Delacroix's *Cheval au Pâturage* and Cézanne's *Pommes*; they are now on loan to the Fitzwilliam Museum, Cambridge.

& then the laying on of the paint; & the time he'd spent, & how he'd altered it, & why, & when he'd painted it— We carried it into the next room, & Lord! how it showed up the pictures there, as if you put a real stone among sham ones; the canvas of the others seemed scraped with a thin layer of rather cheap paint. The apples positively got redder & rounder & greener. I suspect some very mysterious quality of potation [?] in that picture. All day it rained, & L. was out to tea, & brought Goldie home to dinner. Goldie was "humiliated" by the fall of Bailleul,[30] but told his neat well groomed stories, & I went to the Guild, which pleased me, by its good sense, & the evidence that it does somehow stand for something real to these women. In spite of their solemn passivity they have a deeply hidden & inarticulate desire for something beyond the daily life; I believe they relish all the pomp of officers & elections because in some way it symbolises this other thing. They recanted their abuse of the woman on syphilis, which I think to their credit.[31] Since then they have learnt, they said that she only spoke the truth. They wish me to get them a speaker on Sex Education, Mrs Hiscoke telling us that she had had to get a friend to explain the period to her own daughter, & she still feels shy if the daughter is in the room when sexual subjects are discussed. She's 23 years old.

On Wednesday [*17 April*], L. went to lunch with Rowntree, & accomplished another stage of his progress to the Editor's chair. A dummy copy is to be prepared. R. still hedges, on the question of expense, but remarked all the same "Thou art the man!" L.'s hand shook so that he had no luncheon. This came entirely of discussing the question before he went up. I went to Caslon's, & sat in that solid impressive room among the empty desks & smooth tables while they went to fetch me 1/6 worth of h's (lower case) & the Printer of the bank of England ordered 2,000 lbs of type to be conveyed at once in a van, the weight being beyond the capacity of a taxi.[32] I find immense satisfaction in hearing the talk of these solid, competent business men, who give their orders with such weight & simplicity & never a word wasted, & such character of a plain sort, in every movement & feature. To tea at the 17 Club; & Alix & Bryn & Noel there, & I rather disliked them all. On Thursday we took a little walk, but in the teeth of such wind that there was little pleasure in it. Then L. had to dine with Margaret. He is becoming almost a diner out. But in our circle

---

30. Bailleul was evacuated by the British Second Army on 15/16 April during the Lys offensive by the Germans.

31. On 23 January 1917, at Hogarth House, the Richmond Branch of the Women's Co-operative Guild had been addressed by Mrs Bessie Ward, a speaker from the Council of Civil Liberties, whose references to 'moral' questions and to venereal disease had shocked and offended her audience.

32. Typefounders, whose premises, known as the Caslon Foundry, were then in Chiswell Street, EC1.

this is a matter more of business than of pleasure. One goes either to meet someone, or to settle something, or to say goodbye to a prisoner. Bertie's case still hangs fire however. Today I got Desmond's book, sent, I'm sorry to say, by request of the author. Richmond, when I asked for D.'s & Lytton's books said "Certainly—if you can keep it secret". I couldn't promise to do this, & therefore wrote to tell him not to send them. And now I must inform Desmond & Lytton. They won't suffer really I believe, but they will be anxious instead of safe, & I'm in two minds as to whether I'm glad or sorry. I think I could have said some very clever things, & a few true things, but undoubtedly one cant avoid a certain uneasiness in writing formally of people one knows so well.

Friday 19 April

A day of gigantic effort for L. Eight pages printed it off. He went at 1.30 & is still (6 P.M.) at the printers, standing in the cellar & slipping page after page between the pins, having had only a short time off for tea. By tonight I shall have 8 pages to diss. & then to set up; though the type runs to 9 pages, 3 lines with the new h's: t being the one to give out at last. Snow, storms of wind, bitter cold, & occasional sunshine.

Sunday 21 April

How many poor people, clergymen & retired officers for the most part, must be tapping the glass & looking gloomily at their lawns covered with withered blossom—withered still half closed, & then blown off the twig. Orchards must be ruined by this time. At Kew yesterday the magnolias were a most melancholy sight; the great pinkish buds just ready to burst into the most magnificent of flowers, & now browned & shrivelled never to open, & while they ve to be ugly. We noticed several branches ending in white gloves, according to L. a sign that some experiment in grafting is being tried. Even the daffodils are all blown crooked. Fruit trees brown & nipped. The weather goes on with its wind & rain & occasional snow. I went to a concert at the Palladium this afternoon; but on the whole I regretted it. A man called Julian Clifford played Mozart as if it were a Dream Waltz, slowly & sentimentally & with a kind of lugubrious stickiness which spoilt my pleasure in the G. Minor.[33] L. to Staines. I must now write to Desmond, who has been telephoning, I fear, with thoughts of that review.

Friday 26 April

There are five or six days missed out—I don't remember why, but partly at least because there wasn't much to say. On Monday [*22 April*] I

33. Julian Clifford (1877-1921), conductor, pianist, and composer.

remember having tea at the Club & meeting Fredegond, Ermengard, a lady farmer & someone I took to be Bryn, but she answered to the name of Daphne.[34] The Shoves are driven to the land again; had left it to the very last moment of course, & being under compact to have a job by Monday were still in doubt whether to try Cambridge, Hertford, or Hampshire. I talked mainly to Ermengard—a rare visitor, but somehow familiar. As L. remarked these country women get a slow bovine manner, rather refreshing to my taste. She breeds prize bulls, plays a double bass in the evening, & writes improper stories for children. She seems to have settled into a corner absolutely fitted for her, where she exists pleasantly, having a Quaker faith now to round her off. I got the impression of some large garden flower comfortably shoving its roots about & well planted in the soil—say a Stock, or a holly-hock.

On Tuesday [23 April] Wright dined & slept here. I listened with respect to a long conversation, in which both L. & he played their parts with perfect knowledge of the rules of the game. Such was the impression that their deliberate, easy & yet concise manner of speech made upon me. How far W. minded his fate it was difficult to say.[35] The rules of the game require complete urbanity. He was extremely nice to play so well of course. He offered to help as much as he could. His opinion of his own powers as Editor being naturally higher than ours or indeed than the Trustees, this was very nice of him, but I expect there's truth in his own saying that he'd rather get what he wants done by others than do it himself. He labours under a variety of diseases, & is very deliberate, taking twice the time to finish a meal that we do, & perhaps 4 times as long to finish a sentence. The question of salaries was discussed. W. thinks this will be referred to him. He suggests from £200 to £250 for Miss Matthaei; between £300 & £400 for L. This is more than we expected. However it depends on more people than Wright (Eagle here rings up to say he's standing for Parliament—a labour candidate— At that rate the Manx cat has a chance).[36]

On Wednesday [24 April] Lottie spilt half a case of type on the floor, so that I had to spend 4 hours in sorting every compartment—about the

---

34. Ermengard Maitland (1888-1966) was Fredegond's elder sister and farmed in Gloucestershire. Daphne Olivier (1889-1950) was the third of the four Olivier sisters.

35. *The International Review*, with LW as editor, was intended by the Rowntree Trust to supersede *War and Peace* which Harold Wright had edited. (See *III LW*, 223.) Harold Wright had been partially crippled since childhood, and suffered from asthma and a heart condition.

36. J. C. Squire stood as Labour candidate for Cambridge University in the General election of 14 December 1918. He polled 641 votes, less than one-eighth of the total cast in his constituency, thus forfeiting the £150 deposit the law required each candidate to lodge.

most trying work there is. She had mixed the letters in thoroughly, thinking or hoping that though divided in compartments the letters were all the same.

On Thursday I was recumbent & L. went to do proofs at the office.

On Friday we set up, & took a short walk. The weather varies between fog & sunshine, saving us at least from raids, though the moon is full.

Wednesday 1 May

There's a fate in saying that we're safe from raids; On Friday [26 April] I went to the Hippodrome, to see life; L. seeing a different variety of it at the 17 Club. The incredible, pathetic stupidity of the music hall, (for surely we could have risen higher, & only politeness made us laugh,) almost made me uncomfortable;[1] but the humour of Harry Tate, though a low grade was still the queer English humour; something natural to the race, which makes us all laugh; why I don't know; & you can't help feeling its the real thing, as, in Athens one might have felt that poetry was. Home about 11. At 12 the usual maroons, & even extra whistling. The fine night made this likely; we bundled our bedding into the kitchen & took up our appointed stations; L. and I lying by the grate; N. & Lottie whispering in the cellar. After 20 minutes, I thought I heard bugles. One's ears can imagine so much that I said nothing. Ten minutes later Nelly burst out "The bugles!" So they were. We went upstairs, inclined to blame some clerk whose ears played him tricks which the night made into certainties. But Desmond tells us that 3 American aeroplanes crossing the coast without giving the signal caused the false alarm, which woke the whole of London, though ignored by the press.

On Saturday [27 April] we went to Hampton Court, the first visit for a long time. But this weather (I am unjust though; Saturday was fine). We had a tremendous talk about the Equator. In the middle of a demonstration with two pebbles, Jack Radcliffe passed (or so I thought).[2] This diverted my attention. A serious reprimand had to be administered. It was discovered that I took the Equator to be a circular mark, coloured dull red, upon the end of a football. The ignorance & inattention combined displayed in this remark seemed so crass that for about 20 minutes we couldn't speak. However, I was forgiven, & told about the tropics of

1. The London Hippodrome was a very large music hall just off Leicester Square. VW saw Harry Tate (d. 1940), a master of comic solo sketches, in a revue called 'Box o' Tricks'.
2. Probably one of the sons of Judge (F. R. Y.) Radcliffe, whose wife was a cousin of Kitty (Maxse) and Susan Lushington, friends of the Stephen family from Hyde Park Gate days.

Cancer & Capricorn. The question originally was about the time of moon
& sun rise & setting in different months.

On Sunday [*28 April*], Desmond came to dinner; that is after dinner.
He has the hard sea worthy look of an old salt, cased in stiff black, with a
few gold scrolls about him, & boots made out of plain leather.[3] But within
this shell he is as tender & vague as ever, & very tired after his days work
which results, he is alarmed to find & so are we, in practical action upon
his evidence. His mind had a factitious spryness about it, as if still working
under the official eye; but this wore off, & he yawned, & couldn't stir
himself up, though L.'s yawns were partly the cause of his. Late at night
he took to reading Joyce's ms. aloud, & in particular to imitating his
modern imitation of a cat's miau, but L. went to bed, & though capable
of spending a night in this manner, I had compunction, & decoyed
Desmond upstairs, collecting books as we went. Next morning, having
observed that breakfast at 8.30 would possibly be early enough, he stayed
talking about books till 10, & rambled off quite out of tune for his office.
L. dined with the Webbs. At this point it would be useful could I command the pen of some intelligent & well informed diarist, with an eye for
the future; someone who could put down what were the really interesting
things that Sir Wm Tyrrell, Camile Huysman, & the Sidney Webbs said.

[*In LW's hand*]

> Went to dine at Webbs. Camille Huysmans & Sir William Tyrrell
> there.[4] The latter is now Head of Commercial Intelligence Dept &
> is engaged on drawing up complete dossier of our terms for the
> Peace Conference. A small, round, grey, friendly man, more like
> a well-mannered literary man—if there be such—than a diplomatist.
> Very frank—ostensibly—& talked incessantly of policies & people.
> "A friend of mine was at Kiel on the day of the murder of the Arch
> Duke & saw the Kaiser immediately after he had heard the news.

3. Desmond MacCarthy was now on the staff of Naval Intelligence at the Admiralty;
he held the rank (and wore the uniform) of Lieutenant in the Royal Naval Volunteer
Reserve.

4. Camille Huysmans (1871-1968), Belgian socialist writer and politician, from 1904 to
1921 Secretary General of the Labour and Socialist International Bureau in Brussels,
was a personal friend of Lenin and most of the socialist leaders. He was elected to
the Chamber of Deputies in 1910 and held various high offices after the war,
including Minister of Education, Mayor of Antwerp, President of the Chamber of
Deputies and, for seven months in 1946-47, Prime Minister of Belgium. Sir William
Tyrrell (1866-1947), diplomatist, had from 1907 to 1915 been the influential
principal private secretary to the Foreign Secretary Sir Edward Grey. He was now a
member of the Phillimore Committee set up to study the possibility of a League of
Nations.

The K. said: "Es ist ein Verbrechen gegen das Germantum".[5] When I heard that, I knew it meant war." "Lichnowsky has a poor mind.[6] He is a sort of village idiot. His Polish blood however gives him a kind of intuition so that he sees further sometimes than cleverer men —the intuition of the village idiot." The only hope, he said, was for the Allies definitely to declare themselves for a League of Nations & define its constitution. We should be surprised, if the German offensive fails, at the stiffness of the German terms even then. "Wilson under certain circumstances will be the most immoveable of Never-endians."[7] "The most impertinent thing ever written was Kuhlmann's answer to the Pope.[8] A friend of mine met K. & K. told him when he came to England to ask me what I thought of it. I said: 'Tell K. I think exactly what he thinks of it!' He said he had always thought that the greatest mistake the Allies ever made was to refuse to allow our men to go to the Stockholm Conference.

On Tuesday [*30 April*] I went to London. In fact, I went to the printers in Farringdon Street, & got wind of a second hand press; but how far this is the usual talk of shopkeepers I don't know.

On Wednesday May 1st we were to have printed off; our 8 pages were ready, & a 9th too (w. gave out this time). But the printer has his magazine on the press & wont be free till Saturday. These impediments are inevitable but jarring— We were getting along so well.

On Thursday, we tried printing the title page on the small press. Nothing would make it come right. The disease escaped us. We had to give up in despair—irritation at least. All these days as black as November; & a high cold East wind.

5. Archduke Francis Ferdinand of Austria and his wife were assassinated by a Bosnian revolutionary on 18 June 1914, an event which led to the German declaration of war on Russia and the Allies. "It is a crime against Pan-Germanism."

6. Prince Charles Max Lichnowsky (1860-1928), German Ambassador in London 1912-14, at this time employed in Berlin by the German Foreign Office. In 1904 he had married Countess Mechtilde Arco-Zinneberg (1879-1958), a writer and collector of modern painting who had been before the war one of the most brilliant hostesses in London. She was a friend of Roger Fry's.

7. Thomas Woodrow Wilson (1856-1924), President of the U.S.A. In January 1918 he had issued his Fourteen Points towards the restoration of peace with Germany.

8. Richard von Kühlmann (1873-1948), German diplomat, Secretary of State for Foreign Affairs for ten months in 1917-18. Although he believed in a compromise settlement to the war, Kühlmann had rejected the proposals for peace made in Pope Benedict XV's note to the powers of 16 August 1917. He was dismissed from office after having told the Reichstag, on 24 June 1918, that the war could not be decided by military measures alone.

Friday 3 May

L. to London to see Henderson.[9] In course of seeing Henderson he saw all the celebrities of the day. Webbs, Goldie & so on. I went to a Registry Office in the King[s] Rd. to get a servant for Nessa. The woman true Chelsea; marked as China is, by her dress, manner, & refinement. She has a servant, which is more to the point. On then, by Bus & tube to Hampstead, & to tea with Margaret. I almost mistook Lilian semirecumbent upon a green pillow for a Persian cat. Janet was there in those decorous purple draperies with which people compromise between art & fashion in Hampstead. Margaret immensely fat & broad; all black; she had stood two photographs of Ottoline opposite my plate. I felt this to be the heart of the woman's republic. L. came in, & we had a long semi-political argument arising out of Milk combines, about government. Margaret's carpet is there to give an air of austerity to the room.

"Ah yes, my lifes a compromise—all a compromise" she said. I was struck as usual, by her genuine character, & also by the unadorned sense of Lilian, always to the point, & surprisingly ready with her views, considering her air of modesty. As a matter of fact I believe she comes at things better than most women, being entirely unencumbered by any vanity; as she may well be; in clothing, manner, appearance, she is of the most ordinary type possible; & thus her talk, & her pipe, come with force. Janet shows signs of real old age; acquiescent; not blunted, so much as increasingly meditative—shakes her head a little. But she looked very well.

Saturday 4 May

Hodson came to lunch.[10] A soldier now, though by profession a civil servant. A hard, straightforward man, all about him seeming as close cropped as his head. A man of average gifts, I suppose, & thus a sample of what the world does to human beings. He has no special gift or fortune to palliate life. In this light I thought him rather sad; so grim, unpretending, & taking what comes as if it were anyhow good enough for him. He didn't like the war, but joined "as a duty". First the bachelors went, then the married men, then those who could afford to. His passage cost him £200. But there was no trace of heroism in this: mere "such is life". He went to Kew with Leonard. I to the printer who remains shut. The first

9. Arthur Henderson (1863-1935), trades-unionist politician and pioneer of the Labour movement, who in 1916 was made a member of Lloyd George's original War Cabinet of five. Both he and LW played leading parts in winning Labour party support for the League of Nations.

10. T. A. Hodson had been Superintendent of Police, Hambantota District, Ceylon, when LW was Assistant Government Agent there, 1908-11.

fine day since April 1st, or thereabouts. Hot, blue sky, no wind. Birds singing; & people swarming.

Sunday 5 May

But when the wind turns to East, it pours. Such a spring I can't remember, though for blackness the summer I spent in bed at Twickenham matched it.[11] According to Nessa the country has the same climate. This being so, we walked out in our mackintoshes, up the river & down the Avenue. Scarcely a couple to be seen. I pitied the orange barrows, half covered over, with some wet man sheltering near under a tree, his Sunday sales demolished. The tea gardens, too, look dishevelled, with their daffodils bent & drenched. Outside Dysart House we heard a cuckoo, inside some forlorn week end party was listening to a pianola.[12] Desmond put us off, I confess to our relief; his mother burnt her face lighting a gas stove. L. was rather headachy, perhaps owing to a swollen tooth.

Monday 6 May

L. was so uncomfortable this morning that we went out at eleven, for it was sunny & beautiful, the wind being in the East. We meant to sit in Kew Gardens, but they don't open till 12: & therefore we sat on Kew Green, which has been turned into allotment gardens: ugly patches of raw earth, spotted with white paper stuck into sticks. At twelve we entered. To the general loveliness & freshness was added a sense of being out when we should have been at home; this always turns things into a kind of spectacle. It seems to be going on without you. We sat under a tree, & became a centre for sparrows & robins, & pestered by the attentions of a gigantic aeroplane.

L. went to Harrison's, & had his tooth out, for it was very bad & pouring poison into him, sufficient to cause many headaches, so Harrison said. I went to London on my usual round; the one I like best. In my beatific state I forgot the principle thing I'd gone for; a typewriter ribbon; but never mind; that will be another days treat. Mudie's I dont altogether like because I'm kept waiting, but I love Holborn, & the Charing Cross Road, & I rather like turning into the 17 Club, & finding or expecting to find someone I want to talk to. I dont like buying hats though: though

11. In July and August 1910 VW had spent six weeks in Miss Jean Thomas's private nursing home in Twickenham which cared for patients with nervous disorders. She was there again in the summer of 1913, but for little more than a fortnight.

12. Properly called Ham House and in 1918 still the seat of the Earls of Dysart, it was built in the seventeenth century for the Duke of Lauderdale, and faces the Thames at Petersham. It is now administered by the Victoria and Albert Museum, having been given in 1948 to the National Trust.

I've conquered some part of the horror by learning how to look into the eyes of milliners, & make my demands boldly. Eighteen shillings for a hat seems a great price; but I paid it; & it relieves me so much to have bought it that I'm happy again in the end. But what women's faces in the streets! As senseless as playing cards; with tongues like adders. I found James reading the Antigone in the Club. Presently Leonard came, with Adrian. Adrian looks immensely long, & his little bow tie somehow gives him a frivolous rather than distinguished air, as if a butterfly had settled on him by mistake. He has some job in an office. We gossiped. Blood is a very strong tie; so much can be taken for granted, after the first shyness. Then Barbara came in, in her round black hat with the cherry coloured ribbon, as neat as if she'd never been in France; but all the same I think she is a little different. Nick is in hospital, & very irritable. She spends her spare time with Saxon. I daresay the seesaw is not working quite smoothly; but one cant honestly deduce this from a shadow round her eyes! We went on to the London Library, & so home.

Tuesday 7 May

I write expecting Philip Morrell to dinner—not that one need dwell upon that—Wind East & violent rain & grey sky again. A letter from Harry Stephen, suggesting a visit, as if he'd been in the habit of dropping in after dinner once a week all these years.[13] The ties of blood? Something very odd moves in the Stephen brain. L. better, though not entirely right. The tooth was an ancient mammoth. I must read Logan's Trivia now. L. has gone to a [League of Nations] meeting at the House of Commons. I've had a rush of books as usual: three Tchekovs, Logan, Squire, & Merrick hanging over me.[14]

The Woolfs were at Asheham from 17 to 28 May; no entries were made in the Asheham Diary.

Tuesday 28 May

The rush of books was disposed of, & Squire was well drubbed too; at the same time such a rush of people coincided, that I was clogged

13. VW's cousin Harry Lushington Stephen (1860-1945) had until 1914 been a judge of the High Court of Calcutta, and was now an Alderman on London's County Council.
14. VW's reviews of *The Wife and Other Stories* and *The Witch and Other Stories*, both by Anton Tchehov, translated by Constance Garnett, appeared in the *TLS*, 16 May 1918 (Kp C107); of *The Gold Tree* by J. C. Squire, *TLS*, 23 May 1918 (Kp C108); of *Trivia* by Logan Pearsall Smith, *TLS*, 23 May 1918 (Kp C109); and of *While Paris Laughed* and *Conrad in Quest of his Youth*, both by Leonard Merrick, *TLS*, 4 July 1918 (Kp C114).

into complete dumbness, I see; but to take up the pen directly upon coming back from Asheham shows I hope that this book is now a natural growth of mine—a rather dishevelled, rambling plant, running a yard of green stalk for every flower. The metaphor comes from Asheham.

But first let me recall Janet, Desmond, Katherine Mansfield & Lilian; there were others,—yes, there was Harry Stephen & Clive. Each left with me a page full of comments, but useless now partly I think from my habit of telling these incidents over to people, & once told, I don't want to retell them, the telling leaves a groove in my mind which gives a hardness to the memory, stereotypes it, makes it a little dull. But I wandered through Richmond Park in the moonlight with Desmond. We jumped a palisade into Miss Hickman's funeral grove, & found the dark green mounds pointed with red rosettes.[15] The rhododendron is a lovely flower for the moonlight. And we beheld a china watercloset also lovely in the moonlight, the divinity of a sheltered lodger, wedged in among the ferns & the flowering bushes. Desmond, who has been pestering me with inscrutable persistence, over the telephone in letters in visits to lunch with Prince Bibesco, dropped all that, drank a whole bottle, & bubbled like a tipsy nightingale, amorous, humorous, reminiscent, &, remembering the dead, perhaps melancholy in a happy sort of way. But he spoke rather pointedly of the charm & intelligence of Molly.

"Yes, I've never feared tragedy in *your* lives" I said, nor does one, though from what we hear, they strain at the collar now & then. But modern life has the merit of allowing for that. Katherine was marmoreal, as usual, just married to Murry, & liking to pretend it a matter of convenience.[16] She looks ghastly ill. As usual we came to an oddly complete understanding. My theory is that I get down to what is true rock in her, through the numerous vapours & pores which sicken or bewilder most of our friends. It's her love of writing I think. But she is off to Cornwall. Harry Stephen told his old stories, wrinkled his nose, & alluded several times to his great age. He is 58. An undoubted failure; but that has a freshening effect upon people; they are more irresponsible than the successes; but yet one can't call Harry exactly irresponsible either. He is modest; humorous; all his pride for his father & ancestors.

15. Miss Sophia Hickman, MD, a *locum tenens* at the Royal Free Hospital, disappeared on 15 August 1903; in October of that year her decomposed body was found in Sidmouth Wood, Richmond Park, beneath the rhododendrons. VW refers to Dr Hickman's disappearance in a letter to Emma Vaughan of 30 August 1903 (*I VW Letters*, no. 99).

16. Katherine Mansfield's divorce from her first husband George Bowden, whom she left the morning after her marriage to him on 2 May 1909, was made absolute at the end of April 1918; and she and John Middleton Murry, with whom she had been living since 1912, were married on 3 May. She lunched with the Woolfs on 9 May.

He still takes out an enormous pocket knife, & slowly half opens the blade, & shuts it.[17] Janet was decidedly more spirited than of late. She discussed Greek with L. She is still puzzling out theories about Plato: very open minded, & ready to understand whatever one may spring on her. I sprang first, Joyce's novel, then the Murrys; who are to be neighbours.[18] Lilian read a paper to the Guild in a thoroughly co-operative spirit; I think I should take exception to their maternal care of the women's souls, if I were connected with the movement. But I see the terrible temptation of thinking oneself in the right, & wishing to guide & influence.

Then Clive was in his best man-of-the-world vein, fresh from Max Beerbohm, & inclined to think himself one of our foremost. He sent me his book, where I find myself with Hardy & Conrad; & Nessa & Duncan bracketed first.[19] He babbled & prattled & hinted at all his friends & parties & interests—not offensively, to me at least. He gives, or wishes to give the impression that he sits drinking in the Café Royal with Mary, & the young poets & painters drift up, & he knows them all, & between them they settle the business.[20] His book is stout morality & not very good criticism. He seems to have little natural insight into literature. Roger declares that he doesn't know about pictures. On the other hand, he has the strong English sense of morality. At Asheham we had Roger, a picnic, & I spent a night at Charleston. That is by way of company. But the important thing was the weather. The heat was such that it was intolerable to walk before tea; we sat in the garden, I indolently reading, L. not sitting but gardening. We had the best display of flowers yet seen—wall flowers in profusion, columbines, phlox, & as we went huge scarlet poppies with purple stains in them. The peonies even about to burst. There was a nest of blackbirds against the wall. Last night at Charleston I lay with my window open listening to a nightingale, which beginning in the distance came very near the garden. Fishes splashed in the pond. May in England is all they say—so teeming, amorous, & creative. I talked a good deal with Nessa—much about servants & other

17. Cf Peter Walsh in *Mrs Dalloway*, p. 62: 'Putting his hand into his pocket he took out a large pocket-knife and half opened the blade.'

18. In the summer of 1918 the Murrys took a house, 2 Portland Villas, East Heath Road, to which they moved in July; Janet Case lived at Windmill Hill, Hampstead.

19. Clive Bell's *Potboilers* was published on 9 May 1918. In the foreword he refers to 'our three best living novelists—Hardy, Conrad and Virginia Woolf'. In 'The Mansard Gallery' (p. 199) written about the exhibition arranged by Roger Fry which VW visited at Heal's on 17 October 1917 (see above) but not previously published, he pays particular attention to the work of Duncan Grant and Vanessa Bell but as much to that of Mark Gertler.

20. The Café Royal (Nicol's) at the Piccadilly Circus end of Regent Street was a particular rendezvous of writers, artists and foreigners.

possibilities. Roger, of course, came up from Bo-Peep,[21] & there was Mrs B[rereton]. burnt brown, solid, stolid, institutional, & very competent. Roger & I croaked a kind of frogs chorus together—how we loved & admired & were only snubbed for our pains—Nessa sitting almost silent, stitching a dress by lamplight. Roger is growing more egoistical, or it is more apparent to me; & his complaints were more genuine than mine. All interesting people are egoists, perhaps; but it is not in itself desirable. There were numbers of Belgian Hares, & equal numbers of children to judge by the sound, though they are kept to their own rooms & hours by Mrs B. & don't appear at all. Saxon & Barbara arrive at Asheham as we go—this being our compromise, for we didn't want them as visitors as they, coolly enough, proposed that we should have them.

Thursday 6 June

These gaps are accounted for by the weather. Its not weather for drawing up to the fire & settling in. Indeed, I find some difficulty in reading. The windows are both open; the children next door are playing in the garden; the usual song comes from the singing teacher's room above the laundry; the birds are vocal in the trees. I want to be wandering down grassy spaces. Its impossible to concentrate. Things therefore pass unrecorded. A good deal of sociability goes on in this weather—Adrian & Karin dined with us on Sunday; she resolutely artistic in a distressing way; bright green, with sturdy embroidery let in. They live rather apart from our world; from all worlds, I cant help feeling, though this may be wrong. A. never troubles himself to see anyone & together they make too dense a block to be good guests at a party. A. was amusing, however. Prejudice leads me to think my own relations rather distinguished. He certainly makes one laugh with his stories of Saxon "Fifteen minutes it takes him to get from the recumbent to the sitting position." A. is observant, malicious, but more kindly than of old. He has the taste, & she the energy. I've seen Alix too—indeed asked her back here to dine with me, L. being out. I think the faintest ray of dawn is observable on the pitchy black of her horizon. She is able to conceive the possibility of one day finding some book to read. She has tried Bertie's mathematics, relinquished it, but did not altogether dismiss my suggestion of legal history. She wants to work at something that matters to no one; & will never be used, seen, or read, & can be done for no more nor less than 3 hours a day.

Then Carrington came to tea with me, L. making a speech again. (his activities are beyond counting now—what with League of Nations &

21. A farmhouse at the foot of the downs about a mile across the fields to the south-east of Charleston, where Roger Fry had taken rooms for several weeks in the summer of 1918 to be near Vanessa Bell.

all its evil designs. War & Peace, & its possibilities, to which one must add the persistent darkies, & the 17 Club committee). Carrington stayed over 2 hours; & I think that by itself is a sign of youth. She is odd from her mixture of impulse & self consciousness. I wonder sometimes what she's at: so eager to please, conciliatory, restless, & active. I suppose the tug of Lytton's influence deranges her spiritual balance a good deal. She has still an immense strange admiration for him & us. How far it is discriminating I don't know. She looks at a picture as an artist looks at it; she has taken over the Strachey valuation of people & art; but she is such a bustling eager creature, so red & solid, & at the same time inquisitive, that one can't help liking her. She posted me up in all the gossip. Jos has married his deaf governess, & thereby blasted the hopes of Heaven knows how many Marjories.[1] She is dismissed in the harshest way, humiliated in the face of all her friends—or so I should feel it. Lytton complains that the critics haven't attacked his judgments. They have copied each other & complimented him without much fineness. Still his book goes into another edition; the praise from the elderly, the Ottolines & the Goldies, is lavish. I haven't yet read it through; indeed, I've rather shirked formulating my own opinion, expecting to find it rather complicated. At any rate, as I'm on the verge of cooking dinner & going up to hear the Magic Flute I shan't begin now. And Oliver has taken a new mistress, & Barbara & Saxon have left Asheham, & I can think of no more gossip for the time being.

Friday 7 June

One thing Adrian said amused me—how it positively frightened him to see peoples' faces on the Heath "like gorillas, like orang-outangs—perfectly inhuman—frightful" & he poked his mouth out like an ape. He attributes this to the war—though I can remember other pronouncements of the same kind before that. Perhaps the horrible sense of community which the war produces, as if we all sat in a third class railway carriage together, draws one's attention to the animal human being more closely. L. was told the other day that the raids are carried out by women. Women's bodies were found in the wrecked aeroplanes. They are smaller & lighter, & thus leave more room for bombs. Perhaps its sentimental, but the thought seems to me to add a particular touch of horror.

I went to the Magic Flute, & thought rather better of humanity for

1. This news was premature. Josiah Wedgwood's first wife instituted proceedings for divorce in the summer of 1918; he did not marry Florence Ethel Willett, who had been his children's governess and *was* deaf, until 25 June 1919. Dame Veronica Wedgwood, his biographer, suggests that the rumour of his marriage at this time may well have been started by Wedgwood himself for the very purpose of discouraging 'the hopes of Heaven knows how many Marjories'.

having that in them.[2] Goldie was in the same row with me, thinking I daresay much the same thoughts, though the proximity of two youthful men may have coloured them differently. There were Roger & Pippa, & Sheppard & finally Mary Hutch. & Jack & Alix & James—all collecting in the hall for a moment in the twilight, for the sun, at 10 of a hot day, was hardly out of the sky. Mary & Jack in their dress clothes, took me back some 20 years; more accurately they took me back to the New English Art Club, she with her plastered hair, & he with his ruddy face & black riband across his shirt front.[3] Home, & in the carriage I saw Jean [Thomas], & remained hidden behind an officer. I dodged her successfully on getting out, & then, hurrying up the main road, distinctly heard myself called, "O there's Virginia." I hesitated, but judging such rudeness impossible, turned back, saw Jean! was received with the utmost surprise, for she had been talking about a cab, though thinking, so she said, of me— She introduced me to Ann, who used to figure so when I was in bed; the lady with the romance in India, which Jean prayed she might have strength to overcome. I could only see a featureless shape, & strode on again, Jean begging to come & see us, very cordially.

I admit it may be vanity; but people do certainly show themselves very cordial & anxious to come all the way out here—I think we make a good mixture—at any rate, here are the Sangers, Kot & Gertler, Pippa all waiting to be fitted in,[4] while Ottoline never ceases to gape wide for a week end. And we've promised one to the Waterlows.

Monday 17 June

Another gap of ten days takes me to the conclusion of our Waterlow visit. With the sort of clumsiness one might expect of them, they've

2. It was in the repertory of Sir Thomas Beecham's 'Summer Season of Grand Opera in English' performed at the Theatre Royal, Drury Lane.

3. St John ('Jack') Hutchinson (1884-1942), Winchester and Magdalen College, Oxford; Barrister-at-law, unsuccessful Liberal parliamentary candidate, and a Progressive member of the London County Council, 1912-16; he was at this time a legal adviser to the Ministry of Reconstruction. In 1910 he had married Mary Barnes (see above, 15 February 1915, n 8), a cousin of the Stracheys. The Hutchinsons were rather more fashionable than the Woolfs, and in the world of the arts they were friendly both with the *avant-garde* and with an older generation—in particular with George Moore and his friends of the New English Art Club.

4. Charles Percy Sanger (1871-1930), Chancery Barrister, friend and contemporary of Bertrand Russell at Trinity College, Cambridge, and like him an Apostle. A man of brilliant gifts with an unassuming and kindly disposition, VW found him more sympathetic than his wife Dora (see above, 13 April 1918, n 19). Mark Gertler (1891-1939), painter; born of poor Austro-Jewish parents in the East End of London, his remarkable gifts and vitality brought him to the Slade School (1908-1912), where he fell in love with Carrington. See his *Selected Letters*, edited by Noel Carrington, 1965, and *Mark Gertler* by John Woodeson, 1972.

pitched upon a house in the village of Oare; taken it for 28 years; in spite of the way it misses all the good qualities one might have had, with such a range to choose from.[5] You have a view of a dull farmyard; only a glimpse of down, & the house stands in the village street, too much in a hollow to be capable of a view. Sydney has mellowed & grown less susceptible to the good & bad opinions of his friends. She is a gnome like figure; but acute as the unattractive women tend to be, depending upon hard work for their wages. She produced excellent food, & manages the two unattractive children without a nurse. "All is black round me" she said, during a discussion on Saturday night, "I get no acute sensations; I wonder if its worth while." S. talks of taking to literature again. The defect of the household lies in their relationship. She has no admiration for him; he no romance about her. Clear eyed people could scarcely feel otherwise; but how I hate the average! Strictly speaking, they're both above the average. The average is a very queer study though: humble, aspiring, & without illusions.

None of these qualities are common with the people we see for the most part. I must run over the names of those we've seen in 10 days, so far as I can remember them. Ray for the night; Molly for dinner & also for the night; the Sangers & Murry;—the others are now forgotten. Ray lectured the W.C.G. How strange it is to see one's friends taking their fixed shape! How one can foretell middle age for them, & almost see them with the eyes of the younger generation! "Rather a terror", I think they'll say of Ray. She has the look of conscious morality which is born of perpetual testifying to the right. She has grown heavier, more dogmatic; her attitudes are those of the public speaker & woman used to knocking about the country. She speaks in all the counties of England.[6] She has lost such feminine charm as she had; she seems mature. But she is made of solid stuff; & this comes through & pleases me, & L. likes her better than the cropheads. We discussed the moral eminence of Moore, comparable to that of Christ or Socrates, so R. & L. held.[7] They challenged me to match him in that respect by any of my friends. I claimed for Nessa Duncan Lytton & Desmond something different but of equal value. R. tends to think us a set of gifted but good for nothing wastrels. Her days work gives her some claim to look down upon us; but it would be unfair to say that she condescends or judges.

5. Parsonage House, Oare, which lies between Pewsey and Marlborough in Wiltshire.
6. Ray Strachey, honorary Parliamentary Secretary of the National Union of Women's Suffrage Societies 1916-21, and chairman of the Women's Service Bureau 1916-34, was an assiduous speaker in support of women's rights.
7. George Edward Moore (1873-1958), philosopher, an Apostle, was elected into a Fellowship of his College (Trinity) in 1898, and subsequently became University lecturer in Moral Science (1911-25) and Professor of Philosophy at Cambridge. His greatest and most influential book, *Principia Ethica*, was published in 1903.

She merely makes one aware of a different ideal. What ideal does Molly live for? A very wandering will o' the wisp—but she chases it, & sticks in the bog, poor woman, & hasn't the clearest of notions as to what she's after. She has Desmond's Character on her mind. She imagines that he is much talked about, & greatly derided. Its worth noting for my own benefit how very little talk goes on compared with the victims notion of what must go on. She had ready an elaborate defence of D. but finding it unneeded, she confessed to the truth—that she finds him a little spoilt, terribly without a will, & much at the mercy of any fine lady or gentleman with good wine. I couldn't deny all this. I believe she worries herself acutely. Let alone the worry of money; she has a sense of failure, of decadence, & infulfilment. She means to give up London & live in the country, as an attempt at cure. But there's something sordid about it now—no longer pure fun. She finds his mind vitiated; his views no longer so interesting.

Murry & the Sangers came here to supper last Sunday. Dora becomes increasingly ungainly. She has become so lame that in order to take off her boots, she has to kick out one leg, & then hunch herself round into an attitude where she can crook hold of it again. Indeed, I had to do it for her. Murry was pale as death, with gleaming eyes, & a crouching way at table that seemed to proclaim extreme hunger or despair. Charlie has his wintry brightness still; but weighed down by all this cadaverous company, he scarcely chirped his best. And after dinner such a duet of despair was croaked by Murry & Dora as warmed the cockles of Dora's heart.

"At Christmas, said Murry, I was near suicide; but I worried out a formula which serves to keep me going. Its the conception of indifferentism. I have hope no longer. I live in 2 layers of conscience." (but I forget what these were.) Dora egged him on, & sounded his praises when we went through the struggle with the boots again.

But to us he seemed less nice, perhaps more anxious for effect, this time than before. Despairing young men who have worked out philosophies & describe them remind me too much of Henry Lamb. But there's more than that in Murry. I expect he is used to being an oracle in the underworld.[8]

8. Henry Lamb (1883-1960), younger brother of Walter Lamb, abandoned the study of medicine in 1905 and took up painting, being greatly influenced by both the art and the way of life of Augustus John. Before the war—during which he served in the RAMC and as an official war Artist—he had been patronised by Lady Ottoline Morrell and was for some years the object of Lytton Strachey's affections; and though never a close friend of VW's, she had no doubt heard a good deal about him. 'The Underworld' is a barely definable term used by both LW and VW, roughly equivalent to 'Grub Street' (the abode of literary hacks), but with a suggestion of social inferiority.

Then Leonard went to the annual dinner, which was almost a dinner in honour of Lytton; but not very interesting to L. at least; & I went to Don Giovanni, to my infinite delight;[9] & last Friday [14 June] we went to the League of Nations meeting. The jingoes were defeated by the cranks. It was a splendid sight to see.[10] The chief jingo was H. G. Wells, a slab of a man formidable for his mass, but otherwise the pattern of a professional cricketer. He has the cockney accent in words like "day". He was opposed by Oliver [Strachey], Mrs Swanwick & Adrian. There were also present such gnomes as always creep out on such occasions—old women in coats & skirts with voluminous red ties, & little buttons & badges attached to them—crippled, stammering men, & old patriarchs with beards, & labour men, & ourselves. Lord Shaw presided, & Sir W. Dickinson. It was comical to see their polite horror at the sight of our party, but Hobson won, by virtue, I expect, of his academic appearance. Wells, when he found himself thwarted lost the sort of effervescent good temper he has, & struck out as wildly as he could, & spat sarcasms at Williams & Hobson; & finally left the room; but we found him caballing in the hall with McCurdie & Spender, & L. is now in London hearing the result at a meeting of the executive.[11]

9. Mozart's *Don Giovanni* was performed on Thursday 13 June at the Shaftesbury Theatre in the 'Season of Grand Opera in English' given by the Royal Carl Rosa Opera Company. LW's Apostles' dinner took place the evening before.

10. The annual meeting on 14 June of the League of Nations Society—of which LW, with Lord Bryce, G. L. Dickinson, Sir Willoughby Dickinson and J. A. Hobson were among the founders—was the occasion (according to LW's diary) of 'a great row over the Constitution'. This was due to an attempt to force a resolution committing the Society to work for the formation of a League from which Germany was at first to be excluded. A leader in this move was Herbert George Wells (1866-1946), the author, who saw in the defeat of German militarism a step towards the destruction of all nationalisms, hence was able to reconcile his enthusiastic early support for the 'war to end war' with his present advocacy, in a period of flagging morale, of the post-war ideal of a League of—but not of all— Nations. Mrs Helen Maria Swanwick, *née* Sickert (1864-1939), sister of Walter Sickert the painter, had been at Girton College, Cambridge, with Margaret Llewelyn Davies and Janet Case, and was a tireless supporter of the League of Nations and other progressive causes.

11. Thomas Shaw (1850-1937), lawyer and politician, had been a Liberal MP until his elevation in 1909 to a life peerage as a Lord of Appeal. Sir Willoughby Dickinson (1859-1943), Liberal MP and chairman of the London Liberal Federation, was chairman of the League of Nations Society. Charles Albert McCurdy (1870-1941), Liberal MP, was one of the founders of the League of Nations Union (see below). John Alfred Spender (1862-1942), editor of the Liberal daily *Westminster Gazette* from 1896 to 1922, was the most influential political journalist of his day.

The 'caballing' might have been one of the first steps in the formation of the rival peace society, the League of Free Nations Association, variously dated as

Monday 24 June

The League of Nations intrigue hasn't stayed in our favour, owing to various chicaneries practised by Sir Willoughby after the General Meeting.[12] But I'm not competent to give a clear account of them. The amusing thing to me is to see Adrian transformed into an orator, an agitator, a man with convictions. I can't take it quite seriously; I mean I attribute it partly to his need of defending his own attitude as a C.O. He is a little sheepish; & yet works out points, circulates letters, whips up converts, & organises meetings of the godly at the 17 Club, where they plan the most extreme measures. Its odd how people invariably fall into these separate groups, & can't be united, each asserting a complete grasp of the right. But all this week has been harassed beyond any enjoyment by the great servant question. As I haven't traced the stages, I won't begin now. The question was whether N. & L. should go to Nessa for 3 months. At first they agreed with gladness; then they hesitated; then they asked for assurance that we would have them back; then they formally accepted; then they violently refused; then Trissie arrived, on a sudden, as ambassador; spent the night, argued, won her case & lost it again. Finally she and I found a widow & child in Soho who take the place; & now all is as it was, after more conversations, emotions, letters, telegrams, parleyings, compromises & diplomacies than would have set Europe in flame. Trissie's character, so far as I can make out, is the one thing irretrievably damaged in our eyes; the rest have slightly risen in value. At one stage in this agony, Gertler & Kot dined with us.[13] Gertler is a plump white young man, got up for the occasion very sprucely in sponge bag trousers. His face is a little tight & pinched; but the word he would wish one to use of him is evidently "powerful". There is something condensed in all Jews. His mind certainly has a powerful spring to it. He is also evidently an immense egoist. He means by sheer will power to conquer art. But bating this sort of aggressiveness, he was well worth talking to. L. noticed his amazing quickness. He would soon have told us the story of his life. I felt about him, as

---

being formed in July or September, but which was in October to merge with the League of Nations Society to form the League of Nations Union.

12. Possibly a reference to the preparation which took place at about this time of a report to be presented to the Society in September under Sir Willoughby's name, proposing that the League should be formed by 'those nations whose Governments are willing to co-operate with each other'. This formula would presumably have been unacceptable to those who wished at all costs to include Germany.

13. The stages in the agony are more fully traced in VW's letters to Vanessa Bell, April to July (see *II VW Letters*) and are reverted to below (see 27 June 1918). Gertler and Kot dined on 18 June.

about some women, that unnatural repressions have forced him into unnatural assertions. He examined our furniture & pictures. He likes shiny lodging house things best, he said. He has never felt akin to anyone. He thinks himself very much cleverer than most painters. Kot sat indulgently silent, professing scarcely to notice what was before his eyes. They both described their Jewish families. On Gertler, as upon Murry & Katherine, rests to my feeling the shadow of the underworld. You could put no trust in him; on principle, I can imagine, he is unscrupulous. Kot is different—rather in the style of the solid lodging house furniture, but with an air of romance.

We had a visit from Margaret; which opened with a tremendous broadside of cooperative shop; lamentations, aspirations & too sanguine expectations; all exaggerated, so I felt, in comparison with their real value. The vote at Congress against Peace seems to her of unspeakable importance & horror. She still talks of resigning next year; but we were interrupted in this by a strange attack in one of L.'s eyes; he dashed off to the chemist, & left alone with Margaret I became purely ribald. L. got Fergusson to take out a small fly; came back, & went on again, & M. stayed till the last train.[14] She is a fine specimen of the public woman; a type, after all, no less marked than the literary type, though not yet so fully observed & recorded. Their eccentricities keep me amused, when to tell the truth, I've ceased to follow their plots & denunciations. They have the habit of considering themselves driven to death, overwhelmed with work, without a possibility of rest; & never once since I've known her has Margaret owned to any state of health save that of being very tired. But these peculiarities are not more than jokes to me; & the directness & superb vigour of her character always overcome me with admiration. Given a keener mind, or a subtler, or some sort of discipline that she's never had, she might have done marvels. I sometimes guess that she thinks her work less good than it should have been. Or it may be only the terrific shadow of old age, in to which no one, not Roger or Goldie or any of them, can enter without a shudder.

But these remarks on public servants might be written over again for Ka too. She dined with us last night & slept, leaving punctually for her office this morning. With an effort she will talk of other things, but she seems bent & bowed under a load of responsibility, which I

14. Margaret Llewelyn Davies came to tea and dinner with the Woolfs on 22 June. The Women's Co-operative Guild 1918 Congress, held in Bradford on 10 and 11 June, had rejected by 399 votes to 336 a motion entitled 'A People's Peace' which called, among other points, for immediate peace negotiations, universal disarmament, world-wide substitution of co-operation for capitalism and the founding of a people's government. Dr D. J. Fergusson, a partner in the general practice of Gardiner, Fergusson and Saward of Mount Ararat Road, was the Woolfs' doctor in Richmond.

believe to be timber at present. In addition, she broods over the war. Her own happiness, I suppose, went out very completely with Rupert's death; & I fancy she's making up her mind to a life infinitely poorer & colder than she expected.[15] If this is so, her illusion about the value of a desk in the shipping office, & her hallucination about her own driven, exhausted, harassed condition are merciful. To us, they seemed a little excessive. Its the atmosphere bred in an office as much as anything, the common attitude. She's been offered a Hall at Newnham. So we all step into the ranks of the middle aged, the responsible people, the burden bearers. It makes me a little melancholy. Failure would keep us young at any rate.

Before tea this afternoon I finished setting up the last words of Katherine's stories—68 pages.

Thursday 27 June

The echoes of the great Charleston affair may still be heard, especially in the region of the kitchen.[16] But it will be needless I hope to take action on their account any more; I wasted Tuesday afternoon writing first a violent & then a pacific letter to Nessa with my version of our Virtue & Trissie's baseness. L. took proofs meanwhile. The Labour Congress of course makes it impossible to bring that book to a close. L. was there all day yesterday, & had the sensation of Kerensky's surprise visit.[17] I still find it difficult to make head or tail of Labour party politics, or indeed

15. Rupert Brooke (1887-1915), the poet who died of blood poisoning on active service in the Aegean in April 1915, had written to Ka Cox in case of his death: 'you're about the best I can do in the way of a widow'. Their troubled relationship is described and documented in Christopher Hassall's biography *Rupert Brooke*, 1964.

16. In April Vanessa had confided to VW that she was pregnant; also that her cook Trissie Selwood was to leave in the summer to be married; she had no housemaid, and the problem of maintaining her large household at Charleston was worrying her. Deeply concerned for her sister's welfare and failing, after vigorous exertions, to secure more than unsatisfactory temporary help for her, VW proposed sending Nelly and Lottie to Charleston in July for three months, with the unavowed option that they might stay permanently. LW's reluctance to agree to this scheme, the servants' own doubts and speculations and Vanessa's increasing desperation, involved VW in time-consuming and exasperating trouble. In the end Nelly went for a short while, and Vanessa found other solutions, though her domestic situation was precarious and unsatisfactory for a considerable time to come.

17. 'That book' refers to Katherine Mansfield's *Prelude*. The 1918 Labour Party Conference was held in the Central Hall, Westminster, and LW attended on 26 and 27 June. Alexander Kerensky (1881-1970), who from July to November 1917 was Prime Minister of the provisional government of Russia until the Bolshevik revolution, attended on the 26th and was greeted by an ovation. (See *III LW*, 214.)

of any other; but with practice I suppose it wouldn't be harder than reviewing Mr Merrick. The interest in politics thrives among our friends just now. Adrian & Karin have become rebels & extremists & are seen in every gallery & meeting place. L. had to repeat the whole story twice over after dinner, first for Margaret & then for Bella. Bella is anti-Bolshevik; but the significant thing is that everyone takes some side or other. Everyone makes the state of the country his private affair.

Mrs Woolf & Herbert dined with us on Tuesday. She has, I think, the qualities of a person who has never altogether grown up, in spite of 9 children & all her cares. She gossips & enjoys herself & bursts into tears because she feels she ought to burst into tears; but she tells her memories with spirit, & somehow deals with life very freely & easily & with the liveliest, childlike interest in it all, mixed with the most absurd conventions. She chattered away about her first marriage, & how they'd travelled in Austria, & how she'd had a set of sables, & bought her trousseau at Swan & Edgars. "But Rasselas says the truth—a very fine truth" she observed. "Happiness is never perfect—I've never found perfect happiness—always something missing, Virginia,"[18] & there she was taking back a bunch of cornflowers to Bella because it was the anniversary of Dick's death. Herbert cordial, distant, & detached as usual.

At the Club yesterday I picked up the Times & read of Aunt Minna's death 2 days ago at Lane End.[19] She is buried there today. She was in her 91st year. A more composed, & outwardly useless life one can't imagine. She merely lived all that length of time, without adventures, sorrows, difficulties, doubts, actions. She was always unperturbed. I think her great quality was her good sense. She was never in any way absurd or tiresome, & if necessary she would have been a person to ask some sorts of advice from. I saw her a few weeks ago, apparently unaware of death, taking her house for 4 years further, & saying precisely what she'd said any time—about good & bad novels, about George & Margaret & how Dalingridge wasn't really good country, but of course one mustn't say so.[20] An elderly toady was with her, who had been a

18. *The History of Rasselas, Prince of Abyssinia*, a didactic romance by Samuel Johnson, published 1759.
19. Sarah Emily Duckworth (1828-1918), 'Aunt Minna', was the wealthy sister of Herbert Duckworth, VW's mother's first husband, thus not strictly an aunt of the Stephen children. She occupied herself with watercolours and family affairs, and lived in Hyde Park Gate and at what was then called a cottage but would now be regarded as a substantial house, Lane End, at Bank in the New Forest.
20. George Duckworth had married Lady Margaret Leonora Evelyn Selina Herbert (1870-1958), second daughter of the fourth Earl of Carnarvon, in 1904; they had lent their country home, Dalingridge Place, near West Hoathly in Sussex, to the Woolfs for two months in 1913 when VW was recovering from her suicidal depression.

great beauty once, & was still fine looking, & a kind woman, according
to Aunt Minna. I expect that the poor old lady was more stoical than
she let on: certainly she never seemed selfish or callous; always had her
own small affairs which gave her just as much interest as she wanted, &
she was too level headed, too clear sighted to pretend for a second to
feel more than she did or to ask for expressions of feeling. Gerald I
think she was fondest of; his change of mood troubled her a good deal.
She was very proud of George & Margaret. She thought it necessary to
tell me that at her age she couldn't ride a bicycle. I believe too much
money had always kept her more at a distance from life than was good
for her. She was a great supporter of the Duckworth family, & dies the
last of them all.

Monday 1 July

Just back from tea at the Club, laden with 2 cloths had on approval
from Souhami's.[1] L. at the League of Nations. We've talked a great deal
since I wrote last. First there was the party at the Club on Friday. I
came late & met Lytton first & then little Sanger with his name written &
pinned to his buttonhole. All sorts of people one half knew from the
papers—men with shaggy hair & great eyebrows—women cadaverous
or flamboyant—Macdonald, Huysmans, Mrs Despard, Thomas & so on.[2]
I was pitched strangely enough into the arms of Widow Creighton who
remembered me, she said. Age perhaps has toned her dogmatism. I
found her easy enough; a sincere fine old thing, her face emerging out of a
mist of flesh, & looking infinitely seamed & worn, like an immensely
old sun shining through the mists. She said middle age was happier
than youth. I was shot on again. We dined with A. & K.: a good dinner
downstairs, & then sat by their open window looking on to Parliament
Hill.[3] At 9 we went on to Ray's party—a dull affair, neither respectable

1. Joseph Souhami, importer of oriental carpets and textiles, had premises in Newman
   Street off Oxford Street, and later transferred to Princes Arcade, Piccadilly.
2. LW's diary for 28 June records: 'Club At Home to for. delegates. Large party'—
   presumably delegates to the Labour Party Conference. James Ramsay MacDonald
   (1866-1937), who in 1924 became Britain's first Labour prime minister, was treasurer
   of the Labour Party, an active leader of the ILP and the UDC, and at this time MP
   for Leicester—a seat he was to lose at the end of the year because of his unpopular
   pacifist attitude towards the war. Mrs Charlotte Despard (1844-1936), elder sister
   of Field-Marshal Viscount French of Ypres, was an heroic and distinguished
   militant suffragist and social reformer, founder of the Women's Freedom League
   and, during the war, of the Women's Peace Crusade; a member of the ILP, she
   stood (and was defeated) as Labour candidate for Battersea in December 1918.
   J. H. ('Jimmy') Thomas (1874-1949), railwayman, trade union leader and politician,
   MP for Derby 1910-36.
3. Adrian and Karin were living in Tanza Road, Hampstead.

nor bohemian, inundated with Belgians. I talked to Jack [Hills] however; very much like our version of him—emphatic, sententious, & very trusty & kind. I felt him pathetic too; so much seems to have gone wrong for him. On Saturday I went to tea with Janet—but my hand shakes so with carrying parcels that I can't write.

Tuesday 2 July

My hand shakes no longer, but my mind vibrates uncomfortably, as it always does after an incursion of visitors; unexpected, & slightly unsympathetic. One's talked nonsense; one's ashamed; they've been uncomfortable; the contact of one with the other was difficult. I was reading Macaulay's Life over my tea. (L. seeing Snowden in London) when Mrs Woolf was announced.[4] Edgar & Sylvia called in on their way through Richmond. He is a good deal nicer than she is; as I think I've recorded earlier in this book, I take her to be as near the average of her sex, class, & age as may be; given Putney as birthplace, & middle class origin & rather moderate means. The great machine turns out millions like her every year. However they are supplied with a number of ready made remarks into the bargain, so we talked away our 20 minutes,—& now they are gone. But what led him to marry her? "My dear boy" she calls him. I started folding K.M.'s story this afternoon; & went round to the printers, who will only give half a promise to have his press free tomorrow. Every conceivable obstacle is flung across our road, though we do our best to come out this next week. Influenza, which rages all over the place, has come next door.

Thursday 4 July

We had a great bout of people yesterday, as we tend to do nowadays. Mary Hutch. Clive, & Borenius. They had been seeing pictures at Sir Cook's house, & came in later, elegant, frivolous, all garrulous except Mary who scarcely speaks, wanting tea.[5] L. was printing; so I sat in

4. *The Life and Letters of Lord Macaulay* by his nephew George Otto Trevelyan was first published in 1876. Philip Snowden (1864-1937), son of a Yorkshire weaver, was at this time Socialist MP for Blackburn, national chairman of the ILP, a pacifist and champion of conscientious objectors.

5. Tancred Borenius (1885-1948), the Finnish art historian, settled in England c. 1910, and lectured at University College, London, where he was to become Professor of the History of Art, 1922-47. Sir Frederick Cook's notable private collection of old master paintings was housed at Doughty House on Richmond Hill; Borenius had catalogued the Italian pictures (*Catalogue of the Collection of Sir Frederick Cook*, vol. i (Italian Schools) 1913). Clive Bell wrote to Vanessa Bell on 10 July 1918 (CH, Camb.): 'I had arranged for [Borenius] to go before dinner, but Virginia pressed him to stay so graciously that he staid.'

the midst and we engaged in conversation. Borenius is I fancy a good-natured bore of the foreigner type. They tell long very explicit stories, launching out on them on the least provocation; but for one evening it did very well. They dined here; & again we assembled in the drawing room & talked till we could scarcely see each other. B.'s stories filled considerable space; how he'd been made a Count & other stories encroaching upon Asquiths & Cunards.[6] Clive jolly & jovial, cracking his whip & kicking up his heels; & we discussed pictures & jealousy, & derided a good many of our contemporaries. But, as usual, I enjoyed it; L. not quite so much. I took Mary Hutch. over the house; a very shy, or somehow unforthcoming woman; nice I expect, beneath such a fuss & exquisiteness of dress & get up that one has doubts whether she can be nice. She is going to write a story for us, if she can ever leave off scratching it out.

Today, Friday [5 July], L. printed off the last of Prelude, only the title page & dedication still to do. Today the printers machine is running, rather to our alarm, as he seems ignorant of it. We may have his press for £25. Very fine & hot.

Tuesday 9 July

I cant fill up the lost days, though it is safe to attribute much space in them to printing. The title page was finally done on Sunday. Now I'm in the fury of folding & stapling, so as to have all ready for glueing & sending out tomorrow & Thursday. By rights these processes should be dull; but its always possible to devise some little skill or economy, & the pleasure of profiting by them keeps one content. Yesterday we had a day off, & went, together for a wonder, to Souhami's; & I hereby make a vow to buy all draperies, covers, cloths, rugs from him in future and never again go near the Omega or the Burnet's. We have obliterated that painful staring check under a pale green & blue persian cloth—infinitely preferable. L. up in London seeing Bonwick about the dummy copy, & at 17 Club meeting. An Indian is now established in that institution perpetually playing chess. Saxon, by the way dined with us on Saturday, & supplemented this dinner by a long unnecessary intimate discussion of his feelings & health on the telephone. He doesn't get on with Nick, he says, though Barbara manages all right. I believe he takes natural pleasure in feeling himself preferred in spite of the awkwardnesses. Now to my stapling.

6. Margot Asquith, wife of the ex-Prime Minister, and Maud ('Emerald') Cunard, American wife of the wealthy Sir Bache Cunard, were celebrated hostesses whose invitations constituted a recognition of social, intellectual or artistic arrival.

Wednesday 10 July

We have sent off our first copies this evening, after spending the afternoon in glueing & covering.[7] They surprised us when done by their professional look—the stiff blue cover pleases us particularly. I must read the book through after dinner, partly to find possible faults, but also to make up my mind how much I like it as literature.

Adrian & Karin dined here last night, & he spoke to the Guild on Peace—very composed, clear, well spoken, putting on his spectacles & reading in his pleasant intellectual voice from notes. He has traces of the judicial mind & manner. The women were more stirred than usual, though their reasoning isn't very very strong; & they are of course ignorant. But they would all have peace tomorrow, on any terms, & abuse our government for leading us on after a plan of its own. When asked to join a Peace Meeting in Hyde Park on Sunday, Mrs Langston, as spokeswoman, intimated that on no account could they violate the Sabbath.[8] What a terrible grip Xtianity still has—she became rigid & bigoted at once, as if God himself had her in his grasp. That I believe is still the chief enemy—the fear of God. But I was tactful enough to keep this view dark. Karin very voluble with her advanced views, though I never see how she comes by them. One can't trace any passion.

Rain for the first time for weeks today, & a funeral next door; dead of influenza.

Friday 12 July[9]

Just back from the Club, & therefore in the restless state most safely to be appeased by writing; reading, though I've Don Juan, the Tragic Comedians, Verrall upon Meredith, Crees upon Meredith, the poems of Heredia & the poems of Laforgue to read, to say nothing of the Autobiography of Tagore, & the life of Macaulay, being out of the question before dinner.[10] Mudies, I confess, sickens me of reading: I feel disinclined

7. Ruth Elvish Mantz, *The Critical Bibliography of Katherine Mansfield*, London 1931, gives the date of publication of *Prelude* as 16 May 1918; this mistake is repeated in *The Memories of L.M.* [Ida Baker] 1971. 300 copies were printed, and the price was 3/6d.

8. This meeting on Sunday 14 July was held under the auspices of the British Workers' League.

9. VW has wrongly dated this entry *July 5th*, the week before.

10. *Don Juan* by Lord Byron, published 1819-24. VW had for review J. H. E. Crees's *George Meredith: A Study of his Works and Personality*, 1918 (see *TLS*, 25 July 1918, Kp C116); in this connection she was reading Meredith's contemporary romance *The Tragic Comedians* (1880) and Professor A. W. Verrall's essay on 'Diana of the Crossways' in his *Collected Literary Essays, Classical and Modern*, 1913. José-Maria de Hérédia (1842-1905) and Jules Laforgue (1860-1887) were French poets; Sir Rabindrath Tagore (1861-1941), the Indian poet, published his *My Reminiscences* in 1917.

even to write, what may become one of these books, so like bales of stuff upon a drapers shelves—only with out the solid merit of good wool. I stood there with the pallid & respectable & got my allowance. Great storms have been beating over England the last 3 days, the result of the Bishop's importunity, God being, as usual, spiteful in his concessions, & now threatening to ruin the harvest.[11] I owe God a grudge for his effect upon the Guild.

At the Club we met Lytton by appointment, & had tea downstairs, talking mainly of his book, & his success, & the violent attack upon him by Mrs Ward in the Lit. Sup. yesterday. She sees German brutality in his picture of Nightingale & Clough, professing to let the coarse caricature of Arnold pass. How this lights up the stuffed world of the first class railway carriage that she lives in! Lytton is getting Walter Raleigh to answer, though I think nothing short of a coronet will impress her imagination.[12] He stays this week end with the Dutchess of Marlborough, whom he met in the Cunards' box at the opera; & was fresh from Mrs Asquith. Mrs A. is of opinion that the Autobiography of Haydon is superior to the Confessions of Rousseau. She pressed upon him a copy of Hubert Crackanthorpe's works.[13] He is under no illusion so far about the brilliancy or desirability of this set as familiars, though very happy & comfortable & mellow in his success. Country Life begs him to continue the series in its pages. Lalla Vandervelde is going to act a

11. *The Times* on 9 July published a long letter from the Duke of Rutland suggesting that the bishops should instruct their clergy to read the Prayer for Rain in church since, in view of the disastrous effect of two months' drought on food crops, this appeared more urgent than the services of humiliation and intercession which they were due to conduct. The following day brought a rejoinder from a correspondent who declared that rain was already being prayed for, as few of the clergy needed to wait upon the bishops' assessment of the 'correct meteorological moment . . . to call their people to pray for those "moderate showers" which the parched fields so sorely need'.

12. Referring to the praise lavished upon *Eminent Victorians*, Mrs Humphry Ward in her letter published in the *TLS*, 11 July 1918, asked: 'Is this a moment when the same spirit of sheer brutality which we are fighting in the military field should be allowed, without resistance, . . . to penetrate the field of English letters?' Lytton Strachey had poked mild fun at Arthur Clough's devoted service to Florence Nightingale. Dr Arnold of Rugby, another of his subjects, was Mrs Ward's grandfather. Sir Walter Raleigh (1861-1922), Professor of English Literature at Oxford, and a connection by marriage, had been the most influential figure in Lytton's intellectual development before he went to Cambridge. No defence by him of *Eminent Victorians* appeared in the correspondence columns of the *TLS*.

13. Hubert Crackanthorpe (1870-96), considered a daring innovator in the field of the short story, was a contributor to the *Yellow Book*.

play of his.[14] His only anxiety is whether fame will continue. Maynard watches eager for him to be converted; but I see no chance, unless pleasure will be his doom: no, I think he's safe, & really improved, as I suppose most people are by encouragement.

Yesterday & the day before we spent glueing the book, & have now paid all our debts; so that I suppose a great many tongues are now busy with K.M. I myself find a kind of beauty about the story; a little vapourish I admit, & freely watered with some of her cheap realities; but it has the living power, the detached existence of a work of art. I shall be curious to get other opinions. L. rather gloomy now about the prospects of his Review. Thomas has taken his name off the Board, on the ground that the Trade Unions have the same end in view. This is rather cool, as L. gave them the idea. I have bet 1 shilling that all will be settled by Oct. 1st; & L. editor; & the Review in being.

Tuesday 16 July

On Saturday [13 July] we took it into our head to do a little marketing, since the book is off our hands temporarily; & so went to Kingston with a basket, but found peas & beans much the same price there as here. L. bought a vellum Grotius at a bookshop which promised better than it produced.[15]

On Sunday, a wettish cloudy day as all these days have been since the Duke of Rutland fell on his knees, we went to Staines to say goodbye to Philip who has notice to go to the front on Monday. I cant help having a good deal of sympathy with my mother in law, not only in this parting but in her general attitude to life. It is so lacking in self-consciousness; & has a natural kind of rightness & wisdom, though she never says a clever thing, & in fact says many foolish ones, & her conventions are so absurd that they scarcely count. We walked up & down a narrow lane between beds of Herbert's vegetables; & she cried; & laughed; & then gave me 2 large eggs; & ran about among all her children, very lively & haphazard, & affectionate, evidently liking this sort of miscellaneous company of sons & their wives better than anything on earth. But to give this effect I should need a chapter, & rather hope one of these days to take one.

14. *Country Life*, the illustrated weekly devoted to English country matters, architecture and decoration, was not an obvious vehicle for Lytton's craft. Lalla Vandervelde, *née* Hélène Fréderique Speyer (1870-1964), wife of the Belgian Socialist politician Emile Vandervelde, spent the war years in England, where she became a close friend of Roger Fry. Lytton had written *Quasheemaboo or The Noble Savage* for her and St John Hutchinson to perform at a charity gala.
15. This was *De Imperio Summarum Potestatum Circa Sacra* by Hugo Grotius, Amsterdam 1677. (See *Holleyman*, VS I, p. 8.)

Monday, was as usual a day for London & tea at the Club. I was so foolish as to fritter 3/—1/6 on the blue penholder with which I write, &, when I dont write suck; 1/6 on paper, at a grossly extravagant shop in Pall Mall. I justified these extravagances by the fact that you can get into the National Gallery for nothing. I spent an hour wandering there, & then came back & tried to describe my impressions to Vanessa.[16] But I see why I like pictures; its as things that stir me to describe them; but then only certain pictures do this; & I insist (for the sake of my aesthetic soul) that I don't want to read stories or emotions or anything of the kind into them; only pictures that appeal to my plastic sense of words make me want to have them for still life in my novel. But the atmosphere of picture galleries, always gloomy, is worse than ever now, when the glory of war has to be taught by a life size portrait of Lord Kitchener, & almost life size battle scenes; though as the battles are 18th century battles, one can only look upon them as scenes in a gymnasium on rather a large scale.[17] I forget now who was at the Club for tea; but one may still safely seat Alix in one chair, & dress her in green gray coat & skirt with a leather belt round her waist, & a despatch box by her side. As she's not doing work for Alix one can't tell whats in the despatch box.[18]

Tuesday was a day when I stayed at home & folded & stapled paper. A French secretary from Mr David Davies interrupted me.[19] L. makes Tuesday a kind of receptacle for shooting meetings into.

On Wednesday 17th we glued 50 copies of Prelude. So far our present supply is ample. It seems doubtful whether we shall sell more than a hundred. Clive writes a tolerant but not enthusiastic letter about it. "Doesn't set the Thames on fire, or turn his fastidious head" so he

16. In this letter (*II VW Letters*, no. 951) she expounds at some length what she calls her aesthetic views.

17. The portrait of Lord Kitchener, painted in 1890 by Sir Hubert von Herkomer and F. Goodall, was on loan from the National Portrait Gallery; the four large battle-pieces by Horace Vernet (1789-1863), representing the victories of Napoleon, had been bequeathed by Sir John Murray Scott, 1914 (NG nos. 2943, 4, 5, & 6).

18. This would make more sense if VW had written *Leonard* in place of *Alix*.

19. David Davies (1880-1944), a public-spirited Welshman who inherited enormous wealth, much of which he applied to benefactions, was Liberal MP for Montgomeryshire, 1906-29 (and later 1st Baron Davies of Llandinam); he was appointed Parliamentary Private Secretary to Lloyd George in 1916 but his critical attitude led to his dismissal after a year. He became increasingly interested and involved in plans for a League of Nations, being a proponent of the view that it must be equipped with military means to combat aggression. After the failure of the attempt to commit the League of Nations Society to endorse this principle (see above, 17 June 1918, n 10), he and others founded the League of Free Nations Association.

says.[20] Bob Trevelyan dined with us, & Adrian came in late. Bob has been through the great crisis of his life—which will find him in talk for many a day. He has escaped the army, & may now go either to France or Holland. His literary work is interrupted very seriously. He upset me so by his statement that in his absence Bessy would "live with Crompton Davies—I mean stay with him.— In fact she's there tonight to see how she likes it—" that I did nothing but laugh, at discreet intervals.[21] Leonard & Adrian joined in. He is a ridiculous figure precisely like the false Mandrill, especially now that he's bent with the rheumatic, & can only creep & crawl. He is one of our egoists; what's more he manages to be more malevolent than anyone I know, under a cover of extreme good nature. He reminds me of the man with the pointed stick, who picks up scraps of paper. So Bob collects every scrap of gossip within reach—& even stretches after those that are still beyond his reach. He told me that "he'd heard I was taking my book about to publishers", who presumably, refuse to take it. Then he lamented the failure of K.M.'s story; accepting my corrections of both statements, but so half heartedly that he'll repeat them wherever he goes. He insisted, too that he had met me at the Verralls', when he was an undergraduate in the 90ties[22]— And he rambled over a long argument about great musicians & great writers; & he praised our friends books with one breath & found rather more fault than he had given praise with the other. But his relish of all this gossip & malevolence is such that you can't grudge it him. He went off at 9.30 this morning with L. & talked all the way up in the train about his experiences before the Tribunal.

Thursday 18 July

L. spent 3 hours trying to make sense of Sir Willoughby Dickinson & the rest; & at 4 I met him in the Reading Room of the London Library. First, however, I met a milk white horse in St James' Square, wearing

20. See Clive Bell's letter from Garsington, dated 13 July 1918, MHP, Sussex.

21. Trevelyan was granted non-combatant status and was attached to a Quaker 'mission' in Paris providing books for refugees. In 1900 he had married Elisabeth (Bessy) des Amorie van der Hoeven (1874-1957), a Dutchwoman. Crompton Llewelyn Davies (1868-1935), one of Margaret's six brothers was a close friend and brother Apostle. He was Solicitor to the Post Office, but was dismissed because of his wife Moya's ardent Sinn Fein sympathies. In the event Bessy remained at their own home in Surrey during Bob's absence.

22. Arthur Woolgar Verrall (1851-1912), Fellow and lecturer of Trinity College, Cambridge, and, though primarily a classical scholar, from 1911 the first King Edward VII Professor of English Literature in the University. The Verrall and Stephen families had been on friendly terms, and it is not impossible that VW might have been seen with them while staying with her aunt Caroline Stephen, who settled in Cambridge in 1895.

an ancient Spanish saddle, mounted upon red embroidered velvet. An old men led it. No sign of advertisement was visible. Perhaps some great Duke rides abroad like this. We went on to tea at the Club—& what a tea! Two dry biscuits, so that we had to resort to cake on coming home. All the copies that we glued yesterday have gone white in the back. We dont know the cause. Richmond rang up to offer me Rupert's Life for next week. I told him that I should like to explain Rupert to the public. He agreed that there was much misunderstanding. "He was a very jolly sort of fellow"; he said. I'm trying to get letters out of James.[23]

The Germans are not succeeding this time, & the weather is windy, hot, violently wet, & sunny all in turn. We are once more getting safe through the moon.

Tuesday 23 July

I think it was on Friday that I was given my green glass jar by the chemist—for nothing! Its a jar I've always coveted; since glass is the best of all decorations, holding the light & changing it. At Lewes for round jars, the chemist asks £2.2. On Friday anyhow, Jack Hills & Pippa dined here. All went very easily & freely. Jack has weathered life with great credit, upheld so Pippa says, by his human sympathies, & turned by them in the direction of woman's suffrage, reform, education for the poor & so on, though remaining nominally a conservative. I'm somehow reminded of an excellent highly polished well seasoned brown boot by the look of him. He always seems fresh from the country. He gave us a long & very vivid account of his campaigning, from which one could easily gather his immense virtues as leader of men.[24] To my surprise too, he knows about Georgian poetry, & has read Lytton's book, & condemns the Victorians. Perhaps one was inclined to be supercilious; to confound him with George & Gerald. Pippa spent the night. She appreciates Waller immensely. We talked about the future of women next morning. She is head of a kind of exchange for finding places & training women who want work, & sees the future in those terms of course.

On Saturday [20 July] we went to Tidmarsh.[25] From the point of view

23. VW's review of *The Collected Poems of Rupert Brooke: With a Memoir* appeared in the *TLS* of 8 August 1918 (Kp C117). Brooke's close friends and contemporaries as well as VW felt that the memoir by Edward Marsh (1872-1953), a considerably older man who knew Brooke only towards the end of his life, was inevitably partial and distorted. James Strachey had been his friend both at preparatory school and at Cambridge.

24. John Waller Hills rose to the rank of Lieutenant-Colonel in the Durham Light Infantry: he had been wounded in September 1916.

25. Lytton Strachey and Carrington had been living in the Mill House since the previous Christmas. Tidmarsh is on the river Pang, which runs into the Thames at Pangbourne about a mile to the north.

of country there is nothing that we at least can say for it; though the house & garden are nice enough. The river brings such a flood of cheap humanity down to it; red villas perched everywhere; people spending the week end at Pangbourne with leather cases & fishing rods. Lytton & Carrington were alone. No servant was visible & most of the waiting seemed to be done by Carrington. She is silent, a little subdued, makes one conscious of her admiring & solicitous youth. If one were concerned for her, one might be anxious about her position—so dependent on L. & having so openly burnt the conventional boats. She is to run her risk & take her chances evidently. Lytton was fresh from the Dss of Marlborough & Dabernon, who is taking his play in hand.[26] Whatever there is in the way of London society is, I suppose now open to him. He is making his investigations not with a view to a permanent settlement; rather to round off his view of human nature. He declares he knows more different sorts of people than any of us; but we disputed this. A great deal of talk about Rupert. The book is a disgraceful sloppy sentimental rhapsody, leaving Rupert rather tarnished. Lytton very amusing, charming, benignant, & like a father to C. She kisses him & waits on him & gets good advice & some sort of protection. He came up with us on Monday, to lunch with Dabernon. Margaret dined with us. I lay on the sofa & caught only a few unintelligible phrases.

Tuesday. L. went as usual to his committees. There are difficulties about the Review. Macdonald wants to make it part of his Socialist Review.[27] Then there are difficulties about the League of Nations. Unwin is bringing out the Cooperation book, but all these movements are as difficult & as much hindered by jealousies and spites as well can be.

With this entry, V.W. finishes the book; the next (Diary V), is of similar format, the title-page inscribed:

Saturday, July 27th 1918
Hogarth House
Richmond

Saturday 27 July

As usual, this diary has skipped a day or two. But first one must pause to say that here a new volume starts, the third, & therefore there is every appearance of a long, though intermittent life. If it survives the

26. Consuelo, Duchess of Marlborough, *née* Vanderbilt, the American heiress who married the 9th Duke in 1895, and divorced him in 1920. Edgar Vincent, 16th Baronet, 1st Baron and later 1st Viscount d'Abernon (1857-1941), financier and diplomatist, became ambassador to the Republic of Germany in 1920.
27. For Ramsay MacDonald's equivocal behaviour, see *III LW*, 224-5.

summer, when the evenings are unfavourable to writing, it should flourish in the winter. Perhaps the lack of coal may kill it. We may have to live entirely at the 17 Club. But to look ahead is disastrous, considering how much has still to be recorded of time past. On Wednesday [24 July], I had one of my field days. To London, first to meet James at the Club. He was to tell me about Rupert for my article. His first words however were, "Have you heard of Ka's engagement?" "To Hilton?" I asked. "No, to Arnold Forster." This annoyed me considerably. I am glad that she should marry, though she bade fair to be a marked spinster, but marriage with W.A.F. will be merely a decorous & sympathetic alliance, making her more of a servant of the state than ever. Then, as James had a medical examination, we couldn't say much about Rupert, save that he was jealous, moody, ill-balanced, all of which I knew, but can hardly say in writing. Fredegond appeared next; I took her half way to Charing Cross. She had been having confidences from Alix, & was in the flood of affection for her. These emotions are too much in the Fisher spirit for my comfort. Her poems are soon coming out.[28] Then, having spread my rumour about Ka, which only comes through Bob, through a letter from A.F. & thus may not be true, & I hope it isn't, I went up to Gordon Sqre; where the vans were taking the furniture, Nessa in & out of the room all the time;[29] & of course Clive & Mary appeared; & then everything goes over the same little rapids. We all dined at the Mont Blanc.[30] Clive has never forgiven me—for what? I see that he is carefully following a plan in his relations with me—& resents any attempt to distract him from it. His personal remarks always seem to be founded on some reserve of grievance, which he has decided not to state openly.

"You've wrecked one of my best friendships" he remarked; "by your habit of describing facts from your own standpoint—"

"What you call God's Truth" said Nessa.

"One couldn't have an intimacy with you & anyone else at the same time— You describe people as I paint pots."

"You put things in curl, & they come out afterwards" Mary murmured from the shadow of her sympathetic silence.

Clive however had bitterness of some sort in what he said. He meant me to see that somehow I had ended our old relations—& now all

28. *Dreams and Journeys* by Fredegond Shove was published by Blackwell in 1918 as No. 21 in their "Adventurers All" series of Young Poets Unknown to Fame, 2/6d each.

29. In 1916 when Maynard Keynes had taken over the lease of 46 Gordon Square from the Bells, the latter kept some accommodation and a good deal of their furniture there; but Vanessa, in an effort to make Charleston a more permanent and comfortable home, had now decided to remove some of her furniture and household equipment from London to the country.

30. A small French restaurant in Gerrard Street, Soho.

is second best. It was clear also that he lives in dread of some alliance between Mary & me which shall threaten his position with her. He protested that to show her letters of his would be unfair, on my part or on Nessa's. She is a blank book after our much written, rewritten & scratched out torn out pages. The situation is complicated & delicate enough. He can't make up his mind to cut adrift from me altogether. But he paid for my dinner, & we wound up good temperedly. The rain pelted down, & I rushed for my train. I wish I had had the patience to write down the more intelligent parts of our talk: criticism of books & life, & not of people & feelings. But I become too critical of badly written criticism, & write so hurriedly that it would certainly be bad.

On Thursday we had a day off; in which we glued some more copies of Prelude; I think only one more order has come in. People complain that though clever & all that, the story isn't complete.

On Friday, 26th, L. went on his round of League of Nations, & Club. I to Omega for Roger's new paper, to Gordon Sqre for pictures, & then, laden intolerably, to the Club for tea.[31] By rights of importance I should remark that today L. was asked to stand for Parliament.[32] I haven't yet turned my mind that way. A natural disposition to think Parliament ridiculous routs serious thought. But perhaps it is'nt so ridiculous as speeches make one suppose. Journalists were given tea at the Club. I went upstairs, hid behind a door, & saw Mrs Hamilton for the first time, or rather heard her, holding forth like a jolly club man; for I didn't dare look.

James to dinner. He promises to send us Rupert's letters to typewrite at Asheham; but some queer Strachey intrigue is at work on the matter.

Monday 29 July

I'm paralysed by the task of describing a week end at Garsington. I suppose we spoke some million words between us; listened to a great many more, chiefly from the mouth of Mrs Hamilton, who strains at her collar like a spaniel dog, & has indeed the large hazel staring eyes of

31. Paper probably produced by Roger Fry as suitable covering for Hogarth Press books. On 15 July VW had written to Vanessa Bell (*II VW Letters*, no. 951) asking if she would lend her some more pictures; she later (8 August) wrote (no. 956) to say that she could only find 'the one in the frame' at Gordon Square. There is no knowing what this was, though it was probably one of Vanessa's own paintings.

32. LW records (*IV LW*, 33) that after the 1918 election he reluctantly agreed to become a parliamentary candidate; presumably he rejected this earlier approach, which he does not mention.

one of them. There was Gertler; Shearman & Dallas for tea;[33] Brett.
Ottoline, 3 children & Philip. The string which united everything
from first to last was Philip's attack upon Murry in The Nation for his
review of Sassoon.[34] He was half proud of himself & half uncomfortable;
at any rate, I was taxed with being on Murry's side before 10 minutes
was out; & then to prove his case Philip read Murry's article, his letter,
& his letter to Murry, three times over, so I thought, emphasising his
points, & lifting his finger to make us attend. And there was Sassoon's
letter of gratitude too. I think Ott. was a little bored. Happily the weather
was fine, the food good, & we flowed about happily enough, & without
serious boredom, which is more than one can ask of a week-end. In fact,
for some reason I was rather well content. My bed was like layer upon
layer of the most springy turf; & then the garden is almost melodramati-
cally perfect, with its grey oblong pool, & pink farm buildings, its soft
whitish grey stone & enormous smooth dense green yew hedges. Down
these paths we wandered; once or twice with Ott.; once with Mrs
Hamilton. She is a working brain worker. Hasn't a penny of her own;
& has the anxious hard working brain of a professional, earning her
living all the time. I'm not sure though that she didn't compare very
well with Ott. Some time after tea we three meandered off "to the
woods". But we never got there of course. Ott. sat upon a gate very
soon & discussed the character of Ly Margaret Sackville; & as usual
Ott. deplored & marvelled at the very characteristics which, one would
have said, she knew at first hand.[35] However, her drift is always almost
bewilderingly meandering; & I believe she often doesn't know her own
motives for taking a special line. The difficulty is that anyone listening
perceives some motive unconfessed; & this gives her talk rather a

33. Sir Montague Shearman (1857-1930), a KC and a judge, was a collector of pictures
    and a particular friend and patron to Mark Gertler; Patrick Dallas was a friend of
    both, and was at this time 'going to pieces'. See Mark Gertler: Selected Letters,
    edited by Noel Carrington, 1965, p. 162.
34. On 13 July 1918 The Nation printed a long unsigned analytical review of Counter-
    attack, and other Poems by Siegfried Sassoon (1886-1967). The writer (who was
    Middleton Murry) characterised the verses ('they are not poetry') as incoherent
    cries of torment, touching the sense rather than the imagination. The Morrells,
    warm admirers of Sassoon, were indignant and Philip Morrell wrote a splenetic
    letter in protest against such detraction of 'a gallant and distinguished author'. The
    poems were mostly written while Sassoon, an officer in the Royal Welch Fusiliers
    with the MC, was in a Scottish home for neurasthenics as a consequence of
    publishing an open letter to his commanding officer refusing to serve further in
    the army in protest against the political conduct of the war.
35. Lady Margaret Sackville (1881-1963), a daughter of the 7th Earl de la Warr, was
    a poet and a pacifist, and at this period a close friend of Ramsay MacDonald, with
    whom she had visited Garsington.

distracting wearying effect. Halfway up a hill in the sun, she stopped, leant on her parasol, looked vaguely across the landscape, & began a discourse upon love. Some wind seems to blow half her words away—another reason for finding her difficult to listen to—

"Isn't it sad that no one *really* falls in love nowadays? Its the rarest, rarest thing—I mean they dont see each other ideally. They dont feel that every word is something too wonderful just because the other has spoken it. Bertie does of course—but then his choice is so often unfortunate."

Here, chiefly in order to get us home, I said that love meant a great many different things; & that to confine it to romantic love was absurd. I also maintained that one could love groups of people, & landscapes. Unluckily this remark led Ott. to lean on her parasol once more, & look longingly at a wheatfield.

"Yes. I love that—just for itself—the curve of that wheatfield seems to me as divine as any human being. I've always been like that ever since I can remember. I love literature too—"

"I love quite absurd things—the I.L.P. for instance", said Mrs Hamilton.

At last we got moving again, & we asked the poor old ninny why, with this passion for literature, she didnt write.

"Ah, but I've no time—never any time. Besides, I have such wretched health— But the pleasure of creation, Virginia, must transcend all others."

I said it certainly did; though I think the remark ought to have been made to include Mrs Hamilton too. We trailed back through the village, where all the peasants were lounging in the road, with their pipes & their dogs & their babies. The most affable, & I'm afraid, obsequious greetings were exchanged; the dazzling appearance of Ott. & her pearls seeming to strike the agricultural labourer neither as wrong nor ridiculous, but as part of the aristocratic show that he'd paid for. No one laughed. Old ladies in black were eager to stop & talk about the hot weather. They seemed all a little excited & very anxious to please. "Very nice people, aren't they?" she said when we came in; & I daresay nothing for the next 300 years will make them otherwise.

I was taken to Gertler's studio & shown his solid 'unrelenting' teapot (to use Brett's word).[36] He is a resolute young man; & if good pictures can be made by willing them to be good, he may do wonders. No base motive could have its way with him; & for this reason I haven't great faith in him. Its too moral & intellectual an affair; or perhaps the natural gift is not abundant enough to cover his conscience & will power. He says straight out what he thinks, sits very upright; everything tight curled,

36. Inscribed: *Mark Gertler July 1918*, this oil painting is now in the Tate Gallery (no. 5835).

tense, muscular about him; his art an agony often, as he told me. But at last he understands that he wishes to paint form in the brightest colours. Form obsesses him. He sees a lamp as an imminent dominant overwhelming mass of matter. Ever since he was a child the solidity & the shapes of objects have tortured him. I advised him, for arts sake, to keep sane; to grasp, & not exaggerate, & put sheets of glass between him & his matter. This, so he said, is now his private wish. But he can think pianola music equal to hand made, since it shows the form, & the touch & the expression are nothing.

Wednesday 31 July

Arrived at Asheham. I sit as if in the open air—the drawing room providing only a shell of shade in the intense heat. The air dances over the field; & the smoke of the farm on the meadows mixes with the haze. The garden is overgrown, & the flowers crushed out. However, at this moment L. is cutting our beans for dinner.

We spent yesterday doing jobs in London. I saw a dead horse on the pavement—a literal case of what politicians call dying in harness, & rather pathetic to me—to die in Oxford Street one hot afternoon, & to have been only a van horse; & by the time I passed back again he was removed. This shows what my business was. Mudies. The Club. I loitered past jewellers windows looking for a stone to replace my sapphire lost in the train going to Garsington. Pale cracked emeralds of doubtful value tempt me greatly. Lytton & Alix at the Club—the last scene of that familiar drama. Lytton was on his way to catch a train. Alix, I suppose, never catches them. Terrible though it is to think of, she is sitting in the 17 Club at this moment—a kind of Fate, surveying the passage of moral generations. Lytton had lunch with Lord D'Abernon together with Lord Ribblesdale & a vulgar appreciative little manager, who asked to read his Chinese play & gave hopes of producing it.[37] Lytton affects to think poorly of it. I've forgotten what I think. I complimented him on the change in Carrington—he has improved her. "Ah, but the future is very dark—I *must* be free. I shall want to go off." I suggested that she might follow suit, which did not perhaps quite please him. In the street we passed Oliver & the flashing Inez;[38] & were then stopped by Kot. who wanted us to come & meet D. H. Lawrence—or perhaps to ask him here. Kot's blood shot eyes, & general sordidity

37. Lytton Strachey's 'Chinese' play *A Son of Heaven*, which he had nominally finished in 1912, was eventually produced at the Scala Theatre in 1925. Thomas Lister, 4th Baron Ribblesdale (1854-1925), Margot Asquith's brother-in-law, was a Trustee of the National and National Portrait Galleries.

38. Inez Ferguson (b. 1895), an Oxford graduate, became General Secretary of the National Federation of Women's Institutes in 1919; in 1923 she married.

struck us, in the middle of St James Square. He is a mysterious figure—not only in his occupations, but in his desire to be a friend of ours, though he seems without many friends. Anyhow, he was the last person we saw in London, since Mr Cox of the London Library doesn't count.[39]

Today the servants were off by a 7 o'clock train; & we came by Clapham, & meant to go by East Grinstead, but found places in the Lewes train after all, & got to Glynde about 2.30—not a bad journey.[40] Everyone congratulated themselves on finding room at all, after the rumours about crowds that have been put about. In my carriage we were "a family party", according to the extremely capable, friendly dogmatic Jew business man who took us in charge. These are queer meetings; so impressed on one at the time; then so rubbed out. Already I've half forgotten the soldier with the nickel knee plate & the metal arch to his foot, though he talked at the top of his voice, & boasted, & made me hate him; & I have forgotten the women with children, who drank a few drops of whiskey, & how we were all offered drinks of tea, & bites of sandwiches—& were helpful & kindly & on our best manly & womanly behaviour. We ate our lunch under some trees coming from Glynde.

Saturday 3 August

There's nothing but rustic news to record, since as we expected the Murrys have put us off. Katherine writes that she's ill.[1] I cant help guessing that she may be rather hopelessly ill. Anyhow its out of the question that she should come here. The weather hasn't held good. Yesterday was as wet a day as England often produces. Almost always the afternoon is dry in England; & so it was more or less. We went mushrooming in the evening, & got a handkerchief full. So one of our great excitements has begun again. One ripe blackberry was found at

39. Frederick James Cox (1865-1955) joined the staff of the London Library when he was sixteen and worked there until the year of his death. Installed near the entrance, he acted both as sentry and encyclopaedia.

40. On the blank page facing this day's entry is written:

    12   Vict. via E. Grinstead

    2.29

    County Garage or Slaughter

    (these were firms in Lewes from which a taxi or a fly might be hired). The London, Brighton, and South Coast Railway had alternative routes from Victoria *via* Clapham Junction to Lewes and thence to Glynde.

1. On 3 August 1918 Katherine Mansfield wrote to Lady Ottoline Morrell (who had written to her about *Prelude*): 'we are supposed to have fought our way over to Asheham to-day—hung with our own meat and butter, but I couldn't face it'. (See *The Letters of Katherine Mansfield*, 1928, vol. I, p. 207.) She had in truth been very weak and ill for some months.

the top. As I lay in the grass a hare loped past me. Perhaps we're rather pleased to be alone after all.

Better weather today, though a black sky is about the ugliest thing in nature. L. to Lewes. He went to fetch a parcel from the New Statesman which wasn't there. I round M.'s walk, & over the top. My record must be solely of beetles & butterflies. A ray of sun brings out the brown heaths in any number. Over Newhaven an airship floated, & the sky being blue for a space the sea was too. It struck me as odd to think of all the blazing blue safely burning behind the clouds; & how a ray on the earth made a different place of it. I must go and pick 'shrooms, the sun being out.

Monday 4 August

While waiting to buy a book in which to record my impressions first of Christina Rossetti, then of Byron, I had better write them here. For one thing I have hardly any money left, having bought Leconte de Lisle, in great quantities.[2] Christina has the great distinction of being a born poet, as she seems to have known very well herself. But if I were bringing a case against God she is one of the first witnesses I should call. It is melancholy reading.[3] First she starved herself of love, which meant also life; then of poetry in deference to what she thought her religion demanded. There were two good suitors. The first indeed had his peculiarities. He had a conscience. She could only marry a particular shade of Christian. He could only stay that shade for a few months at a time. Finally he developed Roman Catholicism & was lost. Worse still was the case of Mr Collins—a really delightful scholar—an unwordly recluse—a single minded worshipper of Christina, who could never be brought into the fold at all. On this account she could only visit him affectionately in his lodgings, which she did to the end of her life. Poetry was castrated too. She would set herself to do the psalms into verse; & to make all

2. Charles Leconte de Lisle (1818-1894), French poet and leader of the 'Parnassians'. Besides four volumes of poetry, he published a series of translations from classical authors, and it was possibly upon some of these that VW had spent her money. Among her books at LW's death was *Sophocle. Traduction Nouvelle par Leconte de Lisle* (*Holleyman*, VS VII, p. 4), as well as his *Iliade* and *Odyssée*, and she had a great respect for his translations from the Greek. (p.i. QB.)

3. VW must have been reading William Michael Rossetti's 1904 edition of *The Poetical Works of Christina Georgina Rossetti*, to which he added a 'compendious Memoir of her uneventful and rather secluded life'. In the subsequent passage, VW has confused the names of James Collinson (1825?-1881), the pre-Raphaelite painter, whose adherence to Roman Catholicism caused Christina Rossetti to terminate their engagement about 1850, and her second suitor, the scholar Charles Bagot Cayley (1823-83), whom she later rejected. His life in fact ended eleven years before hers.

her poetry subservient to the Christian doctrines. Consequently, as I think, she starved into austere emaciation, a very fine original gift, which only wanted licence to take to itself a far finer form than, shall we say, Mrs Browning's. She wrote very easily; in a spontaneous childlike kind of way one imagines, as is the case generally with a true gift; still undeveloped. She has the natural singing power. She thinks too. She has fancy. She could, one is profane enough to guess, have been ribald & witty. And, as a reward for all her sacrifices, she died in terror, uncertain of salvation.[4] I confess though that I have only turned her poetry over, making my way inevitably to the ones I knew already.

Wednesday 7 August

Asheham diary drains off my meticulous observations of flowers, clouds, beetles & the price of eggs; &, being alone, there is no other event to record.[5] Our tragedy has been the squashing of a caterpillar; our excitement the return of the servants from Lewes last night, laden with all L.'s war books & the English review for me, with Brailsford upon a League of Nations, & Katherine Mansfield on Bliss.[6] I threw down Bliss with the exclamation, "She's done for!" Indeed I dont see how much faith in her as woman or writer can survive that sort of story. I shall have to accept the fact, I'm afraid, that her mind is a very thin soil, laid an inch or two deep upon very barren rock. For Bliss is long enough to give her a chance of going deeper. Instead she is content with superficial smartness; & the whole conception is poor, cheap, not the vision, however imperfect, of an interesting mind. She writes badly too. And the effect was as I say, to give me an impression of her callousness & hardness as a human being. I shall read it again; but I dont suppose I shall change. She'll go on doing this sort of thing, perfectly to her & Murry's satisfaction. I'm relieved now that they didn't come. Or is it absurd to read all this criticism of her personally into a story?

Anyhow I was very glad to go on with my Byron. He has at least the male virtues. In fact, I'm amused to find how easily I can imagine the

4. Christina Rossetti died of cancer in 1894, aged 64.
5. There are daily entries in the Asheham Diary from 31 July to 6 October inclusive, with the exception of four days, 9-12 September. They are written in the laconic style of those of the previous summer (see above, 3 August to 4 October 1917) and deal of the matters VW here mentions. They are not included here as neither in style nor content do they significantly supplement the much fuller diary she was now keeping.
6. The August number of the literary monthly *English Review* (edited by Austin Harrison) contained the first publication of Katherine Mansfield's *Bliss*, and the League of Nations' Prize Essay *Foundations of Internationalism* by H. N. Brailsford.

effect he had upon women—especially upon rather stupid or uneducated women, unable to stand up to him. So many too, would wish to reclaim him. Ever since I was a child (as Gertler would say, as if it proved him a particularly remarkable person,) I've had the habit of getting full of some biography, & wanting to build up my imaginary figure of the person with every scrap of news I could find about him. During the passion, the name of Cowper or Byron or whoever it might be, seemed to start up in the most unlikely pages. And then, suddenly, the figure becomes distant & merely one of the usual dead. I'm much impressed by the extreme badness of B.'s poetry—such of it as Moore quotes with almost speechless admiration. Why did they think this Album stuff the finest fire of poetry? It reads hardly better than L.E.L. or Ella Wheeler Wilcox.[7] And they dissuaded him from doing what he knew he could do which was to write satire. He came home from the East with satires (parodies of Horace) in his bag & Childe Harold. He was persuaded that Childe Harold was the best poem ever written. But he never as a young man, believed in his poetry; a proof, in such a confident dogmatic person, that he hadn't the gift. The Wordsworths & Keats' believe in that as much as they believe in anything. In his character, I'm often reminded a little of Rupert Brooke, though this is to Rupert's disadvantage. At any rate Byron had superb force; his letters prove it. He had in many ways a very fine nature too; though as no one laughed him out of his affectations, he became more like Horace Cole than one could wish.[8] He could only be laughed at by a woman, & they worshipped instead. I haven't yet come to Lady Byron, but I suppose, instead of laughing, she merely disapproved. And so he became Byronic.

Friday 8 August

In the absence of human interest, which makes us peaceful & content, one may as well go on with Byron. Having indicated that I am ready, after a century, to fall in love with him, I suppose my judgment of Don Juan may be partial. It is the most readable poem of its length ever

7. VW was probably reading *The Life and Letters of Lord Byron* by Thomas Moore in the 'new and complete edition' published by John Murray in 1866, of which Leslie Stephen's copy, inscribed by him 'Windermere Station, May 11th 1871' she rebacked and recovered herself. (Property of QB.) Letitia Elizabeth Landon— 'L. E. L.' (1802-38), and the American Ella Wheeler Wilcox (1850-1919) were both poets of considerable natural gifts and facility who enjoyed enormous popular success.

8. (William) Horace de Vere Cole (1881-1936), a picturesque figure educated at Eton and Trinity College, Cambridge, who had been much in evidence as a friend of Adrian's when he and VW lived at Fitzroy Square. Cole was the ringleader in the 'Dreadnought Hoax' and other elaborate practical jokes.

written, I suppose; a quality which it owes in part to the springy random haphazard galloping nature of its method. This method is a discovery by itself. Its what one has looked for in vain—a[n] elastic shape which will hold whatever you choose to put into it. Thus he could write out his mood as it came to him; he could say whatever came into his head. He wasn't committed to be poetical; & thus escaped his evil genius of the false romantic & imaginative. When he is serious he is sincere; & he can impinge upon any subject he likes. He writes 16 canto's without once flogging his flanks. He had, evidently, the able witty mind of what my father Sir Leslie would have called a thoroughly masculine nature. I maintain that these illicit kind of books are far more interesting than the proper books which respect illusions devoutly all the time. Still, it doesn't seem an easy example to follow; & indeed like all free & easy things, only the skilled & mature really bring them off successfully. But Byron was full of ideas—a quality that gives his verse a toughness, & drives me to little excursions over the surrounding landscape or room in the middle of my reading. And tonight I shall have the pleasure of finishing him—though why, considering that I've enjoyed almost every stanza, this should be a pleasure I really dont know. But so it always is, whether the books a good book or a bad book. Maynard Keynes admitted in the same way that he always cuts off the advertisements at the end with one hand while he's reading, so as to know exactly how much he has to get through.

Everyone so far has failed us: Katherine ill: Ka & Will A.F. obliged to work next Sunday; so, in a wild desire to couple Bonwick with someone who will mitigate his tedium, we've wired both to Marjorie Strachey & Mrs Hamilton. Rather wickedly I dwelt to Marjorie, upon the fair hair of B. but she has drawn it upon herself by her confession, or rather statement, that she intends to marry.

Monday 12 August

(I believe this is near about the anniversary of our wedding day, 6 years ago) [10 August 1912]. Bonwick came; but Marjorie & Mrs Hamilton only sent telegrams. Being a man of business he made the most of his holiday, & came toiling up the hill to find us, where we were picking blackberries. A straight commonplace rigid kind of man; impervious to anything at all different from the usual. Going down the hill he told us that he spent a fifth of his income on Prisoners of War, in order to justify his exemption as a C.O. Our talk was almost wholly about The Nation. It was his only topic. The poor man has a strong Cockney accent; a persevering aspiring selfsatisfied mind, making great play with his literary connections, & pretending to be the most important part of "We" when he speaks, as he always does, of the Nation. To tell the truth, I got my first inkling of the lure of gold through hearing him talk. He gave out that he deals in hundreds & thousands. They are Rowntree's hundreds & thousands, but Mr B. has the easy powerful air of one who deals in them. "Rowntree asked me if the Nation could afford it (1000 a year) & I said yes. So he did it— Yes, we pay our writers increased rates now. Hobson chanced to say that he had never made so little by the Nation, so I told Rowntree the fees ought to be raised." I imagine him sitting at a desk in an ante room & opening the door for people who want to see Massingham. He told us that Mrs Phillimore has been offered £500 for a book of her religious sketches.[9] He told us lots of gossip. how Edward Garnett was turned out; & how they got scores of letters against Roger's articles; & madmen write to them "I am the son of God". But I was more impressed by his commercial bearing than by his anecdotes. He told them a little as if he were superior to all these literary people—(but I confess that the mosquitoes are biting my toes, & a moth is dropping perpetually from the lamp, so that I can't remember all the things I meant to say about Mr Bonwick. Leonard is staying with him at "my place" near Croydon tonight, & goes tomorrow to York to see Rowntree. L. declares that the profound psychologist would find B. chiefly remarkable for a complete lack of humour.

Friday 16 August

My visit to Charleston & L.'s to York are both partly responsible for this skip. But I've skipped too much to give a very full account of one or of the other. Bonwick's villa precisely expresses Bonwick: & a stuffy smell thrown in; windows curtained in thick white; pictures of Niagara. They spent 17 hours in travelling to York & back; & the result, still to await another meeting of Trustees, though Bonwick is sure they mean to agree. The Labour people are to be dropped. My visit to Charleston was spent mostly in sitting in the drawing[room] & talking to N. while she made herself a small brown coat. Duncan wandered in & out; sometimes digging a vegetable bed, sometimes painting a watercolour of bedroom china, pinned to a door. In the evening there was the lumpish Bunny, inclined to be surly; & N. inclined to take him up sharply. What did we discuss? There was Ka's engagement, concerning which Duncan had a good deal to say; one of his statements being that A.-F. is 45, & always has been. Another is that he lent to certain affections & practised them in an Italian villa. I made out a description of Garsington.

9. Henry William Massingham (1860-1924), journalist, from 1907 to 1923 editor of the Liberal weekly *The Nation* owned by the Rowntree Trust, of which Bonwick was business manager. Mrs Phillimore was probably Lucy ('Lion'), wife of the Hon. R. C. Phillimore, who was to publish several books of a religious cast.

The hunger of poor Ottoline for some recognition in Sussex is proved by her offering herself for *any* day in the summer after July 8th. She was abruptly told that none suited—which explains her eagerness to insert her foot here. Then we discussed the A[drian]. S[tephen]'s: he a dead weight, & she a live one, according to N. who warns me we shall repent of asking them here—this in front of Duncan too, who said nothing to contradict. So our relationships change, imperceptibly enough. When N. & I were alone, I supposed we discussed the two parrokeets & money, which is not any longer such a distant, speculative sort of commodity as it used to be—at least to her. We discussed the children too; the sort of talk that runs on when one knows all the facts, but wishes to ascertain how they've changed position— What for instance is Lytton's view of Mrs Asquith; & hers of him; & Maynard's of them both. Gertler's notions of painting: his views of *their* painting; Duncan's fame: Bunny's socialism. Bunny thus defines his position: all capitalists are wrong; therefore for him to live upon Vanessa is good, inasmuch as she enjoys money that she has no right to, & could not possibly spend her interest better than by maintaining him. This evolved from a sentimental declaration by him that he ought to spend his life in giving honey to his friends for nothing. His brain must be a tangle of sentiments & half-realised socialism. I bicycled back on Wednesday & found L. & we were very happy, until it came to the fat bacon—when, alas—!

Monday 19 August

Its possible that we may have solved the problem of having visitors—not to see them. At this moment A. & K. are in the house, as an occasional sound from the drawing room proves. But we only meet at meals; so that it is possible to think of things to say in the intervals. I find that deafness imposes itself upon the mind as well as the voice; it frightens away the quicker shyer deeper thoughts so that all the talk that reaches a deaf person must be of the same hearty, plain, matter of fact kind. Try as one will, one can't do otherwise. Carrington came for the weekend.[10] She is the easiest of visitors as she never stops doing things—pumping, scything, or walking. I suspect part of this is intentional activity, lest she should bore; but it has its advantages. After trudging out here, she trudged to Charleston, & only came in at eleven last night, just as we were shutting the windows. Poor lugubrious Bunny escorted her, protesting that a 10 mile walk was nothing compared to the joy of having some one to talk to. She trudged off again this morning to pack Lytton's box or buy him a hair brush in London—a sturdy figure, dressed in a

10. Carrington came to stay with the Woolfs from Saturday to Monday; Adrian and Karin Stephen, for whom VW had found temporary lodging near by, moved in to the house as she departed.

print dress, made after the pattern of one in a John picture;[11] a thick mop of golden red hair, & a fat decided clever face, with staring bright blue eyes. The whole just misses, but decidedly misses what might be vulgarity. She seems to be an artist—*seems*, I say, for in our circle the current that way is enough to sweep people with no more art in them than Barbara in that direction. Still, I think Carrington cares for it genuinely, partly because of her way of looking at pictures.

I finished by the way The Electra of Sophocles, which has been dragging on down here, though it's not so fearfully difficult after all. The thing that always impresses me fresh is the superb nature of the story. It seems hardly possible *not* to make a good play of it. This perhaps is the result of having traditional plots which have been made & improved & freed from superfluities by the polish of innumerable actors & authors & critics, till it becomes like a lump of glass worn smooth in the sea. Also, if everyone in the audience knows beforehand what is going to happen, much finer & subtler touches will tell, & words can be spared. At anyrate my feeling always is that one can't read too carefully, or attach enough weight to every line & hint; & that the apparent bareness is only on the surface. There does, however, remain the question of reading the wrong emotions into the text. I am generally humiliated to find how much Jebb is able to see;[12] my only doubt is whether he doesn't see too much—as I think one might do with a bad modern English play if one set to work. Finally, the particular charm of Greek remains as strong & as difficult to account for as ever. One feels the immeasurable difference between the text & the translation with the first words. The heroic woman is much the same in Greece & England. She is of the type of Emily Brontë.[13] Clytaemnestra & Electra are clearly mother & daughter, & therefore should have some sympathy, though perhaps sympathy gone wrong breeds the fiercest hate. E. is the type of woman who upholds the family above everything; the father. She has more veneration for tradition than the sons of the house; feels herself born of the father's side, & not of the mother's. Its strange to notice how, although the conventions are perfectly false & ridiculous, they never appear petty or undignified, as our English conventions are

11. Augustus John (1878-1961), celebrated as Bohemian and painter; his characteristic women models wore dresses with close-fitting bodice and sleeves and full-length gathered skirts.
12. Sir Richard Claverhouse Jebb (1841-1905), the Greek scholar, whose chief work was his edition of Sophocles which, in addition to the Greek text, has a translation into English prose, critical notes, and a commentary. His volume on *Electra* was published in 1894.
13. Emily Brontë (1818-48), poet and author of *Wuthering Heights*, who combined a passionate and visionary spirit with an uncompromising independence of character.

constantly made to do. Electra lived a far more hedged in life than the women of the mid Victorian age, but this has no effect upon her, except in making her harsh & splendid. She could not go out for a walk alone; with us it would be a case of a maid & a hansom cab.

Saturday 24 August

I had to look carefully before I wrote Saturday; stranger still one won't know that its Sunday tomorrow, I suppose. If I weren't too lazy I think I should try to describe the country; but then I shouldn't get it right. I shouldn't bring back to my own eyes the look of all those old beautiful very worn carpets which are spread over the lower slopes of the hills; nor should I convey the look of clouded emerald which the downs wear, the semi-transparent look, as the sun & shadows change, & the green becomes now vivid now opaque. However I confess that I shirk almost equally the task which has accumulated for 7 days of describing our visitors. They are with us for another week, so I need not try to hit them this very moment. Bridge has broken down the partition between our sitting rooms. L. is playing at this moment, 5.40, binding himself to stop at 6; but it is doubtful if he will. I hesitate a little to write evil of my guests, nor do I think evil—exactly. I refer, in rather crablike fashion, to something coarse, material, insensitive about Karin. One would never find much interest in her; though nothing despicable or mean. No: but she's a capable American, who will get all that can be had for the asking; & nothing that can't.[14] I have a theory that if one sense fails another does double work; she eats enormously. She has no concealed vices. Would she be more interesting if she had? She is not stupid; or dull; or trivial; on the contrary she is bright, capable & stirring: stirring Adrian to read books upon economics, & even stirring him to learn shorthand which according to her is useful in a literary career. She intends him to have a career. At any rate she is going to ask for that, too; for certainly Adrian will never ask for anything for himself. Yet (I confess it is "yet" to me) he is happy; gives one the sense of being well provided for, as he provides her with good manners, good looks, & good taste. I feel myself frightfully superior, so refined as to be almost apologetic to Leonard; so full of fine feelings, sub[t]le perceptions, intellectual tastes & the rest that I almost blush to sit here alone, writing or reading Milton. She informs me that I with my tastes would have much

14. Karin's maternal grandparents (Pearsall Smiths) were American Quakers who settled in England; her father was Anglo-Irish and a Catholic; after her mother left him to live with Bernhard Berenson (whom she later married), Karin and her sister Rachel remained under the care of the American grandmother. They both made an extended visit to the United States with the Berensons in 1908, and attended Bryn Mawr.

in common with Hope Mirrlees; "with my tastes" indeed![15] This account emphasises our points of difference; outwardly we are all good friends, talkative & in agreement, & not relying on gossip merely to despatch dinner with. We talk about the Labour party, & politics, & anarchy, & government. She understands an argument, deals with an article manfully — And in her way she's a nice honest creature, not so sure of herself when it comes to taste; & knowing it too—though taste has led her, alas, to embroider a pair of shoes which A. obediently wears. I must leave what I have to say about Milton, the German prisoners, life, & other subjects for next time.

Tuesday 27 August

Now I confess that I have half forgotten what I meant to say about the German prisoners; Milton & life. I think it was that ? (all I can remember now (Friday, Aug. 30th) is that the existence of life in another human being is as difficult to realise as a play of Shakespeare when the book is shut. This occurred to me when I saw Adrian talking to the tall German prisoner. By rights they should have been killing each other. The reason why it is easy to kill another person must be that one's imagination is too sluggish to conceive what his life means to him—the infinite possibilities of a succession of days which are furled in him, & have already been spent. However, I forget how this was to go on. The prisoner, who looks very lean & hopeless, seemed to like talking; I met him later & we smiled, but the sentry was not there.

Here we are almost at the end of August, & finishing off A. & K.'s visit. They go to Charleston tomorrow. Its odd how in a visit of this kind one wears through different stages. My stages are on the whole nearer to warmth & liking than to irritation; though there is an element of criticism in our relationship, based partly on K.'s manners, appetite & appearance. Which last, poor woman, she can't altogether help; still there seems no need to emphasise the natural process by an orange dressing gown, held in by a broad band.[16] Her appetite is frankly a schoolboy's. "What beef!" she exclaimed today. "Dont you feel elated at the sight of good meat?" Meals add a sort of romance to her life such as I in [my] way get, shall we say, from the post or the newspapers. I can imagine Karin, for instance, thinking with a little thrill that next day is the day for salt beef; as I think perhaps I shall get my book from the Times, or an interesting letter. L. on the other hand, is irritated, & being irritated

15. (Helen) Hope Mirrlees (b. 1887), after relinquishing theatrical ambitions, studied classics at Newnham College, Cambridge, where she was contemporary with Karin, with whom she also studied French in Paris.
16. Karin was six months pregnant. Her first daughter Ann had been born in January 1916.

by superficial disagreeables finds deeper causes for them than I altogether agree with. Our usual method is to begin "Why did Adrian marry her?" Then I say "I can quite understand it—she has energy" & so on. Then L. says "I'd a thousand times rather have married Ka—In fact I'd rather have married any one in the whole world. I couldn't sit in the same room with her." Still, I do see why Adrian married her. First & foremost she makes him like other people. He has always, I believe, a kind of suspicion that whereas other people are professionals, he remains an amateur. She provides him with household, children, bills, daily life, so that to all appearances he is just like other people. I believe he needs constant reassurance on this point; & takes constant delight in her substantiality. Yes, one wants to be found doing the ordinary things when one's friends call. I too have this feeling to some extent. I suppose indeed that I share many of A.'s feelings. A feeling comes over me when I am with him that instead of being comfortably obtuse we are crepuscular to each other; & thus, among other things, fearfully shy when we are alone. With other people in the room we get on much better. We had a walk to the post marked by those cloggings of the wheels, which are so discomfiting; nothing seems possible; then with an odious jerk one jars on again. This was better managed than of old. He lost his diffidence & air of hearing himself talk when he told me about Karin; how deaf she is, & how depressed she gets, & how she thinks that people won't talk loud on purpose, & thus dislikes all Stracheys & others of the low voiced mumbling family. He is very proud of her vitality. I suppose it provides him with a good deal of the stuff of life, which he does not provide for himself.

Yesterday, 22nd, I bicycled to Charleston, lunched, & came home in the evening.[17] It was the first autumn day, warm, softly blue, & blurred with haze. Duncan spent the night before with us. He stumbled along until, by means which he only knows the secret of, he had us all laughing until the tears came. His chief effort was a description of Lady Strachey reading aloud Laurence Housman's The Dying ploughboy speaks from the Grave—[18]

"I hear the bells jingling, & I lie in my mothers bed. The finest poem in the language too." Then we discussed the bursting of people's bladders, the National Gallery, incest, perhaps, & other gossip. All sitting in the

---

17. VW has confused the date of two successive Thursdays: it was on 29 August that she went to Charleston.

18. Probably Duncan Grant's garbled version of 'Blind Love' by Laurence Housman (1865-1959), published in *The Heart of Peace and other Poems*, 1918.

> '. . . There's a grumble of guns on the hill, lass;
> But under it, where I lie,
> The ground of my grave is still, lass;
> And stiller beneath am I.' Etc.

drawing room, until it grew too dark to see. We have lamps almost at dinner; but not quite. I gossiped with Nessa. A new plan is on foot to supply her with Liz for a cook. Trissie is going—but never again into service. She is one of the transition cases—the servant not yet turned lady, but past servanthood.[19] Karin & A. have gone into Brighton to see a specialist about her ear.

Tuesday 3 September

Pernel came on Saturday;[1] & her coming was to have coincided precisely with the Stephens' going; but there was a hitch here; as the fly refused to take them, & thus we enjoyed another meal with Karin. I regret to say though that either nature's protests or our mute ones have diminished her appetite, so that she was no longer a show piece for a visitor. She announced her intention of being wheeled to Charleston on Adrian's bicycle; which considering her shortness, breadth & great pillar like legs, produced a comic picture, & so I think Adrian judged it, for he dissuaded her from mounting till they were at the bottom of the drive.

I think the best way to sum up the impression of Pernel is to quote our simultaneous exclamation on going to bed on Saturday night "What a relief to talk to a human being!" Part of the relief, of course, is the effect of her good ears; but beyond this she is sub[t]le, finely graded, with fine shades of understanding & perception which are not, after all, entirely a matter of ears. I suppose if Karin were witness in her own behalf she might point to a certain faintness, remoteness, & donnishness in Pernel; she does perhaps survey life through a tinted shade, but her eyes are good ones, & she is too sensible, humorous, & indolent to have taken the shape of a professor, or indeed to believe very heartily in Newnham or education or anything but books & ideas & poetry & so on. A more unambitious person does not live; but she has not the dulness & flatness which generally exist in these self effacing unselfish old maids. I wonder what we talked about? Partly about Hope Mirrlees, whom we've asked to write us a story; & Jane, & Lady Strachey, & writing novels, & food.[2] Last night, L. read Hardy's poems aloud. The night

19. In September Trissie Selwood married Gerald Stacey, a son of Vanessa's landlord, a prominent local farmer.

1. (Joan) Pernel Strachey (1876-1951), the fourth of the five daughters of Sir Richard and Lady Strachey; she was Vice-Principal of Newnham College, Cambridge and, from 1923 to 1941, its Principal.

2. Jane Ellen Harrison (1850-1928), Greek scholar and Lecturer in Classical Archaeology at Newnham College, Cambridge from 1898. Hope Mirrlees became her 'ghostly daughter' in her old age, and they lived in Paris and London together after Jane Harrison left Cambridge in 1922. See her *Reminiscences of a Student's Life*, published by the Hogarth Press in 1925.

before we discussed complexes. Then it turned out that she had been to a lecture upon potato blight. I should never be surprised to find that she knows everything about Turbines or Bees: everything that can be learnt from books that is. She lacks the ambition, perhaps the power, to handle the things themselves. Here Karin again has a plea to be considered. I suppose she has done more things than Pernel. The weather was very windy, but the mushrooms have come again. She was rather unable to see them; & I suspect she mooned rather than looked about her. She always arrives here provided with two shilling books with bright covers one to read coming, the other going. During the week end she always reads one classic & one nonsense biography, such as Lady Jeune.[3] I suppose however that she is in her quiet dreamy way obstinately conscientious, & something of a martinet towards herself.

"Nothing would ever induce me to marry" she said, with the utmost conviction. Indeed I should fancy that her bachelor life, with many women friends, & a great many books, & lectures to prepare on French literature suit her perfectly.

This is written on the return from our great Brighton treat. Everything succeeded. L. foretold a wet day by the light on our shutters, but on opening them we found a perfect September morning. The sun is thinner but very clear, & the air sparkling, now that we are past August. The colours are being burnished on the trees too. The shadows seem lighter & paler. No one could confuse the 3rd of September with the 31st August. A perfect treat must include a visit to the 2nd hand bookshops. (I bought the life of Col. Hutchinson);[4] sweets (we found chocolate unlimited) lunch at Mutton's; the band on the pier; some human grotesques; tea at Booth's; Buns at Cowley's;[5] a trail past shops with many temptations to buy, for the most part resisted; & a debauch at some stationer; & so home, to find the downs & this house lovelier than ever. All these things we did; & we had too a feeling of lightness because of the villages won in France. Queant & Lens are taken, as we learnt from a shop window. Can't one see the curtain lifting, very slightly, & some promise of a world of food & so on beyond? I couldn't help thinking that the sight of an English gentleman walking the stubble after partridges with his sons & his retriever was a foretaste of better days.

3. *Memories of Fifty Years*, 1909, by Lady (Mary) St Helier, who before her husband was created 1st Baron St Helier just prior to his death in 1905, had published under the name (Lady) Mary Jeune.

4. *Memoirs of the Life of Colonel Hutchinson . . . by his widow Lucy*, first published in 1806 and often reprinted. John Hutchinson (1625-64), as MP for Nottinghamshire, was one of Charles I's judges and signed his death-warrant in 1649.

5. Mutton's Restaurant on the sea front, Cowley's bakery in Pool Valley and Booth's in East Street were all within a short radius of the pier. LW knew them from his preparatory-schooldays (see *I LW*, 70).

SEPTEMBER 1918

Sunday 8 September

At anyrate today I am the wife of an Editor. Leonard got a letter from Bonwick to tell him that he is to get his first number out in January. He wants to know what office accommodation L. will require. It is, I think, a great triumph to have steered through the shoals of MacDonald, Trades Unions, Rowntrees, Bonwicks & all the rest.[6] The idea is very amusing & stimulating too. I like playing with imaginary offices, & sheets of notepaper, & little boys with buttons, & myself walking up the steps to take a cup of tea, & surveying the Strand from the window. Perhaps there'll be a shake down bed in the corner. Then Miss Matthaei in her little stall, & long galley proofs: distinguished foreign visitors; telegrams from distant capitals; general importance & glory; everything a solid improving success; yes, a very nice prospect even on its picturesque side, which I admit is the one most perceptible to me. At the same time we had a letter from Hoper offering to let us have Asheham on a yearly tenancy, in case he may ever want the house—but theres no present prospect of this. We feel fairly safe again. Ka, another letter says, is to be married at 11 tomorrow. I can't help reading into her letter a sort of protest as to the merits of Will, & her love for him. Yet even so, I own that when I think of her I see her as a rounder warmer more complete person than she was single. I suppose I had got into the habit of seeing her faithful solitary lonely till the end of time; I like happiness too well to be very fastidious about the husband.

What has happened this last week—following upon the superb success of Brighton? For one thing the weather has been so tremendously generous, giving us after a veil of morning mist, such an endowment of sun & such clouds of alabaster firmly laid against the blue, that even people like—shall I say Melian Stawell?—must have felt jovial & random & unencumbered with high moralities.[7] Or are they always bothering how to share the sunshine? I remember lying on the side of a hollow, waiting for L. to come & mushroom, & seeing a red hare loping up the side & thinking suddenly "This is Earth life". I seemed to see how earthy it all was, & I myself an evolved kind of hare; as if a moon-visitor saw me.[8]

6. LW's own account of the preliminaries to his becoming editor of the *International Review* is in *III LW*, 223-6. The editorial offices were to be in Red Lion Court, Fleet Street (a continuation of the Strand); Miss Matthaei (see above, 9 April 1918, n 14) was to be assistant editor.

7. Florence Melian Stawell (1869-1936), sometime classical scholar of and lecturer at Newnham College, Cambridge; she was closely connected with the Society for Psychical Research. A friend of G. L. Dickinson and Roger Fry, she was described as 'lovely in person and mind'.

8. Perhaps an association with a Stephen family story of a young painter's spectacular success, which he could never repeat, with his 'Earth Rise from the Moon'.

A good life it is, at such moments; but I can't recapture the queer impression I had of its being earth life seen from the moon.

Yesterday poor Bunny came for the night, bringing 8 combs of honey, for which he charges 2/6 each. How we were robbed at Brighton! 3/- for a mixture of milk & saccarine. Poor old Bunny! He is as if caked with earth, stiff as a clod; you can almost see the docks & nettles sprouting from his mind; his sentences creak with rust. He can only lay hands on the simplest words. I suppose his vocabulary is now surpassed by Mrs Attfield & equalled by Fred. However, by dint of kindly treatment we softened him; & I must confess that for 20 hours we did very well. We wanted to know about mushrooms; & upon all funguses he is an authority; indeed he discovered one of the smallest for the first time. Then he could tell us about the agricultural labourers' Union, which is being half secretly organised even among our Freds & Wills. He has a humanity which is not all theoretical, though he will insist upon breaking his brains over possible Labour parties. He talks to the German prisoners, who are social democrats, only fought because they would be shot for refusing, & consider the whole war a device of the artistocracy. Bunny looks forward to a democratic future. I sacrificed half my morning & sat with him hemming handkerchiefs. As an example of his uncouth absurdity which one can't help liking he described to me a scene with Hope Mirrlees in Paris. He was furious—the creature is a most enthusiastic friend—because Lawrence's novel was reported burnt. Hope was staying in the same hotel. He burst out to her upon the iniquity of burning books. They had never met before. She was so much of his way of thinking that he exclaimed "You darling!"—& offended her—although, as he explained, he was on the far side of the room, & used the word 'darling' in its other sense. I suppose he never had a rich vocabulary. Anyhow, Hope hinted that he ought to be in the army. Bunny could see nothing wrong or odd in calling a young woman "you darling!"[9]

"Virginia, he said, intimately, I want to ask you to give me a photograph of—Alix." He had one in mind, which I was forced to give him, to muse over, as I can fancy, by the hour, in his half sentimental simple good hearted way, while he ploughs Mr Hext's fields with the motor plough. But I was interested by his story of the attempted rescue of Sovercar, an Indian.[10] Bunny appeared like the manly, serious, romantic hero of a Meredith novel.

9. In November 1915, when over 1000 copies of his friend D. H. Lawrence's *The Rainbow* were seized by the police and condemned to be destroyed, Bunny Garnett was staying in an attic room at the Hôtel de l'Elysée, rue de Beaune, hoping to start work at the Institut Pasteur. Jane Harrison and Hope Mirrlees were in Paris to learn Russian. See David Garnett, *The Flowers of the Forest*, 1955, pp. 94-98.

10. Mr Hecks of New House Farm, near Firle, employed both Bunny Garnett and Duncan Grant. The story of Vinayak Damodar Savarkar is related in the first volume of Garnett's autobiography, *The Golden Echo*, 1953, chapter VII.

Tuesday 10 September

I spend the first five minutes with this book before me trying to fish two drowned flies out of my ink pot on the tip of my pen; but I begin to see that this is one of those undertakings which are quite impossible —absolutely impossible. Not Darwin or Plato could do it with the tip of my pen. And now the flies are increasing & dissolving; today there are three. At Asheham I naturally bethink me of Darwin & Plato; but in this I am not singular. My intellectual snobbishness was chastened this morning by hearing from Janet that she reads Don Quixote & Paradise Lost, & her sister Lucretius in the evenings. I thought that no one in Sussex was reading Paradise Lost at this moment. Janet holds the characteristic view that Don Quixote is more humorous than Shakespeare. The coarseness of Shre I can see would distress her; she would deal with it intellectually. All her generation use their brains too scrupulously upon books, seeking meaning rather than letting themselves run on for pleasure, which is more or less my way, & thus naturally richest & best. Margaret is said to be not so well. I'm inclined to be hard hearted, as I expect to learn to my cost one of these days—about elderly ailments in general & Margaret's in particular. She seems to me to live in an atmosphere where cold feet are more important than bronchitis elsewhere—part of the romance of life, as food is to Karin & reviewing books is to me. And then what an attentive solicitous echo is provided by Lilian & Janet! Margaret dominates, & they taking pleasure in unselfishness, lavish sympathy & somehow make out a different scale of health for M. than for the rest of the world—but this is a little fantastic, & rises partly from the thought that I would, if I were kind, write a long affectionate amusing letter to M. I am deterred from doing this by my prejudice against the patronage of the elderly. I want neither to be patronised, nor to patronise; & I feel that the sort of letter one writes on these occasions is an act of kindness, & so neither to be offered nor received. Inevitably the social worker approaches the non-social worker with a view to getting what they can give & very slightly disparaging the giver, who can be nothing better than a giver of amusement. Boredom is the legitimate kingdom of the philanthropic. They rule in the metropolis.

Though I am not the only person in Sussex who reads Milton, I mean to write down my impressions of Paradise Lost while I am about it. Impressions fairly well describes the sort of thing left in my mind. I have left many riddles unread. I have slipped on too easily to taste the full flavour. However I see, & agree to some extent in believing, that this full flavour is the reward of highest scholarship. I am struck by the extreme difference between this poem & any other. It lies, I think, in the sublime aloofness & impersonality of the emotions. I have never read Cowper on the Sofa, but I can imagine that the sofa is a degraded substitute for Paradise Lost.[11] The substance of Milton is all made of wonderful, beautiful, & masterly descriptions of angels bodies, battles, flights, dwelling places. He deals in horror & immensity & squalor & sublimity, but never in the passions of the human heart. Has any great poem ever let in so little light upon ones own joys & sorrows? I get no help in judging life; I scarcely feel that Milton lived or knew men & women; except for the peevish personalities about marriage & the woman's duties. He was the first of the masculinists; but his disparagement rises from his own ill luck, & seems even a spiteful last word in his domestic quarrels. But how smooth, strong & elaborate it all is! What poetry! I can conceive that even Shakespeare after this would seem a little troubled, personal, hot & imperfect. I can conceive that this is the essence, of which almost all other poetry is the dilution. The inexpressible fineness of the style, in which shade after shade is perceptible, would alone keep one gazing in to, long after the surface business in progress has been despatched. Deep down one catches still further combinations, rejections, felicities, & masteries. Moreover, though there is nothing like Lady Macbeth's terror or Hamlet's cry, no pity or sympathy or intuition, the figures are majestic; in them is summed up much of what men thought of our place in the universe, of our duty to God, our religion.

Wednesday 18 September

I have let the first freshness of the Webbs fade from my mirror; but let me bethink me of another metaphor which they imposed upon me, towards the end of Sunday. I was exalted above a waste of almost waveless sea, palish grey, & dented with darker shadows for the small irregularities, the little ripples which represented character & life love & genius & happiness. But "I" was not exalted; "I" was practically non-existent. This was the result of a talk with Mrs Webb. In truth though they deserve more careful handling. I wonder how I can recapture the curious discomfort of soul which Mrs Webb produces each time I see her again? In the intervals one forgets; in a second it comes over one again. There's something absolutely unadorned & impersonal about her. She makes one feel insignificant, & a little out of key. She represses warmth or personality.

11. Book I of *The Task*, the poem in blank verse published in 1785 by William Cowper (1731-1800), was entitled 'The Sofa' and begins:

'I sing the Sofa. I who lately sang
Truth, Hope and Charity, and touch'd with awe
The solemn chords . . . .
Now seek repose upon an humbler theme.'

A copy of an edition of 1817, with a label by VW, was among the Woolfs' books at LW's death (see *Holleyman*, MH VII, p. 3).

She has no welcome for one's individuality. She divines a little what one's natural proclivities are, & she irradiates them with her bright electric torch.

It was a pouring wet day, on Saturday; not a day for geniality. Webb however has some coat to shake; she is as bare as a bone. We sat down to tea, without George Young. They eat quickly & efficiently & leave me with hunks of cake on my hands. After tea we were soon disposing of our topics, & I began to feel nervous, lest our cupboards should be bare. Then G. Young appeared, having like all Youngs, rejoiced in his battle with distance & wet. Liked the walk, he said.[12] While he changed Mrs Webb rapidly gave me her reasons for saying that she had never met a great man, or woman either. At most, she said, they possessed remarkable single qualities, but looked at as a whole there was no greatness in them. Shakespeare she did not appreciate, because a sister, who was a foolish woman, always quoted him wrong to her as a child. Goethe might conceivably have been a great man. Then, this having been dealt with, down came L. & G. Young & they all pounced together upon some spot of interest floating far out beyond my ken. I think it was to do with the General Election & the views of the private soldiers. Young came provided with facts, but I rather think these did not stand much investigation. He is a slow, stiff, kindly man, with all Hilton's romance, but less than Hilton's brain; & through following his ideals he has left the diplomatic service, & is now a marine officer at Portsmouth. After dinner Mrs Webb plunged from brisk argument to unconcealed snoring. Then Sidney had his turn. I thought he spoke a little quick to conceal the snores, but you have only to ask him a question & he can go on informing you till you can hold no more. He sketched his idea of a Supernational authority, & the future of Bills of Exchange. The work of Government will be enormously increased in the future. I asked whether I should ever have a finger in the pie? "O yes; you will have some small office no doubt. My wife & I always say that a Railway Guard is the most enviable of men. He has authority, & he is responsible to a government. That should be the state of each one of us."

And then we discussed L.'s plan of a state so contrived that each person has to do some work. Here there was a long argument upon the

12. George Young (1872-1952), the eldest brother of Hilton Young (see above, 18 March 1918, n 29), was to succeed his father as 4th Baronet in 1930. A man of considerable and varied gifts, he had served nearly twenty years in the Diplomatic Service, but during the war worked for Admiralty Intelligence; in March 1918 he enlisted as a private soldier, and was then commissioned in the Royal Marine Artillery. After the war he stood several times unsuccessfully for Parliament as a Labour candidate. VW's Asheham Diary for Saturday 14 September records: 'A wet day without stopping; Webbs arrived for tea. G. Young later. Very windy & cold.'

growing distance between men of different social grades & professio
Young affirming it, the Webbs denying it. I asked (in reporting conversations one's own sayings stand out like lighthouses) one of my most
fruitful questions; viz: how easy is it for a man to change his social grade?
This brought down a whole shower bath of information, but let us say
that the Webbs' shower baths are made of soda water. They never sink
one, or satiate. Webb told us how many scholarships were won in London
in a given year, & also reported upon the educational system of E. Sussex,
which bad though it is, is slightly better than that of W. Sussex. "I
myself" he said "came too early to profit by secondary education. My
parents were lower middle class shopkeepers, possessed, like so many
of their kind, with a blind determination to educate their sons somehow,
but without a ghost of a notion how to set about it. They hit on the
plan of sending me & my brother abroad to France & Germany; & so
we learnt French & German at least. I can still read them, though I seldom
do." Our talk must have dealt fully with education, for I remember
that Mrs Webb woke with a start & delivered herself of a statement
upon the German 'wrong turning', & put Young right on some point
about the division of character & intellect. He was simple enough to
separate them & to prefer what he was quite unable to define. She thrust
him through & through with her rapier, but he persisted.

Next day, which was said to begin for the W.'s at 5.30, when they
begin tea-drinking in their bedrooms, I had to withdraw in order to do
battle with a very obstinate review of Wells' 'Joan & Peter'.[13] My ideas
were struck stiff by the tap of Mrs W.s foot, up & down the terrace, &
the sound of her rather high, a rather mocking voice, discoursing to L.
while she waited either for W. to come or the rain to stop. They walked
on the downs, till lunch. I must now skip a great deal of conversation &
let us suppose that Sidney & Beatrice & I are sitting on the road side
overlooking Telscombe, smoking cigarettes, in bright sunshine, while
the Silver Queen slowly patrols above Newhaven. The downs were at
their best; & set Mrs W. off upon landscape beauty, & recollections of
India, which she turns to when lying awake at night, relishing the
recollection more than the reality. Sidney, one perceives, has no organ
of sight whatever, & pretends to none. Mrs W. has a compartment
devoted to nature. So briskly narrating their travels & impressions,
which were without respect for British rule, we set off home. I saw
them from behind, a shabby homely, dowdy couple, marching with the
uncertain step of strength just beginning to fail, she clutching his arm,
& looking much older than he, in her angularity. They were like pictures
in French papers of English tourists, only wanting spectacles & Ba[e]dekers

13. VW's review of *Joan and Peter* by H. G. Wells appeared in the *TLS* of 19
    September 1918 (Kp C122).

. Their clothes looked ill dusted, & their eyes peering in
. My few private words came, as I knew they would come,
W. detached us two together, passing Southease Church.
me about my novel, & I supplied her with a carefully arranged
hed, so at least I said, to discover what aims drive people on,
er these are illusory or not. She promptly shot forth: "Two
ve governed my life; one is the passion for investigation by
scientific means; the other the passion for producing a certain good
state of society by those investigations." Somehow she proceeded to
warn me against the dissipation of energy in emotional friendship. One
should have only one great personal relationship in one's life, she said;
or at most two—marriage & parenthood. Marriage was necessary as a
waste pipe for emotion, as security in old age when personal attractiveness
fails, & as a help to work. We were entangled at the gates of the level
crossing when she remarked, "Yes, I daresay an old family servant would
do as well." On the way up the hill she stated her position that one should
wish well to all the world, but discriminate no one. According to her the
differences are not great; the defects invariable; one must cultivate
impersonality above all things. In old age people become of little account,
she said; one speculates chiefly upon the possibility, or the impossibility
of a future life. This grey view depressed me more & more; partly I
suppose from the egotistical sense of my own nothingness in her field
of vision. And then we wound up with a light political gossip & chapter
of reminiscences, in which Mr & Mrs Webb did their parts equally. & so
to bed; & to my horror, in came Mrs W. early next morning to say
Goodbye, & perched in all her long impersonality on the edge of my
bed, looking past my stockings drawers & po. This has taken so long to
write that we are now arrived at

Monday 23 September,[14]

& so many things have accumulated, that I can hardly proceed to that
masterly summing up of the Webbs which I intended. I intended in
particular to dwell upon the half carping half humorously cynical view
which steals into one's description of the Webbs. I had meant to point
out the good qualities which come from such well kept brisk intellectual
habits; how open minded they showed themselves; how completely &
consistently <u>sensible</u>. That, I think, deserves a line under it. Good sense
seems to me their invariable characteristic. How sensible it was not to
fuss about goodbye, or a Collins; how sensibly they approach every
question whether of servants or politics, putting their minds at your

14. VW's Asheham Diary records that George Young left on Sunday and the Webbs
on Monday 16 September; on Tuesday 'Scene with Lottie about pumping. The
servants went on holiday', and VW bicycled to Charleston.

service without the least ostentation or flummery. Their horizon is entirely clear, unless in the case of Mrs Webb, as the medium said, a cloud of dust surrounds them; they have no illusions; they survey the whole panorama, which is amazingly clear to them, stoically, both for the race & for themselves as individuals. Sidney is the warmer & more human of the two, & one could even commit the impropriety of liking him personally, which one can hardly do in the case of Mrs Webb. How stoically with his perpetual little smile, he remarked that they are now 60, & therefore may expect a stroke within the next 5 years; but if he could arrange things with the divine messenger, he would compound somehow to die precisely at the same moment with "my wife".

By rights Lottie should have a whole chapter to herself at this point; but to live through those things is unpleasant enough without reviving them here. At this moment owing to what she overheard L. say to me before breakfast, I am uncertain whether we have 2 servants or not, & to tell the truth, completely indifferent, such is the relief of being without them for a fortnight. Considering their unimportance they must be compared to flies in the eye for the discomfort they can produce in spite of being so small. But let us change the subject.

I went over to Charleston last Tuesday & was shown his shells by Quentin; sat with Nessa & laid bare my sorrows, which she can more than match; & then Clive & Mary arrived in a motor car for tea—so many were their parcels & bags; & indeed Mary produced chocolates, cakes & sweets in abundance. I'm ashamed to say that that is my chief impression, but I left soon after, & they promised to spend a night here, so that I left unsaid & unasked all my ideas & questions. She was, as usual, mute as a trout—I say trout because of her spotted dress, & also because, though silent, she has the swift composure of a fish. I walked home shoving my bicycle, too badly punctured to ride.

Well then the Times began to shower books upon me, & I was reduced at one point to writing my review in the afternoon, nor can I discover any reason why one's brains should be unavailable between 3 & 5. When the telegraph girl rode up with a telegram from Clive to put us off, owing to some disease of Mary's, we were both immensely relieved, & I threw down my pen, as they say, & ate a large tea, & found my load of writing much lessened. When I have to review at command of a telegram, & Mr Geal has to ride off in a shower to fetch the book at Glynde, & comes & taps at the window about 10 at night to receive his shilling & hand in the parcel, I feel pressed & important & even excited a little. For a wonder, the book, Hudson, was worth reading.[15] Then on Saturday

15. VW's review of *Far Away and Long Ago* by W. H. Hudson appeared in the *TLS* on 26 September 1918 (Kp C123). Mr and Mrs Geall lived in one of the nearby cottages, and now gave occasional help in house and garden in place of Mrs Attfield.

we went to Lewes by train & bought a two handled saw, & fish, & envelopes, & then met Gertler at the station & came out here.

Whether our exclamations on parting from our guests are good evidence, I don't know, but on this occasion we both cried "Good God, what an egoist!" We have been talking about Gertler to Gertler for some 30 hours; it is like putting a microscope to your eye. One molehill is wonderfully clear; the surrounding world ceases to exist. But he is a forcible young man; if limited, able & respectable within those limits; as hard as a cricket ball; & as tightly rounded & stuffed in at the edges. We discussed—well, it always came back to be Gertler. . "I have a very peculiar character . . . I am not like any other artist. . . My picture would not have those blank spaces . . . I don't see that, because in my case I have a sense which other people don't have . . . I saw in a moment what she had never dreamt of seeing . . ." & so on. And if you do slip a little away, he watches very jealously, from his own point of view, & somehow tricks you back again. He hoards an insatiable vanity. I suspect the truth to be that he is very anxious for the good opinion of people like ourselves, & would immensely like to be thought well of by Duncan, Vanessa & Roger. His triumphs have been too cheap so far. However this is honestly outspoken, & as I say, he has power & intelligence, & will, one sees, paint good interesting pictures, though some rupture of the brain would have to take place before he could be a painter.

VW's Asheham Diary records that Gertler departed on the afternoon of 23 September. There were no further visitors to stay, and LW went twice to London for the day. Domestic and daily life, in the absence of the servants, occupied VW's attention and no doubt left little time for writing in her main diary. The coal almost ran out, there was no more to be had, it turned cold, and they had to cut up wood each day for burning. On 27 September VW records 'News that Bulgaria makes peace'. The next day they were both ill, which VW attributed to poisoning by bad meat, or flies; she stayed in bed most of the following day with a headache. On Tuesday 1 October the Sturgeons—LW's sister Flora and her parents-in-law who lived at Ashcombe House, near Lewes—walked over and were given tea.

Wednesday 2 October

No, I can't write to Margaret Davies. I spent on her the first flush of ideas after tea— It is fatal not to write the thing one wants to write at the moment of wanting to write it. Never thwart a natural process. I had so much to say here too. First, how the weather has changed, & we are on the verge of winter. Our clocks were put back on Sunday night; simultaneously I went into thick clothes; the sun lost half its heat, the nights became bitterly cold; we began to burn wood before tea; to dine by lamplight; & to shiver without fur coats on our beds. But the impulse that was to unite & fashion & give sequence to my head full of ideas perished on the ill suited page to Margaret Davies.[1]

Monday 7 October

I infinitely regret my generous impulse to write a letter describing the Webbs to Margaret; that evening my mind was full of ideas; & Asheham deserved some richer farewell than I am able to give it, disturbed as I am by the briskness [?] of homecoming, & a little agitated by the servant problem that I have to face tomorrow. I am inclined to dwell upon the warmth & beauty of this room. I have bought another glass jar for 2/-. These things are in the foreground. It is partly due to them & partly to the dampness of the Harmsworth press that I don't write first & foremost of the German offer of peace.[2] Certainly it made our hearts jump at Asheham this morning. But as the Times insists upon minimising it, not much exhilaration remains.

We came up by East Grinstead to avoid the crowd, a long journey therefore, stopping at all the dullest places in Sussex—West Hoathly among others. We lunched at Valcheras, & there looked into the lowest pit of human nature;[3] saw flesh still unmoulded to the shape of humanity— Whether it is the act of eating & drinking that degrades, or whether people who lunch at restaurants are naturally degraded, certainly one can hardly face one's own humanity afterwards.

Saturday 12 October

The first week in London is always one of the richest; & the rich weeks always tend to pass unrecorded. I have my anniversary to celebrate also; this diary is one year old, & looking back I see how exactly one repeats one's doings. For example this week we went to buy an overcoat for L.; last year we bought boots. Again there was the question of a party; again what I may euphemistically call an 'argument'. Nessa was in London too; & I dined with her & Clive, only there was Duncan

---

1. This letter (if sent) does not survive.
2. After ten weeks of almost uninterrupted reverses for the German army, the defeat of Turkey, the defection of Bulgaria, and the near-collapse of civilian morale, Prince Maximilian of Baden was appointed Chancellor of Germany on 3 October; the following day the German and Austrian governments addressed through Switzerland a note to President Wilson inviting the opening of peace negotiations on the basis of his Fourteen Points, and asking for the immediate conclusion of an armistice. Wilson's reply of 8 October stipulated, *inter alia*, the evacuation of all occupied territory by Germany and her allies.
3. A restaurant in the Quadrant, near Richmond station.

too, & we dined at Gordon Square. But Lord Grey's meeting has no counterpart last year;[4] nor could I possibly have written then, as I can now write that tomorrow morning's paper may bring news of an armistice. Possibly the fighting will be over this time next week. Whatever we have done this week has had this extraordinary back ground of hope; a tremendously enlarged version of the feeling I can remember as a child as Christmas approached. The Northcliffe papers do all they can to insist upon the indispensability & delight of war. They magnify our victories to make our mouths water for more; they shout with joy when the Germans sink the Irish mail; but they do also show some signs of apprehension that Wilson's terms may be accepted.[5] L. has just come in from Staines with a paper which says, with obvious gloom, that the rumour is that Germany agrees to evacuation. She is not, of course, they add, to be allowed to make any sort of terms. Meanwhile Philip is in the thick of it, & Maurice Davies' son has been killed.[6]

Grey's meeting was impressive as meetings go, which is not saying very much of course; but it does amount to saying that Grey himself struck me as a solid straightforward English Squire, curiously like Uncle Herbert magnified, in appearance, & with the kind of open air honour & sagacity which one feels to some extent in a man like Waller[Jack Hills].[7]

4. On 10 October 1918 a great meeting was held at Central Hall, Westminster, at which Lord Grey of Falloden, the first President of the League of Nations Union, formed by the merging of the League of Nations Society and the League of Free Nations Association, made an important speech on its policy. The armistice hoped for by VW on the morrow was in fact brought nearer on 12 October by the German agreement to President Wilson's demand that they evacuate all occupied territory.

5. On 10 October the Irish mail boat *Leinster*, carrying 650 passengers and a crew of 70, was torpedoed and sunk shortly after leaving the port of Kingstown in Ireland, with a loss of 451 lives. *The Times* of 11 and 12 October gave the incident full coverage, referring to it in one article entitled 'The War Brought Home to Ireland' as that country's 'first real blow from German barbarity'. Alfred Harmsworth (1865-1922), 1st Baron (1905) and 1st Viscount (1917) Northcliffe, founder of the *Daily Mail* and chief proprietor of *The Times*, maintained and propagated belligerent anti-German views in his newspapers, contending that the war should be continued until Germany was, not merely defeated, but devastated and humiliated. Since February 1918 Northcliffe had been Director of Propaganda in enemy countries in Lloyd George's administration.

6. Roland Arthur Llewelyn Davies, a Lieutenant in the Royal Fusiliers, was killed in action on 4 October 1918; he was the only son of the second of Margaret Llewelyn Davies's six brothers.

7. Herbert William Fisher (1826-1903), the father of H. A. L. Fisher and husband of VW's Aunt Mary, had been tutor and from 1860 to 1870 private secretary to the Prince of Wales; in 1890 he was appointed to the office of Vice-Warden of the Stannaries.

He said nothing but what one has read & agreed with about a League of Nations, but he said it simply, & for a 'great statesman' to have sense & human feeling & no bombast does produce an odd sense of wonder & humility in me, as if human nature were worth something after all. I don't extend my charity to Lord Harcourt however, who sat in front of us, or to Mrs Asquith & Elizabeth;[8] they were in no way venerable or even striking; but one sees that Mrs A. has triumphed by virtue of a whipcord vitality; she is as tense as a stretched bow; as lean & wiry as a whippet; vibrating like a fiddle; but not a trace (I'm judging by my view of her profile) of any thing more profound or interesting, & as for poor pasty Elizabeth she seemed to have come straight from behind Marshall & Snelgrove's millinery counter. There was an enormous audience, & as we left people were passing about the rumour that the Kaiser had abdicated.

I went on to my dinner at Gordon Square; thence to the Coliseum with Nessa, where we had to sit out an infinite length of Miss Clarice Mayne, after which we saw our ballet—Sche—(I can't achieve either the spelling or the speaking of it) which isn't one of the best, & when I saw it I remembered it better done at Covent Garden.[9] Maynard who has the generosity & something of the manner now of an oriental prince, had hired a brougham for Nessa—an infinitely small, slow, antiquated carriage drawn by a very liverystables looking quadruped. Roger, Duncan, Maynard, Nessa & I all crammed in & padded along slowly across London to Chelsea. Somehow we passed Ottoline, brilliantly painted, as garish as a strumpet, displayed in the midst of omnibuses under an arc lamp; & she reappeared in the Sitwell's drawing room.[10] I had made acquaintance with the two Sitwell brothers the day before [at

8. Lewis Harcourt (1863-1922), politician, Liberal MP 1904-16, and a minister in Mr Asquith's administration; created Viscount in 1917. Elizabeth Asquith (1897-1945) was the only daughter of the former Prime Minister and his second wife Margot; in 1919 she was to marry the Roumanian diplomat Prince Antoine Bibesco.

9. The Diaghilev Ballet Company had begun a season at the London Coliseum—where it shared the bill with Music Hall artistes, including Clarice Mayne and "That"—on 5 September 1918. Leonide Massine was *premier danseur* and choreographer, Lydia Lopokova *première danseuse*, though she had no part in *Scheherezade* which was performed on 10 October. Maynard's princely consideration was due to the fact that Vanessa was pregnant; a brougham was a four-wheeled closed carriage.

10. Edith (1887-1964), Osbert (1892-1969) and Sacheverell (b. 1897) Sitwell, the three children of the eccentric Sir George Sitwell of Renishaw Hall, Derbyshire, were beginning to make a name for themselves in the literary world. Edith edited, and they all contributed to, *Wheels*, an annual anti-Georgian verse anthology. VW's review of recently published poetry, including Edith Sitwell's *Clown's Houses*, appeared under the heading 'Adventurers All' in the *TLS* (Kp C125) on 10 October 1918, the actual day of the Sitwell's party in Carlyle Square, Chelsea.

46 Gordon Square], & been invited to the party. That very morning a review by me of Edith Sitwell's poems had appeared in the Times. It's strange how whole groups of people suddenly swim complete into one's life. This group to which Gertler & Mary H. are attached was unknown to me a year ago. I surveyed them with considerable, almost disquieting calm. What is there to be excited about, or to quarrel over, in a party like this, I asked myself; & found myself saying the most maternal things to Gertler, who was wearing evening dress, bought from the tipsy Mr Dallas, for the first time. We stood & compared our sensations. Edith Sitwell is a very tall young woman, wearing a permanently startled expression, & curiously finished off with a high green silk headdress, concealing her hair, so that it is not known whether she has any. Otherwise, I was familiar with everyone, I think. Nina Hamnet, Mary H., Jack H., Ottoline, Sheppard, Norton & so forth. I found myself discoursing to Sheppard about Sophocles.[11] Never before have I seen him even momentarily serious.

"I think of nothing but Greek plays, he said, & people— And I'm not sure that I don't always see people as if they were in Greek plays." I liked him better than before; still I think he found it awkward to stand discussing Sophocles seriously; & so we parted. My complete mastery of evening parties is shown by the indifference with which I am deserted, & the composure with which I decide upon my next choice. I was a good deal impressed by this; & how calmly too, I looked at my watch, & saw it was time to leave, & went out alone, & drove to Sloane Square, not excited, not depressed, but contemplative & introspective.[12]

Tuesday 15 October

I did not think I should so soon have to describe a meeting with a cabinet minister—though I admit that we seem to be drifting, without much desire on our part, into a circle where the great officials are sometime to be found. This is the doing of the [International] Review, mainly; but Herbert Fisher's visit wasn't due to the Review; it was very obviously due to old family affection. I was sitting down alone to tea on Sunday with my odious penny paper to read (the Germans having agreed to

11. John Tresidder Sheppard (1881-1968), scholar of King's College, Cambridge, of which he became Fellow, Lecturer in Classics (1908-33), and later (1933-54) Provost; elected an Apostle in 1902 at the same time as Lytton Strachey. He was a persuasive expositor of Hellenic ideas and civilisation. During the war he was employed on intelligence work by the War Office, and lived with Maynard Keynes and others in the Bell's old home at 46 Gordon Square, Bloomsbury.

12. LW had dined with G. L. Dickinson, and met VW at Sloane Square, so that they could travel home to Richmond together. The earlier sentence, 'What is there to be excited about, or to quarrel over, in a party like this,' suggests that LW had tried to dissuade her from going.

evacuate late on Saturday night)[13] L. being gone to Sutton to speak about our colonies & the servants out, when the bell rang & I saw several figures against the glass. On opening the door I really couldn't at first collect my wits; there were Olive & M. Heseltine & Herbert Fisher.[14] The H's. went off, & Herbert came in, as they had arranged beforehand. Was I nervous or proud, or anything but interested & anxious to pick his brains for news? I don't think I felt a moments agitation. For one thing he has lost his lean intellectual look; his hollow cheeks are filled; his eyes with that pale frosty look which blue eyes get in age; his whole bearing very quiet, simple, & when not speaking rather saddened & subdued. The number of deaths in his house caused this perhaps;[15] but I can't help thinking that London life has rid him of his desire to say clever things to undergraduates all the time. Anyhow we talked without stopping & without difficulty.

"We've won the war today" he said, at once. "I saw Milner this morning, & he says we shall have peace by Christmas.[16] The Germans have made up their minds they can't fight a retreat. The General staff has faced the fact, & they've had what I think the considerable courage to admit it. Of course we can't accept their present terms. Why, that would leave them still the greatest military power in Europe. They could begin again in ten years time. But it rests with the French. Lloyd George is going to Paris on Monday; but they are holding out for the evacuation of Alsace Lorraine as a guarantee. We shall probably demand the disarmament of certain regiments too. But we've won the war."

He then told me how we'd won the war, which was, according to him, by taking a tremendous risk some time in July & leaving the English line held without reserves, & withdrawing the army to reinforce Foch in his blow, which was timed with French precision 10 minutes before the German attack. If it had failed there was nothing between the Germans & the Channel ports.[17] There is now a good prospect of a complete

13. See above, 7 October 1918, n 2.
14. Olive Heseltine was H. A. L. Fisher's sister-in-law (see above, 18 March 1918, n 29); born Ilbert, she married Michael Heseltine, of the Civil Service, in 1912; the marriage was unsuccessful and was dissolved in 1921.
15. Fisher's mother and two of his brothers had died within the last two years.
16. Alfred Milner (1854-1925), created Viscount in 1902, was a member of Lloyd George's War Cabinet in 1916 and in April 1918 had become Secretary of State for War.
17. In the second battle of the Marne (15 July to 5 August 1918) the decisive French counter-attack was supported by the British XXIInd Corps, which had been held in reserve to deal with an expected German offensive on the Ypres front. The French General Gouraud, on the Eastern flank of the battle, forestalled the enemy by unmasking his batteries and using them against German troops massed for the assault on his front.

defeat of the German army; Foch says "I have not yet had my battle". Despite the extreme vindictiveness of our press & the French press, Herbert believed that we are going to baulk Foch of his battle, partly because the Germans will accept any terms to avoid it. "Lloyd George has told me again & again that he means to be generous to the Germans. "We want a strong Germany", he says. The Kaiser will probably go. O I was a great admirer of the Germans in the beginning. I was educated there, & I've many friends there, but I've lost my belief in them. The proportion of brutes is greater with them than with us. They've been taught to be brutal. But it hasn't paid. Each one of their crimes has turned out badly. No one can face another war. Why in 10 years they could blot out London by their aeroplanes. It cost us £1,000 to kill a German at the battle of the Somme [1916]; now it costs us £3,000. But the proportion of men who have never been hurt, or even seen anything horrible is very large. Seeley told me the other day that he'd spoken to thousands & thousands of soldiers, & they all wanted the war conditions of life to go on "without these bloody shells."[18] There'll be trouble when they come back. They'll find their old lives too dull. I'm going to educate them, its true; but that won't begin yet—not in my time. I want to reform the Universities next, & then I shall have done. I can't stay in Parliament without office. Very likely I shall go back to Oxford to teach."

So we talked on, not altogether [?un]like a Mrs Humphry Ward novel. I tried to think it extraordinary but I found it difficult—extraordinary, I mean, to be in touch with one who was in the very centre of the very centre, sitting in a little room at Downing St. where, as he said, the wireless messages are racing through from all over the world, a million miles a minute; where you have constantly to settle off hand questions of enormous difficulty & importance—where the fate of armies does more or less hang upon what two or three elderly gentlemen decide. Herbert thinks there are 2 or 3 geniuses in the cabinet (L. George, Balfour, & possibly Winston Churchill—his definition being that they make everything appear different) & a number of mediocrities.[19] His qualities I suppose are balance & foresight & culture. Importance seems to smooth away surface eccentricities; to give people an appearance of simplicity;

18. Major-General John Edward Bernard Seely (1868-1947, later 1st Baron Mottistone), had been Secretary of State for War from 1912 to 1914; he spent most of the war years in command of the Canadian Cavalry Brigade, but in 1918 returned to Whitehall, becoming deputy Minister of Munitions.

19. Arthur James Balfour (1849-1930), statesman, had been Conservative Prime Minister 1902-05; from 1914 he was a member of the 'War Council' and became Foreign Secretary in Lloyd George's coalition government 1916-19. Winston (Leonard Spencer) Churchill (1874-1965), who held an army commission from 1895 to 1916, had entered parliament in 1900 and after heading various ministries from 1906, was now Minister of Munitions.

they are very courteous; but somehow no longer spontaneous people; the taint of the family butler is on them. But this was more visible when L. came in. Alone with me H. was very friendly & quiet; & gave himself no airs of dignity.

Friday 18 October

Its quite obvious of course that for some reason perhaps not creditable to me I think H.F. worth many more words than Ka say, or Saxon, both of whom have dined here since. My theory is that for some reason the human mind is always seeking what it conceives to be the centre of things; sometimes one may call it reality, again truth, again life—I dont know what I call it; but I distinctly visualise it as a possession rather more in H.F.'s hands than in other peoples. For the moment he makes all the rest of the world's activities appear as ramifications radiating from him. But this is roughly stated—

Old Ka anyhow is not in the knot in the middle of the web. She came alone, Will having hurt his knee; & not being there in the flesh, one didn't trace him in the spirit. She seemed unchanged; but I think decidedly happier, a little defiant on Will's behalf. The poor little gentle, weakly creature is stated to be wild & queer & his action in giving up his patrimony & refusing to go to Balliol is brought forward as proof. For myself I distrust young men who return to nature on the Wiltshire Downs, paint pictures of the sky only, & want more than anything to fly. I own though that I'm judging from my ancient view of him at Fitzroy Sqre. Saxon, we assume, has found complete consolation in Mrs Stagg & a new set of gold teeth.[20] We have never seen him so sprightly, bold & communicative. He is already talking of his next visit to Bayreuth. He did not knit Barbara's child's drawers; & only showed a slight asperity when Nick was mentioned. But I write hurriedly, giving no account of the Albert Museum,[21] nor of our suspension over what one of the papers calls 'the precipice of peace', since I must read a little about Voltaire before going up to hear a Promenade Concert at the Queen's Hall. The truth is that nothing much more definite is yet known about peace. Wilson's second note came out on Tuesday, in which he used the word 'peradventure'; so far the Germans have not answered. But their Retreat goes on, & last night, beautiful, cloudless, still & moonlit, was to my thinking the first of peace, since one went to bed

20. Mrs Stagg was Saxon's landlady at Great Ormond Street.
21. VW had been to the Victoria and Albert Museum and among other things had seen the collection of works presented to the British Nation by the sculptor Auguste Rodin in 1914. (See *II VW Letters*, no. 980.)

fairly positive that never again in all our lives need we dread the moon-light.[22]

Wednesday 23 October

I went up to the concert, & heard the ghosts of lovely things, since the substance somehow escaped me; partly owing to my mood, partly to the usual vulgarity of Wood. Even so the ghosts of two Bach pieces (one for a duet of violins) were exquisitely lovely.[23] Edith Sichel, whose entire soul is now open to me through her letters, makes me determine to write descriptions neither of pictures nor of music.[24] She makes me consider that the gulf which we crossed between Kensington & Bloomsbury was the gulf between respectable mum[m]ified humbug & life crude & impertinent perhaps, but living. The breath of South Kensington lives in her pages—almost entirely, I believe, because they would not mention either copulation or w.c.'s. However this brings me to our dinner with the MacCarthy's, when I borrowed this book. The book has a sort of fascination for me. I see the outside of that world so clearly, & take a kind of ribald pleasure in putting those figures into action—sending them slumming, to Pops [concerts], to the National Gallery, always full of high thoughts, morality, kindliness, & never seeing beyond High St. Kensington. Molly, thanks to Bloomsbury, has escaped the Ritchie touch.[25] Her book is anyhow giving her some exquisite pleasure, & pain too. Her head, so Desmond said, shrank to the size of an apple; it is now swelling to normal again. They were both in the best spirits—

22. On 14 October President Wilson's second note to the Germans was virtually a demand for absolute surrender; it insisted that the Allies should dictate the manner in which occupied territories were to be evacuated (see above, 7 October 1918, n 2); it also, with the object of excluding both the Emperor and the army, stipulated that negotiations must be with a properly constituted government: 'It is indispensable that the [Allied] governments should know beyond a peradventure with whom they are dealing.' This was accepted by the Germans on 20 October.

23. Sir Henry Joseph Wood (1864-1944), conductor and musical director of the Promenade Concerts at the Queen's Hall from their inception in 1895. The Bach pieces were Suite No. 2 for flute and strings, and Concerto No. 3 for two violins and orchestra; the programme also included works of Beethoven, Mozart, Glück and Dvorak.

24. Edith Sichel (1862-1914), authoress. VW was reading her *New and Old*, published with an introduction by A. C. Bradley in 1917. In 1905 she had written a review of a book by Edith Sichel on Catherine de' Medici—her second task for the *TLS*; it was turned down.

25. Molly MacCarthy's mother Blanche Warre-Cornish was born a Ritchie, a large family with extensive ramifications in the upper-middle-class world of Kensington, the civil service, India, literature and so forth. VW had read Molly's novel, *A Pier and a Band*, while she was at Asheham in September.

extraordinary if you consider that they were in their own house, & no wine allowed. They gave us an excellent meat dinner; D. has some hopes that if Turkey makes peace he will be discharged, & will then take to wandering & writing more articles.[26]

Thursday 24 October

The degradation of steel pens is such that after doing my best to clip & file one into shape, I have to take to a Waterman [fountain pen], profoundly though I distrust them, & disbelieve in their capacity to convey the nobler & profounder thoughts. Yes, I can speak of myself with more confidence today as noble & profound; I am capable of standing for Parliament & holding office, & becoming just like Herbert Fisher perhaps.[27] To me the vote was as surprising as to some retired cleric in the vales of Westmorland, who will see in it the death knell of liberty, I daresay, & preach a sermon to that effect next Sunday. Then the great lady at Stocks must be feeling uncomfortable, though I am malicious enough to suppose that if by some process of selection she alone could represent Belgravia in the House of Lords, the change would not seem so devastating. Imagine her neatly accoutred in black trousers (so my imagination sees her) upon the bench at the Hague Conference![28] Her book, the reviews say, lays emphasis upon the fact that her novels were once thought beauties.

We are just in from Kingston—today being a holiday, L. not going up to London, & printing not started. McDermott is generally invisible, & when we caught him was just going out "partly in your interests, I may say", & threw out ominous hints as to the decline of his business, which threatens our seven pounds, so we imagine (back again to the superior fluency & cogency of steel). However, having walked across Bushy Park, & heard a stag grating his throat in a very surly manner, his doe being couchant by his side, we took tram to Kingston & there heard the paper boys shouting out about the President's message, which we bought & devoured in the [train.] The main points are that he is

26. Turkey signed the Armistice of Mudros on 30 October 1918.
27. As a natural corollary to the extension of the vote to women over thirty granted under the Representation of the People Act of March 1918, the House of Commons on 23 October passed a Bill making women eligible as MPs.
28. Stocks was the country home in Hertfordshire of Mrs Humphry Ward, an ardent and vociferous opponent of votes for women. The Hague Conference (for peace) was first held in 1899, and again in 1907. (A third, planned for 1915, was prevented by the war.) After the war the League of Nations was to replace the periodic Hague Conferences as an instrument for regulating international disputes, but the International Court of Arbitration there set up at the outset still functions. Mrs Humphry Ward's *A Writer's Recollections* was published in October 1918.

keeping negotiations going, though the Times came out with a great headline "No parley" this morning. He discriminates too, between the German people & the Kaiser; he will consider an armistice with the one but only complete surrender with the other. Anyhow, the question is now laid before England & France; & so another step in the tedious business is begun.[29]

Privately our minds are exercised about the question of going to Tidmarsh on Sunday. Lytton wired to beg us to yesterday, saying "desolation extreme". The difficulties are the nuisance of moving; work to be done; Herbert [Woolf] & his Freda dining here on Sunday. Yes, Herbert has been accepted by a certain Miss Freda Major—who she is or what she is, except that she is reported very active, I do not know.

Saturday 26 October

Here I am experimenting with the parent of all pens—the black J. *the* pen, as I used to think it, along with other objects, as a child, because mother used it; & therefore all other pens were varieties & eccentricities. What I have to record with it is the cheerful news that I am once more (see p. [?67] for the last occasion) in hot water—this time owing to Gertler, —Monty Shearman—Mary—Clive—Vanessa;—who exploded upon my head with reproaches for having almost brought her to disaster. My conscience is clear; but I'm coming to think that friendships maintained in this atmosphere are altogether too sharp, brittle, & painful. I have written to Charleston to this effect.[30] If I could have letters from Mary & Clive I should feel myself rewarded. L. is down at Tidmarsh, & I write to relieve myself of the feeling which comes over me in his absence of being a besieged city.

We had a day in London yesterday—somehow the charm of those days is not quite what it was. Am I getting blasé—is the 17 Club less enthralling? We went to the Omega show, met Roger, were invited to tea at his studio, discussed the change in Duncan's style, his father's burial, half Church of England, half Quaker, representation, reality, &

---

29. The headline 'NO MORE PARLEY' above a *Times* despatch from Washington dated 23 October, related to American political reactions to the German acceptance on 20 October of President Wilson's second note (see above, 18 October 1918, n 22); his third note, of 23 October, agreed to transmit to the Allies the German request for an armistice, first put forward on 4 October.

30. See *II VW Letters*, no. 983 (oddly enough dated *Sunday*, the day following this entry). VW was supposed to have told Mark Gertler that Vanessa did not admire Mary Hutchinson; the dissemination of this story caused great perturbation both to Clive and to Vanessa, who was anxious to remain on good terms with both Clive and Mary.

so on again, Waley coming in as we left.[31] We dined at a very hot place in Soho, where you have perhaps a stone's weight of food given you for 2/3. On again to the Club, where Leonard made his speech about Austria Hungary.[32] As usual I find him not only very clear but with the right degree of passion to be interesting. The audience, as usual at the 17 Club, seemed made of curiosities whose aberrations of feature had driven them up & up the backwaters of life, where they dwell in semi obscurity, only issuing from their huts to plant arrows in the sides of the sleek town dwellers. If it weren't so ugly, it might be picturesque. Or is it merely that the body resents much use of the brain?

Monday 28 October

L. found Lytton with a swollen finger & 2 or 3 spots on his hand sitting over the fire, & only moving when enveloped in a silk tablecloth, & wrapping his hand also in silk handkerchiefs & complaining of the cold, & describing nights of agony when a pain like toothache seizes upon him & develops into frantic agonies only to be allayed by morphia. This has been going on for a month, & Carrington is at her wits end, very naturally. Anything like pain is abhorrent to all Stracheys, but making all allowances for the exaggerations & terrors of the poor creature, he has had a sufficient dose of horror, I imagine, & the doctor privately warns Carrington that shingles may last months. However, Lytton is probably moving in to Mary in a day or two, avoiding London, because of the influenza[33]—(we are, by the way, in the midst of a plague unmatched since the Black Death, according to the Times, who seem to tremble lest it may seize upon Lord Northcliffe, & thus precipitate us into peace). But I am far from peace. A fortnight ago all Bloomsbury rang with my crimes; M.H. was conveyed about London in a fainting condition in taxicabs; Lytton was appealed to come to her rescue; Duncan Clive Vanessa—all were in agonies & desperations. Why no one charged me with it then, I don't know; my private theory is that Clive inspired V.'s letter as a precaution against further indiscretions, giving strict orders that his name should not be mentioned. I soothed myself by denouncing the spy system, & now am quite unable even to feel irritated. It all comes,

31. Roger Fry's father, the Rt Hon Sir Edward Fry (1827-1918), a High Court judge, died at his home at Failand, near Bristol, on 18 October. The family were Quakers, and his funeral took place at the local parish church on 22 October. 'Waley' was probably Hubert (1892-1968), Arthur's younger brother, who sometimes did work for the Omega.
32. The cornucopia was Molinari's, 23 Frith Street. At the 1917 Club, LW opened a discussion by the International Group.
33. The St John Hutchinsons had rented a country house, Glottenham, near Roberts-bridge in Sussex, and Lytton stayed there most of November.

so I think, from the indiscreet way in which people like M.H. accept positions which they are unable to fill, & thus flinching & shying constantly, keep everybody in a state of discomfort. I announce my intention to keep clear of that set in future; & as I write this, the post brings a letter from Eliot asking to come & see us.[34]

To my great surprise a voice upon the telephone developed into the voice of Lady Mary Murray; asking us to lunch yesterday.[35] We changed lunch to tea & went off to More's Gardens, a block of flats on the Embankment, where after ringing for some time, a gigantic knock was answered by Lady Mary in person. L. was half inclined to think her an untidy but cordial housemaid. The Fisher Williams' were there.[36] A tea party is the least natural of situations, & produces the utmost amount of discomfort I think. Then the F.W.'s possessed only the brain of one moderate sized rabbit between them. Still it was the respectability that weighed me down, not the absence of intellect. There are certain dun coloured misty days in autumn which remind me of the Murray's atmosphere. The cleanliness of Gilbert was remarkable; a great nurse must rub him smooth with pumice stone every morning; he is so discreet, so sensitive, so low in tone & immaculate in taste that you hardly understand how he has the boldness to beget children. She is a wispy elderly lady, highly nervous, a little off hand & much of an aristocrat in her dashing method, kindly, fussy, refined too—O yes, they are all refined. I sat & talked to Gilbert first about our love of sweets, then about the Greek love of wine, then

34. Thomas Stearns Eliot (1888-1965), the American-born poet, having married Vivienne Haigh-Wood in 1915, was now making his living as an employee of Lloyds Bank, and also acting as assistant editor of *The Egoist* (see above, 28 January 1918, n 45). The Woolfs knew of him and they clearly had common friends; but, although LW may have met him, it does not appear that VW did so until 15 November 1918. In September VW, writing to Clive Bell, asked him to ask Mary Hutchinson to send her Eliot's address again, as she had lost it; thus it seems probable that she had now written suggesting he should visit them and bring some of his poems. He wrote to her from 18 Crawford Mansions, W1, on 12 November saying that he should look forward to Friday with much pleasure.

35. Lady Mary Henrietta Murray, *née* Howard (1865-1956), eldest daughter of the 9th Earl of Carlisle, in 1889 married Professor (George) Gilbert (Aimé) Murray (1886-1957), the classical scholar and internationalist. He was active in the promotion of a League of Nations Union, having been one of the group (loosely termed 'jingoes' by VW, see above, 17 June 1918) which set up the League of Free Nations Association after failing to alter the constitution of the League of Nations Society. The two bodies were merged in October 1918 to form the Union, of which Gilbert Murray became Chairman and Lord Grey President.

36. John Fischer Williams (1870-1947), liberal, lawyer, and internationalist, was at this time serving in the Aliens Branch of the Home Office. Like Murray a fellow of New College, Oxford, their common interest in Greek literature and the League of Nations ideal united their two families in friendship.

about his standing with the Government. He has, he says, refused many honours, but was reprimanded for sending a review of a book on Job to America. Maliciously enough, I felt that his simplicity was maintained in the face of years of worship & adulation, & that the proper thing to say is "How wonderfully simple dear Gilbert Murray is!" But his niceness was unmeasured. The Toynbees came in. I had a long rigmarole with Arnold about his office & his learning & so forth; I think I frighten him; or perhaps I'm not used to the Oxford manner. Its suavity & politeness are strange to me. He is so shortsighted that he has a painful look of pinkness round the eyes, as if he were a grammar school boy exalted by the most assiduous industry to positions above his station. I'm always surprised to find how well meaning & even outspoken he is in spite of this.

Home to find Freda Major marooned at the station, so that L. had to fetch her. Herbert came after a field day; he'd been out since 6. & took F. home, & caught the last train to Staines. Freda is merely a toy dog enveloped in human flesh, but retaining the pretty, plaintive, rather peevish ways of her canine existence. She has stimulated Herbert to talk with greater fluency & enthusiasm than usual about the policeman strike & Ford's motor cars.[37]

Wednesday 30 October

Just in from a walk in the Park on this incredibly lovely autumn day. Various houses have orange berries growing upon them; the beech trees are so bright that everything looks pale after you have looked at them. (How I dislike writing directly after reading Mrs H. Ward!—she is as great a menace to health of mind as influenza to the body.) We talked of peace: how the sausage balloons will be hauled down, & gold coins dribble in; & how people will soon forget all about the war, & the fruits of our victory will grow as dusty as ornaments under glass cases in lodging house drawing rooms. How often will the good people of Richmond rejoice to think that liberty has been won for the good people of Potsdam? I can believe though that we shall be more arrogant about our own virtues. The Times still talks of the possibility of another season, in order to carry the war into Germany, & there imprint a respect for liberty in the German peasants. I think the distance of the average person

37. On 31 August 1918 the London police had struck for better conditions and the right to belong to their own Union; the strike ended on 2 September when a conciliatory Lloyd George agreed to all their demands save that concerning the union, recognition of which might be granted after the war. (In the event a bill outlawing the Police and Prison Officers' Union was passed by Parliament in 1919.)

from feelings of this sort is the only safeguard & assurance that we shall settle down again neither better nor worse.

We had a day in London yesterday; ending for me in talks with Ka & James at the Club, which now renews its life apparently. Ka has ceased to be a bureaucrat owing to Will's illness; shed power as a chestnut its husk; & remains untouched within. James just back from Cornwall, where he had the influenza. Alix back too; without having the influenza & ready, I suppose to begin her autumn campaign, which Oliver bets that she will win.[38] I here note that I bought my new battery on Tues. Oct. 29th; so far of extreme brilliance.

Sunday 3 November

On Friday night I went up to dine with the Arnold Forsters, partly I own, to avoid Mr Seymour Cox's lecture upon the Secret Treaties, since I thought I knew already what Mr Seymour Cocks would say.[1] Ka & Will live just past the Spectator office in the little semicircle of houses standing off the road, but tolerably noisy nevertheless.[2] Here he lived before his marriage. He looked unusually small, drawn & pallid, like a face seen under a gas lamp, owing to his disease; & no longer young. He reminds me rather of one of those old ladies, who have yellow hair & very pink cheeks, but you can count their years in the way the flesh is drawn tight across the bone, & crinkled with very delicate fine lines. His person & manners are against him. He makes an impression of being very sharp, rather fretful, & acid. I think all this is largely due to his peevish voice, & little angular body, which he jerks about when he gets excited, & very little makes him emphatic. Nor did I like the pale acid decorations of the room—the lavender walls, & the one white rose drooping against them; nor did I like his niggled & emotional picture of the downs. There seemed a lack of warmth, depth, & substance. Perhaps none of this very much matters. His principles are those of the modern husband—freedom & independence for the wife—equal pleasures. Principles matter too. Ka will be happy with him. We talked very briskly. I dont think I should like his taste in books; I don't like his slang; or his

---

38. Eventually she did—she and James Strachey were married in June 1920.

1. Frederick Seymour Cocks (1882-1953), author and journalist (and later a Labour MP) spoke to a meeting of the Richmond Branch of the Union of Democratic Control held at Hogarth House on 1 November. He was the editor of *The Secret Treaties and Understandings* published by the UDC in the spring of 1918, of which a copy was among the Woolfs' books at LW's death (see *Holleyman*, VS V, p. 2).

2. Lancaster Place, where the Arnold-Forsters were living, faced Somerset House to the north of Waterloo Bridge; the road continuing northwards across the Strand becomes Wellington Street. The *Spectator* offices were then at No. 1.

admirations; but I liked his excitement over the war office gazette. I suspect he has an able excitable rather febrile mind, which, on principle, has taken to painting pictures; I could wager my own head full of brains that he'll never paint a good one.[3]

On Saturday, we had one of our Hampstead afternoons, L. going to Margaret, I to Janet. I've done the same thing so often. I've found her in that green distempered room, with the ugly pictures. How well I know the benevolent look of the late Mr Case as a young man, drawn upon yellow paper & very slightly tinted on the cheeks, larger than life, framed in gold, by the late Mr Richmond.[4] I know the photographs of young soldiers, & the silhouettes, & Janet's books, which never seem to be read, & the greek dictionary with the piece of paper sticking out of it. Then theres Diana who takes up a lot of attention; but is now a reformed character. Emphie vagulates in & out of the room. Tea is prepared. I am pressed to eat more of everything. Questioned about butter & coal. Yesterday Emphie had a new kind of methylated spirits to show me, which you can only get in Highgate. Mr Marshall rather varied the proceedings—a well kept middle aged gentleman of Hampstead who proclaimed his wish to rule the world; & his fear lest America should rule it instead. Here was a Times leading article in the flesh. But he was also a chatty old gossip; & he & Emphie had noticed so many houses unlit, newcomers who were almost unknown, trees that wanted lopping, motor cars waiting for Mr Galsworthy, preparations for opening the Y.M.C.A., that it was like Cranford, to listen.[5] And then they went & Janet talked to me about literature, & I fell into a passing gloom. She says that a great many novels are written, & it seems fairly evident that none are "immortal". I suppose I referred this to my own novels; indeed, she urged me to write a biography for Basil Williams. But I fancy that what depressed me was not only the personal question, but the smell of musty morality. None of us came up to the scratch—not Lytton or Forster or anyone; but I felt beyond this fairly safe criticism the depressing effect of talking to some one who seems to want all literature to go into the pulpit; who makes it all infinitely worthy & safe & respectable. I

3. Although he continued to paint throughout his life, after the war was over Will Arnold-Forster joined the Labour Party and devoted much of his time and energies to the cause of internationalism.

4. William Arthur Case, the father of Janet and her five elder sisters, with his wife Sarah ran a co-educational school called Heath Brow at Hampstead, where they were all educated. His portrait was probably by George Richmond, RA (1809-96). Diana (perhaps a cat) and Mr Marshall have not been identified.

5. The novelist and playwright John Galsworthy (1867-1933) lived at Grove Lodge in Hampstead from 1918 until his death. Cranford, Mrs Gaskell's record of genteel daily life in a village early in the nineteenth century, was first published in book form in 1853.

was led into trying to define my own particular search—not after morality, or beauty or reality—no; but after literature itself; & this made Janet a little anxious & insistent, as if, conceivably, she might have missed something. Where did I find it? How did I explain it? We agreed upon a certain passage in Sophocles; but as she capped this with one in Lear, I think we were talking of different things. And she pressed me to tell her what I meant; & of course I came nowhere near it, & at length she said that she thought she was beginning to find what I meant—after all these years of reading Greek! Yes, I was depressed at her age, at something unstable about her; but I was also depressed at the implied criticism of The Voyage Out, & at the hint that I had better turn to something other than fiction. Now this seems to me foolish, & I wish I could make up a cure for it, to be taken after such encounters, which are bound to happen every month of one's life. Its the curse of a writers life to want praise so much, & be so cast down by blame, or indifference. The only sensible course is to remember that writing is after all what one does best; that any other work would seem to me a waste of life; that on the whole I get infinite pleasure from it; that I make one hundred pounds a year; & that some people like what I write. But Janet would only admit that love counted, & said that her friends had succeeded only in "coming off" in life, not in art.

Monday 4 November

Since I'm back from the Club & waiting for L. (who has gone to see Mr Hawkins of the Temple [unidentified]) I had better assuage my fretfulness with pen & ink. I have a pen of ⟨malachite⟩ vulcanite(?) which perhaps serves the purpose of a babies coral. I've had no letter from Charleston which makes me feel rather sent to Coventry, though I suppose communications are going on between Clive & Mary; & then I can't help fancying that Janet's chill falling upon the last pages of my novel still depresses me. The depression however now takes the wholesome form of feeling perfectly certain that nothing I can do matters, so that one is both content & irresponsible—I'm not sure that this isn't a happier state than the exalted state of the newly praised. At least one has nothing to fear, & the sheer pleasure of writing seems singularly unalloyed. It proves itself so genuine that no amount of Hampstead cold water can impair it. Praise? fame? Janet's good opinion? How beside the mark they all are!

I keep thinking of different ways to manage my scenes; conceiving endless possibilities; seeing life, as I walk about the streets, an immense opaque block of material to be conveyed by me into its equivalent of language. (Lottie's fire has to be nursed like a dying kitten—its my fire now, her's being dead of course, & I've taken 25 minutes to get a trickle of flame between the coals.) In the intervals I've been thinking a good deal about this melancholy state of impending age. From the way Janet took certain remarks of mine about 60 as an age limit (for the Webbs) I felt that she took age to be a shameful disease that one shrank from hearing named. At anyrate, it is obvious that she must think about it privately, not facing it, turning away from it. And then it seems as if she were now always playing for safety. She has a kind of personal resentment against anyone, like Lytton for example, who laughs at what she holds sacred; she falls into the insidious trap of believing that any departure from the great is ephemeral & impertinent; & she argues this with personal feeling as if her own reputation depended on theirs. And all the time she's so anxious to be in the front, to share what the young feel. But if I represent the young, my feelings tend to develop on such different lines that I can only wave my hand over leagues of Sea.

To Souhami's; Mudies & the Club.

Saturday 9 November

Lord Mayor's day among other things, & one of the two last of war, I suppose.[6] It's just possible that Lottie may bring us news that the armistice is signed within an hour. People buy papers at a great rate; but except for an occasional buzz round a newspaper boy & a number of shop girls provided with The Evening News in the train one feels nothing different in the atmosphere. The general state perhaps is one of dazed surfeit; here we've had one great relief after another; you hear the paper boys calling out that Turkey has surrendered, or Austria given up, & the mind doesn't do very much with it; was the whole thing too remote & meaningless to come home to one, either in action or in ceasing to act? Katherine Murry, whom I saw on Wednesday, inclines to think that most people have grasped neither war nor peace. Two or three weeks ago I heard a citizen holding forth to a lady in the train, who asked him whether he thought there would be peace.

"I hope *not.* . . . We're giving them everything they want & getting nothing." Since then it is difficult to see how the most bloodthirsty citizens can squeeze anything more out of Germany. The Kaiser still wears a phantom kind of crown.[7] Otherwise there is revolution, & a kind of partial awakenment, one fancies, on the part of the people to the unreality of the whole affair. Suppose we wake up too?

6. On the second Saturday in November each year the new Lord Mayor of London, accompanied by a splendid procession, proceeds in full state from the City to the Royal Courts of Justice in the Strand to make his statutory declaration before the Lord Chief Justice.
7. It was in fact on this very day that the German Emperor Wilhelm II (1859-1941) was compelled finally to take off his crown and go into exile in Holland.

We began to set up Kew Gardens this week—Thursday was the first day of it, I think. MacDermott has surrendered his £7: after a little ineffective shuffling. On Wednesday I went up to Hampstead; found the tall ugly villa-looking over the valley where the Murrys live.[8] Katherine was up, but husky & feeble, crawling about the room like an old woman. How far she is ill, one cant say. She impresses one a little unfavourably at first—then more favourably. I think she has a kind of childlikeness somewhere which has been much disfigured, but still exists. Illness, she said, breaks down one's privacy so that one can't write— The long story she has written breathes nothing but hate. Murry & the Monster [LM] watch & wait on her, till she hates them both; she trusts no one; she finds no 'reality'.

Monday 11 November

Twentyfive minutes ago the guns went off, announcing peace. A siren hooted on the river. They are hooting still. A few people ran to look out of windows. The rooks wheeled round, & were for a moment, the symbolic look of creatures performing some ceremony, partly of thanksgiving, partly of valediction over the grave. A very cloudy still day, the smoke toppling over heavily towards the east; & that too wearing for a moment a look of something floating, waving, drooping. We looked out of the window; saw the housepainter give one look at the sky & go on with his job; the old man toddling along the street carrying a bag out [of] which a large loaf protruded, closely followed by his mongrel dog. So far neither bells nor flags, but the wailing of sirens & intermittent guns.

Tuesday 12 November

We should have done well, I think, to be satisfied with the aspect of peace; how the rooks flew slowly in circles, & the smoke drooped; but I had to go to Harrison, & I think we were both conscious of a restlessness which made it seem natural to be going up to London. Disillusionment began after 10 minutes in the train. A fat slovenly woman in black velvet & feathers with the bad teeth of the poor insisted upon shaking hands with two soldiers; "Its thanks to you boys &c &c". She was half drunk already, & soon produced a large bottle of beer which she made them drink of; & then she kissed them, & the last we saw of her was as she ran alongside the train waving her hand to the two stolid soldiers. But she & her like possessed London, & alone celebrated peace in their sordid way, staggering up the muddy pavements in the rain, decked with

8. In July 1918, with LM (Ida Baker) to 'look after things', the Murrys had settled at 2 Portland Villas, East Heath Road, which they nicknamed 'The Elephant'.

flags themselves, & voluble at sight of other people's flags. The Heavens disapproved & did their utmost to extinguish, but only succeeded in making feathers flop & flags languish. Taxicabs were crowded with whole families, grandmothers & babies, showing off; & yet there was no centre, no form for all this wandering emotion to take. The crowds had nowhere to go, nothing to do; they were in the state of children with too long a holiday. Perhaps the respectable suppressed what joy they felt; there seemed to be no mean between tipsy ribaldry & rather sour disapproval. Besides the discomfort tried every one's temper. It took us from 4 to 6 to get home; standing in queues, every one wet, many shops shut, no light yet procurable, & in everyone's mind the same restlessness & inability to settle down, & yet discontent with whatever it was possible to do.

[*End of book*]

The next portion of the diary, including the entries for 20, 22 and 24 January 1919, is written at the other end of a hard-backed exercise book which VW had begun to use in January 1918 for notes on books she was reading or reviewing (Diary VI).

Friday 15 November[9]

I've no money to buy another book; besides by waiting the paper question may once more take its place in the scale of my pleasures; good books, cheap books, books that make one wish to finish them in order to have the pleasure of buying another may be built up against the wall in stationers shops. Peace is rapidly dissolving into the light of common day. You can go to London without meeting more than two drunk soldiers; only an occasional crowd blocks the street. In a day or two it will be impossible for a private to threaten to knock out the brains of an officer, as I saw done the other day in Shaftesbury Avenue. But mentally the change is marked too. Instead of feeling all day & going home through dark streets that the whole people, willing or not, were concentrated on a single point, one feels now that the whole bunch has burst asunder & flown off with the utmost vigour in different directions. We are once more a nation of individuals. Some people care for football; others for racing; others for dancing; others for—oh, well, they're all running about very gaily, getting out of their uniforms & taking up their private affairs again. Coming home from the Club tonight I thought for a moment that it must still be sunset, owing to the sharp bright lights in Piccadilly Circus. The streets are crowded with people quite at their ease; & the shops blazoning unshaded lights. Yet its depressing

9. VW has mistakenly written the date as *Friday November 16th 1918.*

too. We have stretched our minds to consider something universal at any rate; we contract them at once to the squabbles of Lloyd George, & a General Election.[10] The papers are unreadable. One's sense of perspective is so changed that one cannot see at first what meaning all this gossip of parties can possibly have; one can't be interested. Other people have more right to be sluggish than I have. One predicts a year or two of laxity save on the part of the professionals. They will have things their own way. Masses [?] will play football & cricket & take shooting in the country. The first effect of peace on our circle is to set Desmond loose, & to bring Gerald Shove up to London saying that he must find a way of making £500 a year. Before long the crowd of out of work intellectuals looking for places will be considerable. Desmond is doing what he knows how to do supremely well—going later & later to the office every day & taking longer for lunch, & sometimes not going back again. This he proposes to continue for a fortnight; then to fold up his blue & gold coat for ever—unless by cutting off the brass buttons he can make it do for an ordinary coat. His spirits are very high, though depressed occasionally by the question of earning a living. It came out that he means to suggest himself for Solomon Eagle's place on the New Statesman; for the Eagle is flying higher.[11] "I know so many people who write well" he said; & if that were all, he would make a perfect editor. After tea he told us the last section of the Ireniad. I suppose it would fill a book, from start to finish. It ended, characteristically, with his promising to go to lunch—& waiting eleven years before he saw her again. The story brought her back very plainly; perhaps his conclusion was right— one ought to pity any woman who is engaged to a young Cambridge man who has never been in love before—a young Cambridge man, I should add, who has read & has by heart all the novels of Henry James.

I was interrupted somewhere on this page by the arrival of Mr Eliot. Mr Eliot is well expressed by his name—a polished, cultivated, elaborate young American, talking so slow, that each word seems to have special finish allotted it. But beneath the surface, it is fairly evident that he is very intellectual, intolerant, with strong views of his own, & a poetic

10. There had been no general election since the Liberals were returned in December 1910, Lloyd George's coalition government having supplanted Asquith's administration in December 1916. Following the armistice, the Labour Party seceded from the government and a general election was announced on 14 November; Parliament was to be dissolved on 25 November, and polling day was fixed for Saturday 14 December. Lloyd George and his Conservative chancellor, Bonar Law, offered a continuation of coalition government; the Asquithian Liberals and the Labour Party opposed it. Owing to the servicemen's vote, the result could not be announced until 28 December.

11. J. C. Squire was vacating the literary editorship of the *New Statesman* to found his own monthly *The London Mercury*; Desmond MacCarthy did succeed him.

creed. I'm sorry to say that this sets up Ezra Pound & Wyndham Lewis as great poets, or in the current phrase "very interesting" writers. He admires Mr Joyce immensely.[12] He produced 3 or 4 poems for us to look at—the fruit of two years, since he works all day in a Bank, & in his reasonable way thinks regular work good for people of nervous constitutions. I became more or less conscious of a very intricate & highly organised framework of poetic belief; owing to his caution, & his excessive care in the use of language we did not discover much about it. I think he believes in "living phrases" & their difference from dead ones; in writing with extreme care, in observing all syntax & grammar; & so making this new poetry flower on the stem of the oldest.

As an illustration of Eliot's views I may add what Desmond has just (Thursday 21st Nov.) told me; D. asked him how on earth he came to add that remark at the end of a poem on his Aunt & the Boston Evening Transcript that phrase about an infinitely long street, & "I like La Rochefoucauld saying good bye" (or words to that effect). Eliot replied that they were a recollection of Dante's Purgatorio![13]

Thursday 21 November

I am overwhelmed with things that I ought to have written about; peace dropped like a great stone into my pool, & the eddies are still rippling out to the further bank. Has Nelly Cecil sunk beyond recall? & that concert at Shelley House, presided over, so appropriately by Bruce Richmond?[14] For the sake of the good report of my diary let me record the fact that Nelly Cecil met the Kaiser at Hatfield: & said he appeared a small man, in a grey suit, & "his people were afraid of him—

12. Ezra Loomis Pound (1885-1972), the American-born but Europe-based poet, a supporter, both critically and materially, of the *avant-garde*, which included at this period Eliot himself, James Joyce, and Percy Wyndham Lewis (1882-1957), the writer and artist. Lewis's first novel *Tarr* had been published in July by The Egoist, Ltd., the firm started by Miss Harriet Weaver as an offshoot of her periodical *The Egoist* (of which Eliot was still assistant editor).

13. 'When evening quickens faintly in the street,
Wakening the appetites of life in some
And to others bringing the *Boston Evening Transcript*,
I mount the steps and ring the bell, turning
Wearily, as one would turn to nod good-bye to Rochefoucauld,
If the street were time and he at the end of the street,
And I say, 'Cousin Harriet, here is the *Boston Evening Transcript*."
From *Prufrock and other Observations*, 1917. Faber, London, Harcourt Brace Jovanovich, New York.

14. Nelly Cecil (1868-1956) had been a friend of VW's since early in the century. Born Lady Eleanor Lambton, third daughter of the 2nd Earl of Durham, she had married in 1889 Lord Robert Cecil, third son of the 3rd Marquess of Salisbury who, as Prime Minister, had entertained the Kaiser at his family seat, Hatfield House, on

They were afraid to tell him if his motor car was late. . . . He was romantic—very romantic."

Too much space would be needed for an accurate description of Shelley House: briefly speaking it is a luxurious sham in imitation of the 18th century; but as people like the St John Hornbys never put all their eggs in one basket, the Italian renaissance is represented too; &, I should guess, Arthur Hughes shows that they patronise English art; but mainly they put their faith in George the Third.[15] How much the annual income of the audience amounted to, I should not like to guess; they wore a substantial part of it on their backs: the furs were richly dark; the stuffs of the best black. And then the lovely music offered up before this congregation—among whom, as they say, I noticed Mrs Rathbone, Pearsall Smith, Hervey Vaughan Williams, & Mrs Muir Mackenzie.[16]

However peace came & dissipated all that; & now where are we? According to Roger, on the brink of revolution; this is strictly speaking, according to Ray, & Ray, who is standing for Parliament as a Coalition candidate, says that if ever she were tempted to hoard food, now would be the time.[17] The Lower classes are bitter, impatient, powerful, & of course, lacking in reason. For example they demand houses with 10 rooms at Guildford; & they have a prophet, Ditcher by name, who knows the truth; he knows what the brain is made of; & he has no use for the "middle class idealism" which cherishes doubts about some matters, & preaches liberty, toleration, & other humbug; for Ditcher knows the truth.[18] These are a few facts that I gathered from Roger over a dish of tripe & leeks. I cheered him a little by reminding him of the existence of football & of King George. How they crowd—my

---

11-13 July 1891. The Woolfs had been to tea with Lady Robert on Sunday 10 November, and went on with her to a quartet concert at Shelley House, No. 1 Chelsea Embankment, the home of St John Hornby (1867-1947), printer, connoisseur, and partner in W. H. Smith & Son. This appears to have been one of a series of private subscription concerts organised by Bruce Richmond.

15. Arthur Hughes (1832-1915), painter and book illustrator, adopted the principles of the Pre-Raphaelites but was not actually of the brotherhood. VW would have regarded him as very stuffy.

16. Mrs Rathbone was Mrs Bruce Richmond's mother; Hervey Vaughan Williams was the elder brother of the composer Ralph Vaughan Williams who had married VW's cousin Adeline Fisher; the Hon. Mrs Muir-MacKenzie had lived in the next house to the Stephens in Hyde Park Gate.

17. This was incorrect: Mrs Oliver Strachey stood as an Independent candidate in Middlesex, Brentford and Chiswick, against the Conservative-Unionist coalition and the Labour candidates.

18. I have unfortunately been unable to discover anything about this interesting character.

memories of the past week! Mention of King George recalls Harry Stephen who sat like a frog with his legs akimbo, opening & shutting his large knife, & asserting with an egoism proper to all Stephens, that he knew how to behave himself, & how other people ought to behave, which science he taught, with success according to him, upon the Bench at Calcutta. He has need of the Royal Family; he wants someone descended from Egbert upon the throne; not a schoolmaster, like Wilson. The impenetrable wall of the middle class conservative was never more stolid; dynamite may smash it to powder; but—it is impervious to reason, or imagination or humanity; an educated version of the prophet Ditcher.

Poor James Strachey was soft as moss, lethargic as an earthworm. James, billed at the 17 Club to lecture on "Onanism", proposes to earn his living as an exponent of Freud in Harley Street. For one thing, you can dispense with a degree.[19]

But the real news of the past week is of a confidential nature. [Gilbert] Murray has asked L. to be his secretary if, as is possible, he is chosen to represent England on the League of Nations Committee at the Peace Conference. This would mean a visit to Paris. More than this need not be said; but it is an important possibility.[20] Coming after it, the news that I today wrote the last words of my novel reads a little flat. Five hundred & thirty eight pages!

Saturday 30 November

I see I've been rather slack, & I cant remember now exactly what's made me slack. Certainly not the General Election. I've reduced my reading of newspapers, though the D[aily]. N[ews]. has an extra sheet. They somehow keep it up. Mrs Dacre Fox bellows in the High St.[21] McDermott demands a government which will make the Germans pay. He prints poster after poster in red ink. I've a new niece, Judith, not welcomed, but made the best of; & Barbara has a Judith too;[22] & Saxon dined here, talking of death without enthusiasm. He knew for certain that he would die on a certain day last summer & then—didn't.

19. James Strachey had embarked upon a medical training with a view to becoming a psychoanalyst; these studies were abandoned because of illness, but in 1920 he was to go to Vienna to study under and be analysed by Freud.

20. Nothing more is heard of this possibility. VW's novel was *Night and Day*.

21. Mrs Dacre Fox, who had been a militant suffragist, stood as an Independent candidate for Richmond. Her election address read (in part): '. . . if the faith of the people is to be restored, the leaders of the nation must prove their sincerity by clearing out from the councils of state and public life all those who belong by blood or connexion to the race with whom civilization is at war.'

22. Karin and Adrian Stephen's second daughter Karin Judith was born on 20 November; Judith Bagenal on 8 November.

One night we went to the Russian dancers; & it was incongruous enough to see what they offered the tolerant good tempered public who had been bellowing like bulls over the efforts of a man to nail a carpet down.[23] They were tolerant, but, as I fancied, a little bit contemptuous of all this posing & springing against a flat blue wall. What a queer fate it is—always to be the spectator of the public, never part of it. This is part of the reason why I go weekly to see K.M. up at Hampstead, for there at any rate we make a public of two. On Thursday Murry came in, & we had an awkward, interesting talk; too self conscious to be enkindling. I think something or other is a little inharmonious in both of them;—in my arrogance, I suppose I feel them both too much of the underworld, with all sorts of nostrums of their own; & all this talk about being artists. I dont express what I mean. Perhaps all I mean is that they seem suspicious— Beneath the surface I expect that they are both very anxious for appreciation, not at all sure of themselves, & Murry wrings his brains dry, & becomes more & [more] hopeless of finding anything to believe in. I dont like married couples where the husband admires the wife's work immensely.

Arthur Ponsonby came up & spoke to us at the Club the other day. He is standing somewhere, & wants to get in, if only to prove that his side has a good case; he said he didn't much care to be in Parliament itself.[24] A weak, moderately intelligent, kindly man, permanently puzzled, & worried too, by the strange order of the world. Living in a social class different from the one he was born into may account for this. Then we had Dr Leys to lunch on Wednesday (27th, I put in by way of mark).[25] He has spent 17 years in East Africa, & being a very sterling direct Scotchman has a terrible tale to tell about the natives. How they concentrate, how bare of superfluity they are, these professional intellectual men!

Printing off on our little machine began today, & now I must give

23. On 28 November the Woolfs went to the London Coliseum to see Lydia Lopokova and Leonide Massine in 'Carnaval'; the Diaghilev Ballet company shared the variety bill with, among other items, a recital of popular music, Beatie and Babs in 'Frivolous Fragments', and Will Evans in 'Laying the Carpet'.

24. Arthur Augustus William Harry Ponsonby (1871-1946), later 1st Baron Ponsonby of Shulbrede (1930), author, politician and pacifist, who throughout the war had urged a negotiated peace. Since 1908 he had been a Liberal MP, but standing for Dunfermline as an Independent Democrat in December 1918 was decisively beaten. His father had for twenty-five years been private secretary to Queen Victoria.

25. Dr Norman Maclean Leys, MB, DPH (d. 1944), who had retired from the Public Health Service of Kenya, was to write several books on African questions which were published by the Hogarth Press.

my very best attention to Murry's manuscript, A Fable for Critics, which I brought home in my bag, with a view to printing.[26]

Tuesday 3 December

(What odd stray of knowledge makes me think that this is Carlyle's birthday? Perhaps because I'm reading about Froude;—I go on to wonder whether any one else is thinking of Carlyle's birthday, & if so whether it gives him any pleasure; & again of the curious superstition, haunting literary people, of the value of being remembered by posterity— but I had better rein myself in).[1]

I have to read for a second time Murry's poem, which I found hard to read; from reasons the opposite of those that make Eliot hard to read: Murry has a plethora of words; his poem is intricate & involved & as thick as a briar hedge; he does his thinking aloud; not making you fetch it from the depths of silence as Eliot does. We've been walking by the river, & indeed sitting beside it, so hot it is, bland, milky, & without thrill in the air. The gulls were letting themselves be carried down stream, for a diversion I suppose; little companies of three & four gliding down, & then one dives & reappears. We discussed the origin of my present fit of melancholy, & I was divinely reassured by L. so that here I sit comfortable & secure; once more established in that degree of belief which makes life possible. But I leave out the analysis, which I have gone into sufficiently. I fancy all people have these spiritual tides in them —Heaven knows why. Altogether the more one thinks of it the stranger one's own organisation appears.

On Sunday, that is the 1st December we had a dinner party. Six people make a dinner party. They destroy private conversation. You have to be festive. We had Nick, Carrington, Mrs Manus & Sanger: & I think it was a successful party. We were sufficiently springy & spontaneous I think. Charlie made his little jokes. Nick was nearly silent, but apprecia-tive. I foresee a testy middle age for Nick. Mrs Manus enjoyed her dinner. Carrington has more merit than most of the young. We had chairs down and abolished the sofa. I can't for the life of me remember what we talked about, save that Charlie emphatically despised both Herbert

26. This poem dated October 1913, and retitled *The Critic in Judgment or Belshazzar of Baronscourt*, was published by the Hogarth Press on 12 May 1919.
1. Thomas Carlyle was born on 4 December 1795 (and died in 1881); Leslie Stephen (who knew him) wrote his life for the *Dictionary of National Biography*. J. W. Froude (1818-94) was Carlyle's literary executor and wrote his biography. VW was reviewing Froude's *English Seamen in the Sixteenth Century* together with Richard Hakluyt's *Voyages, Travels and Discoveries of the English Nation*; her article appeared in the *TLS* on 12 December 1918 (Kp C133).

Fisher & Gilbert Murray. He doesn't like to be asked to meet people because they're interesting he said. I said no, you only like failures. On Monday I went first to Harrison's with L. then walked across Regent's Park & had tea with Barbara. Regent's Park at 4.30 on a December afternoon is a dreary place. So many purple leaves seem to be flattened on the path. Then the park keepers begin whistling, & I remember being afraid of being shut in, as a child. Then the mist rolls up over that vast open space. On one side of you the commoner animals in the zoo grunt & growl—chiefly pigs now, for war purposes I suppose. This did not produce a cheerful frame of mind in which to visit an invalid; & to my horror I found that she shares a room with another, a widow, whose husband was killed; & there poor woman, she sat, pretending to read a book & not to look my way, while Barbara & I gossiped, without much spirit. B. would have preferred a son; sons, she says, are more troublesome, nervous, naughty, from birth; I suppose this is the natural feeling, though not a very desirable one; assertiveness seems to her interesting. Her own baby, with Nick's nose, slept in a cradle; grumbling a little, but very good she said. The future seemed to oppress her.

Saturday 7 December

For some reason, not connected with my virtues I think, I get 2 or even 3 books weekly from the Times, & thus breast one short choppy wave after another. It fills up the time while Night & Day lies dormant; it gives me distinct pleasure I own to formulate rapid views of Henry James & Mr Hergesheimer; chiefly because I slip in some ancient crank of mine.[2] But this sort of writing is always done against time; however much time I may have. For example here I have spent the week (but I was interrupted 2 days, & one cut short by a lunch with Roger) over Hakluyt: who turns out on mature inspection to justify over & over again my youthful discrimination. I write & write; I am rung up & told to stop writing; review must be had on Friday; I typewrite till the messenger from the Times appears; I correct the pages in my bedroom with him sitting over the fire here.

"A Christmas number not at all to Mr Richmond's taste, he said. Very unlike the supplement style."

"Gift books, I suppose?" I suggested.

"O no, Mrs Woolf, its for the advertisers."

But to retrace. On Thursday I lunched with Roger in order to hear the following story.

2. VW's review of *The Method of Henry James* by Joseph Warren Beach appeared in the *TLS* on 26 December 1918 (Kp C138); and of *The Three Black Pennys* by Joseph Hergesheimer on 12 December 1918 (Kp C134).

Mrs McColl to Mr Cox of the London Library:[3]
"Have you The Voyage Out by Virginia Woolf?"

"Virginia Woolf? Let me see; she was a Miss Stephen, daughter of Sir Leslie. Her sister is Mrs Clive Bell I think. Ah, strange to see what's become of those two girls. Brought up in such a nice home too. But then, they were never *baptised*."

Roger & I get on very well now; more genuine & free than we were, under the shadow of Gordon Square. We agree on many points; & he, at least, perceives the isolation of our little group in the large hostile world of MacColls & Duckworths. Then we discuss prose; & as usual some book is had out, & I have to read a passage over his shoulder. Theories are fabricated. Pictures stood on chairs. Here I become rather random & desperate. Wolfe brings in a picture— The question is about a slice of green on the midmost apple. Does it interpose with the violet on the edge of the potato? "Cut it out: see the way the colours show up over there:—well try varnish then." "I think its the best thing I've done yet." "O yes, there's more life in it—its very strong, Wolfe, very strong."[4]

At last, inevitably late, I go on to the 17 Club, where Mrs Manus & L. sit in the upper room, correcting proofs, but Couch [?printer] has only sent a batch. Anyhow, I was too late to help; but not to pour out tea for Miss Matthaie. Why should a woman of her sense apologise all her life long because she is an unattractive woman? She looks up sidelong, like a child who has done wrong. And yet she has more in her head than all the cropheads put together. Alix I found intoning pompously downstairs, with a perverted likeness to a colonel of the upper classes holding forth upon the iniquity of Bolshevism. Her theme is the iniquity of colonels; the method seems much the same; even the voice.

Friday, as I say was spent writing by me; by Leonard in having lunch with Will A.F. & correcting more proofs. No sooner had I done a little type setting, & ruled off the hour & a half before dinner in which to read my distinguished American novelist [Hergesheimer] recommended by Mr Galsworthy, than Lottie admitted Sydney Waterlow. My only hope for passing the time was some sort of introspective confidence on his part; but no such luck. He is prosperous, complacent, self assured even to the extent of confronting the disapproval of Gordon Square unabashed. He is now on the round of his friends, not, he was careful to explain in order to test us, but to enjoy our society. Mary Sheepshanks

3. Andrée Desirée Jeanne MacColl, *née* Zabé (d. 1945), the French wife of the painter and art critic D. S. MacColl, at this time Keeper of the Wallace Collection. She was a great friend of Roger Fry.
4. Edward Wolfe (b. 1897), painter, born in Johannesburg, studied at the Slade 1916–1918 and worked in the Omega Workshops with Roger Fry.

had been summoned to dine with us in order to discuss the Review, &
MacDonald's treachery.[5] Paler, perhaps thinner, fading into middle age
imperceptibly, with the same flavour of bitterness against a world—a
world of upper class women, it is at the present moment, who ask for
an indemnity. Yet, compared with the greater variety of my acquaintance,
she comes out abler, better informed, more rational than I remembered
her in the days of Fitzroy Square. But still she accepts her "nice evening"
as the grudging poor accept a charity which is rather less than they
deserve.

Tuesday 10 December

Sunday was memorable to me for another visit to Shelley House—
where I actually shook hands with Miss Sands, Katie, & Elena Rathbone.[6]
All expressed great surprise at seeing me, as if I were a strange bird
joining a flock of the same species. I felt strange enough; but oddly
familiar with their ways after the first. Elena was almost like an old friend—
a very old friend who persists, remembering what went on before I took
my dive & she hers. She pressed me, almost affectionately, to come &
see them. I shall do it with misgivings. Suppose we have absolutely
nothing to say? All her charming frank caressing manner may vanish.
And then there is the eternal, & insoluble question of clothes. Katie
rather ensanguined & flesh covered, but with a great dignity & amplitude
of feature, sitting very up right, eyes half closed, in the front of the
room, listening to Ravel & Schumann, which she said she admired
equally.

On Monday I paid what has now become my weekly visit to Katherine.
Murry was there; which makes it a little stiff, though I like them both, &
her better as a wife. He scarcely speaks; makes one feel that most speaking
is useless; but as he has a brain of his own I don't mind this. Besides it
is more shyness than purpose. I told such stories as I could think of;
Murry then explained that he had a confession to make. It only amounted
to the fact that he has bought his brother a hand press, upon which

5. Mary Sheepshanks (*c.* 1870-1958), daughter of a bishop, was from 1899 effective
principal of Morley College, and had persuaded VW to teach there in 1905; she
retired in 1913 to devote herself to the cause of international women's suffrage.
Ramsay MacDonald's treachery is described in *III LW*, 223-6, and lay in his
blowing first hot then cold upon LW's projects for the *International Review*.

6. Ethel Sands (1873-1962), painter, born at Newport, Rhode Island, studied in Paris,
worked with Sickert, and was a foundation member of the London Group. Well-
to-do and sociable, she became a British subject after the war. Katie was Lady
Cromer, *née* Lady Katherine Thynne (1865-1933), second wife of Evelyn Baring,
1st Earl of Cromer. VW had known her and her sister Beatrice since Hyde Park
Gate days. Elena Rathbone was Mrs Bruce Richmond.

some short poems of his are to be printed, beautifully, like Kelmscott books. Arthur is learning at a Polytechnic, & wishes to do 'art' printing. I rather suspect Arthur's views of art.[7] But anyhow we are to do what we like with Murry's long poem. At present to give it McDermott seems the most feasible plan, when the great red posters are all issued, which have begun to paper Richmond during the past few days. "Payment, Punishment . . ." & some other P. is the policy they advocate. We shall probably vote for no one. A wet day; but we went out having "practically" finished Kew Gardens; I mean it is all ready to print save a few lines. Light in my study gives out about 3.30. Now I shall try to do a few lines of Eliot before we go away. There is one of the usual kitchen intrigues to have Liz & children to Asheham for Christmas. Nelly doesnt like to ask me; Lottie makes up a rigmarole about saving us expense & this being the last time that she will be able to leave home. How terrible it is to be in this position to other grown people!

Monday 16 December

Back from a week end with Roger. Lips, therefore, rather sore with talk, though his range is so wide, & we both have such a number of things to say that I, certainly, was neither bored nor satiated. Pamela was there, very rounded, supple, with a likeness to some naked wood creature in an Italian picture; she has the yellow brown complexion too. I suspect that children take the shape of their parents the other way about; a vivacious sociable enthusiastic father produces a quiet, unselfish, rather passive daughter. She is only sixteen, but mature in manner, as the result of living with grown up people.[8] It was polling day on Saturday in Guildford, as in other parts of the world, & Roger very gloomy about the future of the world. No doubt he will soon forget about politics. The war is already almost forgotten. All Sunday, in spite of rain & fog he painted till the sky was black, having been grey through the time of daylight. I feel little hope about his pictures, but had to counterfeit an opinion as to the effect produced on the solidity of a bowl by a mornings work on it. He said that he grudged every hour of daylight spent not painting, since age draws near, & he must say what he wants to say before he dies. Age he proposes to spend alone, working all day long.

7. Murry's only brother Arthur (called Richard) was some twelve years younger than he. The press was installed in the Murry's Hampstead house, and one of Katherine Mansfield's stories was the first production of the 'Heron Press'. The Kelmscott Press had been founded by William Morris in 1890 at Hammersmith. The Woolfs were not interested in 'art' printing in the productions of the Hogarth Press.

8. Agnes Pamela (b. 1902), daughter of Roger Fry and his wife Helen. She had been brought up almost entirely by her father and his sisters, her mother having been confined to an asylum since 1910.

At last he seems to do what he has always tried to do. We had some melancholy revelations about the treachery of certain friends towards the Omega.[9] Roger's great point is that though superficially unbalanced & exaggerated his sense of balance is always right in the end; he is always magnanimous & forgiving, however much weight he may lay upon imaginary or semi-imaginary grievances. The Omega case is that his artists accept commissions independently of the Omega. For that & other reasons the poor shop has been a source of unmitigated disillusion to him—a weariness & grievance. People hate art & him for loving it is now a frequent burden of his talk. Nor did I show myself one of the elect, with regard to painting at least. We visited the National Gallery together this morning; I thought a Rembrandt "very fine" which to him was mere melodrama. A little El Greco conveyed little until he illumined it; showed how it held more real colour than any other picture there. Then the Ingres was repulsive to me; & to him one of the most marvellous of designs. I always feel, too, that to like the wrong thing, or fail in sufficiently liking the right jars on him, like false notes, or sentimentality in writing.

Tuesday 17 December

This I cannot help fearing will be my last opportunity for writing before I go to Asheham on Friday, though I shall continue there, God being willing, in some form of new book. Tomorrow I go to K.M. Thursday I have tea with the Richmonds, & perhaps dine at the Club; so Friday is reached without any interval between tea & dinner; & even today I am stealing what belongs to Sophocles, before Mrs Hamilton arrives at 7 to address the Guild. Suppose I buy a block, with detachable leaves, I think I shall snare a greater number of loose thoughts. No doubt this is pure fancy, but then so much of one's mental affairs are controlled by fancy. Nessa has asked us to have the children for a fortnight when the new baby is born. This is now imminent, & she fixes the 28th for the exact day. The servants go to Guildford for a week, in order that we may be free from Liz & her offspring. We shall have one week entirely alone, at Asheham, the greatest & most unmixed pleasure this world affords; enhanced very much in my mind by the absence of servants, so that often we are alone in the house. I am going to read through my novel & determine what to do with it. L.'s book is almost done; February

9. During the past summer Duncan Grant and Vanessa Bell had decorated a room in River House, Hammersmith, for Mary Hutchinson. Roger Fry was deeply wounded by what he felt to be their disloyalty to the Omega Workshops, of which they were directors, in disregarding the obligations of their position by undertaking a direct commission.

will see it finished most likely.[10] We have printed off the text of Kew Gardens, & got an estimate from McDermott for printing Murry's poem. He asks £4.10. which to us seems little, for 200 copies of a 24 page book. We supply the paper, & the cover. Possibilities are opened up I think.

Weather has been so warm that I dont think I've had a fire in my study more than 3 or 4 times, & that only when we were printing in the afternoon. Influenza seems to be over, though Lottie had an attack lasting an hour or two on Saturday. Iced cakes are possible, but so far no more than that. As for public news, the war already seems an unimportant incident; one of our political dodges, & at this moment the news boys are shouting that Russia prepares for war.[11] It is difficult to see how even a jingo can now believe in any good from war, or any ideal, or anything, one feels tempted to add undertaken by bodies of human beings in concert. It is said that Labour did well, & the Coalition only moderately, at the polls. Ray is said to have a good chance;—we voted on Saturday, but L. overcome with panic, very likely voted for Mrs Dacre Fox.[12]

10. At the instigation of Sidney Webb, LW in 1917 began the preparation of a report on international trade for a committee of the Labour Research Department. In the summer of 1917 VW had helped by copying out relevant statistics from books and reports lent to LW by the library of the London School of Economics. LW later decided to restrict his study to Africa, and Alix Sargant-Florence helped him with the research. The book was finished in February 1919 but did not appear until the beginning of 1920, when it was published jointly by the Labour Research Department and Allen & Unwin under the title *Empire and Commerce in Africa, A study in Economic Imperialism*.

11. The Bolsheviks had invaded Esthonia, capturing Narva, and British naval intervention was reported on 17 December.

12. This proved over-optimistic: the results of the poll on 14 December (declared on 28 December) showed an immense majority for the Lloyd George-Bonar Law coalition—526 seats out of 707; Labour secured 59. Mrs Strachey polled 1263 votes as against the Conservative-Unionist's 9077 and Labour's 2620. Mrs Dacre Fox (see above, 30 November 1918, n 21) was the runner-up at Richmond, polling 3615 votes as against the Conservative-Unionist's 8364.

1919

1919

The entry dated 17 December was the last for 1918. VW went to Asheham on Friday 20 December, a day before LW. Maynard Keynes and Duncan Grant came to tea on Christmas day, on which day Vanessa gave birth to her daughter by Duncan, three days sooner than was expected. Julian and Quentin Bell, whom VW had undertaken to look after during Vanessa's confinement, were fetched from Charleston by LW on Saturday 23 December, and returned with the Woolfs to Hogarth House on 1 January 1919. On this day VW had bad toothache, and next day a tooth extracted, followed by bleeding and headaches. The boys were returned to their father at Gordon Square on 9 January, and VW remained in bed until 16 January.

When she resumed her diary, VW continued to write it in the improvised book she had been using since 15 November (Diary VI). Entries for 20, 22, and 24 January are made there; and these were copied out, with emendations and additions, at the beginning of her new book for 1919 (Diary VII), headed, on the first page:

Hogarth House
Paradise Road
Richmond
January 1st 1919

This text follows her revised version; for the earlier version, see Appendix 2.

Monday 20 January

I mean to copy this out when I can buy a book, so I omit the flourishes proper to the new year. It is not money this time that I lack, but the capacity, after a fortnight in bed, to make the journey to Fleet Street. Even the muscles of my right hand feel as I imagine a servants hand to feel. Curiously enough, I have the same stiffness in manipulating sentences, though by rights I should be better equipped mentally now than I was a month ago. The fortnight in bed was the result of having a tooth out, & being tired enough to get a headache—a long dreary affair, that receded & advanced much like a mist on a January day. One hours writing daily is my allowance for the next few weeks; & having hoarded it this morning, I may spend part of it now, since L. is out, & I am much behindhand with the month of January. I note however that this diary writing does not count as writing, since I have just reread my years diary & am much struck by the rapid haphazard gallop at which it swings along, sometimes indeed jerking almost intolerably over the cobbles. Still if it were not written rather faster than the fastest typewriting, if I stopped & took thought, it would never be written at all; & the advantage of the method is that it sweeps up accidentally several stray matters which I should exclude if I hesitated, but which are the diamonds of the dustheap. If Virginia Woolf at the age of 50, when she sits down to build her memoirs out of these books is unable to make a phrase as it should be made, I can only condole with her & remind her of the existence of the fireplace, where she has my leave to burn these pages to so many black films with red eyes in them. But how I envy her the task I am preparing for her! There is none I should like better. Already my 37th birthday next Saturday is robbed of some of its terrors by the thought. Partly for the benefit of this elderly lady (no subterfuge will then be possible: 50 is elderly, though I anticipate her protest & agree that it is not old) partly to give the year a solid foundation, I intend to spend the evenings of this week of captivity in making out an account of my friendships & their present condition, with some account of my friends characters; & to add an estimate of their work, & a forecast of their future works. The lady of 50 will be able to say how near to the truth I come; but I have written enough for tonight (only 15 minutes, I see).

To resume; I admit I dont like thinking of the lady of 50. Courage however; Roger is past that age, & still capable of feeling, & enjoying & playing a very considerable part in life.

Wednesday 22 January

Today is Wednesday, Jan. 22nd. Two days more were spent in bed, & today counts as my first of complete health. I even wrote a sentence of alterations and additions this morning. I have a book on Meredith to do for the Times,[1] & we walked this afternoon, so I am back again nearly in my old position. As I can't get up to London, & only see little framed pictures of Alix & Fredegond sitting by the fire here, I might attempt that solid foundation which I think desirable.

How many friends have I got? There's Lytton, Desmond, Saxon; they belong to the Cambridge stage of life; very intellectual; cut free from Hyde Park Gate; connected with Thoby; but I can't put them in order, for there are too many. Ka & Rupert & Duncan, for example, all come rather later; they belong to Fitzroy days; the Oliviers & all that set are stamped as the time of Brunswick Sqre; Clive I put a little aside; later still there are the cropheads, Alix, Carrington, Barbara, Nick, Bunny. I must insert too the set that runs parallel but does not mix, distinguished by their social & political character, headed perhaps by Margaret & including people like Goldie, Mrs Hamilton, & intermittent figures such as Matthaei, Hobson, the Webbs—no, I can't include either the darkies, or Dr Leys,

1. VW's review of *George Meredith: His Life and Friends in Relation to his Work* by S. M. Ellis appeared in the *TLS* of 13 February 1919 (Kp C140).

though they stand for the occasional visitor who lunches
room to talk seriously. I have not placed Ottoline or Roger
are Katherine & Murry & the latest of all, Hope Mirrlees
Pernel & Pippa & outlying figures such as Ray & Oliver. Ge
omit (& Mary Hutch. too) for reasons which if my account gets
might give; & Eliot I liked on the strength of one visit & shall p
see more of, owing to his poems which we began today to set up.

This is a very partial account, but I shall never place half of
accurately unless I start straight away. Lytton & Desmond & Saxon then.
Well, I cherish a considerable friendship for each of them; the worst of it
is how seldom we meet. With Lytton & Desmond till last month tethered
to a stool in the Admiralty, months pass without a sight of them. The
season of letter writing is over for all of us, I think; or perhaps we need
different correspondents. Brilliant letters we wrote each other once, partly
for the sake of being brilliant, & we were getting to know each other then,
& there was a thrill about it (I speak of my own feelings.) But when we
do meet, there is nothing to complain of. Lytton is said to be more tolerant
& less witty; Desmond, they say, needs a glass of wine; Saxon has his
rheumatics & his hopeless love affair. Lytton again is famous these last
six months, but as that was a matter of course since his first six months
there is not much surprise or change in it. Moreover, I hear he has abandoned his Asquiths or they are provided with some later light. Nothing
is easier or more intimate than a talk with Lytton. If he is less witty, he is
more humane. Presumably, judging from precedent & taking into account
the demobilisation of the army, he is now preparing to fly, but as his
alliance is not with me the direction he flies in makes very little difference.
I like Carrington though. She has increased his benignity. O yes, if he
were to walk in at this moment we should talk about books & feelings &
life & the rest of it as freely as we ever did, & with the sense, on both sides
I think, of having hoarded for this precise moment a great deal peculiarly
fit for the other.

Friday 24 January

Oddly enough, the day after writing this sentence I got into touch with
Lytton, after a lapse of six months or so, on the telephone. & he is to dine
here next Friday. But to resume. There are three words knocking about
in my brain to use of Stracheys,—a prosaic race, lacking magnanimity,
shorn of atmosphere. As these words have occurred automatically, & will
tease me till written down, I daresay there is some truth in them. All the
unpleasantness that I wish to introduce into my portrait of Lytton is contained in them, as if in deep wells. I shall only need one drop of this gall
for his portrait, but I fancy a tinge of the kind is perceptible in him too—
far more in James, Oliver & Marjorie. Roger's version is that all, except

y S., lack generosity. It is an air, a vapour, an indescribable taste of dust in the throat, something tickling & irritating as well as tingling & stimulating. But then one must combine with this a great variety of mental gifts, & gifts of character—honesty, loyalty, intelligence of a spiritual order. One might almost attribute what I mean in Lytton's case at least to lack of physical warmth, lack of creative power, a failure of vitality warning him not to be spendthrift but to eke out his gifts parsimoniously, & tacitly assume his right to a superior share of comfort & opulence. In matters of emotion this has a slightly stingy appearance, nor is he ever unthinkingly generous & magnanimous, risking himself. Mentally of course it produces that metallic & conventionally brilliant style which prevents his writing from reaching, to my judgment, the first rate. It lacks originality, & substance; it is brilliant, superbly brilliant journalism, a supremely skilful rendering of the the old tune. Written down these words are too emphatic & linear; one should see them tempered & combined with all those charming, subtle & brilliant qualities which compose his being in the flesh. But when I think of a Strachey, I think of someone infinitely cautious, elusive & unadventurous. To the common stock of our set they have added phrases, standards, & witticisms, but never any new departure; never an Omega, a Post Impressionist movement, nor even a country cottage, a Brunswick Square or a printing press. We Stephens, yes, & even Clive, with all his faults, had the initiative, & the vitality to conceive & carry our wishes into effect because we wished too strongly to be chilled by ridicule or checked by difficulty. Even in the matter of taking Tidmarsh Lytton had to be propelled from behind, & his way of life insofar as it is unconventional, is so by the desire & determination of Carrington.

Thursday 30 January

Such is the cold today that I doubt whether I can go on with my disquisition. On such a day one would need to be of solid emerald or ruby to burn with any flame, & not merely dissolve in grey atoms in the universal grey. I saw no one in Richmond High Street who seemed to be burning with the intensity of ruby or emerald—poor pinched women, absolutely mastered by circumstances, though I did hear one speak of going home to get tea ready, which suggested the possibility of some individual life for her. A child threw her hat into the area which I had to recover, & made a whole row of them laugh by tossing it up twice so that it fell into the area again; then the Poles require copies of the In[ternational]. R[eview]. to be sent to Paris; & here is Nelly to say two servants may call in to see me about Nessa's place.[2] To my chronicle of Lytton I can only

2. For the background to and progress of this domestic saga see *II VW Letters*, no. 1002 etc., and also below, *passim*.

add that he writes today to put us off, being fled to Tidmarsh, since "Calvé is ill, & cannot meet me at Heinemann's".[3] What he should be doing with Calvé, I dont know; but the information thus vouchsafed, suggests—well, further speculations of mine upon fame, jealousy, vanity, & so forth which I wait a more congenial season to unfold. Owing to this incubus of my friends I have said nothing of a visit from Alix, from Norton, from Fredegond, nor traced some rather interesting revelations, or developments, which may bear fruit one of these days. Alix is thinking of taking a house in Gordon Sqre "chiefly in order to live with James" she said;[4] & this, as she announced it to L., me, & Saxon, had some quality in it that for the moment made my blood run cold. Now, to tune myself up I am going to shut Mrs Watts upon George Frederic, & open the Antigone of Sophocles. One second—I must note for future use, the superb possibilities of Freshwater, for a comedy. Old Cameron dressed in a blue dressing gown & not going beyond his garden for 12 years, suddenly borrows his son's coat, & walks down to the sea. Then they decide to proceed to Ceylon, taking their coffins with them, & the last sight of Aunt Julia is on board ship, presenting porters with large photographs of Sir Henry Taylor & the Madonna in default of small change.[5]

Friday 31 January

Here I solace my restlessness as usual upon returning from the Club upon this book. I visited the Omega, & heard Roger wheedling a fat German lady to buy stuff, & doing his best to be polite to Mr Powell, an art gentleman who makes glass in South Kensington I suppose, & can

3. See *VW/GLS Letters*, p. 77. Lytton Strachey had been a guest in September 1918 at a house-party in Northumberland and there had met William Heinemann (1883-1920), the publisher. He had no doubt invited Lytton to a party to meet Mme Emma Calvé (1886-1942), the celebrated operatic singer, but had cancelled the invitation because of her illness. A performance Mme Calvé had been due to give at the Queen's Hall on 25 January was postponed, presumably owing to her indisposition, until 8 February.

4. Alix Sargant-Florence and James Strachey rented the whole of 41 Gordon Square—which remained theirs until 1956—living at first in the two top floors and letting off the lower floors.

5. The two volume biography of her husband *George Frederic Watts, The Annals of an Artist's Life*, was published by Mary Fraser Watts in 1912. The description of the Camerons' departure for Ceylon, which inspired VW's play *Freshwater* (written 1923; re-written and performed 1935; first published with an introductory essay by Lucio Ruotolo, 1976), occurs in vol. 1, pp. 300-1. Charles Hay Cameron (1795-1880), jurist, served on the Indian Law Commission, 1835-48; VW's great-aunt Julia, the photographer, was his wife; Sir Henry Taylor (1800-1886), the author of *Philip van Artevelde* (1834) was one of her favourite sitters.

believe.[6] Thence through streets of frozen mud, snow, slush, slippery & congealed into little knobs like those on an astrachan coat, to the Club (& here I am interrupted by the voice of my dear old friend, Desmond, upon the telephone—10 minutes discourse. Yes, he's taking a house at Oare, perhaps, & wishes us to be near him, & will come on Tuesday to bring a story, & is lodging at Littlehampton, & will subscribe to the Review, & send a flimsy for 10/—no, 12/- of course, & they've let Wellington Square, & propose to live cheap & spend half the year in the country, which he doesn't much like, but there it is. Here, with sympathetic enquiries about my health & tooth, we ring off.[7]) Yes, its sympathy that Desmond has; & thus I'm switched back again to old Lytton. But old Lytton I must at once acquit of wishing to impress me with his Calvés & his Heinemanns; I think he mentioned a concert, & this is it. Let me try to account for the fact that he has 'dominated' (why, even the word is his) a generation at Cambridge, & make it square with my disparaging remarks. How did he do it, how is he so distinct & unmistakable if he lacks orginality & the rest? Is there any reputable escape from this impasse in saying that he is a great deal better than his books? or am I too chary of praise for those books? Am I jealous? Do I compare the 6 editions of Eminent Victorians with the one of The Voyage Out? Perhaps there's a hint of jealousy; but, if I underrate, I think the main cause is that while I admire, enjoy up to a point & up to a point agree, I'm not interested in what he writes. Thomas Hardy has what I call an interesting mind; so have Conrad & Hudson; but not Lytton nor Matthew Arnold nor John Addington Symonds.

Tues. Feb. 4th

Life is getting crowded out altogether. But life hasn't been very enjoyable these last few days. Conceive a conspiracy of fog, frost, strike on Tube railways,[1] & on top of that servant hunting for Nessa. This last has ended disastrously. I braved Mrs Abbey once more yesterday, snatched my Phoebe Crane from the jaws of mistresses innumerable, only to hear

6. Possibly Harry J. Powell of the Whitefriars Glass Works, Tudor St., EC1, who, like Roger Fry, showed work at the Arts and Crafts Exhibition held at the Royal Academy in the winter of 1916. VW's 'South Kensington' appears to be arbitrary.

7. The MacCarthys did take a house, opposite to the Waterlows', in the village of Oare, near Marlborough, Wiltshire, letting their London house, 25 Wellington Square, Chelsea. 'Flimsy' was a slang term for a banknote, and hence for a postal order; 12/- was the price of an annual subscription to the *International Review* of which LW was editor.

1. The motormen on the London Underground ('Tube') railway came out on strike on 3 February, in support of strikers on the Clyde and in Belfast. The District Railway—normally used by the Woolfs—closed down on 4 February. The strikes were settled by 7 February but full services were not restored until the 10th. Richmond was however also served by the main London and South-Western Railway from Waterloo.

now that she's not wanted, & must be put off with a pound no
her. This is the imposing pinnacle to my fortnights castle bui.
Budge & the rest; the cards fall down & things are as they were
upon letters have been written in that bold hand & business like s.
natural to me, telegrams sent, Nelly entreated, brains ransack
journeys of penitence made with the result that 32/- is now scattered among
undeserving people.[2] But I must record a little sunshine today, less cold;
&, to balance that, the district railway on strike.

Desmond has *not* rung up. That is quite a good preface to the description of his character. The difficulty which faces one in writing of Desmond is that one is almost forced to describe an Irishman: how he misses trains, seems born without a rudder to drift wherever the current is strongest; how he keeps hoping & planning, & shuffles along, paying his way by talking so enchantingly that editors forgive, & shopmen give him credit & at least one distinguished peer leaves him a thousand in his will.[3]

Saturday 15 February

What a disgraceful lapse! nothing added to my disquisition, & life allowed to waste like a tap left running. Eleven days unrecorded. Still I think if I were a painter I should only need a brush dipped in dun colour to give the tone of those eleven days. I should draw it evenly across the entire canvas. But painters lack sub[t]lety; there were points of light, shades beneath the surface, now, I suppose, undiscoverable. The predominant tint was furnished by the need I was under of visiting Registry Offices in the coldest weather of the year. It seems to me that I must have visited a dozen; three was in truth the utmost. But then one was on the verge of civilisation, on the outskirts of Fulham; & how hard, contained, & disillusioned the eyes of the women at the desks become, as if glued in front of them they saw eternally a cook of doubtful character! They can scarcely draw a veil of politeness over them at the sight of me, dressed up in red velvet & fur for their benefit. In the end somehow, Nelly had to go to Charleston for a week, & Phoebe Crane recovered from her illness, & was despatched there, so that peace is temporarily renewed.

Yesterday, Friday, I had one of my occasional galas. Dressed in my

2. Mrs Abbey ran a registry-office (or domestic agency) at 37 Berners St., W1, from where VW engaged Phoebe Crane as a stop-gap servant for Vanessa, whose domestic situation was chaotic. Vanessa at first repudiated and then accepted VW's arrangements; Phoebe Crane fell ill but did finally go to Charleston a week or so later. Budge was Nelly Boxall's sister. There had been expectations—which were to be renewed in October 1919—that she would become Vanessa's cook: expectations disappointed by reason of Budge's 'misfortune' (an illegitimate baby).

3. This was Auberon Thomas Herbert, 8th Baron Lucas and 11th Baron Dingwall (1876-1916), a member of the government 1908-15, and an airman, killed in action over the German lines. The sum involved *was* £1000.

best I went to Sickert's pictures, which I here pronounce the pleasantest, solidest most painter-like show in England.[4] & there I met Clive & Mary; Clive in his fur coat, Mary in the more subdued style of the New English [Art Club]. Put a yellow cane in Clive's hand, & hang a ribbon from an eyeglass, & he would step out of a sporting print—no, a caricature tinted with pinks & yellows. He introduced me to young Nevinson, with the Prince Albert whiskers—making allusion to our both being "such celebrated figures", which Nevinson did not appreciate.[5] Later, Clive, Mary & I strolled chattering like a perch of parrokeets, to Verreys, with its blue paint & gilt devices. Mary had a dutiful visit to pay her husband in hospital. So we sat & talked in an inner room,—a pleasant, dissipated place, parquet floor—curved bar, little tables—green & gold flourishes, dilapidated George the 4th style, & empty at this hour, save for some dubious ladies. We talked. We vibrated in sympathy. We billed & cooed. Rosy lights shone on his cheeks. Our intercourse was very gay, vibrant, like that of stringed instruments. Duncan passed through—a strange shaggy interlude, but, always & inevitably harmonious. He blinked as if newly exposed to the light, crumbled his brioche, & gulped down his coffee, stammering out his half articulated but immensely expressive words; & saying, I remember, how Art & Letters was the dullest & dreariest of papers ("I'll show it you—no, its not in that pocket—no, I don't know where it is.")[6] & how Julian & Quentin were so much cleverer than most children. Somehow, too soon, he hoisted himself into an astonishing long straight black coat, like a non-conformist ministers, hitched down his red waistcoat, & started off in a vague determined way to Victoria Station. And then we sat on, Clive & I, talking of writing, of my writing chiefly, which he praises sufficiently to give his strictures a good deal of force. As I half suspected, he found grave faults in that crude laborious novel of mine; & excessive merits in the Mark; the best prose, he said, written in our day.[7]

4. Walter Richard Sickert (1860-1942), a master painter, and an eccentric. He had studied under Whistler and knew several of the French Impressionists. Settling in London in 1905, he was associated with the Camden Town and London Groups, and was thus well known to Clive and Vanessa Bell. The exhibition of Sickert's paintings and drawings to which VW went was held at the Eldar Gallery, 40 Great Marlborough Street; the catalogue had a preface by Clive Bell.

5. Christopher Richard Wynne Nevinson (1889-1946), the painter and a foundation member of the London Group, son of Henry Woodd Nevinson, the war correspondent. In 1917 young Nevinson had been appointed an official war artist and his semi-cubist paintings had attracted considerable attention. Verreys was a café and restaurant at 229 Regent Street, W1.

6. *Art and Letters*, an illustrated quarterly, edited by Frank Rutter, Charles Ginner and Harold Gilman, began publication in July 1917.

7. 'The Mark on the Wall' was VW's contribution to *Publication No. 1. Two Stories* of the Hogarth Press, printed entirely by the Woolfs themselves and issued in July 1917 (Kp A2). The novel criticised by Clive was *The Voyage Out*.

Mary came in & interrupted, or rather influenced the current of our discourse, for she hardly spoke, & then we turned out into Regent Street where the lamps were lit, & the shop opposite had all its windows full of bright clothes against a green stage scene, & so strolling in the spring twilight & laughing still we made our way through Soho, & I left them, in a street with many jewellers windows.

Tuesday 18 February

Here I sit waiting for Alix, who can't be coming to disburden herself of confidences as I supposed; & thus my mind returns by way of her fickleness to my friends. Where was I? Desmond, & how I find him sympathetic compared with Stracheys. It is true; I'm not sure he hasn't the nicest nature of any of us—the nature one would soonest have chosen for one's own. I dont think that he possesses any faults as a friend, save that his friendship is so often sunk under a cloud of vagueness, a sort of drifting vapour composed of times & seasons separates us & effectively prevents us from meeting. Perhaps such indolence implies a slackness of fibre in his affections too—but I scarcely feel that. It arises rather from the consciousness which I find imaginative & attractive that things don't altogether *matter*. Somehow he is fundamentally sceptical. Yet which of us, after all, takes more trouble to do the sort of kindnesses that come his way? who is more tolerant, more appreciative, more understanding of human nature? It goes without saying that he is not an heroic character. He finds pleasure too pleasant, cushions too soft, dallying too seductive, & then, as I sometimes feel now, he has ceased to be ambitious. His 'great work' (it may be philosophy or biography now, & is certainly to be begun, after a series of long walks, this very spring) only ⟨takes shape⟩ appears, I believe, in that hour between tea & dinner, when so many things appear not merely possible but achieved. Comes the day light, & Desmond is contented to begin his article ; & plies his pen with a half humorous half melancholy recognition that such is his appointed life. Yet it is true, & no one can deny it, that he has the floating elements of something brilliant, beautiful—some book of stories, reflections, studies, scattered about in him, for they show themselves indisputably in his talk. I'm told he wants power; that these fragments never combine into an argument; that the disconnection of talk is kind to them; but in a book they would drift hopelessly apart. Consciousness of this, no doubt, led him in his one finished book [*Remnants*], to drudge & sweat until his fragments were clamped together in an indissoluble stodge. I can see myself, however, going through his desk one of these days, shaking out unfinished pages from between sheets of blotting paper, & deposits of old bills, & making up a small book of table talk, which shall appear as a proof to the younger generation that Desmond was the most gifted of us all. But why did he never do anything? they will ask.

At any rate in his own intermittent way Desmond is faithful. So much [one] may affirm of Saxon too, who comes next on my list. But Saxon's fidelity is almost that of the senile colly, or broken down ass—the pensioner who can draw upon a memory of the past for a seat at one's table in perpetuity. His present condition makes him appear almost exclusively in the character of almoner. He has little to give at the moment, life has not been generous to him. His possessions are old friendships, old memories —things we've talked of ages ago. Unlike the rest of us he has had no renewal of life in marriage; his hopes in that direction have been crushed. Therefore he comes to me disconsolately, grudgingly, ungenerously were the cause not one beyond his reach, asking rather than giving; asking at this moment that I shall accept Barbara at his hand—return her to him enriched with the glow of my approval. And Barbara does not appear to me somehow of that metal—that rarity— However, poor Saxon's life is now in the uncomfortable & unbecoming season which is so painfully well reproduced out of doors. Sleet, & mud & chill, & nothing growing; no warmth, no brilliancy, not even a modest domestic glow. He lodges with Stagg in Great Ormond Street, & has summed up his own position accurately as that of one who finds himself lonely if alone, & bored if in company. But faithful—there is something worth having in Saxon's fidelity; something that makes his most meagre visitation not altogether fruitless. One is aware, even after two hours of tepid & almost entire silence, that he is strictly true, genuine, unalloyed. You would never find him wanting; never find him callous, insincere, or grudging the last farthing of his possessions. Granted that he is not richly supplied with the gifts one might need, still I come to think in my weary age that safety— a modest competence—a truth as flawless as diamond or crystal—is not negligible, nor without its curious flashes of high remote beauty. At any rate I rest on the thought of Saxon with some relief after hovering for the past two months in a state of uncertainty over the thought of Katherine Murry. I might turn round what I have written of Saxon in order to make a background on which to paint a portrait of Katherine. It is at this moment extremely doubtful whether I have the right to class her among my friends. Quite possibly I shall never see her again. Upstairs I have letters in which she speaks of finding the thought of me a joy, dwelling upon my writing with excitement; I have letters making appointments, pressing for visits, adding postscripts of thanks & affection to visits already paid. But the last is dated December, & it is now February. The question interests, amuses, & also slightly, no, very, decidedly pains me. If it were not that I suspect her of wishing to produce precisely these emotions, save that of amusement, I should be still more put out. As it is—well I should need to write a long description of her before I arrived at my queer balance of interest, amusement, & annoyance. The truth is, I suppose, that one of the conditions unexpressed but understood of our friendship has been precisely that it was almost entirely founded on quicksands. It has been marked by curious slides & arrests; for months I've heard nothing of her; then we have met again upon what has the appearance of solid ground. We have been intimate, intense perhaps rather than open; but to me at anyrate our intercourse has been always interesting & mingled with quite enough of the agreeable personal element to make one fond—if that is the word—as well as curious. I was at pains to go up to Hampstead every week since mid October or November, I suppose. And then what happened? I go away for Christmas, & we send small bright presents, carefully timed to arrive on Christmas day. I add to mine one if not two long & affectionate letters; I propose to come as soon as I get back. My time in bed prevented this. But meanwhile, for no reason given or to be guessed at with any certainty, she falls silent; I get no thanks, no answers, no enquiries. So suspecting but willing to make every test before coming to conclusions, I asked Murry whether she would like a visit; to which he replied cordially & without the shadow of hesitation. I proposed to go yesterday. About eleven she, or rather the female who keeps house, rang up & put me off, saying that K.M. was too unwell for my visit; but making no suggestion of another time, nor have I any word from her or K. this morning.

Friday 21 February

But all this is made to appear rather fine drawn & exaggerated by the simple fact that I have a letter this morning from K.M. herself asking me to tea on Monday & explaining how some new treatment gives her fever for two days & makes it impossible for her to see people. Also I am asked to write for the Athenaeum, so that little scratch in my vanity is healed.[8] Not that I want to review any more books than come my way already. But owing to my laborious, & it appears rather misleading, accounts of my friends life has been too much neglected. Let me recollect. On Sunday last Saxon & Barbara dined here; but did little more than dine, since she had to return to feed her baby. She came frisking into the room; but her mind is a sedate literal mind; the pity is that she cant always be in a state of bodily frisk. That is her natural element, I'm sure; to expect quiet talk is against nature. Saxon watches her, judging I suppose that her charms

---

8. The *Athenaeum* (founded in 1828) had been bought after the war by Arnold Rowntree, who early in 1919 reconstituted it as a weekly journal of literature and the arts, offering the editorship to J. Middleton Murry. Murry had already asked Lytton Strachey and probably other of VW's friends to contribute, but she had not hitherto been approached. See *The Letters of Katherine Mansfield* edited by J. Middleton Murry, 1928, vol. 1, p. 224 for K.M.'s letter to VW.

provide for them both. I let myself in for a visit to Faith's; a tea, to see the Baby. Faith will shortly add to the race herself.[9] A discontent is roused in me at this proceeding on her part. I'm a human being myself; I scarcely feel that Faith will do us credit. She is a lax satirical woman, finding sharp things to say, & already at 28 possessed of a grievance. There she lounges over her fire arranging little mosaic patterns of all of us in a peevish way, & making it appear that she has no other interest in life. One feels her mind a very magpies larder of gossip. Oh yes, she knew of my meeting with Hope Mirrlees; & informed me that she supposed I was one of those unstable friends, rejoicing in quarrels. She had apparently given the matter some thought. In contrast to her Barbara was 'very nice'; direct, unaffected, sympathetic, as far as her wits will carry her; & in some queer fashion of her own a personality. I wonder what this rises from. On the doorstep in the dark she hinted her concern for poor old Saxon. And then Saxon rang me up to apologise for not staying longer, & suggest another visit.

Tuesday 25 February

Well, I haven't even quarrelled with Mirrlees—my literary ladies are faithful, though intermittent, whether purposely or not, I don't undertake to say. But these speculations obliterate what I see I call 'life'. The truth is I shirk the gigantic task of giving an account of Sundays teaparty, at which I met Sir Val. Chirrol, Sir Henry Newbolt & Lady, Lady Cromer, the Bruce Richmonds, & a scattering of gallant bald cavalry officers, & mounds of South Kensington dowager respectability who must be nameless.[10] Sir Val & Katie both foretold a revolution, & seemed to picture themselves meeting death nobly for the principle of respectability at the hands of the Russian Jews. Russian Jews invest every great city—a people of enormous energy & unscrupulosity—& then, as Sir Val remarked, 1914 will never come again—"not that anyone could accuse *me* of pacifism". Meanwhile Sir Henry confessed that music, especially the music of strings, moves the fount of poetry in him, & "something always comes of a concert—something will come this evening"—he assured me, as a priest foretelling a miracle, or a conjuror producing a rabbit. But the amiability of South Kensington is disarming. A kind of modesty veils what is so prominent & disagreeable in the intellectuals. They have an air of saying "I am no one—no one at all. My only function is to be agreeable. Another cup of tea? Do for goodness sake take this arm chair—& let me fetch you a slice of bread & butter—" Thats my impression of the

9. Her son was born on 1 April 1919; the baby on view was her niece, Barbara's child.
10. Sir Valentine Chirol (1852-1929), traveller and journalist, had been the influential head of the foreign department of *The Times*, and, like Sir Henry Newbolt, was known to VW personally through her father.

moment; though for some reason it doesn't encourage one to say anything more interesting than Thank you & please dont trouble, & other
phrases of the kind. Of no 23 Cromwell Houses, fronting the stuffed
beasts, & quite capable of staring them out of countenance, I will only say
that it is furnished on the great South Kensington principle of being on the
safe side & doing the thing handsomely.[11] Good Mrs Samuel Bruce went to
the Autotype Company & ordered the entire Dutch school to be sent
round framed in fumed oak. And so they were; & just covered the
staircase walls, leaving an inch or two's margin in between. The drawing
room—no, I cant write it all out; memory preserves only the shoulders of
a horse on a gilt easel, & three large seascapes, like slabs of thick bread &
butter. The company was decorous & fur bearing as usual; & the music
like the voice of spirits in another world enticing the hopelessly damned.
Sir Henry wrote a patriotic song to the tune of it. But how nice they are
too!—Katie shouldering her way along the streets afterwards, & letting
fall sentences of curious remote force, as though she were on top of a
mountain, or lost in a mist, as I can't help feeling these aristocrats are.

Not, however, Lord Eustace Percy. But at him my pen boggles, since
I cannot delve any further back into the week. How modestly he started,
smoking his pipe like any commoner, like poor rubber faced little Ewer
himself, or wry-necked Burns, & then by degrees how authoritative &
masterly he became, & beat the table to make his points, & pulled his
audience up short, & bade them "Wait a second", or asked them "Well,
What do you suggest then? What is your answer to that?" like some
transcendent head master, to whom the rest of us are but little children
spelling out their lesson, very badly stumbling over the long words; &
Lord Eustace, in his goodness, undertakes to enlighten us. I got the
impression of a very able man & a very aristocratic man, & a very nice
man—a combination that is so irresistable as to be alarming. He explained
the League of Nations draft.[12]

Very well: but now we come to another of the ornate & decorated
tribe; try as she will she can never lay aside her coronet; I mean poor dear

11. The home of Mrs Samuel Bruce in the Cromwell Road, opposite the Natural
History Museum, was the *venue* for a Sunday afternoon concert like those at
Shelley House (see above, 21 November and 10 December 1918).
12. On 22 February the Woolfs attended a conference on the League of Nations draft
treaty, chaired by Lord Eustace Percy (1887-1958), a son of the Duke of
Northumberland, who had served in the Diplomatic Service and Foreign Office
since 1910 and was to attend the Peace Conference in 1919 with Lord Robert Cecil,
assistant Secretary of State for Foreign Affairs. William Norman Ewer (b. 1885),
was a political journalist who became foreign editor and diplomatic correspondent
of the *Daily Herald* in 1919. Cecil Delisle Burns (1879-1943), social philosopher,
was until the war a University extension lecturer; he was now working for the
Ministry of Reconstruction.

old Ottoline. We dined at Gatti's together last night. I fetched her from the family bosom of Garlands Hotel.[13] She has the slim swaying figure of a Lombardy poplar—the ridges & hollows of the cheeks are the only sign of her years (47 I make them); & a feeble mincing step on the street, like that of a cockatoo with bad claws.[14] She has an indomitable spirit—plucking life out with those same gouty claws as if she were young & had illusions by the score. She had swooped down upon the land agents wife, & upon Rosa Allatini—for no reason save that the land agents wife writes novels, & Rosa Allatini has had her novel burnt by the hangman.[15] Allatini was a bad choice, save that she almost fainted & had to be fed on bath buns, which Ottoline had by her—& confided, of course, the story of her unhappy love, which made it necessary for her to be fed on Bath Buns. Birrell had been to tea, remarking how Queen Victoria liked nothing better than the sight of a drunken man; Lopokova had been discoursing all the afternoon.[16] As we sat a[t] dinner Ott picked up scraps of talk from the other diners, & admired their profiles. And so round to Gordon Square where we found Clive at the top of the house, where I used to stand & write, in the largest arm chair ever seen, by the finest fire, with a screen across the door to keep the draught out, as affable as a cockatoo & as brightly coloured as a macaw.[17] I left them together & lost my train.

13. Gatti's Restaurant lay between the Strand and Adelaide Street, near Charing Cross; Garland's (formerly Garlant's) Hotel was in Suffolk Street, east of Haymarket.
14. Lady Ottoline was forty-five (b. 16 June 1873).
15. Rosa Allatini's *Despised and Rejected*, published in 1918 under the pseudonym A. T. Fitzroy, had been the subject of charges under the Defence of the Realm Act. At the Mansion House on 10 October 1918, Alderman Sir Charles Wakefield judged that the book was 'likely to prejudice the recruiting, training and discipline of persons in His Majesty's Forces'. He fined four people representing the publishers, C. W. Daniel Ltd., the maximum of £100 each plus £10 costs and ordered them to forfeit all 234 copies of the book in their possession. The author was not proceeded against. Lady Ottoline's other quarry was Constance Holme (1880-1955), wife of the agent to her brother Lord Henry Cavendish Bentinck's estate, Underly Hall at Kirkby Lonsdale in Westmorland. See also *II VW Letters*, no. 1024.
16. Augustine Birrell (1850-1933), the author and Liberal statesman who had been President of the Board of Education 1905-07, and Chief Secretary for Ireland 1907-16. He was an old friend of Ottoline's and VW had met him before the war at her house, 44 Bedford Square. Lydia Lopokova (b. 1891), the Russian ballet dancer, came to England with Diaghilev's company, and during the winter season 1918/19 was appearing at the London Coliseum, partnered by Leonide Massine. Maynard Keynes, whom she married in 1925, first met her at the party given by the Sitwells in Carlyle Square on 10 October 1918, a party at which both Ottoline and VW had also been present (see Diary entry for 12 October 1918 above).
17. 46 Gordon Square, to which the four Stephens moved after their father's death in 1904, and which subsequently became the home of Clive and Vanessa Bell, was

Wednesday 5 March

Just back from 4 days at Asheham, & one at Charleston; I sit waiting for Leonard to come in, with a brain still running along the railway lines, which unfits it for reading. But oh, dear, what a lot I've got to read! The entire works of Mr James Joyce, Wyndham Lewis, Ezra Pound, so as to compare them with the entire works of Dickens & Mrs Gaskell; besides that George Eliot; & finally Hardy.[1] And I've just done Aunt Anny, on a really liberal scale.[2] Yes, since I wrote last she has died, a week ago today to be precise, at Freshwater, & was buried up at Hampstead yesterday where 6 or 7 years ago we saw Richmond buried in a yellow fog. I suppose my feeling for her is half moonshine; or rather half reflected from other feelings. Father cared for her; she goes down the last, almost, of that old 19th Century Hyde Park Gate world. Unlike most old ladies she showed very little anxiety to see one; felt, I sometimes think, a little painfully at the sight of us, as if we'd gone far off, & recalled unhappiness, which she never liked to dwell on. Also, unlike most old Aunts she had the wits to feel how sharply we differed on current questions; & this, perhaps, gave her a sense, hardly existing with her usual circle, of age, obsoleteness, extinction. For myself, though, she need have had no anxieties on this head, since I admired her sincerely; but still the generations certainly look very different ways. Two or perhaps three years ago L. & I went to see her; found her much diminished in size, wearing a feather boa round her neck, and seated alone in a drawing room almost the copy, on a smaller scale, of the old drawing room; the same subdued pleasant air of the 18th Century & old portraits & old china. She had our tea waiting for us. Her manner was a little distant, & more than a little melancholy. I asked her about father, & she said how those young men laughed in a "loud melancholy way" & how their generation was a very happy one, but sel-

---

leased to Maynard Keynes in 1916, but Clive retained accommodation there. VW had had a high desk constructed, at which she could stand to write, in emulation of her sister who normally stood before her easel to paint.

1. Possibly in preparation for her article 'Modern Novels', *TLS*, 10 April 1919 (Kp C147).
2. Anne Isabella (1837-1919) was the elder of W. M. Thackeray's two daughters, the younger of whom was the first wife of Leslie Stephen. In 1877 she married her second cousin, (Sir) Richmond Ritchie (1854-1912); they had two children, Hester and William. Lady Ritchie was a prolific writer; and the model for Mrs Hilbery in VW's novel *Night and Day*, published in October 1919. After her husband's death she had moved from 109 St George's Square, SW1, to a smaller house in St Leonard's Terrace, Chelsea. The last three years of her life were spent at The Porch, the cottage at Freshwater, Isle of Wight, she had owned since the 1860's. VW's obituary notice of Lady Ritchie appeared in the *TLS* on 6 March 1919 (Kp C142).

fish; & how ours seemed to her fine but very terrible; but we hadn't any writers such as they had. "Some of them have just a touch of that quality; Bernard Shaw has; but only a touch. The pleasant thing was to know them all as ordinary people, not great men—" And then a story of Carlyle & father; Carlyle saying he'd as soon wash his face in a dirty puddle as write journalism. She put her hand down I remember, into a bag or box standing behind the fire, & said she had a novel, three-quarters written— but couldn't finish it—nor do I suppose it ever was finished. but I've said all I can say, dressing it up a trifle rosily, in the Times tomorrow. I have written to Hester, but how I doubt the sincerity of my own emotions!

Asheham was, I suppose, a qualified success only—at any rate for L. because of the discomfort; for me the discomfort such as it was was chiefly due to Philip [Woolf]'s presence. One couldn't sink back before the log fire & read Shakespeare. That form of exalted egotism was checked, & I think perhaps Philip felt himself a little of a hindrance, as no doubt, he always feels himself now—an outsider, a spectator; unattached & very lonely. Duncan came over involved in domestic difficulties, & gave him a letter to Mr Hecks the farmer, which he was to deliver yesterday morning, in the worst downpour of the year. But we had two lovely afternoons of spring, when I kept asking myself "Now where are we? What point have we reached? Is this spring or September?" waking with a start to the fact that we are launched on another summer. Those little grey green tassels were decorating the woods, like the design on a Japanese screen. Starting out to fetch milk on one of these days we met Gunn & heard our fate. We're to go in September. He wants Asheham to live in with his old mother. Oh dear Oh dear!— Each time I walked up the drive I though[t] how nothing was ever so perfect. If it weren't for the devil of starting something new in me, I should be in despair. L. thinks it easy to make a fetish of a house; which is true; meanwhile we hang suspended. But the need of looking for another house is a source of great pleasure. It drove us all along the Rodmell Road to Mr Stacey's & there we heard from a pair of drab females in a chaise that Mr Robinson of Iford is going to let;[3] so on we went, to Iford, a thickly set little village on the plain; & found a house with three green columns, a stuffed up drawing room, & a Mrs Robinson, made so L. declared & the number of her children attested, for breeding purposes. Art lamps & iridescent plates attached to the wall demonstrated the gentility of her farmer husband. Evidently they have made themselves very snug, & will want more than we can

3. James Stacey, who lived at Swanborough Manor on the west side of the Ouse valley, was the lessee of several farm properties (including Charleston) on the estates of Viscount Gage to the east of the river. Joseph Colgate Robinson lived at Oatlands, Iford.

pay; even if the country there were better than it is. On the whole we incline to aim at Itford farm house—a house that could be made very attractive, with its view & its sun.[4] We have grown out of gentlemen's houses.

Charleston is by no means a gentleman's house. I bicycled round there in a flood of rain, & found the baby asleep in its cot, & Nessa & Duncan sitting over the fire, with bottles & bibs & basins all round them. Duncan went to make my bed. Their staff at this moment consists simply of Jenny, the sharp Jewish looking cook; & she having collapsed, spent the afternoon in bed. By extreme method & unselfishness & routine on Nessa's & Duncan's parts chiefly, the dinner is cooked, & innumerable refills of hotwater bottles & baths supplied. One has the feeling of living on the brink of a move. In one of the little islands of comparative order Duncan set up his canvas, & Bunny wrote a novel in a set of copy books.[5] Nessa scarcely leaves the babies room, or if she appears for a moment outside, she has instantly to go off & talk to Dan, Jenny's young man & the future support of Charleston, or to wash napkins, or bottles, or prepare meals.[6] Mrs B. & the children run rapidly to & fro between their rooms. I had an immense long talk with Ann [Brereton] about the health of the Persian cat, which, according to Mrs B. was fatally injured internally while being washed to cure it of nits; so that she demanded chloroform, which Nessa refused, & the cat recovered. Then Quentin had just been suspected of measles— The atmosphere seems full of catastrophes which upset no one; the atmosphere is good humoured, lively, as it tends to be after three months of domestic disaster. In these circumstances, I daresay I had no more than 30 minutes consecutive talk with Nessa, chiefly devoted to the great epic of the Dr the nurse & Emily.[7] But as happens after disaster upon disaster a sudden lightening of calamity appeared this morning: Dan & his mother being engaged, a letter then arrived from a nurse who against all probability seems to wish to come if she may bring a friend. But I broke

---

4. The Itford farm house, which Mr Gunn the farm bailiff would vacate when he moved a mile north to Asheham, did not become available to the Woolfs. See *II VW Letters*, no. 1026.

5. David Garnett's novelette *Dope Darling* was published in 1919 under the pseudonym Leda Burke by T. Werner Laurie. For Garnett's account of the book and its writing, see his autobiographical volume, *The Flowers of the Forest* (1955), p. 197.

6. Dan Pitcher, from Lewes, was employed as gardener at Charleston; it was hoped his mother would come as housemaid, and that they would act as caretakers when the family were away in the winter.

7. Vanessa's daughter, born on Christmas day, did not thrive under the care of an incompetent doctor and a timid nurse. Dr Marie Moralt, a friend of Noel Olivier's, took charge and saved the child. Life at Charleston was made more difficult by Emily Paton, an unmarried mother found by VW as housemaid for Vanessa in July 1918. She was thought to be stealing clothes and food, and was dismissed.

off in full tide, & had to trudge through mud to Glynde—such mud that when I went into Powell, the land agent, the sleek little clerk looked from my head to my boots in expostulation—as if such a figure couldn't possibly require a house with 7 bedrooms & a bathroom.[8] Unhappily there seems little chance of finding one. I've said nothing of my niece, who must be called so formally, since they've cancelled Susanna Paula, & can think of nothing else.[9] She is a wistful, patient, contemplative little creature, examining the fire very meditatively, with a resigned expression, & very large blue eyes. I suppose not much larger than a big hare, though perfectly formed—legs, thighs, fingers & toes—both fingers & toes very long & sensitive.

Friday 7 March

Having smashed my ink pot, I have recourse to safety pots again & purple ink I see dwells in this one; but I can't use with any effect the muffled respectability of a fountain pen.

Yesterday I had a tooth out, to which the bag of a large abscess had attached itself. Harrison showed it me, previous to putting it in the fire; a token of much pain he said. The queer little excursion into the dark world of gas always interests me. I came home in the Tube wondering whether any of the people there suspected its existence. I wake from it, or seem rather to step out of it & leave it to go on hurtling through space while the world of Harrison & Dr Trueby engages my attention— "Open your mouth, Mrs Woolf— Now let me take out this little bit of wood." Suppose one woke instead to find the deity himself by one's side! The Christians believe it, I suppose.[10] L. has met an immense number of people these last few days; & I should have told how Sidney Webb finds his book a most remarkable piece of work, & how it is to be printed directly by Clark of Edinburgh, & will be out, perhaps, by June.[11] And my poor old sluggard, Night & Day, is to be taken in a parcel to Gerald [Duckworth], as soon as I can get through with these niggling, bothersome corrections.

8. Humphrey Powell was the Agent to the extensive Firle estates of Viscount Gage; his offices were in the High Street, Lewes, which VW reached by train from Glynde.

9. The child was first registered as Helen Vanessa, to which Angelica was later added.

10. Cf VW's essay 'On Being Ill', first published in January 1926 in *New Criterion* (Kp C270) and reprinted in *The Moment and Other Essays* (1947): '. . . when we have a tooth out and come to the surface in the dentist's arm-chair and confuse his "Rinse the mouth—rinse the mouth" with the greeting of the Deity stooping from the floor of Heaven to welcome us—'.

11. See above, 17 December 1918, n 10. LW's *Empire and Commerce in Africa* (1920), was printed by R. & R. Clark of Edinburgh.

Lady Wolseley who seems a lady of the utmost distinction since she writes to the Editor of the Times in pencil, finds L.'s memoir of Aunt Anny 'most admirable', & the delicacy of his touches 'a proof of Genius in *him*'.[12] To balance this satisfactorily my article, according to B.R., is received with acclamation in the office, at home, & in my Club. The Richmonds want to take a house for April & May—possibly we may consider letting them Asheham. If I had L.'s experience I could here give a little story of the Coal Commission & Lloyd George behind the scenes, as reported by Mrs Webb.[13]

Wednesday 12 March[14]

Sunday was one of my Shelley house afternoons. There I met Clive, & in his company I was less than ever in touch with the gathering—as dusky, fur-clad & discreet as ever, though I fancy that I am less impressed by it all than I was, & even take Shelley House more or less as an ordinary house. I had to talk to Elena about Asheham, & find her so slow in her mind, so accustomed I suppose to the position of an ornate & handsome ornament that she positively can't understand & scurries in her replies, as if she were a fat spaniel crossing a busy road. And her eyes are without depth. Clive gave me dinner at the Café Royal, which did not much interest me as a show, rather to his disappointment. However towards the end of dinner a woman of doubtful character dining alone with a man threw her glass on the floor, made a great rattle of knives & plates, upset the mustard pot & marched out like an indignant turkey Cock. Was this moment, with the eyes of the diners upon her, what repaid her? Was it for this that she protested? Anyhow she left her man very crestfallen, trying to appear nonchalant; & I daresay that was what she wanted. I couldn't help thinking of the dreary scene in the flat next morning—the tears, the recriminations, the reconciliation—& next Sunday they'll dine, I suppose, at another restaurant.[15]

12. An obituary notice of Lady Ritchie had appeared on 28 February 1919 in *The Times* which, following its principle of not divulging names of anonymous contributors, forwarded to LW a letter dated 'Hampton Court Palace, 1.3.19', from Louisa, dowager Viscountess Wolseley, widow of a Commander-in-Chief of the British army. LW must have acknowledged both her letter and his authorship, for she wrote direct to him on 13 March, again in pencil for she was ill, a 'dissertation on novels'. See MHP, Sussex.
13. LW saw Beatrice Webb on 5 March, the day VW returned to Hogarth House from Charleston; her 'little story' is told in *Beatrice Webb's Diaries, 1912-24*, edited by Margaret Cole, 1952, pp. 146-152.
14. VW has dated this entry *Wed. March 11th*.
15. The incident involving the 'woman of doubtful character' is echoed in *Jacob's Room*, pp. 79-80.

Dining with Clive now I always feel that we mark the change in our circumstances & views; our present is acted on a background of the past. The present is more amiable, considerably gayer than the past; though not perhaps so interesting. Its interest is different, rather, for I was interested in what he told me of Nessa & R. & D.—& in what I could guess of his own attitude; so happy; so vibrant, so epicurean—& yet has he his moments, not exactly of disillusionment, but of feeling that things might have been rather on a larger scale? I doubt it; I fancy he has found his level, & hence his comfort.

On Monday [10 March], I think, we had a day of industry. We are coming to the end of Eliot's poems—but I've forgotten Saturday, when we had Marjorie Strachey, & the Shoves & Saxon to dinner. Saxon, like the sand in the oyster, was the origin of the whole pearl. We cannot quite face Saxon alone; & had recourse to telephone & telegraph to summon others. I doubt that he likes this. He wants more attention than one can give him in company, & he sits silent, outside the magic circle; no lure draws him in. To me the most interesting object that evening was Gumbo; instantly & undoubtingly I thought her changed. She has come to some decision; she has passed some stage. Doesn't Conrad say that there's a shadow line between youth & middle age? Well, since I saw her last she has crossed it into the smoother greyer waters beyond.[16] She has just had notice to leave her school on account of her short sight. In old days this would not have mattered much; she would have been on with something new; but when I spoke of her as the acrobat flying from trapeze to trapeze she shook her head; no that is all over. She now has her two rooms in Kensington, lives on her earnings, comes home & is glad to be quiet there, glad to find that her charwoman has lit the fire— Things haven't turned out well. Jos's fault, I suppose. The prospect is drearier than I could face in my own case. I begin to see, now, how my friends' lives are shaping. It looks a little as if Marjorie was to be one of the failures—not that I rank marriage or success in a profession as success. Its an attitude of mind— the way one looks at life.

I must notice that though the sky is as black as water one has washed one's hands in, a bird is singing romantically & profusely at the window. On our walk today we passed almond trees in full flower. The daffodils are on the point of bursting. But so far I doubt if we've had one day of blue sky, or any heat; nor is there any shadow at Kew, where the shade is universal.

Last night Miss Fox, aged perhaps 26, earning her living, living in rooms with a friend, daughter of an Oxford don & Pippa's secretary,

16. *The Shadow Line* (1918) by Joseph Conrad, a sea tale which the author described in a note (1920) as dealing with 'the change from youth, care-free and fervent, to the more self-conscious and more poignant period of maturer life'.

dined here & lectured the Guild on equal pay. Leonard is preparing to dress for the first time since marriage in an assortment of clothes to dine with David Davies & Venizelos.[17] This morning we had notice to quit from Hoper, & the further blow that he will not let us have the [Itford] Farm.

Saturday 15 March

Today was to have been the happiest of the week, & then among my letters was one from Duncan, which looked to me ominous, & proved of course to contain a demand for Nelly as soon as possible. What else but a demand is it when he says that Nessa is becoming completely knocked up by incessant work & responsibility? So I have wired to say she will go if possible for 3 weeks; & the prelude to the wire was unpleasant, & the postscript will be still more so.[18] For the moment this house represents a little island of refuge to the childbearers; Karin rang up last night to suggest that we should take Ann, Judith & Mabel for a fortnight, which fortnight they are going to spend at Asheham. But no one can see how difficult it is to detach a cook or to take in children when one's organisation is framed on a different scale—however its enough to live one's disagreeables without writing them. Moreover we refused to take Mabel & Ann & Judith.[19]

On Thursday Bruce & Elena dined here—rather an event. But it went off peaceably enough. They, at least, are well beyond the shadow line; I found him mellower & milder & less spruce than I expected, which pleased me in the admiring editor of my works. As for Elena her distinction in black with a jade jewel is undeniable; her white hair too, on the top of a face coloured like almond blossom; & with all this stateliness & repose an air, if I mistake not, of melancholy, as of hopes not realised & acquiescence accepted instead of something warmer, which slightly touched me, guessing the cause of it. Her notes are very few. But she could discuss the Indian Bill with L. & Indian religions; so that I daresay her slowness & apparent stupidity are only that she finds herself out of her

17. LW was going to a League of Nations dinner. Eleutherios Venizelos (1864-1936) was the Prime Minister of Greece, and represented his country at the Peace Conference. For David Davies, see above, 16 July 1918, n 19. Nothing has been found to add to VW's description of Miss Fox.

18. Nelly had already been lent to Charleston for five days in February to tide over a domestic crisis there. LW, more interested in his wife's health than his sister-in-law's difficulties, had been reluctant to spare her then, and this second demand from Charleston no doubt aggravated the friction between him and VW on the subject. See II VW Letters, no. 1023 etc.

19. Mabel Selwood had moved on from the Bells to become nurse to the Stephen children.

element with me.[20] We talked, much about Asheham of course, & the evening passed quietly, sedately, & with only one or two of those awkward pauses which I remember in their house. He treats her rather as a large magnificent child. "O you'll like that" he said when I offered her a bulls eye, & she told me she had noticed a very nice sweetshop in the street. I fancy that Bruce is a kindly & very unambitious man, who has been quite pleased to spend his time in doing kindnesses to poverty stricken young men & fitting the articles into the advertisements in the Supplement, which he says is not such as easy job as it looks. "When the great catastrophe happens" he said, alluding to Lord Northcliffe, there is a Walter who is going to buy back the Times, & make it into a decent paper again.[21] They went down to see Asheham on Friday, but the result is not yet known to us. L. is right I think in saying that Elena's place ought to be in a big house in a village, distributing alms. I asked vaguely for a compositor & she undertook very scrupulously to find me one, being in touch of course with various organisations.

On Friday I went to London & had tea with Mrs Hamilton—Molly that is: I had to correct myself half a dozen times. L. has now got into the habit of lunching in London twice a week, & so appeasing the gaping maws of Green & Matthew.[22] Murry is in the next room & has asked L. to do the social, I mean social reform, side of the Atheneuam, pressing upon him a large yellow book for review. James [Strachey] has extracted the post of dramatic critic. Eliot may be sub-editor. The first number comes out on April 4th.[23] These little bits of literary gossip strike me as slightly discreditable. They point perhaps to one's becoming a professional, a hack of the type of Mrs W. K. Clifford, who used to know exactly what everyone was paid, & who wrote what, & all the rest of it. I

---

20. The Government of India Bill finally received Royal Assent in December 1919. Plans for the devolution of power were complex, and a compromise was reached known as the Montagu-Chelmsford scheme of 'dyarchy' in which some departments were handed over to popular control and others were reserved for the British administrators.

21. *The Times* was founded by a John Walter in 1785. Lord Northcliffe acquired it in 1908 but chairmanship of the board of directors was retained by a member of the Walter family, first by Arthur Fraser Walter and then, in 1910-23, by the founder's great-great-grandson, John Walter. In 1923, following Northcliffe's death, *The Times* was in fact bought by John Jacob Astor (later Lord Astor of Hever).

22. Miss Matthaei was LW's assistant editor, and Miss Minna Green the secretary on the *International Review*. In undertaking to edit the review, LW had stipulated that he should not be required to attend the office more than once or twice a week.

23. There is nothing signed by LW in the *Athenaeum* during its period under Murry's editorship (April 1919 to January 1921) but LW's diaries show that he began receiving payments from the periodical in April 1919. Eliot did not become sub-editor, but was a contributor.

can see father listening with disapproval but secret enjoyment.[24] Mrs Hamilton made me feel a little professional, for she had her table strewn with manuscripts, a book open on the desk, & she began by asking me about my novel; & then we talked about reviewing, & I was interested to hear who had reviewed Martin Schüler, & was a little ashamed of being interested.[25] She told me a curious thing about the sensibilities of my family—Adrian had asked her to tell me how much he'd liked The Voyage Out, which he has just read for the first time, & is too shy to write & tell me so himself. She has 2 or 3 sisters, all artists according to her,[26] though the designs for stained glass that I saw didn't seem to me to prove it; & one is a poet, who surrounds herself with sketches of projected books on every conceivable subject, & has written a long poem which she wants us to consider publishing. "She is a poet—certainly a poet", she said, which roused my suspicions. The truth is that Molly Hamilton with all her ability to think like a man, & her strong serviceable mind, & her independent, self-respecting life is not a writer. But we exchanged the plots of our novels, & said "How very interesting—"

Wednesday 19 March

Life piles up so fast that I have no time to write out the equally fast rising mound of reflections, which I always mark down as they rise to be inserted here. I meant to write about the Barnetts, & the peculiar repulsiveness of those who dabble their fingers self approvingly in the stuff of others' souls.[27] The Barnetts were at any rate plunged to the elbow; red

24. Mrs W. K. Clifford (d. 1929) and her mathematician husband who died in 1879, had been friends of VW's parents; Leslie Stephen considered her 'a little too much immersed in the journalistic element' for his taste, though he respected her gallantry in providing for herself and her two daughters. She was a prolific writer, publishing over two dozen books (novels, stories, plays) and a great deal of journalism.

25. *Martin Schüler*, a novel about a German musician by Romer Wilson, was briefly and jingoistically noticed in the *TLS* of 10 October 1918, and received serious praise in a longer review in the same paper on 7 November 1918. Though the novel was assumed to be the work of a man, the author was in fact a woman.

26. Mary Agnes Hamilton, whose father Robert Adamson had been Professor of Logic at Glasgow University, had three younger sisters, Una and Sarah who were painters and craftworkers, and Margot, a poet and writer, who had already published a book of poems, *A Year of War* (1917).

27. The Rev. Canon Samuel Augustus Barnett (1844-1913) and his wife Henrietta (1851-1936) were indefatigable social workers, particularly concerned with the education of the poor. Canon Barnett was the first warden of Toynbee Hall, the adult educational settlement he had helped to found in Whitechapel. In 1918 his wife published in two volumes *Rev. Canon S. A. Barnett: His Life, Work and Friends*.

handed if ever philanthropists were, which makes them good examples; &
then, unquestioning & unspeculative as they were, they give themselves
away almost to the undoing of my critical faculty. Is it chiefly intellectual
snobbery that makes me dislike them?—is it snobbery to feel outraged
when she says "Then I came close to the Great Gates"—or reflects that
God = good, devil = evil. Has this coarseness of grain any necessary connection with labour for one's kind? And then the smug vigour of their self-
satisfaction! Never a question as to the right of what they do—always a
kind of insensate forging ahead until, naturally, their undertakings are all
of colossal size & portentous prosperity. Moreover, could any woman of
humour or insight quote such paeans to her own genius? Perhaps the root
of it all lies in the adulation of the uneducated, & the easy mastery of the
will over the poor. And more & more I come to loathe any dominion of
one over another; any leadership, any imposition of the will. Finally,
my literary taste is outraged by the smooth way in which the tale is
made to unfold into full blown success, like some profuse peony.
But I only scratch the surface of what I feel about these two stout
volumes.

On Monday after many failures I met Murry at the Club & we had our
talk about the Athenaeum. Success has already begun to do for Murry what
I always said it would do. He is more freshly coloured, even in the cheeks,
than when we last met; & his mind has its high lights. Why, he chuckled
like a schoolboy; his eyes shone; his silences were occupied with pleasant
thoughts, I think; not that he would admit that to edit the Athenaeum was
much more than preferable to a place in a government office.[28] He talked
so much about his plans, & with such zest that we sat there from 4.45 to
6.30, or past, & I had to rush. In fact I only caught my train owing to my
skill as a psychologist. We were discussing his poetry, & his standing as
a poet, with some intensity on his part, so that he lay back, & looked very
intently at the ceiling. I was interested but guilty about dinner waiting.
So I said "Yes, its true writing for one's own press is very pleasant—
Now next week I have to take my novel to Gerald Duckworth—" "Ah"
his eyes came down from the ceiling at once. "What's it called?— Oh
yes—it'll be out in the autumn I suppose. Well, d'you know I'm afraid
I must be going."

Murry is much of a small boy still, I think, in spite of his tragic airs.
I suspect his boast will come true; the Athenaeum will be the best literary
paper in existence in 12 months.

"What will you write Virginia?" he asked. Am I too modest in thinking
that there was a shade of the perfunctory in the question? Anyhow I
didn't persecute him with any degree of pressure. I offered to look in on

28. From 1916 until the end of the war Murry had been attached to the Political
Intelligence Department of the War Office.

Thursdays sometimes & get a book;[29] sometimes to suggest an article; he agreed quite cordially. We went over all his names, & tried to think of others, but agreed that once our intimate friends were gone through the field was mown of its poppies. The younger generation promises very little so far. An editor naturally sweeps the young writers very carefully. I doubt that I was so much of an incubus to Richmond as I thought. While we were demurring a little to the idea of James as dramatic critic, the dramatic critic looked in & saw us. I recommended Desmond for the star part. Katherine will do 4 novels every week—pray to God she don't do mine! I feel the acid in her once more—since she doesnt take the trouble to write a card to fix an engagement; but I shall try to go up there tomorrow & judge the situation with my own eyes. Today we finished printing Eliot's poems—our best work so far by a long way, owing to the quality of the ink. MacDermott has done Murry's poem with such blots & blurs that we must at any rate reprint the title page.

Saturday 22 March

Today among other things the coal strike is postponed, & the Guards march through London.[30] L. might have seen them, but thought it not worth the loss of his seat in the Tube. As to private news, our new bookcase came & one part has been set up in the drawing room: the other is too large to get upstairs to my room. Further we have decided to take 2 cottages at Tregerthen if we can get them; & this brings me to Katherine Murry from whom I heard of them.[31] The inscrutable woman remains inscrutable I'm glad to say; no apologies, or sense of apologies due. At once she flung down her pen & plunged, as if we'd been parted for 10 minutes, into the question of Dorothy Richardson; & so on with the greatest freedom & animation on both sides until I had to catch my train.[32]

29. The editorial office of the *Athenaeum* was at 10 Adelphi Terrace, near Charing Cross.

30. This conjuncture was apparently fortuitous: the Guards' march was a triumphal progress; the threatened general strike by the miners was averted by the Prime Minister promising to expedite the final Report of the Sankey Commission on conditions in the coal industry, which recommended nationalisation and improved wages and conditions.

31. In 1916 Katherine and Murry had stayed at Tregerthen, near St Ives in Cornwall, in one of the cottages D. H. Lawrence rented during the war. There were two buildings, but the smaller was divided into two dwellings. Lawrence wrote to LW at this time from Berkshire saying he had heard from Koteliansky of the Woolfs' interest in his cottages and offered to sublet, assuming they intended a limited stay; but meanwhile VW had written direct to the landlord, Captain Short.

32. The writer Dorothy Miller Richardson (1873-1957), whose book *Pointed Roofs*, the first of a novel-cycle of a dozen volumes, was published by Duckworth some

Perhaps its I who live in the suburbs & think it necessary to answer letters; that would be a proper retort to my jest of the underworld. But something—something dark & catastrophic possibly to do with Murry—has taken place since we met. So much she hinted; but said she wished now to forget it—something that had absorbed her, apparently.[33] But this was a momentary revelation as I left. Otherwise, as I say, we chattered about the Athenaeum mostly, & I was much complimented to hear how much they wish for my writing, in proof of which I have a book this morning from Murry. And again, as usual, I find with Katherine what I don't find with the other clever women a sense of ease & interest, which is, I suppose, due to her caring so genuinely if so differently from the way I care, about our precious art. Though Katherine is now in the very heart of the professional world—4 books on her table to review—she is, & will always be I fancy, not the least of a hack. I don't feel as I feel with Molly Hamilton that is say, ashamed of the inkpot. Before this I met Hope Mirrlees at the Club—a very self conscious, wilful, prickly & perverse young woman, rather conspicuously well dressed & pretty, with a view of her own about books & style, an aristocratic & conservative tendency in opinion, & a corresponding taste for the beautiful & elaborate in literature. For example, she had been examining Swift as to his use of words; whether he used them properly, & found him deficient compared with Burke, who writes from this point of view magnificently though detestably from any other. She uses a great number of French words, which she pronounces exquisitely; she seems capricious in her friendships, & no more to be marshalled with the long goose wand which I can sometimes apply to people than a flock of bright green parrokeets.

'Will you write to me, Hope?" I asked.

"O no. I can't write to people."

So we parted in the Charing Cross Road for the next six months, I suppose.

But to tell the truth what I'm thinking about most is neither Katherine nor Hope, but the two cottages at Higher Tregerthen. About now, I suppose, Captain Short of St Ives is opening my letter.

---

six months after *The Voyage Out*. VW had recently reviewed the fourth, *The Tunnel*, in the *TLS* of 13 February 1919 (Kp C141); she wrote: 'The reader is not provided with a story; he is invited to embed himself in Miriam Henderson's consciousness'. Dorothy Richardson was a pioneer of the so-called 'stream-of-consciousness' method.

33. VW had last seen Katherine Mansfield on 17 December; in January the latter had begun a course of injections in the hope of curing her tuberculosis. The nature of her illness and the severity of this treatment, rather than her relationship with Murry, might account for the impression made on VW.

Thursday 27 March

Captain Tregerthen Short has now got my letter, & written me an answer, & even drawn me a sketch, & appears not only willing but anxious to let us have his three cottages, at a rent of £5 a year cach. I have replied, also in the course of these last few days, that we will probably take them, & truth to tell, I have spent the greater part of the time on the slope beneath our house, which Leonard has already planted with fuchsias, or crouched on a rock, watching the great foam swirl of the waves. In a pessimistic walk by the river yesterday L. made this capacity for being happy first at Asheham, then at Tregerthen, the text of a discourse upon the illusory nature of all pleasures & pains; from which he concludes that mankind is a wretched tribe of animals, & even the works of Shakespeare no good save as his skill in doing it excites one's pleasure. Shall I own that I attribute some of this to my wretched family, who asked me up to dine with them, & I went? & also to Night & Day which L. has spent the past 2 mornings & evenings in reading? I own that his verdict, finally pronounced this morning gives me immense pleasure: how far one should discount it, I don't know. In my own opinion N. & D. is a much more mature & finished & satisfactory book than The Voyage Out; as it has reason to be. I suppose I lay myself open to the charge of niggling with emotions that don't really matter. I certainly don't anticipate even two editions. And yet I can't help thinking that, English fiction being what it is, I compare for originality & sincerity rather well with most of the moderns. L. finds the philosophy very melancholy. It too much agrees with what he was saying yesterday. Yet, if one is to deal with people on a large scale & say what one thinks, how can one avoid melancholy? I don't admit to being hopeless though—only the spectacle is a profoundly strange one; & as the current answers don't do, one has to grope for a new one; & the process of discarding the old, when one is by no means certain what to put in their place, is a sad one. Still, if you think of it, what answers do Arnold Bennett or Thackeray, for instance, suggest? Happy ones—satisfactory solutions—answers one would accept, if one had the least respect for one's soul? Now I have done my last odious piece of typewriting, & when I have scribbled this page, I shall write & suggest Monday as the day for coming up to lunch with Gerald. I don't suppose I've ever enjoyed any writing so much as I did the last half of N. & D. Indeed, no part of it taxed me as The Voyage Out did; & if one's own ease & interest promise anything good, I should have hopes that some people, at least, will find it a pleasure. I wonder if I shall ever be able to read it again? Is the time coming when I can endure to read my own writing in print without blushing & shivering & wishing to take cover?

Our dinner last night at the Isola Bella was rather a brilliant affair in the Bohemian style, with a great deal of wine, & talk of books & pictures,

& a general air of freedom & content—though I fancy that Roger—I was specially warned by Nessa not to let him know that she & Duncan were in the bath, which casts some light on his point of view. At the end of dinner the Padrone, as we called him, (Clive chattered Italian with the greatest gusto) brought a large sketch book, in which Nessa & Duncan & Roger all drew pictures, & we were rewarded by a bottle of Marsala. Then home; leaving Nessa & Roger in Fitzroy Street, with Clive, Mary & Duncan following behind.[34] We talked by the way a great amount of Athenaeum gossip, all secretly delighted with our own importance; Clive & Roger to do art criticism, the most brilliant list of contributors on record; & indeed I open this book again solely to record the fact that Murry has applied to me for a signed article, which I shall send him.

Sunday 30 March

I open this book today merely to note that Miss *Eleanor Ormerod*, destroyer of insects, promises well for Murry: should he take kindly to my first (Eccentrics: I myself rather liked it).[35] That note being made & L. not in yet from Staines I may add that I'm writing by the clear shrewd light of the sun, though its five minutes to the half past five. Last night we changed our watches. So the winter gloom is over, for which I am half sorry, since the dark evening over the fire has its charm. Moreover, should I look out of the window I should see snow in the garden. Yesterday morning the glare of white on trees & roofs when I drew the curtains was dazzling, surmounted too by a bright blue sky, as tender as June; but falsely tender, since outside one was scourged by the bitterest east wind, & I've not felt so cold this winter. Cold dashed in one's face, & whirled up ones legs is far more cruel & harassing than a still profound frost. The Almond blossom is all gone, as if it were Cinderella when the clock struck.

I went up to tea at Gordon Sqre on Friday, having first visited Spicer the paper makers in Upper Thames Street. Clive sat at tea; a little grumpy, growing bald, & now showing a forehead rather in the style of Hall Caine.[36] Very queer, as Nessa said, we all felt, united again in that drawing

---

34. The *Isola Bella* restaurant was then, as now, at 15 Frith Street, Soho. It changed hands in 1920, and the sketch book referred to has not been traced. Roger Fry's studio was at 21 Fitzroy Street, W1.

35. 'The Eccentrics' appeared in the *Athenaeum* on 25 April 1919 (Kp C149). VW's essay entitled 'Miss Ormerod', based upon *Eleanor Ormerod, LLD. Economic Entomologist, Autobiography and Correspondence*, edited by Robert Wallace (1904), did not appear in print until December 1924, when it was published in the *Dial*, New York (Kp C257).

36. James Spicer and Son Ltd., wholesale stationers and papermakers, had their head office and warehouse at 50 Upper Thames Street, EC4. (Sir Thomas Henry) Hall Caine (1853-1931), the Manx novelist, whose books achieved an extraordinary popularity.

room as though it were 1907 again, & yet with so complete a re-arrange-
ment of our parts. Perhaps we are all much happier; at any rate more
secure & therefore tolerant towards each other. Then on to the Club, &
dinner with the Shoves & Marjorie, for whom of course we paid, since
they had all come out with no money.[37] Gerald's buttons burst off
too, & his coat came unsewn; & on again across half Mayfair, discreet
& semi-lit, to the Club meeting—where my attention was drawn to a
large picture, the Rape of the Sabines, I daresay, given by Edward
Owensmith in memory of his devoted wife Elizabeth, a Christian
mother who went home Feb. 1907— I find it impossible to keep out
thoughts about all sorts of things, & found that Marjorie listened
attentively; but I can give no record of what happened, save that L. was
elected again, 5th.

Wednesday 2 April

Yesterday I took Night & Day up to Gerald, & had a little half domestic
half professional interview with him in his office. I dont like the Club
man's view of literature. For one thing it breeds in me a violent desire to
boast: I boasted of Nessa & Clive & Leonard; & how much money they
made. Then we undid the parcel, & he liked the title, but found that Miss
Maud Annesley has a book called Nights & Days—which may make
difficulties with Mudies.[1] But he was certain he would wish to publish it;
& we were altogether cordial; & I noticed how his hair is every blade of it
white, with some space between the blades; a very sparsely sown field. I
had tea at Gordon Sqre; Shepherd [Sheppard], Norton, Nessa, Duncan &
later Clive. The disturbing effect of the company is not so great as it was.
Yet I feel that the presence of these very brightly lit brains makes things
go swiftly, & without padding. And then they have different cups &
saucers, & pictures on the walls, & new chair covers. Later I withdrew
with Nessa, though to withdraw is very difficult owing to the regulations
about coal. Much domestic talk; Lil offering herself, as it proves fruit-
lessly.[2] Then dinner at the Isola Bella; talk with Clive & Duncan: Clive
insisting that Eliot dislikes me, & further trying to convince us that Nessa,
Roger, himself, Lytton & I are the most hated people in London; superficial, haughty, & giving ourselves airs—that, I think, is the verdict

---

37. LW records that they dined at the *Mont Blanc* restaurant in Gerrard Street, the
street in which the 1917 Club was also situated.

1. Published by Mills & Boon in 1912; in 1915 Duckworth had published another of
her novels.

2. Lil was Nelly Boxall's niece, and came to work as a temporary servant at Hogarth
House while Nelly was at Charleston. By this time Vanessa had satisfactory
domestic arrangements in prospect.

against the ladies.[3] I admit I hate not to be liked; & one of the drawbacks of Bloomsbury is that it increases my susceptibility to these shades, which are always made very visible by Clive, in so much that I own to have sulked a little under the suspicion that Murry has confided to Clive that he dislikes my article. Home to find L. in bed; a sight to restore confidence. He had dined with Bob Trevy, spoken at South Place, & performed other activities which I give no account of.[4] I mean, he had been to the office, & the League of Nations, & the Labour party, so that between us our range was wide yesterday. Forster is back again, & said by good Dutch Bessy to be 'more serious'.[5]

Thursday 10 April

A great skip, how accounted for I scarcely know. Writing hard at a Times article on novels perhaps used up my desire for activity of the fingers; & then these last few days I've been submerged in Defoe; & only steal 10 minutes from Roxana to write this.[6] I have to read one book a day in order to start on Saturday—such is the life of a hack. I went up to tea with Janet, & noticed the signs of age in her; gentle old ladyish smiles, & turns of speech; for her age will be a profitable season. And the Eliots, Walter & Marjorie dined here on Sunday; I amused myself by seeing how sharp, narrow, & much of a stick Eliot has come to be, since he took to disliking me. His wife a washed out, elderly & worn looking little woman, who was relieved to find Walter Lamb with his stories about the King provided for her; & indeed Walter seemed to both the ideal of manhood.[7] Gumbo held forth in her most vivacious & commanding style. I tried to

3. On 4 April VW wrote to Vanessa, 'By the way, Mary rang me up yesterday in great agitation about Eliot, imploring me to say nothing, denying the whole story, and insisting that he only abused Bloomsbury in general, and not me, and that Clive had completely misunderstood!' (see *II VW Letters*, no. 1032). But VW's suspicions, once aroused, were not so easily allayed, as her subsequent remarks about Eliot and his wife clearly show (see below, 10 April).

4. The South Place Ethical Society, Finsbury Pavement, in the City. VW had written to Ka Arnold-Forster: 'Our only engagement is on April fools day when Leonard is addressing the Ethical Society upon the Rights of Democracy'. See *II VW Letters*, no. 1016.

5. E. M. Forster returned to England from Alexandria early in 1919. He had gone there in October 1915 to work for the Red Cross, his job being to question patients in military hospitals for details of 'missing' comrades. 'Dutch Bessy' was Mrs Robert Trevelyan.

6. 'Modern Novels', *TLS* 10 April 1919 (Kp C147); and 'The Novels of Defoe', *TLS* 24 April 1919 (Kp C148).

7. Vivienne, *née* Haigh-Wood (1888-1947), married T. S. Eliot in 1915, when she was an attractive and vivacious young woman. She suffered increasingly from psychotic illness and this began to show in her appearance.

secure Faulker a nurse for Nessa & failed; went up to the Times on Monday & had an interview with Richmond—a restless vivacious little man, jumping onto a chair to see the traffic over the blind, & chivvying a piece of paper round the room with his feet. He offered many suggestions about houses in Cornwall. Yesterday Desmond appeared, & told us the strange story of Elizabeth Asquith & Hugh Gibson, which I have not time to write down, but it is remarkable that 2 years ago she knew nothing of the physical side of the sexes.[8]

Saturday 12 April

These ten minutes are stolen from Moll Flanders, which I failed to finish yesterday in accordance with my time sheet, yielding to a desire to stop reading & go up to London. But I saw London, in particular the view of white city churches & palaces from Hungerford Bridge through the eyes of Defoe.[9] I saw the old women selling matches through his eyes; & the draggled girl skirting round the pavement of St. James' Square seemed to me out of Roxana or Moll Flanders. Yes, a great writer surely to be thus imposing himself upon me after 200 years. A great writer—& Forster has never read his books! I was beckoned by Forster from the Library as I approached. We shook hands very cordially; & yet I always feel him shrinking sensitively from me, as a woman, a clever woman, an up to date woman. Feeling this I commanded him to read Defoe, & left him, & went & got some more Defoe, having bought one volume at Bickers on the way.[10] Then to the Club; & met Alix, all in a new outfit to match the spring; brown too, & happier than usual, being now mistress of 41 Gordon Square, where James is to lodge, though she declares several dusky Brazilians have made their head quarters there. So home with L. walking over Hungerford Bridge on a fine warm evening & thinking of Defoe as I say. L. is now off to address the Cingalese; & Herbert Fisher has astounded us by asking himself to lunch tomorrow, & we have been to Kew, & seen the Magnolia trees in blossom.

Thursday 17 April

We saw the magnolia tree in blossom next day with the Minister for Education himself. He is a strange mixture of ascetic & worldling. The lean secluded man now finds himself dazzled by office, & with all his learning & culture swept away by men of vitality & affairs. Such a tribute as he paid to Winston [Churchill] might have been paid by some

8. The story has not been retrieved.
9. See the last paragraph of 'Defoe' in *The Common Reader*, p. 131. VW frequently travelled from Richmond by the London and South-Western Railway, and crossed the Thames between Waterloo and Charing X by the Hungerford footbridge.
10. Bickers bookshop was at 15 Charles Street, leading in to St James's Square.

dazzled moth to a lamp. He seems to see nothing clearly, or else some notion of responsibility forbids him to say what he thinks. He hums & haws when asked a plain question & murmurs on in a husky sort of whisper which seems bodiless & blurred as himself. His whole aspect is that of a worn & half obliterated scholar made spruce by tailors & doing his best to adopt the quiet distinguished manner of those who govern. This is his official side. In private he is a kindly, even affectionate gentleman, simple by nature, though tarnished either by Oxford or by his Fisher blood with a supercilious superficial manner which leads him to dally urbanely & in a way which belittles them with art & letters & everything but politics. This used to irritate—now it merely amuses me. He has long passed the shadow line, & his sarcasms seem directed at phantoms. All clever official men, even poor old Goldie, seem smoothed out of likeness to humanity; & impelled to babble on glibly & entertainingly as if they were under a perpetual contract to keep the high table amused. I do H.A.L.F. the credit to say that he does not give himself airs, save those of a person rendered responsible through no particular merit of his own. We took him to Kew, & chatted of Oxford & Walter Pater, & how Chesterton is a genius, & George Moore another, by way of relief from politics. And he approved of nature too, & likened the Thames beneath a shower to a picture in the Louvre. He stood still on the bank for some minutes, taking in the impression, not as a person who is accustomed to looking at things looks, but rather as a man who collects objects for the good of his soul. So it was too with the buds of the magnolia at Kew.

We had Oliver & Inez to dinner. As one of the couples they must be linked together thus. What binds him to her I did not find it easy to see. Animation perhaps, a kind of brisk professional manner, & it appears that she had read modern poetry & can deliver her opinions as if they were her own. I'm a little doubtful, when I find a cheap ready made young woman out of an office in Oxford Street & lodging at Harrow, enthusiastic about Robinson Crusoe; nor do I attribute it wholly to my intellectual snobbery. Her face, unlike the faces of all the other Cropheads, seemed to me vulgar, & unpleasant. One must remember though that Oliver is now verging upon 50; a little grey at the temples; abrupt & inclined to be snappish; so that his choice is not so wide as it was. However one may abuse the Stracheys their minds remain a source of joy to the end; so sparkling, definite & nimble. Need I add that I reserve the qualities I most admire for people who are not Stracheys? It is so long since I have seen Lytton that I take my impression of him too much from his writing, & his paper upon Lady Hester Stanhope was not one of his best.[11] I could fill this page

11. Lytton Strachey's essay on Lady Hester Stanhope had appeared in the first number of the *Athenaeum* issued under Murry's editorship on 4 April 1919. VW had herself written on Lady Hester in the *TLS* of 20 January 1910 (Kp C42).

with gossip about people's articles in the Athenaeum; since I had tea with Katherine yesterday & Murry sat there mud-coloured & mute, livening only when we talked his shop. He has the jealous partiality of a parent for his offspring already. I tried to be honest, as if honesty were part of my philosophy, & said how I disliked Grantorto on whistling birds, & Lytton & so on.[12] The male atmosphere is disconcerting to me. Do they distrust one? despise one? & if so why do they sit on the whole length of one's visit? The truth is that when Murry says the orthodox masculine thing about Eliot for example, belittling my solicitude to know what he said of me, I dont knuckle under; I think what an abrupt precipice cleaves asunder the male intelligence, & how they pride themselves upon a point of view which much resembles stupidity. I find it much easier to talk to Katherine; she gives & resists as I expect her to; we cover more ground in much less time; but I respect Murry. I wish for his good opinion. Heinemann has rejected K.M.'s stories; & she was oddly hurt that Roger had not invited her to his party. Her hard composure is much on the surface.

Sunday (Easter) 20 April

We are, for the first time for many years, spending Easter in London. We had arranged to go, but dissolved all our arrangements in 5 minutes; partly to escape what was said to be the worst journey on record; partly that L. may get 10 clear days, which will be possible at the end of the week. I own to some hopes of a wet Easter; but was disappointed. Both Friday & Saturday were of the texture of full summer. We walked along the river & through the park on Good Friday, & the sun made the crowd to swelter unpleasantly. They tramped placidly along, in their coats & skirts & bowler hats, leading their dogs, save for a random terrier who had secured a muzzle. Meanwhile the green of the leaves thrust at least one inch out of the envelopes, & today the tree against the window has some perfectly shaped small leaves, & the tree at the end of the garden is as green as it will be until September. On Saturday Bruce Richmond came in person to fetch my Defoe article; & we had a little talk about mistakes in proofs. He prides himself upon letting none through his fingers;—& charges such as do get through (& I was under the impression they were by no means rare) to Dalton.[13] And then we walked; & I came out in my summer things, shady hat, thin muslin dress, stockings, & cloak on my arm. Today I'm sitting in a jersey & serge over the fire; but the evening repents, & through an open window the birds sing, & the leaves are yellow green in the sun. L. at Staines.

12. 'Whistling of Birds' by D. H. Lawrence appeared under the pseudonym 'Grantorto' in the *Athenaeum* on 11 April 1919.
13. Frederick Thomas Dalton (1855-1927) was Bruce Richmond's principal editorial assistant on the *TLS* and, for a period, what amounted to the paper's managing editor. He joined *The Times* in 1893 and retired in 1923.

In the idleness which succeeds any long article, & Defoe is the 2nd leader this month, I got out this diary, & read as one always does read one's own writing, with a kind of guilty intensity. I confess that the rough & random style of it, often so ungrammatical, & crying for a word altered, afflicted me somewhat. I am trying to tell whichever self it is that reads this hereafter that I can write very much better; & take no time over this; & forbid her to let the eye of man behold it. And now I may add my little compliment to the effect that it has a slapdash & vigour, & sometimes hits an unexpected bulls eye. But what is more to the point is my belief that the habit of writing thus for my own eye only is good practise. It loosens the ligaments. Never mind the misses & the stumbles. Going at such a pace as I do I must make the most direct & instant shots at my object, & thus have to lay hands on words, choose them, & shoot them with no more pause than is needed to put my pen in the ink. I believe that during the past year I can trace some increase of ease in my professional writing which I attribute to my casual half hours after tea. Moreover there looms ahead of me the shadow of some kind of form which a diary might attain to. I might in the course of time learn what it is that one can make of this loose, drifting material of life; finding another use for it than the use I put it to, so much more consciously & scrupulously, in fiction. What sort of diary should I like mine to be? Something loose knit, & yet not slovenly, so elastic that it will embrace any thing, solemn, slight or beautiful that comes into my mind. I should like it to resemble some deep old desk, or capacious hold-all, in which one flings a mass of odds & ends without looking them through. I should like to come back, after a year or two, & find that the collection had sorted itself & refined itself & coalesced, as such deposits so mysteriously do, into a mould, transparent enough to reflect the light of our life, & yet steady, tranquil composed with the aloofness of a work of art. The main requisite, I think on re-reading my old volumes, is not to play the part of censor, but to write as the mood comes or of anything whatever; since I was curious to find how I went for things put in haphazard, & found the significance to lie where I never saw it at the time. But looseness quickly becomes slovenly. A little effort is needed to face a character or an incident which needs to be recorded. Nor can one let the pen write without guidance; for fear of becoming slack & untidy like Vernon Lee. Her ligaments are too loose for my taste.[14] But to return to life, albeit with something of an effort. I have forgotten to record

14. Vernon Lee was the pseudonym of the English writer Violet Paget (1856-1935) who, born in France and normally resident in Florence, produced over thirty volumes of historical works, travel sketches and fiction, including the pioneering *Studies of the Eighteenth Century in Italy*, 1880. VW probably met Vernon Lee in Florence in 1909; a page of typescript relating to her is preserved in MHP, Sussex (B 10c); and two of her books were critically reviewed by VW in the *TLS* (Kp C9 and C34).

Desmond's visit. His main purpose in coming was to get himself a bed; but I can pardon these self seeking impulses on the part of Desmond very easily. My tolerance in this respect is far greater than poor Mary Sheepshanks', who remarked bitterly that since she has gone to live at Golders Green her friends pay her visits on Sundays, for the sake of the country air. But then I am happy; & Mary S. is not; every virtue should be natural to the happy, since they are the millionaires of the race. I can give little account of Desmond, seeing that I was under contract to write all the morning, & he arrived late the night before. As L. had been kept by trains failing from reaching home till 8.45, he was out of tune for friendship. Desmond is a very sensitive man. He apologised, & did his best to charm; & did so, in both our cases, I think. But, sure enough, L.'s morning wasted in the sun of his laziness; for though he took a chair into the window & supplied himself with books, the books started ideas, & the ideas had to be communicated, & lying in my bath next door I heard fragments of Lord Robert's speech read from the Times; & then a disquisition upon the authenticity of Barbellion's diary; & this had gone on, with one excursion to buy an A.B.C. [Railway Guide] since breakfast.[15] May we therefore be pardoned for inventing a cook's sister, who was spending the holidays with us; without this dear old Desmond would be smoking his cigarettes & talking about catching a train in the arm chair opposite at this moment. As it was, he had reluctantly to take himself off at lunch time, & fling himself upon a world of crowded trains, & accurate hours; directing his steps towards Oare where they have taken a house, which Molly is engaged upon getting into at this moment. Desmond declared that he had despatched a kitchen table to her; but I own that I doubt it. And who can say whether he has yet reached Oare?

Thursday 24 April

On Easter Monday we went up to visit the Murrys & see Hampstead Heath. Our verdict was that the crowd at close quarters is detestable; it smells; it sticks; it has neither vitality nor colour; it is a tepid mass of flesh scarcely organised into human life. How slow they walk! How passively & brutishly they lie on the grass! How little of pleasure or pain is in them! But they looked well dressed & well fed; & at a distance

15. Desmond MacCarthy stayed at Hogarth House on the night of 16 April. In the House of Commons debate on the adjournment that day, Lord Robert Cecil contributed a long speech concerning the League of Nations, which was fully reported in *The Times* the next morning. Lord Robert Cecil (1864-1958), Nelly Cecil's husband, was assistant Secretary of State for Foreign Affairs, and an indomitable champion of the ideals of the League. W. N. P. Barbellion was the pseudonym of Bruce Frederick Cummings (1889-1919), a biologist whose autobiographical *Journal of a Disappointed Man* was published in March 1919.

among the canary coloured swings & roundabouts they had the look of a picture. It was a summers day—in the sun at least; we could sit on a mound & look at the little distant trickle of human beings eddying round the chief centres of gaiety & filing over the heath & spotted upon its humps. Very little noise they made; the large aeroplane that came flying so steadily over head made more noise than the whole crowd of us. Why do I say 'us'? I never for a moment felt myself one of 'them'. Yet the sight had its charm: I liked the bladders, & the little penny sticks, & the sight of two slow elaborate dancers performing to a barrel organ in a space the size of a hearthrug. Katherine & Murry & Murry's brother met us at their door. We thought she would have enjoyed herself, from the likeness of her prose to the scene; on the contrary, she was disgusted. We had rather a stiff tea. Murry's brother is a bumpkin; & the Rhodesian woman under a cloud of lacerated feelings I suppose; Katherine haggard & powdered; & so on. But it was no one's fault; & their talk of Tregerthen combined with the image of it on a hot day made us determine to take it here & now. We have written to this effect to Captain Short. I try not to hope, since I feel sure we shall be disappointed.

"Let it three days ago" or no answer at all; that is what I imagine.

Last night the Coles dined here, & gave me my first view of them.[16] Sharp, positive, hard minds; in tense taut bodies; in Cole's case the mouth seems fixed in a kind of snarl at the world. A positive domineering young man he seemed; & she, with less force, equally sure of herself. A good laugh would do them both good; yet how laugh with those tight stretched drums for cheeks, & those curled sneering lips? I don't accuse either of them of a desire to be savage or destructive: I write from the outsiders unsympathetic point of view. But Leonard, though he works at their works, is still humane & deliberate. Its the perpetual strife that strings them up in this way, I think; no speculative or contemplative or imaginative power seems to be left them. And what's it all for? Who gains, even if they do win their victories. But I fancy that Mrs Cole is not a very clever woman; & such wits as she has use up all their force in keeping nimble. She has nothing left over to play with. This I write from the recollection of them which came to me on waking. "I dont like the Coles" I said to myself, before I had time to set my faculties to work upon this judgment.

Tomorrow we go down to Asheham for 10 days; alone; leaving the servants to clean here, & intending to find a house for £35 if we can, for that is our solution at present. The weather has gone to pieces; the image

16. George Douglas Howard Cole (1889-1959) and his wife Margaret Isabel, *née* Postgate (b. 1893) were forceful and active socialists who had met working in the Labour (formerly Fabian) Research Department, of which he was appointed the first secretary for research in this year.

is a true one; it is much as if some serenely sailing ship had been wrecked on a splinter of rock & left only tatters & spars to be tossed in a swelter of grey sea.

Monday 5 May

The day mother died twenty something years ago.[1] The smell of wreaths in the hall is always in the first flowers still; without remembering the day I was thinking of her, as I often do.—as good a memorial as one could wish.

Now it is a fine evening, the first since I wrote here last; & I'm just back from Asheham, Leonard still to come in. A fine but cloudy day; an immense weight of sun piled up behind the clouds. I race through, so as to have time for a bath. Ah but how happy we've been at Asheham! It was a most melodious time. Everything went so freely;—but I cant analyse all the sources of my joy—& here's Leonard in, to find a stack of books from the New Statesman, & the drawing room floor littered with blue-black papers from Roger. Lottie & Nelly chattering away about their house cleaning.

Wednesday 7 May

& thus my writing got interrupted, but I had the hot bath I remember, after duly, though a little insincerely, admiring what had been done in my absence. To recapitulate the events of Asheham is no longer in my power, or perhaps, since they were mainly of a spiritual nature requiring some subtlety to relate, I'm too lazy to try. Happiness—what, I wonder constitutes happiness? I daresay the most important element is work, & that rarely fails either of us now. Leonard, of course, had his telegram from Sharp, & an article to do in a hurry; but 1500 words now merely fill a morning pleasantly for him.[2] Then there were two moments of some anxiety: first, a letter from Captain Short to say we can have Tregerthen, which we now possess; then a letter from Gerald to say he has read Night & Day with "the greatest interest" & will be delighted to publish it. I suppose, as I go to the trouble of copying his words verbatim, that I was a good deal pleased by them. The first impression of an outsider, especially one who proposes to back his opinion with money, means something; though I can't think of stout smooth Gerald smoking a cigar over my pages without a smile. However, a good deal beyond this letter in importance was Captain Short's. For a day to two I did nothing but put my

1. Mrs Stephen died in 1895.
2. There are no signed articles by LW in the *New Statesman* issues of 10 or 17 May 1919.

pen down or my book & see Tregerthen. Considering the extreme in-
hospitality of Eastbourne agents, I daresay we are well advised from a
practical point of view, to be sure of some retreat. But Asheham, as if to
keep our loyalty, breathed its usual charm. It compares very well with
Charleston; indeed I've never come back to it without that feeling of being
incredulous as one perfection was added to another. This time we spent
most of our day in the house, owing to the weather. L. scarcely left the
garden. One walk insufficiently clothed to Southease was very bitter. I
got over to Charleston, though; & had a night & morning alone with V.
—so far as she can ever be alone. There was Pitcher, the new gardener;
Angelica; Julian & Quentin of course; the new nurse; & a fire which
wouldn't burn. Indeed living is fairly bare at the moment. I had the rare
sensation of its being necessary to eat, in order to support life. They have
bread by the yard, as if slid along a slot; all the necessaries; but not an
ornament. My life, by comparison, seems padded at every turn. But they
all looked as vigorous as possible. The floors strewn with Burnet stuffs
for the Flat;³ & as usual, a good deal of domestic talk; sleep in the ground
floor room at night, where this time last year about I heard the night-
ingales, & the fishes splashing in the pond, white roses tapped at the
window: that night when I was told that Angelica was in evidence. Nothing but wind & rain this time, & no coal in the house.

Yesterday, Tuesday, we both renewed London life in the usual way;
save that I had to buy stuff for dresses, as well as paper labels & glue. Tea
at the Club, where Alix, dusky & dreary, borrowed 10/ in order to give
James his dinner. They were going to hear Bertie lecture; I preferred the
songsters of Trafalgar Square.⁴ The steps of the column were built up,
pyramid fashion, with elderly respectable householders grasping sheets of
music, which they rendered, in time to a conductor on a chair beneath,
with great precision. It was Life boat day, & the elderly people were
singing sailor's chanties & Tom Bowling. This seemed to me a very
amusing & instructive spectacle; & being famished for music, I could not
get past, but stood & felt thrilled with an absurd visionary excitement; &
walked over Hungerford Bridge making up stories.

3. In March 1919 Vanessa took over for a year the lease of the flat at 36 Regent
   Square vacated by James Strachey when he moved to 41 Gordon Square. Her
   intention was to furnish and let it for the summer and move in herself with her
   children in the autumn when Julian would attend Owen's School in Islington.
4. Bertrand Russell delivered a course of eight free lectures on 'The Analysis of
   Mind' at Dr Williams' Library, Gordon Square, on Tuesdays in May and June.
   They formed the basis of his book of the same title which was published in 1921.
   Lifeboat day was marked by an entertainment in Trafalgar Square organised by the
   League of Arts and consisting of Morris dancing and folk songs by a choir of
   500 voices. 'Tom Bowling' is a nautical song by Charles Dibdin dating from the
   late 18th century.

Monday 12 May

We are in the thick of our publishing season: Murry, Eliot, & myself are in the hands of the public this morning.[5] For this reason, perhaps, I feel slightly but decidedly depressed. I read a bound copy of Kew Gardens through; having put off the evil task until it was complete. The result is vague. It seems to me slight & short; I dont see how the reading of it impressed Leonard so much. According to him it is the best short piece I have done yet; & this judgment led me to read the Mark on the Wall, & I found a good deal of fault with that. As Sydney Waterlow once said, the worst of writing is that one depends so much upon praise. I feel rather sure that I shall get none for this story; & I shall mind a little. Unpraised, I find it hard to start writing in the morning; but the dejection lasts only 30 minutes, & once I start I forget all about it. One should aim, seriously, at disregarding ups & downs; a compliment here, silence there; Murry & Eliot ordered, & not me; the central fact remains stable, which is the fact of my own pleasure in the art. And these mists of the spirit have other causes, I expect; though they are deeply hidden. There is some ebb & flow of the tide of life which accounts for it; though what produces either ebb or flow I'm not sure.

But I have written nothing here for a week, & must cramp myself even now, in order to cut some more covers. Tuesday was written down; on Friday [*9 May*] I had tea with K.M. & Murry, with whom I now adopt a manner of motherly badinage; which is less fatiguing than the intellectual pose. He has not yet shed all the husks of clever youth. One feels him very unformed essentially, & capable of running on in an excited uneasy state about life such as I can recall in my own past. One tacitly assumed it to be a mark of genius. On Sunday Margaret & Lilian dined here; Margaret tending to be the flowing matron; she increases in size; & one can fancy her fitting a large arm chair, & reluctant to move. They seriously consider resignation. Lilian, M. whispered, is getting unfit for so much work. Poor Janet is depressed at having lost her job, & being fit for no other, & also very hard up. Indeed this is a melancholy season for them all; but J. has more than the usual shadows to depress her. I laughed to myself over the quantities of Armenians. How can one mind whether they number 4,000 or 4,000,000? The feat is beyond me.[6]

5. *The Critic in Judgment* by J. Middleton Murry, *Poems* by T. S. Eliot, and *Kew Gardens* by Virginia Woolf were all published by the Hogarth Press on 12 May 1919, the two last having been printed and paper-covered entirely by the Woolfs themselves.

6. The Armenian population had been decimated by the Turkish massacres of 1915, and the withdrawal of Russia from the war had exposed them again to attack. Famine resulting from attacks by both Turkey and Egypt was at this time causing a reported 150 deaths daily in one region of Armenia alone.

Friday 16 May

These swarming hot summer days seem to quicken human life as well as vegetable. One becomes a flower oozing honey upon which ones friends cluster—or such is my version of the relationship. This week we've had Ottoline, & Lytton, & I've been to see Violet Dickinson, & tonight the Abrahamsons & Oliver Strachey dine with us; on Saturday Logan comes to tea; on Sunday we lunch with the Webbs, to say nothing of invitations we've refused, & leaving out a great squash at the 17 Club to hear Forster speak on Egypt, when we met Bob, Altounyan, & Dora Sanger, with the usual varieties of old friends.[7] As usual my mind is too crammed to sift all these wares. Let me attempt Ottoline, since her hat & veil on the sofa beside me recall her. She was, I think L. was right in saying, anxious to come out & inspect us. She struck her unmistakable note on entering the room; rayed with green & blue, like the Cornish sea, & magnificently upright & held together; her blue blood giving her the carriage of assurance & self-respect which is rare among the intellectuals. We have taken, this last week, to dining in the garden, & there we sat on the flawless summer night with the apple trees softly snowed under with blossom, & a moon up. Certain layers of powder showed upon the steeps of her face—but when you reflect that she's close on 50—& has cropped her hair like a boy! Of course we talked personalities; investigated the case of Mary Hutch. & Eliot; also Gertler; & she was apparently, & as I believe, genuinely, kindly, & well wishing, though considerably bewildered, & bewailing as usual her disasters in friendship, & inclined to blame everyone but herself, though anxious for reconciliations, & plaintive rather than bitter. L's verdict was that she was "very nice"; the first time he has ever said that. The qualities which one has glimpses of in company were steadily visible in this domestic evening, when there was nothing to stimulate, & no effort to rise to.

Her intuitions are more penetrating than many of the profoundly reasonable remarks of our intellectuals; & to me she always has the pathos of a creature vaguely afloat in some wide open space, without support or clear knowledge of its direction. Perhaps she was on her good behaviour—but if so, she was capable of wrapping herself in her great Spanish cloak, & sallying out into the street without her hat; she's altogether such a fancy dress character that a hat more or less seems immaterial. We put her into

---

7. Violet Dickinson (1865-1948) was for many years VW's most intimate friend. She had disapproved when in 1911 VW set up house with her Bloomsbury friends at 38 Brunswick Square, and from about this period their relationship became more formal. (See *I VW Letters* and *I QB*.) Martin Arnold (1870-1962) and Emma (*née* Hirschsprung) Abrahamson of Copenhagen; he was LW's first cousin. For Altounyan, see below 22 May, n 13.

her train with young officers who looked up startled; & despatched her to Waterloo.

Next day there was Lytton. I need not repeat the stock observations upon his mellow good humour. It is more to the point to chronicle a renewed sense of affection, which has never been seriously in abeyance, & the usual conviction that his wit & what one calls personality are as peculiar to himself as his voice, or his finger nails. And then one thinks that it doesn't much matter if his writing is not profound or original; one begins perhaps to suspect that it may be more original than one thinks. He tells his stories of Cunards & Winston & Lord Ribblesdale admirably; with Marjorie's dramatic talent, & with a finer power of observation. We scrutinised the condition of his soul, with his help, very closely. Ottoline had professed some alarm. We came to the conclusion that it would be absurd not to have this butterfly's season among the great. The comparison between him & the select Norton, Alix, & James seemed entirely in his favour. The touchstone of virtue with them now is whether you attend Bertie's lectures or not. I hereby vow to fuddle Alix completely. We sat on the river bank, & he told us of a visit to Irene Vanbrugh, with his comedy; how the singing of her canary birds almost drowned his voice; & how finally she determined against it, finding a lack of human passion.[8] Therefore the comedy is shelved, for ever, I suspect, & he writes, & will continue to write Eminent Victorians.

Perhaps there was a little melancholy at this confession; perhaps a little desire for commendation of Lady Hester Stanhope, which we withheld; or perhaps I judge other writers' craving for applause by my own. I've had Roger's praise of Kew Gardens by the way, so I suppose I'm still safe, though no longer greeted with such exciting raptures. Indeed the books sell very slowly; & it looks as though the market for such commodities is a small one—infinitesimal; we shan't even pay our expenses it seems. But with such a variety of matter to choose from, this can scarcely be the fault of the books themselves; it was novelty that sold them at first. I broke from Lytton with regret, & paid my visit to Violet; but she would have been hurt had I shirked it, to judge at least by her pleasure at seeing me. Its odd how people of 50 remain exactly 50. She hasn't changed a hair for 20 years, which must be the length of our friendship. We take things up precisely as we left them; a years gap makes no difference; we have had our intimacy; something or other has fused; & never hardens again. Thus I felt in talking to her; it was the usual inconsequent, generous minded, unselfish talk. When I come onto the verge of the respectable classes I'm

8. Irene Vanbrugh (1872-1949), the successful and influential actress, was distantly related by marriage to the Stracheys. Lytton's 'comedy' was probably *The Son of Heaven*, his 'Chinese' play which he made great efforts to have professionally performed; eventually, in 1925, he succeeded.

always struck by their unexpectedness: V. is as much of a democrat as I am; as little of an Imperialist; she blames England; she has no hate of Germany; she sends clothes to Russia; & yet she lives in Manchester Street, consorts chiefly with people like the Horners & the Thynnes, & has Ozzie for a brother.[9] Beatrice Thynne has inherited a quarter of a million; two large properties, & one of the finest libraries in England; she has no idea what to make of them; visits them in a distracted way to see which she'd like to live in; can't make up her mind to settle in either, & finally spends most of her time in Gray's Inn, looked after by a charwoman. Her only acknowledgement of her balance is that now & then she pulls out strings of pearls, & parades the Squares of the Inn, with such effect that Lady H. Somerset has to beg her to remove them.[10]

Sunday 18 May

Our seductive sweetness appears still to be drawing bees from all quarters; last night I went to bed with lips so parched with talking & brain so dazed that I could only tumble into sleep head foremost. As we left lunch & were on the stairs there was a great rapping at the door, & the hall immediately filled with strangers, who eventually became Roger, Pamela, & a strange silent foreign woman whom from her grey hair I took to be Marjorie Fry.[11] We pitched on the grass, under a shower of apple blossom; & there sat until tea; & then Logan came; & we only fell silent at half past six or even later; nor was there a moment of repose, neither for tongue nor brain. It is true that Logan does his turns, which take the form of "delightful adventures—life is like the Arabian Nights—"

9. Violet Dickinson's family home had been at Chapmanslade near Frome in Somerset, where her social circle included the Thynnes at Longleat, the Horners at Mells, and the Duckworths at Orchardleigh, all within a few miles radius of Frome. Oswald Eden Dickinson (1869-1954), the younger of Violet's two brothers, was called to the Bar, and in 1912 became Secretary to the Board of Control (Lunacy and Mental Deficiency) in the Home Office. He lived with his sister.

10. On the death in September 1918 of her younger brother Lieutenant-Colonel Lord Alexander Thynne, killed in action while serving with the Wiltshire Regiment, Beatrice, the third and only unmarried daughter of the 4th Marquis of Bath, inherited the greater part of his property. Lady Henry Somerset (1851-1921), a first cousin of VW's mother, after renouncing her husband on account of his homosexual activities, devoted herself to the redemption of inebriate women. Her London home was at 4 Gray's Inn Square, as was Lady Beatrice Thynne's.

11. Margery Fry (1874-1958), the reformer, was the youngest of Roger Fry's six sisters; she had been warden of a women's university hostel in Birmingham and spent the war years working for Quaker Relief in France. Early in 1919 she set up house with Roger and his children at 9 Dalmeny Avenue, Holloway, which was her home until she became Principal of Somerville College, Oxford, in 1921.

& good stories, quotations, & recitations; but even these required intelligent attention. He is a very well brushed, bright eyed, rosy cheeked man, seemingly entirely satisfied with life, which he appears to have mastered; visiting each of its flowers, like a bee. These flowers he keeps stored in his waistcoat pocket: lines from Jeremy Taylor, Carlyle, Lamb, &c. An epicurean, I suppose: a little frosty, I conjecture; though kindly & humane of course; rather than human. I believe his motive was to get us to print some new works of his; anyhow he welcomed the invitation to submit them; & he lavished offers of help, & suggestions for increasing our sales; & altogether took the Hogarth Press in hand, & promises us a most splendid future. He proposes to become our agent. One must beware of becoming satellites of his set, however; cherishing single lines, & reprinting the Essays of Elia.[12]

Thursday 22 May

A few vegetable notes ought to prelude this page: the weather continues fine; the blue seems eternal; an occasional wind rises; we rock slightly; then steady ourselves, & ride on serenely. The apple blossom, which deluged Ottoline & looked so soft beside her cheeks, is over; 2 red rambler roses are pricking through. We dine of course out of doors to the sound of the fountain. The robins douche themselves there. Last night there were six voices to drown its perpetual dripping—Altounyan, A. & K. & Bob dining with us.[13] I had a vision of Bob as a tory squire; at any rate a conservative, mahogany coloured gentleman, innocent of rhyme. How far this is from the truth may be gauged from the fact that he swells with four separate volumes, & is to be delivered in the autumn. The good shrewd sound Trevelyan stock shows through; moreover he is well cropped & brown for a poet. He is also a comic character, & rises higher in that sphere when he feels himself inspired by laughter. His ungainly compliments to Karin, his eager awkward ways, made us all shout with

12. The miscellaneous essays of Charles Lamb originally contributed to the *London Magazine*, and collected in two volumes in 1823 and 1833. In 1919, Logan Pearsall Smith published *A Treasury of English Prose*; it contained lines from Jeremy Taylor, Carlyle, and no fewer than twenty-one examples from Lamb.

13. Ernest Haig Riddell Altounyan (1889-1962), whose father was an Armenian doctor with his own hospital in Aleppo, was born in England and educated at Rugby and Cambridge with the object of becoming his father's aide. He regarded himself, however, as a poet. E. M. Forster had recommended him to LW in May 1915 on the grounds that he had once been mad and might be of help to VW, who was then in the throes of madness; LW had then invited him once or twice to Hogarth House. (See MHP, Sussex, EMF/LW 20, 24 and 28 May 1915.) Altounyan qualified in 1919 and in October returned to Aleppo with his wife and children to pursue his medical career. His only published work, *Ornament of Honour*, a book of verse, appeared in 1937.

laughter. Altounyan is an effervescent Armenian, shy, but ready to bubble on provocation either of a literary or political nature. But Bob talked us all down. I must omit an exquisitely flattering duet between me & A. when I had a surfeit of praise for Kew Gardens—the best prose of the 20th century, surpassing Mark on the Wall, possessing transcendent virtues, save for one passage, between the women, & highly admired by Clive & Roger. I was at pains to sweeten his enthusiasm with this relish, since his native product is not of the very highest quality perhaps. Yes, authors are rather a despicable race I think. I'd composed myself to face failure so stoically that this unexpected gift was, at the moment, delicious. Forster approves too. But Altounyan has weighted his praises with a thick wad of mss., written, not typed, which we are to read & consider, & upon our verdict depends the whole of his future. Further, he appointed us his literary executors; everything he writes in Armenia is to be sent to us—to do what we like with. He gave us £2 towards our future. Still, to read a novel in manuscript, & settle a young man's future, & his wife's, & his childrens—that is a severe price for 10 minutes of praise. A[drian]. seemed to me to deserve Henderson's saying "He knows the right sneer for every occasion". He strikes me as more & more of a moon to the lusty red sun provided by Karin; & the light he throws upon whatever turns up is more & more bleaching and cadaverous. The truth is he has no occupation.

Sunday 25 May

The day recalls the fact that we lunched with the Webbs this time last week. I have made no note of it. There was the weak distinguished looking & yet vaguely apologetic Noel Buxton; & Arnott, rather self assertive, on the contrary, owing everything to his wits, & without an ounce of distinction thrown in.[14] I cannot get over my distaste for the Fabian type; though if it came to spending a year on a desert island, I suppose I should choose him rather than Buxton. I don't know. The Webbs were very quotable. Mrs Webb's brilliant idea of municipal bricks for children, in-scribed with the names of organisations so that in putting them together they would learn their civic duties was almost too much in character to be

14. Noel Edward Buxton (1869-1948), the high-minded intellectual politician, had become disillusioned with the Liberal Party owing to the harshness of the Paris peace treaties; he had narrowly lost his seat in Parliament in the 1918 election, and joined the Labour Party in 1919. He was to be re-elected as a Labour member in 1922. Robin Page Arnot (b. 1890), economist and social scientist, author of a major history of the mineworkers of Britain, was Secretary of the Fabian (later Labour) Research Department; his publications at this period included *Trade Unionism on the Railways* (with G. D. H. Cole, 1917), and *Facts from the Coal Commission* (1919).

suitable. Even Sidney had his mild joke at her. Noel Buxton obsequiously offered his son for the experiment.[15] Rich men nowadays can be seen divesting themselves of particles of gold with a view to the eye of the needle. Then later in the week Mrs Woolf & Sylvia came to tea, bringing fresh eggs & lilies of the valley. Sylvia amused me by her assurance that the affairs of Putney are of moment to the world; & her anxiety to get stories of her own house hunting adventures corrected—as though these were matters of importance. And Mrs Woolf, as usual, pleased me by her childishness, by which I mean her freshness & inconsequence, as if all her life were still spent among the little incidents & goings on of a large nursery. She couldn't face a play, she told me; but she could just manage lunch at the Carlton. Why the boundary line between the impossible comes there I don't know. And Bella since Bertie's death finds life necessary to keep up her spirits; & is learning to Jazz; & her eyes prevent her from reading much; but she writes her page in Little Folks; & her friends are all very good to her, & she has gone to Bexhill with Martin & Emma. It is predicted that Martin will be made not quite a knight but the next best thing.[16] Martin believes in orders, I gather, & our laughter at the O.B.E. must have saddened him the other night. Philip is cutting off lambs' tails, & they are made into a pie at night— Philip who would step aside to avoid a caterpillar, & once fought Harold for using worms for bait, & was chased by Harold to the next village in the Isle of Wight where they were staying "& I ran after them, miles & miles, thinking that the end of the world had come!"[17] Naturally Mrs Woolf had no time to read Sophocles—nor have I for the matter of that.

Lytton came to tea on Friday & half maliciously assured me that my industry amazed him. My industry & my competence, for he thinks me the best reviewer alive, & the inventor of a new prose style, & the creator of a new version of the sentence. People's compliments generally manage to reserve the particular praise they wish to have themselves. But we are surprisingly honest; we have a clear perception of the others meaning. He asserted that he was disgusted by his own stereotyped ways: his two semi colons; his method of understatement; & his extreme definiteness. Without agreeing, I conveyed my sense of his dangers, & urged him to write plays—stories—anything to break the mould of the early Victorians. After a volume on Victoria, in the same manner, he is going to attempt it. But then money—he must make money—he cant write reviews—& I've to do Addison, & other books, & protested that all the same I'm not a hack, & he runs the risk of becoming a Logan, a superior dilettante. To

15. His eldest son was two years old (born 13 January 1917).
16. For Bella Woolf see above, 1 September 1917, n 1. Her cousin Martin Abrahamson was created K.B.E. in 1920.
17. Since his demobilisation, Philip Woolf was training as a farmer.

which he agreed, & then we talked about Addison, & read scraps of Johnson's lives; & so enjoyed ourselves. He told me about Princess Sophia & the d. of Cumberland.[18]

To the Squire's party.

Monday 9 June (Whit-Monday)

I know I meant to convey my sense of the degradation of the Squire's party; but the sense has faded, & is not worth recapturing. A week at Asheham has intervened—from one Tuesday to another. An odd thing happened to me at Asheham, where I count upon becoming clearer & more concentrated, & reading print as if through a magnifying glass. The very opposite of this took place. I dozed & drowsed & seemed to feel the sun in my brain sending all my thoughts to seek repose in the shadow. I write there at an open window looking onto the field; & the field was gilt with buttercups; the sheep were tempting in their indolence; in short, I used to find the morning gone & only a few lines written, & so it was with my Addison, or whoever it might be, after tea. Our ship rode so steady that one came to disbelieve in motion or the possibility of change; we appeared wedged in the blue. Perhaps one day there was a cloud; but no harbourage was offered it, & congregation of clouds was impossible. The loveliness of Asheham once again brimmed the cup & overflowed. Wild ideas seized us of building a house at the Lay.[1] To give up every foothold in that region seemed unthinkable. L. bicycled round & brought news of an ancient manor house at Denton, which excited hopes, but the sight of it next day completely dashed them. In order to popularise this large stuffy, ill lit, slightly mouldy & decayed mansion the owner, a London publican dazzled into purchasing by the aristocratic name but unable to induce his wife to live there, hit on the ambitious plan of starting a line of omnibuses to run from London, & deliver their loads at the manor house, where tea would be provided. One such feast was held, as long boards stretched on trestles, & a few dozen green wine-glasses testified; but the device failed; the Londoners had seen more seductive sights than Denton Manor, & it is still in the market. With the notion of building a house running strong in my mind I went to Charleston for a night & was there disabused of such fantasies very completely. To recapitulate a story

18. VW's article on Addison was published in the *TLS* on 19 June 1919 (Kp C155). *The Lives of the Poets* (1779-81), biographical and critical studies by Samuel Johnson. Princess Sophia, fifth daughter of George III, was believed to have had an illegitimate son by her brother the Duke of Cumberland. General Thomas Garth consented to pass for the father of this child, although the story was apparently quite untrue. See D. M. Stuart's *The Daughters of George III* (1939).

1. A cottage and group of farm buildings about a mile along the Lewes road from Asheham. Denton is a village some four miles off in the opposite direction.

told verbally several times would be dull. But Nessa & I quarrelled as nearly as we ever do quarrel now over the get up of Kew Gardens, both type & woodcuts; & she firmly refused to illustrate any more stories of mine under those conditions, & went so far as to doubt the value of the Hogarth Press altogether. An ordinary printer would do better in her opinion. This both stung & chilled me. Not that she was bitter or extreme; its her reason & control that give her blame its severity. Anyhow I left in rather a crumpled condition, & paused in Lewes, on L.'s advice, to see a house on the hill. A degree of that refinement & smug efficiency which one finds in Surrey houses set me against the White House; & I trudged down into Lewes again in no cheerful mood, with three hours, moreover, to spend there. To pass the time, more than anything, I asked Mrs Wycherley about houses;[2] & she, after tepidly recommending some that were impossible & sketching the difficulties of the situation, bethought her of one newly on the market, small, old, actually in Lewes, & perhaps a little humble for one used to lodge at Asheham. I pricked my ears; since this is always the way one is told of what one wants. Off I went, up Pipes Passage, under the clock, & saw rising at the top of the sloping path a singular shaped roof, rising into a point, & spreading out in a circular petticoat all round it. Then things began to go a little quicker. An elderly and humble cottage woman the owner, showed me over. How far my satisfaction with the small rooms, & the view, & the ancient walls, & the wide sitting room, & the general oddity & character of the whole place were the result of finding something that would do, that one could conceive living in, that was cheap (freehold £300) I don't know; but as I inspected the rooms I became conscious of a rising desire to settle here; to have done with looking about; to take this place, & make it one's permanent lodging. Perhaps later it will amuse me to read how I went from one grade to another of desire; till I felt physically hot & ardent, ready to surmount all obstacles. I liked the way the town dropped from the garden leaving us on a triangular island, vegetables one side, grass the other; the path encircling the round house amused me; nor are we overlooked. In short I took it there & then, being egged on by Wycherley's hesitation, & hints of a purchaser who had already asked for the refusal. Lewes that afternoon, with its many trees & laburnums, & water meadows, & sunny bow windowed houses, & broad High Street looked very tempting & dignified. The end of the story, which I must curtail, is that we have bought the Round House, & are now secure of a lodging on earth so long as we need sleep or sit anywhere.[3]

2. The White House stands on Cuilfail, the hill dominating Lewes on the east. Wycherley is an estate agent in the High Street.
3. The Round House, a converted windmill, stands on the western walls of Lewes Castle. The windmill tower is truncated and covered by an eight-sided pointed slate roof; a small two-storey cottage is attached.

Tuesday 10 June

I must use up the fifteen minutes before dinner in going on again, in order to make up the great gap. We are just in from the Club; from ordering a reprint of the Mark on the Wall at the Pelican Press;[4] & from tea with James. His news is that Maynard in disgust at the peace terms has resigned, kicked the dust of office off him, & is now an academic figure at Cambridge.[5] But I must really sing my own praises, since I left off at the point when we came back from Asheham to find the hall table stacked, littered, with orders for Kew Gardens. They strewed the sofa, & we opened them intermittently through dinner, & quarrelled, I'm sorry to say, because we were both excited, & opposite tides of excitement coursed in us, & they were blown to waves by the critical blast of Charleston. All these orders—150 about, from shops & private people—come from a review in the Lit. Sup. presumably by Logan, in which as much praise was allowed me as I like to claim.[6] And 10 days ago I was stoically facing complete failure! The pleasure of success was considerably damaged, first by our quarrel, & second, by the necessity of getting some 90 copies ready, cutting covers, printing tables, glueing backs, & finally despatching, which used up all spare time & some not spare till this moment. But how success showered during those days! Gratuitously, too, I had a letter from Macmillan in New York, so much impressed by The Voyage Out that they want to read Night & Day.[7] I think the nerve of pleasure easily becomes numb. I like little sips; but the psychology of fame is worth considering at leisure. I fancy one's friends take the bloom off. Lytton lunched here on Saturday with the Webbs, & when I told him my various triumphs, did I imagine a little shade—instantly dispelled, but not before my rosy fruit was out of the sun. Well, I treated his triumphs in much the same way. I can't feel gratified when he expatiates upon a copy of Eminent Victorians lined & initialled "M" or "H" by Mr & Mrs Asquith. Yet clearly the thought produced a comfortable glow in him. The luncheon was a suc-

---

4. *The Mark on the Wall*, VW's contribution to *Two Stories* (Kp A2), was issued separately by the Hogarth Press as a second edition in June 1919; 1000 copies were printed for them by the Pelican Press (Kp A2b).

5. Maynard Keynes was the British Treasury's chief representative at the Paris Peace Conference in 1919, a position from which he resigned formally on 19 May, in protest against the conditions to be imposed on Germany, which he considered both unjust and inexpedient. By August he was at Charleston writing his polemic *The Economic Consequences of the Peace*, published by Macmillan in December. He was a fellow of King's College, Cambridge.

6. VW presumed wrong. It was in fact written not by Logan Pearsall Smith but by Harold Child (1869-1945), a regular contributor to the *TLS*.

7. Macmillan had published LW in America, and this may have given rise to their interest in VW's books.

cess. We ate in the garden, & Lytton sported very gracefully & yet with more than his old assurance over the conversation. "But I'm *not* interested in Ireland—"

Saturday 14 June

The weather seems unbreakable. A delphinium is out today in the garden & one Sweet William; Lottie was discovered brushing the grass with a hearth broom, as though attending to the coat of some pet animal. They say the strawberry crop will be ruined. This is a serious matter for us as we have just bought 60 lbs. of sugar, & had arranged a great jam making. Strawberries are 2/ a lb. at this moment. Asparagus 6d & 7d, & yesterday at Ray's I ate my first green peas. I had a Hampstead field day; first the Murrys, then Adrian & Karin, & finally dinner—it was 8.30 by the time I got it—with Ray & Dorothy Bussy.[8] A very severe review of Murry, a severe review of Eliot, appeared in the Lit. Sup. on Thursday.[9] Considering their general slackness, I don't see why they choose to come down so hard upon Murry; & I wish they hadn't. I attribute the extreme depression of him & Katherine at least partly to this. And I felt gorged & florid with my comparative success. Poor Murry pretended not to mind, but much like a small boy sticking it out that caning doesn't hurt. A poem is a very sensitive part to be beaten. But Katherine looks so ill & haggard that I suppose health may make a great part of her depression. She is going to San Remo for a year in September. Murry means to live alone in the country. I don't see how, all this being so, they can look forward to their future. And then there's the question of Katherine's writing. Isn't she a little querulous & restless about that? Standing emphatically yet not quite firmly on her rights as an artist; as people do who must insist upon being one. In token of this she told me a long & to me rather distasteful story about her dealings with a man called Schiff, who wanted her to contribute to art & letters, & dared to offer her advice, upon which she got on her high horse, & wrote him such a letter that he replied humbly—in a style that I couldn't make anything of, & indeed the rights & wrongs of the whole business escaped me though I protested, I'm ashamed to say, that I share Katherine's indignation.[10] What a fraud one is in many ways! But

8. Dorothy (1866-1960) was the third child of Sir Richard and Lady Strachey; her family was at first dismayed when in 1903 she married the French painter Simon Bussy and went to live at Roquebrune on the Mediterranean. She later translated many of the works of her friend André Gide into English, and in *Olivia* (1949) gave a revealing picture of her own sentimental education.

9. This review of Eliot's *Poems* and Murry's *The Critic in Judgment* appeared in the *TLS* of 12 June 1919 under the heading 'Not Here, O Apollo'.

10. Sydney Schiff (*c.* 1869-1944) was a wealthy and discerning patron of artists and the arts who with his wife Violet befriended Katherine and sought to help her

then if one's on this footing of being fellow artists & all that, one's relations are queered from the start. Anyhow I went off rather sombre, leaving them to their spare lonely meal, nothing seeming to grow or flourish round them; leafless trees.

Wednesday 18 June

I went off, as I now remember, to call on Adrian, as I was early for Ray; & found that strange couple just decided to become medical students. After 5 years' training they will, being aged 35 & 41 or so, set up together in practise as psycho-analysts.[11] This is the surface bait that has drawn them. The more profound cause is, I suppose, the old question which used to weigh so heavy on Adrian, what to do? Here is another chance; visions of success & a busy, crowded, interesting life beguile him. Halfway through, I suppose, something will make it all impossible; & then, having forgotten his law, he will take up what—farming or editing a newspaper, or keeping bees perhaps. I don't see that it matters at all, so long as they always have some carrot dangling in front of them. Dinner with Ray; talk with Dorothy Bussy of her past; promise of her play, & so home with L. who had dined higher up with Margaret. That morning (Friday 13th to be exact) I got the first proofs of my novel. I've now had 64 pages.

On Sunday we planned to go to Kew & have tea there, but Logan rang us up, & we came home to see him. More stories, a little less carefully told & so more to my liking; & then we came indoors, & he read us his stories from the bible. At this moment we have the following manuscripts or promises of manuscripts. Paris by Hope Mirrlees. Novel by Altounyan. Stories by Logan. Play by D. Bussy. Ray's grandmother's sexual-religious experiences. And old Bob caught Leonard last night at the [Apostles'] dinner & pressed upon him a translation of Lucretius.[12] What steps we're to take is not at the moment clear to me. Whether to become a shop, or remain a small private press—whether to get help or refuse it. Logan, of

with money and hospitality. He published novels under the pen-name Stephen Hudson and was to translate Proust's *Le Temps Retrouvé*. He financed the quarterly *Art and Letters*.

11. Adrian and Karin Stephen studied medicine at University College Hospital, London from 1919, qualifying MB, BS in 1926, and did thereafter practise as analysts.

12. Of these, *Paris* (dated 'Spring 1919') by Hope Mirrlees, and *Stories from the Old Testament* retold by Logan Pearsall Smith, were published by the Hogarth Press in May 1920. Ray's grandmother was Hannah Whitall Smith, a celebrated American Quaker evangelist who had settled with her family in Surrey. Nothing more was heard of Dorothy Bussy's play or Altounyan's novel; R. C. Trevelyan's Lucretius translation was published by Allen & Unwin in 1920.

course, has a charming young man up his sleeve. How futile these elderly people are! There's Maurice Baring gone & printed one copy of an anthology at a cost of £40 to give Lady Diana Manners for a present—& she is one of those vaguely literary people who "sometimes read Shakespeare".[13] Logan approves of this on the whole. He likes to supervise these literary undertakings, & would even give money, but doesn't want to be disturbed out of his habits. He is printing several anthologies himself in the autumn, "I consider that I've done my bit" he said, with a comfortable sigh, after saying that he had been correcting the proofs of these works.[14] He now goes yachting for a holiday.

Yesterday, Tuesday, I was treated to ices at Gunter's by Clive. It was all the same as before. Little tables; long rather dark shop; numbers of gilt chairs; discreet buffet; elderly waitresses in black; & couples scattered all about silently, or almost silently, absorbing ices & sugared cakes. There was an aristocratic small boy got up like a picture of Queen Victoria as a child, with a great sash, & a bow, & a hat wreathed in roses. His mother had brought him in, we thought, from one of the great Berkeley Square houses. Then there was youth, by some misadventure not at Ascot; a coffee-coloured young man, & a semi-transparent girl.[15] We strolled out of this solemn cave & sauntered through the purest 18th Century London to the Green Park where we sat on hard green chairs, & watched people passing down the little slope towards the Palace. This being, I suppose, the 6th week without rain the grass is already haycoloured & slippery. We gossiped, speculated, & reminisced. Very easy, agreeable talk to my mind, & then what an age I've know[n] him! How much we've been through side by side—these infrequent meetings are little islands upon which one stands surveying the flood racing away in the past; looking out over the future, safely & with very little anxiety just at present. He talks of going to Paris in the autumn, to see what's on; & he's given up his book, & finds that articles of 2,000 words exactly suit him. He thinks of subjects in his bath. He makes money. He spends it on ices & dinners at the Café Royal. He dines out every night, enjoys every moment, & feels his senses quicker & stronger as time goes on. We agreed in finding life very delightful, though very different for each of us. Home, to await Miss Barbara Lynch, but she never came. The meeting talked to its hearts con-

13. Maurice Baring (1874-1945), diplomatist, foreign correspondent and man of letters; the anthology was given as a wedding present. Lady Diana Manners, third daughter of the 8th Duke of Rutland, had married Alfred Duff Cooper on 2 June 1919.

14. During 1918-20 Logan Pearsall Smith wrote and published much of the material contained in *More Trivia* (1922). *A Treasury of English Prose* (see above, 18 May 1919, n 12) and Donne's *Sermons. Selected Passages*, were both published in 1919.

15. Gunter's tea-rooms were at 63 New Bond Street. Ascot, the most fashionable event in the racing calendar, was in 1919 held on the four days 17-20 June.

tent. Mrs Whitty & another pressed me for copies of Kew Gardens.[16] But I don't want them to read the scene of the two women. Is that to the discredit of Kew Gardens? Perhaps a little. I've just been there, in the flesh, & sat under a tree, reading The Way of all Flesh, which I have to review tomorrow.[17] According to Fredegond there's been a crisis between Alix & James. She tried to break with him; failed; went reeling off to Tidmarsh in what state of mind I don't quite know, & there is at the moment. James inhabits Gordon Sqre—

Monday 23 June

If I hadn't had since midday to settle myself, I should still be twanging & twittering with Garsington.[18] But parties don't fluster me as they used. I dont much care now about the great question of hair, & doing up dresses; I am resigned to my station among the badly dressed, though Gravé [a dressmaker] & her vagaries, & the speeding up of my blue dress, & doubts as to its beauty scarcely seem to confirm that statement. Here, I think, the great & at present sore, question of aesthetic taste enters in. Why am I calm & indifferent as to what people say of Night & Day, & fretful for their good opinion of my blue dress?

However this may be, I enjoyed Garsington saying to myself "The worst moment will be when I come into the drawing room in my blue dress before dinner." I planned thus to get dressed quick & come in before Ott. which is not difficult as Ott. never gets dressed quick. Mercifully I need not face Garsington squarely & draw its picture. I observed that the sealing wax red drawing room is a good deal smaller this visit than last, & last visit than first. That's what happens to people too. There was young Lord de la Warr walking among the roses & cabbages, a boy of 19, who after sweeping mines as a seaman is now a socialist, under the guidance of Lansbury.[19] But I took a good look at him & noticed the straightness of his body, ease, & certainty of his manner which mark him out from Gertler quite emphatically. Gertler & Nelson strolled up another garden path. Nelson one of the insignificant, I should say, who

16. Miss Lynch was a Women's Co-operative Guild Speaker; Mrs Whitty a Richmond Branch member.

17. VW's review of the eleventh impression of the second edition of Samuel Butler's posthumously published autobiographical novel (1903), appeared in the *TLS* on 26 June 1919 (Kp C156).

18. VW went to stay with the Morrells at Garsington on Saturday 21 June and returned home on Monday; LW did not go.

19. Herbrand Edward Dundonald Brassey Sackville, 9th Earl De La Warr (1900-1976), succeeded his father in 1915; in 1916 he left Eton and served in the Royal Naval Reserve as an able seaman; after the war he went up to Magdalen College, Oxford, and thereafter had a distinguished career in the public service. While at

has attached himself firmly to the comforts of Garsington. His anxiety to accept an invitation to dinner proved his relish for that one of Ottoline's bounties. The population was floating & changing. Goldie & I were permanent; Aldous H. came for one night. I shall leave out several names if I try to count them. Young Lord de la Warr said very little; but I think he would have impressed an American, & good manners conciliate me. I think Goldie was the principle element in the week end, that is to say that he took upon him the brunt of Sunday morning, & meal times; 3 hours sitting on a hard seat with Ott. & me, Philip sometimes, Gertler occasionally, & Aldous off & on was a trial; but for us all it was well surmounted. I did not guess the time once. When Philip suggested a visit to the pigs I was ready but not over-ready. I think we discussed Roger most carefully & Forster, & Bob. Ott. needled away at her embroidery, Philip's bedspread, losing her needle once, & crouching on all fours behind the seat, while Goldie & I went on talking. This seemed to me to typify her modest position; so long as people talk she doesn't much want to interfere, & she listens, especially if people's characters are discussed. She had worked off the great Picasso grievance upon Goldie; I had only vague lamentations, & aspirations for my share.[20] Yet it struck me as strange

Thursday 3 July

What struck me as strange? I cant now remember or even guess; perhaps I meant to finish by trying to define the sense of purposelessness which now & then beset me— Suppose we do settle exactly what Roger's character is, & what degree of spite to allow Clive, & how far Logan has a heart?—well, what then? Are we going nowhere? Does the mist move with us? Well—this is too far gone for recapturing, though there was a queer enough sequel a day or two later at Asheham. We went there on the Thursday following, & came back yesterday. I can't give much space to Philip's letter though, seeing how many matters I must despatch; & how, to purify my mind, I must have a brush with the Ajax before L. comes in. Philip's letter was all about my lack of heart & his terror of me; to which

---

Eton he had been the moving spirit behind the foundation of the College Political Society at the first meeting of which, in December 1917, George Lansbury (1859-1940), the idealistic socialist leader and pacifist, had been one of the speakers.

Geoffrey Nelson (c. 1896-1941) was a painter of Bohemian tendencies for whom Lytton Strachey had harboured a fruitless passion some years before.

20. Picasso was in London during the summer of 1919 in connection with his décor for the Russian ballet; Clive Bell and Maynard Keynes arranged a dinner party for him, which occasioned his refusing Lady Ottoline's invitation to Garsington— and she herself was not invited to the dinner. See *II VW Letters*, nos. 1051, 1053, 1054; also *VW/GLS Letters*, p. 80.

I have rejoined "if I'm Bloomsbury, you're Mayfair"; to his bewilderment, as I hope.[1] But this is moonshine. The solid fact is that we own, besides the Round House, Monks House at Rodmell, with three quarters of an acre of land. We own Monks House (this is almost the first time I've written a name which I hope to write many thousands of times before I've done with it) for ever. It happened thus. As we walked up the steep road from the station last Thursday on our way to inspect the Round House, we both read out a placard stuck on the auctioneers wall. Lot 1. Monks House, Rodmell. An old fashioned house standing in three quarters of an acre of land to be sold with possession. The sale we noted was on Tuesday; to take place at the White Hart.[2] "That would have suited us exactly" L. said as we passed, & I, loyal to the Round House, murmured something about the drawbacks of Rodmell, but suggested anyhow a visit to the place; & so we went on. I think a slight shade of anti-climax had succeeded my rather excessive optimism; at any rate the Round House no longer seemed so radiant & unattainable when we examined it as owners. I thought L. a little disappointed, though just & polite even to its merits. The day lacked sun. The bedrooms were very small. The garden not a country garden. Anyhow it seemed well to plan a visit to Rodmell on the following day. I bicycled over against a strong cold wind. This time I flatter myself that I kept my optimism in check. "These rooms are small, I said to myself; you must discount the value of that old chimney piece & the niches for holy water. Monks are nothing out of the way. The kitchen is distinctly bad. Theres an oil stove, & no grate. Nor is there hot water, nor a bath, & as for the E.C. I was never shown it." These prudent objections kept excitement at bay; yet even they were forced to yield place to a profound pleasure at the size & shape & fertility & wildness of the garden. There seemed an infinity of fruitbearing trees; the plums crow[d]ed so as to weigh the tip of the branch down; unexpected flowers sprouted among cabbages. There were well kept rows of peas, artichokes, potatoes; raspberry bushes had pale little pyramids of fruit; & I could fancy a very pleasant walk in the orchard under the apple trees, with the grey extinguisher of the church steeple pointing my boundary. On the other hand there is little view—O but I've forgotten the lawn smoothly rolled, & rising in a bank, sheltered from winds too, a refuge in cold & storm; & a large earthen pot holds sway where the path strikes off, crowned with a tuft of purple samphire. *One* pot; not two. There is little ceremony or precision at Monks House. It is an unpretending house, long & low, a house of many doors; on one side fronting the street of Rodmell, & wood boarded on that side, though the street of Rodmell is at our end little

1. For the letter in question (and others from Philip Morrell to VW), see MHP, Sussex. VW's rejoinder is *II VW Letters*, no. 1065.
2. The White Hart Hotel in High Street is a large inn facing the Law Courts in the centre of Lewes.

more than a cart track running out on to the flat of the water meadows. There are, if memory serves me, no less than three large outhouses of different kinds, & a stable; & a hen house—& the machinery of a granary, & one shed full of beams of ancient oak; & another stored with pea props; but our fruit & vegetables are said to flow over each summer into these receptacles, & to need selling; though so obliging in its prolific way as to flourish under the care of a single old man whose heart is of gold, & who, for 40 years I think, has spent his spare time in tending these trees for the late Mr Jacob Verrall[3]— All this made a happy kind of jumble in my brain, together with the store of old fashioned chairs & tables, glass & furniture with which every inch of room space is crowded; I came back & told my story as quietly as I could, & next day L. & I went together & made a thorough inspection. He was pleased beyond his expectation. The truth is he has the making of a fanatical lover of that garden. It suits me very well, too, to ramble off among the Telscombe downs, when fine; or tread out my paces up the path & across the lawn when dark or wind blown. In short, we decided walking home to buy if we could, & sell Round House, as we conjecture we can. Eight hundred we made our limit, which, according to Wycherley, gave us a good chance of possession. The sale was on Tuesday. I don't suppose many spaces of five minutes in the course of my life have been so close packed with sensation. Was I somehow waiting to hear the result, while I watched the process, of an operation? The room at the White Hart was crowded. I looked at every face, & in particular at every coat & skirt, for signs of opulence, & was cheered to discover none. But then, I thought, getting L. into line, does *he* look as if he had £800 in his pocket? Some of the substantial farmers might well have their rolls of notes stuffed inside their stockings. Bidding began. Someone offered £300. "Not an offer", said the auctioneer, who was immediately opposed to us as a smiling courteous antagonist, "a beginning." The next bid was £400. Then they rose by fifties. Wycherley standing by us, silent & unmoved, added his advance. Six hundred was reached too quick for me. Little hesitations interposed themselves, but went down rather dismally fast. The auctioneer egged us on. I daresay there were six voices speaking, though after £600, 4 of them dropped out, & left only a Mr Tattersall competing with Mr Wycherley. We were allowed to bid in twenties; then tens; then fives; & still short of £700, so that our eventual victory seemed certain. Seven hundred reached, there was a pause; the auctioneer raised his hammer, very slowly; held it up a considerable time; urged & exhorted all the while it slowly sank towards the table. "Now Mr Tattershall, another bid from you—no more bidding once I've struck the table—ten pounds? five pounds?—no more? for the

3. For the history of Monks House and its previous owners see *III LW*, pp. 61-64, and *IV LW*, pp. 12-15.

last time then—*dump*!" & down it came on the table, to our thanksgiving
—I purple in the cheeks, & L. trembling like a reed—"sold to Mr
Wycherley." We stayed no longer. Out we went into the High Street, &
very nearly quarrelled over the address of Roger's House.

Tuesday 8 July

We went on, however, L. to Asheham, & I to Charleston, where there
was Maynard, & a good deal of brisk talk. He is disillusioned he says. No
more does he believe, that is, in the stability of the things he likes. Eton is
doomed; the governing classes, perhaps Cambridge too. These conclusions were forced on him by the dismal & degrading spectacle of the
Peace Congress, where men played shamelessly, not for Europe, or even
England, but for their own return to Parliament at the next election. They
were not wholly vicious; they had spasms of well meaning; but a fate
seemed to possess the business from the first, driving it all in the most fatal
direction & soon no one had the strength to resist. He resigned, & is now
a don at Cambridge, daily rejecting profitable offers made him by houses
of business, willing, according to Duncan, to pay £4,000 a year for his
attendance for a short time daily. We all came up to London early next day,
Nessa having to see a Mr Cholmondeley about Julian's education.[4] We
had an afternoon's gaiety at the Ballet, & then went back to Gordon Sqre,
everything a little glittering & unreal, as usual after the country & in
Nessa's presence.[5]

Friday, the 4th, I went to tea with Katherine, since I begin to feel my
visits numbered, how seriously I dont know, but once she gets abroad,
what's to bring her back?[6] Murry, poor man, pale & sad as usual, for she
is again only just out of bed. The weather of course is taking its revenge
now for a season of generosity. We have fires every night. Worse than the
cold is the drab coloured sky, so that one's whole existence seems to be
in the shadow.

On Saturday we saw the horse show, & I had a look at Queen Alexandra's poor old effigy, still painted like a wildrose, though she is about 75,

---

4. R. F. Cholmeley (1862-1947) was from 1909 to 1927 headmaster of Owen's School,
Islington—a public grammar school founded in 1613. Julian, who had hitherto been
educated at home, attended the school as a day boy for two years from September
1919.

5. Diaghilev's company were this year performing at the Alhambra Theatre, Leicester
Square; the ballets presented that afternoon were *Carnaval*, *Children's Tales*, and
Scheherezade, with Lopokova and Massine dancing.

6. Katherine Mansfield, suffering from consumption, left England in mid-September
to winter by the Mediterranean. She returned to Hampstead for five months in
April 1920, and again briefly in 1922.

& can only hobble up a ladder like a decrepit washerwoman. Its only on the face that the pretence can be preserved.[7]

On Sunday Mrs Hamilton brought her sister—"the poet"—to dinner.[8] I almost laughed at the sight of her. She stumps, peering & hesitating, into a room, shakes hands with emphasis, & displays a small round pale face, with wisps of brown hair controlled by a tight band of ribbon. A mixture of schoolgirl & German professor to look at; awkward & restless in manner; & delivering herself of rounded periods which would be queer enough in themselves were they not delivered with the oddest rotundity of diction, as of one speaking from a tub,—& in a voice that swells & falls but finally swells like a musical instrument imperfectly controlled. In spite of these curiosities of manner & appearance she seemed perfectly self possessed, & referred to her stock of book learning, which seemed very large & various, with the greatest composure. "As Nietchze says" or, "To quote Dostoevsky", or "In the opinion of the Neo-Cartesians."— Such were her conversational openings, waiting no season but obtruding themselves spontaneously. "I do not myself feel any doubt as to the nature of the good, nor have I indeed ever felt any doubt upon that point"— this was fired off when the talk was not concerned with anything of the kind. Yet one couldn't dislike her, or dub her a very poisonous variety of the prig. I suppose her to be the family prodigy, fed on books, & living up to now in a dark cave until like a creature deprived of light the complexion of her soul is entirely white. She has the mind of an albino. What is to become of her? I don't suspect her a poet. I imagine her one of those prodigies who quite contentedly continue all their lives, in some country village, to absorb learning, & have their circle of correspondents. Her letters must be portentous. Molly watched her with the oddest mixture of pride & uneasiness. What were we thinking of her? Did we realise that these manners & views were only superficial; did we not see how remarkable a product she was—could we not perhaps be made, by artful questions & hints, to see it? Margot is now reading—on Comparative Religions. Margot spent all her life pretending she was a Monk or Rob Roy. We now hesitate whether or not to ask to read her poems.

Thursday 10 July

I have forgotten several people, I see. One is Arundell del Ré, Logan's prize young man, devoted to the cause of good books, & proposing to

7. Richmond Horse Show, a famous two-day event held in the Old Deer Park, was revived in 1919 after being in abeyance during the war. Alexandra (1844-1925), the Danish Queen-consort and widow of King Edward VII, was patroness of 'Alexandra Rose day' in aid of hospitals. She was renowned for her beauty, which was very carefully preserved into old age. She visited the Horse Show on the afternoon of 5 July with a party of royal ladies.

8. Margot Adamson (see above, 15 March 1919, n 26).

start a shop in Chelsea for the promotion of them.[9] He intends not only selling on a select principle, but binding, & printing, & providing a room where book lovers can love books. His weakness & paleness did not impress us; but then, perhaps weakness and paleness are the necessary qualities. At a pinch too, I think, like most men, he has business qualities, & brains enough to be dependable. His most serious contribution to an evening of vague discussion was that he should relieve us of all the business of the Hogarth Press, stock our books, keep our accounts, in return for which we're to give him a few lessons in printing. I suppose something may come of it.

Last night I dined at the Savoy Grill Room with Clive. It is long since eating a meal was such a serious business to me—long since I had taken part in the great ceremony of dinner with others believing in it, assisting at it, & dressing for it. Fish & meat & melon & ices have come to their own again. Clive parted with a good deal of paper money. His appearance never, even now, is altogether smart or wordly; his shoulders are not broad enough, & then his hair— But he was dressed, carried a black cane, & wore a silk hat. Oddly enough my mind went back to my first sight of him years ago. He looked young & had the unselfassured manner of one not used to things, only pretending use. This ceremony of eating takes so long that it was 9 by the time we finished, & the light through the enormous window dusky & almost lamplit. He pointed out to me Picasso & Mdme Picasso making off for the ballet; & behind us sat the little ivory figure of Lopokhova's husband.[10] Thus there was every reason for Clive to feel assured. We drove back to Gordon Square & talked about the problems of literature. On his table lay his 'puff' of me in the New Republic; I daresay I should have preferred not to be bracketed with Eliot & Murry.[11] I wonder if I talk nonsense about writing to Clive? On the whole I believe that he has an odd gift for making one talk sense. He's

9. Arundel del Ré had been assistant editor to Harold Munro on the *Poetry Review* and worked in his Poetry Bookshop before the war. In 1919 he opened the Chelsea Book Club at 65 Cheyne Walk, stocking English and French *éditions de luxe* and exhibiting modern pictures.

10. Picasso's wife at this time was the ballerina Olga Koklova. Lydia Lopokova was married to Randolfo Barocchi, who accompanied her to London for the 1919 Diaghilev Ballet season. According to Richard Buckle (*Essays on John Maynard Keynes*, 1975, edited by Milo Keynes, p. 52), it was on 10 July 1919 that she ran off with a Russian officer. The company officially attributed her absence to 'indisposition caused by the strain of her work'. She did not return to the Ballet during the remainder of the season, which ended on 30 July.

11. Clive Bell's article 'Standards' was published in *The New Republic* (New York) on 14 June 1919, and was reprinted in his *Since Cézanne* (1922), p. 146. He refers to VW as 'the best of our younger novelists', and derides the English critics for not noticing her, Eliot and Murry.

so eager that one should talk sense; his enthusiasm is the engaging thing about him—deducting the tribute of his enthusiasm for me. Moreover, whatever one may think of his taste in life, however one may feel him a little battered & dusty in the pursuit of pleasure, still there's his honesty; his vivacity; his determination not to be bored, & not to bore. In his own way he is somehow a figure.

Saturday 12 July

In public affairs, I see I've forgotten to say that peace was signed; perhaps that ceremony was accomplished while we were at Asheham.[12] I've forgotten the account I was going to write out of the gradual disappearance of things from shop windows; & the gradual, but still only partial reappearance of things. Sugar cakes, currant buns, & mounds of sweets. The effect of the war would be worth describing, & one of these days at Monks House—but why do I let myself imagine spaces of leisure at Monks House? I know I shall have books that must be read there too, just as here & now I should be reading Herman Melville, & Thomas Hardy, not to say Sophocles, if I'm to finish the Ajax, as I wager myself to do, before August.[13] But this dressing up of the future is one of the chief sources of our happiness, I believe. There's still a good deal of the immediate past asserting its claim on me. I met Morgan Forster on the platform at Waterloo yesterday; a man physically resembling a blue butterfly—I mean by that to describe his transparency & lightness. He had been conveying the luggage of 5 Indians from Deptford to Waterloo; Indians seemed to weigh him down. We exchanged compliments on our writing—I'm surprised to find him openly liking a compliment, though its nothing strange in myself; & discussed Altounyan's work a little. He did not at all care for it; no form, no character; no one figure dominating the others. I like Forster very much, though I find him whimsical & vagulous to an extent that frightens me with my own clumsiness & definiteness.[14] Then I bought my bag of coffee, & so up to Katherine, with whom I spent my hour very happily. Indeed, I like her more & more; & think we have reached some kind of durable foundation. Home to a dinner party consisting of the two Altounyans, Ernest & Norah, Carrington (the male), & Herbert Woolf after dinner. Poor scatterbrained A. showed the least pleasant side of himself in discussing his novel, which he

12. The Peace Treaty between the Allies and the German National Assembly was signed at Versailles on 28 June. The Woolfs were then at Asheham in the throes of buying Monks House.

13. VW's essay marking the centenary of Herman Melville's birth on 1 August 1819 was published in the *TLS* on 7 August 1919 (Kp C161). For her reading notes on Melville see MHP, Sussex, B2 l.

14. Vagulous: from the Latin adjective *vagulus*, restless, wandering.

does not merely with passion but with a conceit that would be irritating if it weren't transparently foolish. His only anxiety is to find how many people are capable of understanding him; about the merits of his work he has no doubt, & cut short my laborious critical survey of them. Rather coolly, he proposed that we should be his agents, finding publishers for all his works for ever. This is all rather foreign; as I found it foreign, though pleasantly foreign of him, to tell me how many people had wished to marry his sister—"For she wishes very much to be married." "Yes" she said simply, "if one hasn't a profession, one must marry; one must look after someone." I liked her better than I like him. As for Carrington, he will be a very popular man in the East.[15]

Satuday 19 July

One ought to say something about Peace day, I suppose, though whether its worth taking a new nib for that purpose I dont know.[16] I'm sitting wedged into the window, & so catch almost on my head the steady drip of rain which is pattering on the leaves. In ten minutes or so the Richmond procession begins. I fear there will be few people to applaud the town councillors dressed up to look dignified & march through the streets. I've a sense of holland covers on the chairs; of being left behind when everyone's in the country. I'm desolate, dusty, & disillusioned. Of course we did not see the procession. We have only marked the rim of refuse on the outskirts. Rain held off till some half hour ago. The servants had a triumphant morning. They stood on Vauxhall Bridge & saw everything. Generals & soldiers & tanks & nurses & bands took 2 hours in passing. It was they said the most splendid sight of their lives. Together with the Zeppelin raid it will play a great part in the history of the Boxall family. But I don't know—it seems to me a servants festival; some thing got up to pacify & placate 'the people'—& now the rain's spoiling it; & perhaps some extra treat will have to be devised for them. Thats the reason of my disillusionment I think. There's something calculated & politic & insincere about these peace rejoicings. Moreover they are carried out with no beauty, & not much spontaneity. Flags are intermittent; we have what the servants, out of snobbishness, I think, insisted upon buying, to surprise us. Yesterday in London the usual sticky stodgy conglomerations of people, sleepy & torpid as a cluster of drenched bees, were

15. Altounyan never did publish a novel (see above 16 May 1919, n 13). Noel Lewis Carrington (b. 1894) (Dora) Carrington's younger brother, returned to Oxford University after four years' service as an officer in the Wiltshire Regiment, then joined the Oxford University Press and from 1919 to 1923 represented it in India.

16. On 19 July 1919 official Peace celebrations were held throughout Britain, with processions, massed choirs, firework displays and so forth. The proceedings were marred by almost continuous rain all day.

crawling over Trafalgar Square, & rocking about the pavements in the neighbourhood. The one pleasant sight I saw was due rather to the little breath of wind than to decorative skill; some long tongue shaped streamers attached to the top of the Nelson column licked the air, furled & unfurled, like the gigantic tongues of dragons, with a slow, rather serpentine beauty. Otherwise theatres & music halls were studded with stout glass pincushions which, rather prematurely, were all radiant within—but surely light might have shone to better advantage.[17] However night was sultry & magnificent so far as that went, & we were kept awake some time after getting into bed by the explosion of rockets which for a second made our room bright. (And now, in the rain, under a grey brown sky, the bells of Richmond [are] ringing—but church bells only recall weddings & Christian services.) I can't deny that I feel a little mean at writing so lugubriously; since we're all supposed to keep up the belief that we're glad & enjoying ourselves. So on a birthday, when for some reason things have gone wrong, it was a point of honour in the nursery to pretend. Years later one could confess what a horrid fraud it seemed; & if, years later, these docile herds will own up that they too saw through it, & will have no more of it—well—should I be more cheerful? I think the dinner at the 1917 Club, & Mrs Besant's speech rubbed the gilt, if there were any grains remaining, effectually off the gingerbread.[18] Hobson was sardonic. She—a massive, & sulky featured old lady, with a capacious head, however, thickly covered with curly white hair,—began by comparing London, lit up & festive, with Lahore. And then she pitched into us for our maltreatment of India, she, apparently, being 'them' & not 'us'. But I don't think she made her case very solid, though superficially it was all believable, & the 1917 Club applauded & agreed. I cant help listening to speaking as though it were writing, & thus the flowers, which she brandished now & again, looked terribly artificial. It seems to me more & more clear that the only honest people are the artists, & that these social reformers & philanthropists get so out of hand, & harbour so many discreditable desires under the disguise of loving their kind, that in the end there's more to find fault with in them than in us. But if I were one of them?

17. The decoration of London's streets and buildings was a feature of the celebrations. VW's image of pin-cushions was perhaps prompted by the resemblance between the clusters of coloured electric bulbs and glass-headed pins.

18. Mrs Annie Besant (1847-1933), who, after repudiating orthodox Christianity and with it her clergyman husband, had proceeded by way of neo-Malthusianism and Fabian Socialism to Theosophy, being president of the Theosophical Society from 1907 until her death. From 1895 onwards India had been the scene of her activities. In 1916 she had initiated a Home Rule for India League and in December 1918 had been elected president of the Indian National Congress, but was later rejected in favour of Gandhi. The 1917 Club dinner was given in her honour.

Sunday 20 July

Perhaps I will finish the account of the peace celebrations. What herd animals we are after all!—even the most disillusioned. At any rate, after sitting through the procession & the peace bells unmoved, I began after dinner, to feel that if something was going on, perhaps one had better be in it. I routed up poor L. & threw away my Walpole.[19] First lighting a row of glass lamps, & seeing that the rain was stopped, we went out just before ten. Explosions had for some time promised fireworks. The doors of the public house at the corner were open, & the room crowded; couples walzing; songs being shouted, waveringly, as if one must be drunk to sing. A troop of little boys with lanterns were parading the Green, beating sticks. Not many shops went to the expense of electric light. A woman of the upper classes was supported dead drunk between two men partially drunk. We followed a moderate stream flowing up the Hill. Illuminations were almost extinct half way up, but we kept on till we reached the terrace. And then we did see something—not much indeed, for the damp had deadened the chemicals. Red & green & yellow & blue balls rose slowly into the air, burst, flowered into an oval of light, which dropped in minute grains & expired. There were hazes of light at different points. Rising over the Thames, among trees, these rockets were beautiful; the light on the faces of the crowd was strange; yet of course there was grey mist muffling everything, & taking the blaze off the fire. It was a melancholy thing to see the incurable soldiers lying bed at the Star & Garter with their backs to us, smoking cigarettes, & waiting for the noise to be over.[20] We were children to be amused. So at eleven we went home, & saw from my study Ealing do its best to rejoice, & indeed one fire balloon went so high that L. believed it a star; but there were none showing. Today the rain has left us in no doubt that any remaining festivities are to be completely quenched.

Thursday 24 July

Well, the peace at any rate is over; though the poor deluded servants are spending their day out on a bus to see the decorations. I was right: it is a servants peace. Last night we had Forster & the Bussys. It was not the mixture we should have chosen, since Forster would come out better alone. However, such are the penalties of owning a press. I feel something like Horace Walpole who had to limit the visitors to Strawberry Hill to

19. VW had for review the two-volume *Supplement to the Letters of Horace Walpole* edited by Paget Toynbee, 1918; her article appeared in the *TLS* on 31 July 1919 (Kp C159). For VW's reading notes on these volumes see MHP, Sussex, B2 l.
20. The Star and Garter Home for totally disabled soldiers and sailors replaced the Star and Garter Hotel, pulled down in 1915, at the top of Richmond Hill.

4 daily[21]— Morgan is easily drowned even by the vivacity of the Bussys. He is an unworldly, transparent character, whimsical & detached, caring very little I should think what people say, & with a clear idea of what he wishes. I dont think he wishes to shine in intellectual society; certainly not in fashionable. He is fantastic & very sensitive; an attractive character to me, though from his very qualities it takes as long to know him as it used to take to put one's gallipot over a humming bird moth. More truly, he resembles a vaguely rambling butterfly; since there is no intensity or rapidity about him. To dominate the talk would be odious to him. He subsided in a chair; or strolled about the room, turning over the pages of a book. Even when the B's had gone, we made little direct headway. He will come to Asheham if we pay his fare. He has only £26 in the bank. I liked this simple way of explaining things. And he hates Stevenson; & makes up his novels as he goes along; & sees what I mean about dialogue; there's a lot to say to him, though I don't yet know how to say it. Its absurd at my age, & I feel very middle aged, to be as easily put out & flustered as I am. It takes the form of saying things rashly. "I want to write an article upon you" I said, & that wasn't what I meant to say.

The Woolfs moved from Asheham to Monks House, Rodmell, on 1 September 1919. VW kept no diary between 24 July at Hogarth House and 7 September at Monks House. From LW's diary however we learn that on Saturday 26 July, James Strachey and the Shoves came to tea, and that on the following day the Woolfs had tea with the Murrys in Hampstead. On Tuesday 29 July they went to Asheham, where they had ten days alone. Hope Mirrlees arrived on Friday 8 August to stay for the weekend, and there was a good deal of coming and going between Asheham and Charleston, where Clive and Vanessa Bell, Duncan Grant and Maynard Keynes all were. On Thursday 14 August the Woolfs attended the sale of contents at Monks House. Pernel Strachey and E. M. Forster stayed at Asheham 22-25 August, a dinner party with Clive and Vanessa, Duncan, Roger Fry, Mary Hutchinson and Maynard Keynes as additional guests, took place there on Sunday 24th.

VW wrote the entries from 7 September to 1 October inclusive in Diary VIII, the title-page of which is inscribed:

Monks House
Rodmell
Sept 7th 1919

21. Horace Walpole's management of visitors is explained in a letter of 27 June 1771 to the Countess of Upper Ossory: 'I am forced to confine the rule to four, or as near it as I can; my neighbours wanting to bring all their acquaintance, and taking it ill if they are refused and others indulged'. See *Letters of Horace Walpole*, ed. Mrs Paget Toynbee, 1903-05, vol. viii, pp. 53-4.

Sunday 7 September

I suppose this is the first day upon which I could easily sit down & write in my long suffering & by this time I hope tolerant diary. The lack of table, pen, paper, & ink or rather their dispersion into separate parts of the house was one reason; & then followed domestic crises which I had foretold, but that did not improve their quality when they came. Now the servants are at Charleston, Mr Dedman & his brother are naming apple trees in the orchard to Leonard & if I can resist getting up & joining them I may fill this page.[1]

The move was accomplished in one day, thanks chiefly to the organisation of L. who tied all the books in lots. Two waggon loads, one leaving about ten, another at six did the job, & we managed to roost about the house somehow or other that night. Next morning those troubles began which I will not specify further; then L. had a night in London, & I, sitting down to my book in the dusk, heard a voice asking for me, & then, to my dismay, saw the lean fantatical figure of Altounyan cross the window. He had his wife & friend—Montana or Fontana—outside, & I had to produce ham & coffee for them & entertain my first visitors.[2] A. had come from London on purpose to see us; on purpose, I rather think, to discuss the eternal novel once more, & perhaps contrive to get it issued by us. Mrs Hamilton has read, & found it necessary to quote King Lear. Part of this terrific egotism may be attributed to the Armenian half of him, I think; it is not offensive; but would become intensely boring. But, unhappily, people who come all the way from London & walk 10 miles for the chance of seeing one are almost always bores. I set them on their road about ten o'clock, & could not resist a dark stroll in the garden. The temptation whispers from the window all the time—so pleasant to step out onto the lawn, walk across to the tool house, & survey the downs in day time or the lights of Lewes by night. Much remains to be done inside the house, though the main arrangements are now made. But for some days one's mind is distracted by perpetually dwelling upon the changes round one; it works with an effort. This is wearing off slightly, though I write this as if I were raising 7 stone on my pen instead of the usual number of ounces. However from all the difficulties, advantages & disadvantages of the place, I think the upshot is wholly favourable. One gains much in the way of variety here; there are more walks, & endless interests in the garden, though nothing of the flawless beauty of Asheham.

1. William Dedman, a Rodmell villager, who helped in the garden at Monks House.
2. Ernest Altounyan had married in 1915 Nora, the eldest daughter of W. G. Collingwood, friend and biographer of Ruskin. The third visitor has not been identified.

Thursday 12 September

The weight upon my mind is lessening, though, as I have not yet mastered a writing board, the long leisurely filling of these blank pages which I promised myself becomes something of a mirage. But then Duncan & Nessa have just been over unexpectedly to tea. Other peoples incursions always leave me tremulous. They break in upon a mood of depression, deep according to L.; to me of the consistency of September mist. Why is it, I wonder? Partly that for 10 days I don't think I've had a letter; then I expect something unpleasant from Macmillans.[3] Here I make my forecast. "We have read Night & Day with the deepest interest, but hardly think it would appeal to our public over here." Though I foretell this, & see that written down it is negligible as criticism, yet I want to have that unpleasant moment over. It will infect me for a few days. And the publication of N. & D. may perhaps send an occasional tremor through me for all my boasting. If that is pronounced a failure, I dont see why I should continue writing novels. These are the usual writers melancholies. On top of them, there's been the move, the comparison of this place with Asheham, servants—& so on. Writing has been done under difficulties. I was making way with my new experiment, when I came up against Sir Thomas Browne, & found I hadn't read him since I used to dip & duck & be bored & somewhow enchanted hundreds of years ago.[4] Therefore I had to break off, send for his books (by the way, I have read him fairly often, now I come to think of it) & start little stories. These are always ticklish; a bad morning reduces one to melancholy. But since I began to write this, I've suffered so many interruptions, that my mood is no longer benignant. I think I shall yield to temptation & see what the sun is doing over the meadows. O the thousand appliances one needs for writing even a sentence! No books from The Times either, & as for writing a letter, I cant bring myself to break the virginity of a sheet of paper.

Saturday 13 September

Well, Macmillan's letter came this morning, & is neither so good nor so bad as it might have been. They read with great interest, think N. & D. a fine work, but not likely to appeal to a wide public in America, & too long to be, at this season, worth reprinting. But they propose to take 500 or 1000 sheets from Gerald; the same number of The Voyage Out, & understand that I will offer them my next book. On the whole, I'm rather

3. See above, 10 June 1919, n 7.
4. Sir Thomas Browne (1605-1682), physician and writer, author of several meditative works.

pleased than otherwise. The Voyage Out will be exhausted; certainly this is the only method of becoming known to America, & presumably Macmillans think me worth keeping in view. Heaven knows when my next novel will be ready! The same post brought their refusal of Le's book, they will take sheets of that too. It don't much matter. I shall accept, I suppose, since there's scarcely time to try elsewhere. But I dont think Macmillan had much to do with my depression. Do I envy Nessa her overflowing household? Perhaps at moments. Julian has gone into a preparatory form of breeches; everything flourishing & humane there; perhaps I can't help a contrast which never occurs when I'm in full flood of work. I made these comparisons yesterday, when I lunched there & spent the afternoon & rode home. By the way, I'm an ingrate to nourish the least private cloud in the face of such brightness of sky. The downs all black against scarlet & gold, as I rode home, stopping to look at Asheham, which had its windows open as if lived in. Mr Geal was going up to pick apples. But Monk's House gives one a pleasant little shock as one opens the gate. I found L. & Nelly just back from Lewes with her new bicycle. He had spent the day in London. Seven has struck & I'm tempted to walk upon the flats. I had meant to say something about these queer spiritual states. They interest me, even when I'm the subject. And I always remember the saying that at one's lowest ebb one is nearest a true vision. I think perhaps 9 people out of ten never get a day in the year of such happiness as I have almost constantly; now I'm having a turn of their lot.

Sunday 14 September

Well, I dont think my turn of their lot is a very serious matter. The interesting thing is that one does, normally, keep up a kind of vibration, for no reason whatever. Equally for no reason whatever, the vibration stops. Then one enquires why one ever had it, & there seems no reason why one should ever have it again. Things seem clear, sane, comprehensible, & under no obligation, being of that nature, to make one vibrate at all. Indeed, its largely the clearness of sight which comes at such seasons that leads to depression. But when one can analyse it, one is half way back again. I feel unreason slowly tingling in my veins. If I could have a good morning's work! We went for our first Sunday walk today. In order to counteract the tremendous draw of the garden we have arranged two walks a week, on Sundays & Wednesdays. Today we went on the downs towards Kingston. For the first of many days it was cloudy; a north east wind, a threatening of rain. We saw the sea at Brighton & the sea at Eastbourne to right & left of us. The valley slopes behind the down are very lovely; the down itself rising to some height, but intersected by railings. I think the views are finer this side than the other, though the downs themselves inferior. I must try a little Plato now—to prove that concentration is as easy here as elsewhere.

Sunday 21 September

Why should I pick out the one hour of the week when Church bells jangle to go on with this? A cold bright Sunday; very easy today to remember the feel of winter,—even the look of the winter earth. Yesterday, as I sat reading, Nick came knocking at the door. I had put away his letter unanswered, also, apparently, unread. We had to make ready a room, & prepare a crab, which he brought as offering. He seemed singularly featureless, rather like those chubby little village boys one sees with rosy cheeks & red ears staring in at sweet shop windows. This is I think much his real character, but superimposed is a dab of culture, taking the safe direction of 18th century literature & art. "Thomas Gray knew how to write letters from the country—very witty interesting letters— Have you ever read Thomas Gray?" Then Jane Austen appears. She is his great fan. As for apples & pears, which are now his business, his knowledge is limited;[5] or perhaps it is due to his thin soiled brain that words are very poverty sticken, ideas seem to crawl. Looking up, I saw his face alongside L.'s; & they looked samples of different breeds, or widely spaced stages of development. "Here, the professor might say, pointing his stick at Nick, is a type of primitive man—man yet incapable of concentration or foresight—" Whereas here—well, his remarks upon L. would be highly complimentary. In spite of this grudging scrape of my pen, I liked Nick quite enough to enjoy seeing him; & having a practical, & perhaps, trained mind, we pumped him a good deal about the house. He cannot see a cupboard without discovering how it has been built in, or a pipe without running his finger along, or a brick without lifting it to pry[?] out possible secrets of building. He advises us to ask Hope's advice.[6] Barbara arrived for lunch, in breeches & jersey, scarlet as an apple but maternal, to my eye, & with her vivid little edge of character distinguishing her from the rest of them. She is considerably more distinguished than Nick, & he recognises this abundantly. Perhaps his pride is blown upon by the covetous eyes of Saxon. Anyhow, he thinks B. a most remarkable character, stamped with the precious mark of Gordon Square's approval. O dear—when will that mark be rubbed out? Yet it's vain talking. What would it profit me to gain the praise of the whole world & lose that single voice? This reflection is due in part to the Memoirs of Mrs Humphry

5. Under an Army scheme for training officers after demobilisation, Nicholas Bagenal attended the South-East Agricultural College at Wye in Kent (a School of London University) in 1919-20 to study horticulture.

6. (Philip) Hope (Edward) Bagenal (b. 1888), Nick's elder brother, was a qualified architect.

Ward. By paying 5/ I have become a member of the Lewes public library.[7] It is an amusing place—full of old ghosts; books half way to decomposition. A general brownness covers them. They are as much alike outwardly as charity schoolchildren. Most have shed their boards years ago, & been recovered in brown paper. There is no reason, either, why Mungo Park should not be succeeded by the Sermons of Ebenezer Howard, & then Lord Morley's Recollections, & then White Wings, or a Swallow's Summer, & then Treasures of the Deep.[8] Thats the sort of thing anyhow I could not resist Mrs Ward, & I stand in her unconscionably long hours, as if she were a bath of tepid water that one lacks the courage to leave. But she set me thinking after tea about fame. No one has had a deeper draught of it. The poor woman, now conscious of a little chill, brings out her old praises & hangs them out of her front windows. "See what Henry James said of me—Walter Pater—George Meredith." And indeed these poor old grandees, solicited I suppose by presentation copies & the rest, do seem to have perjured themselves cheerfully, though I can see them winking. My point is however, that all this blare & pomp has no kind of effect upon the sensitive reader, as I claim to be. Perhaps the winks are too evident. The enormous sales, the American editions, the rumble & reverberation—Piccadilly placarded with posters 'Marcella out!'—seem like the drum & cymbals of a country fair.[9] No, nothing of this counts— She herself, setting out to write an intimate account of feelings & thoughts, gives nothing but bills of fare & pass books. At what point did she cease thinking? Long Long ago, I should say; & then came to believe implicitly in the mummery: names of the great serve as umbrellas covering vacancy. But all tea table talk to admonish the young, who are, I suppose, now becoming inquisitive & objectionable. What a picture though of the highest life in intellectual circles in London! What a portrait of the Servants Hall; with Mrs H. W. for housekeeper, & Uncle Matt. the master.[10] A Detestable assembly, as she paints it. Literature served up on plate before them. I have Gosse to review,[11] which makes me rig up some fancy scene

7. *A Writer's Recollections*, by Mrs Humphry Ward, had been published in the autumn of 1918. VW had read it then, and refers to it in *II VW Letters*, nos. 995, 999. The Lewes public library was at Fitzroy House, the Victorian Gothic building at the corner of Friars Walk and the High Street, built in 1862 by Sir George Gilbert Scott.

8. Mungo Park (1771-1806), the Scottish explorer, was famous for his *Travels in the Interior of Africa*, published in 1799; Ebenezer Howard (1850-1928), the originator of the Garden City movement, did not write sermons; Lord Morley did write recollections; *White Wings* (1880) is a novel; the other titles are probably made up.

9. *Marcella*, Mrs Ward's fourth novel, was published in 3 volumes in 1894.

10. Matthew Arnold (1822-1888), the poet, was Mrs Ward's uncle.

11. 'Mr Gosse and His Friends', VW's review of *Some Diversions of a Man of Letters*, by Edmund Gosse, appeared in the *TLS* on 2 October 1919 (Kp C168).

as I stumble about the fields. To Rat Farm with L. this afternoon; & found a hawk moth drowned in the brook—privet? or what?[12]

Sunday 28 September (perhaps the 28th at least)

Cut off as we are from all human intercourse (unless you count the Dedmans) I cannot be sure even of the date. It is said that the entire railways of England are on strike; the miners, & perhaps the transport workers, are with them.[13] This happened yesterday morning, or rather late the night before; & though we got our papers through late in the evening, we are without posts. The signalman [Tom Pargiter] gave us some information yesterday, & believes himself to be striking against a reduction of 14/ a week in his wages. His strike pay comes to 16/ a week. How with prices what they are the strike can be kept up more than a day or two it is difficult to see. He expects a settlement tomorrow; but as he hopes it, one can't trust him, & like all the rest, he knows far less about the reasons & machinations than we do—L. at any rate. At present, what with Sunday & the quiet one imagines on the lines, a queer deep silence seems to lie upon us. We post letters knowing they wont get further than Lewes. There is talk of a motor car service. The Government make a show of courageous determination. We are on war rations, & told to be brave & good. Not since coaching days has the village of Rodmell been so isolated as it is at the present moment. Yet a state of siege has a certain snugness & self sufficiency about it. No one can interrupt. I have given myself a respite from Hope Mirrlees, whose review ought to have been dispatched this morning.[14] If it lasts another day or two the food difficulty will begin. Then there's the question of getting back on Thursday.

Until this strike came our main concern has been L.'s arm. A week ago, or last Monday his wrist & arm broke into a rash. The Dr called it eczema. Then Mrs Dedman brushed this aside & diagnosed sunflower poisoning. L. had been uprooting them with bare hands. We have accepted her judgment, which is confirmed by the case of Mrs Wooler's brother, but that doesn't do away with the fact that its a vile & irritating disease. Today for the first time the swelling is less, & the rash improved. But the week

12. Rat Farm was the Woolfs' name for some deserted farm buildings in the Telscombe downs (see *II VW Letters*, no. 1081); the Privet is a variety of the considerable family of Hawk-moths (*Sphingidae*).

13. The strike by the National Union of Railwaymen, called on 27 September and settled by 6 October, succeeded in defeating the government's attempt to trim back wartime wage gains. The miners and other transport workers did not strike but there was naturally broad support within the trade union movement, most effectively from the printers whose threatened action assured the railwaymen of room to put their case in the national press.

14. VW's review of *Madeleine, One of Love's Jansenists*, by Hope Mirrlees, appeared in the *TLS* on 9 October 1919 (Kp C169).

has been much damaged in consequence. Yesterday we went over to Asheham, plundered the hollow of its mushrooms, & then got in at the drawing room window. Gunn is spending £60 on turning it into a rose pink boudoir—that colour at least predominates. But they have evidently taken a book of patterns & marked out the most respectable bright colours, so that the rooms are all as smooth & impeccable & glossy as can be. There are mustard yellows & pillar box reds. Of course, I couldn't approve, but I should have liked it still less if he had chosen after my own taste, & the house had looked as dim & mysterious as ever. I dont know whether its one's accommodating temper that painted the place a little shut in & dismal, with the vast hollow behind & the straight view between trees in front. I thought it lacking in variety, this time, & colour—but I expect this is one of the devices of the imagination. Anyhow Monk's improves, after the fashion of a mongrel who wins your heart. I should have said a good deal about the garden only the temptation of being there instead of describing it from within has been too much even for my confirmed habits. The green of the turf with the bunch of purple Japanese anemones keeps getting in my eyes. We have been planting tiny grains of seed in the front bed, in the pious or religious belief that they will resurrect next spring as Clarkia, Calceolaria, Campanula, Larkspur & Scabious. I shan't recognise them if they do; we are planting at a venture, inspired by seedsmen's language: how they stand high & bear bright blue petals. Then there's weeding. Very soon, in any occupation, one makes a game of it. I mean (for I'm cold & inept at the moment—church bells ringing, fire just catching, & the great log we sawed about to plunge into fiery caverns) that one gives characters to weeds. The worst is the fine grass which has to be sifted out conscientiously. I like uprooting thick dandelions & groundsel. Then the tea bell rings, & though I sit & ponder over my cigarette, L. runs out like a child allowed to get down & go. And as I say, today we're on our island, which will be boarded tomorrow, oddly enough, by Clive.

I've reviewed Hope; Gosse & Swinnerton, all in the past 10 days so that the great autumn downpour is beginning.[15] It crosses my mind now & then that Night & Day will be one drop of it: but that seems to belong to London—not here. The bore will be meeting people, who think they must say that they have not read it; perhaps worse, that they have. That will last six weeks; then no more.

Tuesday 30 September

This is opened to record the Strike bulletin. Nothing has happened. All railways are silent. I went into Lewes yesterday, & found a kind of modi-

---

15. VW's review of *September*, by Frank Swinnerton, appeared in the *TLS* on 25 September 1919 (Kp C167.)

fied Sunday prevailing; shutters half closed at post & railway station. There were numbers of motors with luggage & the pampered rich. Rumour—shop keepers, that is to say,—predicts a long strike. Who's in the right, they dont say: 'anyhow its bad for us'. In our private world the discomfort is mostly what we imagine for the future. We can make no plans anyhow. Last night Clive did not come, & thinking this implied disaster to N. in London, I telegraphed first thing this morning; no answer yet, & its struck seven. The papers are just in, shrunk to single sheets, & untrustworthy in their extreme—Daily Mail & Herald; truthful in the middle perhaps, Daily News. So far nothing but persistent hostility on both sides; no overtures. To increase our private sense of the ominous, Mr Dean chose this day to move the cupboards.[16] The house is therefore scattered with books & furniture, but we gain a dining room. To appease us, the weather stays fine as possible, clear, cold, still, & sunny. Clive stayed at Charleston nursing a cold. No letters since Saturday morning, save his card, which is local. We shall be without butter, coffee, & cigarettes in a day or two, getting them from London.

Wednesday 1 October

The strike remains, so far as we can judge, the same. On the other hand, rumours of the strike change from hour to hour. A post came this morning. The postman is reported to say that all trains are running as usual. The signalman appears. Situation unchanged; much depressed. Then Dedman comes to pick apples. A notice is in the post office, he says, that trains are as usual. Nelly goes to Lewes. Comes back 'frightened' so she says. A few trains only, into which you get at your own risk. This sickened her of travel, which she had been urging an hour before. We went down to the signalman with books & offers of help. His wife met us; he being at Newhaven. A fiery, impulsive, vigorous woman about to bear her 5th child. She was urging him to give in. Public opinion was against them, she said. Then she explained that they had only saved 6 shillings. With their strike pay this can't long keep off hunger. Then she couldn't see the rights of it, "They're like children who've had their sweet & dont want to give up their penny" she said, often enough to show that she'd used the argument often to him. They must give it up sooner or later, so why not now.

On returning to Hogarth House, VW continues her diary in the book she had used from January to July, Diary VII.

16. Mr Dean of The Forge, Rodmell, the blacksmith and jobbing builder, was called in to do various small building and carpentering jobs in Monks House.

Tuesday 7 October

Home yesterday. The 'docile herds' whom I describe on Peace day are not so deluded after all. They have held the country up for eleven days, I think. We did a little to support them too, & kept one man on strike who would have gone back without our pound. Still, what's to be read in the papers is hardly fit for my private page. I wonder if I could expound the railway strike? What they asked, & what they got? At any rate the strike broke in to our life more than the war did—but I've written my diary, intermittently, & have it at Rodmell. There's a private strike to record too. I should like to write philosophically & analyse what is no doubt a sign—dont they call it?—of the times. We must think out our position. The question is, are we to fling off in a new direction? What do we want? Now at our age, where youth is not quite over, & discretion is fully blown, but not long seated—its not so easy to know what one does want, I meant to add, but that reflection's two days old. Dear old Nelly came in shyly like a school girl & asked to apologise last night; & I see us settled for life, with Hogarth, Monk's House, & two domestics.

9th Oct

I have no time to fill this page, since I must read my review book, (Landor), read Logan's stories, write a letter or two, & I've let the time since tea slip.[1] I began reading the first volume of my diary; & see that its second anniversary is now reached. I dont think the first volume makes such good reading as the last; a proof that all writing, even this unpremeditated scribbling, has its form, which one learns. Is it worth going on with? The trouble is, that if one goes on a year or so more, one will feel bound on that account to continue. I wonder why I do it. Partly, I think, from my old sense of the race of time 'Time's winged chariot hurrying near'— Does it stay it?[2]

Saturday 11 October

Things are once more in swing, though in rather a modified form for me, since I've promised to be careful, which means avoiding the temptation of London, & walking down the sunny drives at Kew. In spite of cold, the sun is still the sun of holiday & country, somehow unfit for the pavement slabs. A record autumn for fineness, I should think, always falsifying the predictions of the Times prophet, who is gloomy. For the first time I went up to London yesterday in the first place to buy gloves;

---

1. VW's review entitled 'Landor in Little' of *A Day-Book of Walter Savage Landor* (1919) chosen by John Bailey, was published in the *TLS* on 16 October 1919 (Kp C170).
2. From Andrew Marvell's poem 'To His Coy Mistress'.

in the second to have tea at Nessa's flat [36 Regent Square]. A comfortable party there, seated on the kitchen floor. Julian in a Norfolk jacket & Eton collar looking a responsible Briton; Quentin still amorphous. The dim & dusky flat of James's day is now at the very opposite pole of culture— the pole of sun & brightness. The rooms overflow with children. The books are the incongruous part of the decoration, & Nessa professed great contempt for them. "Of course, she said, there's Shakespeare & all that on the bottom shelf, but look at that! Doesn't that give James away?" He has all the right books, neatly ranged, but not interesting in the least— not, I mean, all lusty & queer like a writers books. The Stracheys with the exception of Lytton are down in the world. Lytton we ran into at the Club on coming back—composed, agreeable, permanently shone upon, & completely sure of himself—ah, but infinitely charming into the bargain. Success, I believe, produces a kind of modesty. It frees you from bothering about yourself. He was flattering to me, as usual; but then I'm *not* a suc- cess. Did I not hear from Macmillan today that Messrs Duckworth's charges are prohibitive? So my chance of appearing in America is gone. But I'm showered under with review books; &, though I dont suppose I can pretend that any saying by a publisher is a rebuff, still I'm conscious of being almost proof—against Gordon Square? I wonder. Yes, I believe that my well of confidence, or rather pleasure, is so deep sunk as to bubble up in a day or two after any chastening. But this I shall soon be able to test. My review, laboured & well meaning as it was, of Hope's book has so far drawn no letter of thanks from her. I'm not sure that she didn't cherish some boundless dream about it. A whole column, in the middle, com- paring her with the greatest only. Well, I've had my dreams too. At the same time I'm generally rather surprised by the goodness of reality.

Sunday 19 October

A gap of more than a week. Let me see how my hours after tea have been occupied. The Waterlows came last Sunday; on Monday I went up, had my tea at the Club, & met for a second, Molly Hamilton "And when's your novel coming out?"; Tuesday I had to read through 2 volumes of an American scribbler sent me by Murry; Wednesday was crammed with George Eliot, I expect, since Logan & Clive came at 7.30; Thursday I re- joiced in Saxon & Barbara; Friday I had tea with Nessa, & supper too, & went to a Promenade; Saturday I heard L. say his lecture, & then had poor little Dorothy Hornett up to give her her sweets; so here I am with a clear conscience at Sunday, over my fire, waiting for L. to come in from Sutton.[3] Clearly I cant go through the list. That is an unreasonable demand.

3. *Tuesday*: VW's article 'Maturity and Immaturity' reviewing *Joyce Kilmer*, a two- volume work edited with a memoir by Robert Cortes Holliday, and *Edward Wyndham Tennant: A Memoir* by Pamela Glenconner, appeared in the *Athenaeum*

Sydney Waterlow is very well pleased with himself.[4] Yet as his talk becomes more & more complacent, his prospects more & more blooming, I always fancy that I can see a slight wobble in what should be the perfect sphere, like that which used to foretell the collapse of an air ball. He has great designs upon the F.O. nothing less than complete reformation; but if these miscarry he will accept £10,000 a year in the city. But the preposterous man has his endearing absurdity. A third project of his is to settle at Oare & write books in collaboration with Desmond. For ever he clings to the skirts of the Desmonds & Leonards & even Virginias (I'm much admired, momentarily) as if not wholly secure even now. She, Dawks, was squat & vivacious as usual. Some of her intelligent remarks fell flat though—those supposing a knowledge of Sydney's work. He is respectful to her in her own department, & feels that her capacity there is a tribute to him. Saxon & Barbara don't need much licking into shape: he on the sprightly side, she maternal & boyish, a little to my irritation. After all, few people dont act a part of some kind. Logan was rather more aloof & distinguished than my memory of him. Perhaps he disapproved a little of Clive. Clive certainly intended that he should. He described his entire indolence; & then his pleasures: "We dine not very well, & then slip into bed together." "Goodness no—I dont read on a system—Goodness gracious, I dont write every day."—so on. Now Logan's epicurean life is well regulated; self improvement is not despicable in his eyes; his conversation is decorous. We got out 12 volumes of Gibbon, & they capped passages. We have undertaken to get Logan's stories printed.

Tuesday 21 October

This is Trafalgar day, & yesterday is memorable for the appearance of Night & Day. My six copies reached me in the morning, & five were despatched, so that I figure the beaks of five friends already imbedded.[5]

---

of 21 November 1919 (Kp C176). *Wednesday*: VW's article written for the centenary of George Eliot's birth on 22 November 1819, was published in the *TLS* on 20 November 1919 (Kp C175). *Friday*: the Promenade Concert at the Queen's Hall on the evening of 17 October, conducted by Sir Henry Wood, contained works by Beethoven, Mozart, Bach and Chopin. *Saturday*: LW's lecture—on Co-operation—was delivered at Sutton on Sunday. Dorothy Hornett has not been identified.

4. Sydney Waterlow, who had resigned from the Diplomatic Service in 1905, had been employed in Paris at the Peace Conference in 1919. He was now about to re-enter the Foreign Office, which he did in 1920. 'Dawks' was the Bloomsbury nickname for his wife Margery.

5. Trafalgar day was the anniversary of the victory and of the death of Lord Nelson in 1805. VW sent copies of *Night and Day* to Vanessa and to Clive Bell, to Lytton Strachey, Morgan Forster and to Violet Dickinson.

Am I nervous? Oddly little; more excited & pleased than nervous. In the first place, there it is, out & done with; then I read a bit & liked it; then I have a kind of confidence, that the people whose judgment I value will probably think well of it, which is much reinforced by the knowledge that even if they dont, I shall pick up & start another story on my own. Of course, if Morgan & Lytton & the others should be enthusiastic, I should think the better of myself. The bore is meeting people who say the usual things. But on the whole, I see what I'm aiming at; what I feel is that this time I've had a fair chance & done my best; so that I can be philosophic & lay the blame on God. Lovely autumn days come one after another; the leaves hanging like rare gold coins on the trees. Clive was at the Club yesterday, & talked ostensibly to me, but to the whole room in reality some of whom judged him a little bounder, I suppose, & turned round & thanked God when he left the room.

O yes, I should like a good long review in the Times.

Thursday 23 October

The first fruits of Night & Day must be entered "No doubt a work of the highest genius" Clive Bell. Well, he might not have liked it; he was critical of The Voyage Out. I own I'm pleased; yet not convinced that it is as he says. However, this is a token that I'm right to have no fears. The people whose judgment I respect won't be so enthusiastic as he is, but they'll come out decidedly on that side, I think. Moreover, in a way which I can't defend to L., I do respect Clive's judgment. It's erratic, but always springs from a direct feeling. I think I feel most doubtful about Morgan; after getting his report I shall be quite at ease. Three or four people count, & the rest, save as a senseless clapping of hands or hissing, are nowhere. No one of much intelligence, outside my own friends, is likely to read a very long novel. But I must stop; I'm at my hack work, & Ka dines here, & I can't spare time to describe my concert last night. Only room for my own praises. Besides, I must thank C.[6]

Thursday 30 October

I have the excuse of rheumatism for not writing more; & my hand tired of writing, apart from rheumatism. Still, if I could treat myself professionally as a subject for analysis I could make an interesting story of the past few days, of my vicissitudes about N. & D. After Clive's letter came Nessa's—unstinted praise; on top of that Lytton's: enthusiastic praise; a grand triumph; a classic; & so on; Violet's sentence of eulogy followed; & then, yesterday morning, this line from Morgan "I like it less than the

---

6. See *II VW Letters*, no. 1088, mis-dated 30 October. The concert was probably that given by the Allied String Quartet at the Wigmore Hall.

V.O." Though he spoke also of great admiration, & had read in haste & proposed re-reading, this rubbed out all the pleasure of the rest. Yes; but to continue. About 3 in the afternoon I felt happier & easier on account of his blame than on account of the others' praise—as if one were in the human atmosphere again, after a blissful roll among elastic clouds & cushiony downs. Yet I suppose I value Morgan's opinion as much as anybodies. Then there's a column in the Times this morning; high praise; & intelligent too; saying among other things that N. & D. though it has less brilliance on the surface, has more depth than the other; with which I agree.[7] I hope this week will see me through the reviews, I should like intelligent letters to follow; but I want to be writing little stories; I feel a load off my mind all the same.

The rheumatism made me visit the region which is in my mind the mediaeval region. Clive burst in I was going to say like a ruddy sun last night; but I wasn't altogether in the mood, nor he either. The most selfish of men, in some ways; though I don't know why that struck me. Letting his mood have its way, indifferent & frivolous. But I pinned him down, & made him talk about N. & D. which he did, absentmindedly at first; later he warmed to his task; but he was thinking of a jolly time in Paris.

Saturday 1 November

Shall I ever again get time for writing here? Never have I been so pressed with reviewing, for theres George Eliot to fill up all crannies left by other books, & Murry to choke effectually any empty space remaining. I think I might slack off if N. & D. succeeds. No more letters or reviews. A cheque for £25 though, on copies sold before publication. Happily the book begins to recede from the front of my mind, & I begin to be a little surprised if people speak of it (not that anyone has—but meeting Mde Champcomunal yesterday, I was glad she'd not heard of it).[1] This lady whose name I shall never write again, wishes to share Tregerthen: the plan may be the perfect one. She is a grenadier of a woman, high red cheek bones, thin, competent, handsome, unhappy, tailor made & up to date. I met her at Regent Square—all lights out; a single candle, electricians insistent. Sometimes I wish that the old laws of life held good: a husband, a house, servants, establishments. That same afternoon I looked in at the London Group;[2] but saw nothing save people I had no wish to

---

7. This highly favourable review of *Night and Day* is in the *TLS*, 30 October 1919.
1. Mme Elspeth Champcommunal (d. 1976), widow of a French painter, a friend of Roger Fry's, killed in the war; she was visiting Vanessa at 36 Regent Square.
2. An exhibiting society of artists formed in 1913 by an amalgamation of the Camden Town Groups and others. The annual exhibition was held as usual in Messrs Heal's Mansard Gallery, Tottenham Court Road. It included paintings by Roger Fry, Duncan Grant and Mark Gertler, who were members.

see; ran into Noel Olivier walking through the Squares. November descends. Squire's new monthly [*The London Mercury*] out; and now—Middlemarch!

Tuesday 4 November

And now I only steal time from an hour dedicated to Stokoe's poems before Miss Green arrives & we plod off in the foggy cold to address the Guild upon the Russian revolution. The hard scrubbed surface of the lower middle class mind, does not attract me. This refers partly to Mr Osborne.[3] I'm critical, intellectually, of the aristocrats but sensually they charm. I was hauled out of the background to talk to Katie at the Richmond's concert on Sunday.[4] Her beautiful blue eyes all bleared & blood shot now, her skin soft like the skin on an old apple; like an apple's creased at the edge of the mouth, baggy here & there. What sorrow she has had to make her look sad I don't know. The following dialogue went forward.

K. The Cecils have given up their house—couldn't afford it—

V. But he has £5,000 a year!

K. No such thing; besides everyone must economise. My dear Virginia, 'the end is coming. A la lanterne!'

V. For you I daresay; not for me.

K. Ah, there's where you mistake. I go first, but you directly after.

V. Well, after 300 years of Longleat, you deserve it.[5]

K. It was so beautiful—you don't know how beautiful.

V. You rode?

K. I walked in the woods. We had music. I used to read; & always beautiful things to look at; always something new, never the same things twice over. I had it for 13 years; & I used to say I wished I could die when it was over: I wish I had.

V. But you haven't done so badly.

K. I didn't care for Egypt. I dont care for that sort of thing—2 men running before my carriage. I envied them—the only people who got any exercise. Civilisation is at an end. My father always warned

3. Frank Woodyer Stokoe (1882-1952), a friend and contemporary of Altounyan's at Cambridge, was a Fellow of Gonville and Caius College and lecturer in French there. He contributed a number of poems to the *Athenaeum* and other periodicals, and a collection was published in 1922 under the title *Tolkopf on Dreams*. 'Mr Osborne' was probably Frederic James Osborn (b. 1885), town planner and a friend of LW's. His *New Towns after the War* was published in 1918.

4. This appears to have been another in the series of private subscription concerts organised by Bruce Richmond which usually took place at Shelley House, Chelsea.

5. Longleat is the magnificent Tudor house in Wiltshire, built by a Sir John Thynne in 1566-80, which had passed by descent to Lady Cromer's brother, the 5th Marquess of Bath.

us. I've read history. We're all going to go. Painters will be [the] only people wanted—to paint bodies pretty patterns. No one means to work. There'll be no clothes—
So we talked in the intervals of Mozart.

This is the daily talk in Mayfair I suppose. She seemed to be convinced of it; almost grown indifferent; her one desire to save something for her son, & to die before the crash.[6] But spoken with a kind of humorous resignation which foretells a gallant death on the scaffold.

Thursday 6 November

Sydney & Morgan dined with us last night. On the whole, I'm glad I sacrificed a concert. The doubt about Morgan & N. & D. is removed; I understand why he likes it less than V.O. &, in understanding, see that it is not a criticism to discourage. Perhaps intelligent criticism never is. All the same, I shirk writing it out, because I write so much criticism. What he said amounted to this: N. & D. is a strictly formal & classical work; that being so one requires, or he requires, a far greater degree of lovability in the characters than in a book like V.O. which is vague & universal. None of the characters in N. & D. is lovable. He did not care how they sorted themselves out. Neither did he care for the characters in V.O. but there he felt no need to care for them. Otherwise, he admired practically everything; his blame does not consist in saying that N. & D. is less remarkable than t'other. O & beauties it has in plenty—in fact, I see no reason to be depressed on his account. Sidney said he had been completely upset by it; & was of opinion that I had on this occasion 'brought it off'. But what a bore I'm becoming! Yes, even old Virginia will skip a good [deal] of this; but at the moment it seems important. The Cambridge Magazine repeats what Morgan said about dislike of the characters; yet I am in the forefront of contemporary literature.[7] I'm cynical about my figures, they say: but directly they go into detail, Morgan who read the Review sitting over the gas fire, began to disagree. So all critics split off, & the wretched author who tries to keep control of them is torn asunder.

For the first time this many years I walked along the river bank between ten & eleven. Yes, its like the shut up house I once compared it to: the room with its dust sheets on the chairs. The fishermen are not out so early; an empty path; but a large aeroplane on business. We talked very easily, the proof being that we (I anyhow) did not mind silences. Morgan

---

6. Lady Cromer died in 1933. Her son was the Hon. Evelyn Baring (1903-1973), later 1st Baron Howick of Glendale.

7. A long review of *Night and Day* entitled 'Reality and Dream' was featured on the first page of *The Cambridge Magazine* for 1 November 1919; it was written by E. B. C. Jones.

has the artists mind; he says the simple things that clever people don't say; I find him the best of critics for that reason. Suddenly out comes the obvious thing that one has overlooked. He is in trouble with a novel of his own, fingering the keys but only producing discords so far. He is anxious to begin again & moderate reviewing.[8] We timed our walk admirably for him to catch his train, Wc havc promised to go to the Hutchinsons tonight; but as L. is at the Famine Conference, & there's something disagreeable to me about that circle which makes me reluctant to go alone, I don't suppose we shall.[9]

Saturday 15 November

It is true that I have never been so neglectful of this work of mine. I think I can foresee in my reluctance to trace a sentence, not merely lack of time & a mind tired of writing, but also one of those slight distastes which betokens a change of style. So an animal must feel at the approach of spring when his coat changes. Will it always be the same? Shall I always feel this quicksilver surface in my language; & always be shaking it from shape to shape? But if this is so, it is only part cause of my neglect. There have been substantial difficulties. We were with Lytton last Sunday; on Monday I was at Harrisons, & back just in time for Moll H. (to distinguish her from Molly M.): Tuesday I wrote letters; Wednesday, at a concert, with Violet Dickinson immediately after;[10] Thursday Molly M., for tea & after tea; Friday to Margaret & Lilian, & so here I am, sitting after Saturday tea, a large warm meal, full of currants & sugar & hot tea cake, after a long cold walk. If I shut my eyes & thought of Tidmarsh, what should I see? Carrington a little absorbed with household duties; secreting canvas in the attic; Saxon mute & sealed till Sunday night, when he flowered for a time & talked of Greek; Lytton—a more complex situation. Good & simple & tender—a little low in tone; a little invalidish. If I'd married him, I caught myself thinking, I should have found him querulous. He would have laid too many ties on one, & repined a little if one had broken free. He was in his usual health (as they say); but the

---

8. This was probably *A Passage to India*, which Forster had begun to write in 1913 after his first visit to India; he resumed work on it on his return from his second visit in 1921. In 1919-20, his most prolific period as a reviewer, he produced no fewer than 68 articles.

9. LW and Margaret Llewelyn Davies, for the Co-operative movement, attended the International Economic Conference at Caxton Hall, Westminster, on 4-6 November; it was called by the Fight the Famine Council to report on the postwar chaos in Europe.

10. Given by the Classical Concert Society at the Wigmore Hall on 12 November. The works performed were: a trio for pianoforte, violin and viola by Mozart; twenty-four preludes by Chopin, and a quartet for pianoforte and strings by Fauré. Violet's house in Manchester Street was near by.

sense of living so much for health, & assembling so many comforts round him with that object is a little depressing. But I always qualify these strictures, which I'm quick to find I know, with some subconscious idea of justifying myself. I need no justification. And what I feel for Lytton is as true as ever it was. We sit alone over the fire & rattle on, so quick, so agile in our jumps & circumventions. Lytton I suppose if one could dissolve all extraneous surroundings has in the centre of him a great passion for the mind. He cares for more than literature only. On his table were the latest editions of Voltaire. His books were as primly ranged & carefully tended as an old maids china. He talked of his own work, not optimistically, but one must discount the effect of my perhaps excessive optimism about my own writing. I was in the vein to feel very highly 'creative', as indeed he said he thought me. But he declares himself entirely without that power. He can invent nothing, he says; take away his authorities, & he comes to a full stop. Perhaps this is true of all Stracheys, & accounts for the queer feeling—which I will not analyse, since in Lytton's case the rightness, the subtlety, the fineness, of his mind quite overcome my furtive discomfort. Moll H. still strains at her leash like the spaniel of my legend; but foams with enthusiasm for N. & D. It is a rough eager mind, bold & straightforward, but O dear—when it comes to writing! Her courage impresses me; & the sense she gives of a machine working at high pressure all day long—the ordinary able machine of the professional working woman. A tailor made coat costing £16 is essential she said to exact respect in an office. That shows her competent grasp upon life. But why do I always like people & so throw out my judgments? It is true that I always do.

I think Violet Dickinson must be skipped, save that I may note how she has been grave finding in France & planting Lady Horner's rosemarys upon German tombs.[11] All this she enjoyed highly, in her humorous sporting way, & had been most touched by an inscription she found telling how Ainsworth of the hussars had loved his life & loved his horse & dog.

So we skip to Molly who took her tea in the kitchen & drew an amusing sketch of Uncle Gerald Ritchie gone mad & rushing in taxis from fruiterer to fruiterer to buy melons which he showers on his friends in an ecstasy of good temper, pronounced madness by the doctors since he is positively rude to his wife.[12] Lastly, we approach the heights of Hampstead—the immaculate & moral heights of Hampstead. Had I the energy

11. Lady Horner, of Mells in Somerset, an erstwhile country neighbour of Violet's, had lost both a son and a son-in-law in France during the war.
12. Gerald Ritchie was an elder brother of Sir Richmond Ritchie and of Molly MacCarthy's mother, Blanche Warre-Cornish. He married his second-cousin, Margie Thackeray.

left I would write out that scene of revelation & explanation with Margaret, since in 30 minutes we traversed more ground than in the past 3 years. Tentatively she began it—how Janet & she felt that perhaps—they might be wrong, but still in their view—in short my article on Charlotte Brontë was so much more to their liking than my novels.[13] Something in my feeling for human beings—some narrowness—some lack of emotion— here I blazed up & let fly. So you go on preaching humanity, was the gist of what I said, when you've withdrawn, & preserve only the conventional idea of it. But its *you* that are narrow! she retaliated. On the contrary, I shiver & shrink with the oncoming contest as I step up your stairs. I? But I'm the most sympathetic, the most human, the most universal of people. You grant that Janet moralises? I said. O yes, she granted that readily. But the idea of herself as a forcible intense woman, excluding the greater half of the human heart staggered her. She took the blow well. It was as if one had suddenly drawn some curtain. She must think it over, & write to me she said. I plunged down the hill to Lilian's bedside, & she in her serene quiet way said "Ah, I'm glad you told Margaret that; she never will let me say it."[14]

Friday 28 November

This gap can easily be accounted for by recalling the old saying (if it is one) that when things happen, people don't write. Too many things have happened. Within this last fortnight the International Review has come to an end; both servants are going; two publishers have offered to publish N. & D. & V. O. in America; Angelica has stayed with us; Mrs Brewer has told us that she means to sell Hogarth & Suffield, & we are considering buying them both[15]—together with a greater number than usual of diners, letters, telephone calls, books to review, reviews of my book, invitations to parties & so forth. It was the dinner parties that led Nelly to give notice last Monday.[16] She did it in a tentative boastful way, as if to show off to someone behind the scenes which makes me think she would be

13. Probably VW's article 'Charlotte Brontë', published in the *TLS* of 13 April 1916 (Kp C52), a cutting of which is among the Case letters, MHP, Sussex.
14. Lilian Harris was in a nursing home at this time.
15. On 25 March 1915 the Woolfs took possession of Hogarth House, for which LW had obtained a five-year lease at £50 p.a.; it had once formed a single house with the adjoining Suffield House. In January 1920 he completed the purchase of both houses from Mrs Brewer of Bayswater for £1950. Suffield House was let until 1921, when it was sold to a Richmond solicitor; the Woolfs moved to Tavistock Square from Hogarth House in 1924, but did not sell it until 1927.
16. During the eight days before Nelly gave notice, the Woolfs had had three dinner parties and two tea parties; and Angelica Bell, aged 11 months, and her nurse had come to stay in the house.

glad now to change her mind. She would this moment if I asked her. But on the whole I'm not going to ask her. Let alone the recurring worry of these scenes we both incline to try a new system of dailies, which never ceases to attract us & what with Rodmell & a lower income from the I.R. now becomes desirable. My opinion never changes that our domestic system is wrong; & to go on saying this only breeds irritation. We mean to make the attempt now. No one could be nicer than Nelly, for long stretches; at this moment she gives Angelica her bath, & is perfectly friendly & considerate to me; but think of Rodmell—think of the summer she offered to go to Charleston! The drawbacks are too great. But the fault is more in the system of keeping two young women chained in a kitchen to laze & work & suck their life from two in the drawing room than in her character or in mine.

Perhaps I think this our chief event, since I put it first. But the chief event should be the I.R. I'm on the whole glad that we draw our £250 for half L.'s work.[17] That is the solution so far—an amalgamation with the Contemporary. So many afternoons I walked alone, so many evenings L. sat reading proofs or papers; to me the red magazine on the first of the month seemed scarcely worth all of him that he gave. But then to have thrown that away is galling too, & the Rowntree's methods of making arrangements is to smash everything with his heavy hooves. Then I was considerably pleased with the American publishers, & that the old V.O. should set sail again.[18] It is like going into another form. "Mrs Woolf you are now admitted to our society." Yet that sort of compliment means very little so far as praise goes; nor was I elated for more than 2 hours by Eagle [J. C. Squire]'s invitation to make his broad yellow production my mouthpiece. K.M. wrote a review which irritated me—I thought I saw spite in it.[19] A decorous elderly dullard she describes me; Jane Austen up to date. Leonard supposes that she let her wish for my failure have its way with her pen. He could see her looking about for a loophole of escape. "I'm not going to call this a success—or if I must, I'll call it the wrong kind of success." I need not now spread my charity so wide, since

17. LW's annual salary as editor of the *International Review* was £250, a rate at which he was retained when the periodical was taken over by another of Arnold Rowntree's interests, the monthly *Contemporary Review*. In 1920 and 1921 LW regularly contributed an unsigned section called *The World of Nations: Facts and Documents*; in 1922 this was superseded by a signed monthly article entitled *Foreign Affairs*; for this he received £200 p.a. See *IV LW*, pp. 90-91.

18. The negotiations between Duckworth and Macmillan, New York, for the American publication of *The Voyage Out* and *Night and Day* were overtaken by more favourable proposals from George H. Doran of New York, who became VW's first American publishers.

19. Katherine Mansfield's review of *Night and Day* appeared in the *Athenaeum* of 26 November 1919.

Murry tells me she is practically cured. But what I perceive in all this is that praise hardly warms; blame stings far more keenly; & both are somehow at arms length. Yet its on the cards, I suppose, that N & D is a marked success; I expect a letter every day from someone or other, & now I can write with the sense of many people willing to read. Its all pleasant; lights up the first sentences of my writing of a morning. Today, bearing K.M. in mind, I refused to do Dorothy Richardson for the Supt.[20] The truth is that when I looked at it, I felt myself looking for faults; hoping for them. And they would have bent my pen, I know. There must be an instinct of self-preservation at work. If she's good then I'm not. I'm pained to read praise of Legend, a book by Clemence Dane. But it looks as if I had a soul after all; these are revelations, self analyses. I'm reading Ethel Smyth.[21] I wish it were better—(odd that I wrote that genuinely meaning it; but I couldn't have done so with the novels). What a subject! That one should see it as a superb subject is a tribute to her, but of course, not knowing how to write, she's muffed it. The interest remains, because she·has ridden straight at her recollections, never swerving & getting through honestly, capably, but without the power to still & shape the past so that one will wish to read it again. Honesty is her quality; & the fact that she made a great rush at life; friendships with women interest me.

Friday 5 December

Another of these skips, but I think the book draws its breath steadily if with deliberation. I reflect that I've not opened a Greek book since we came back; hardly read outside my review books, which proves that my time for writing has not been mine at all. This last week, L. has been having a little temperature in the evening, due to malaria, & that due to a visit to Oxford; a place of death & decay.[1] I'm almost alarmed to see how entirely my weight rests on his prop. And almost alarmed to find how intensely I'm specialised. My mind turned by anxiety, or other cause, from its scrutiny of blank paper, is like a lost child—wandering the house, sitting on the bottom step to cry.

Night & Day flutters about me still, & causes great loss of time. George Eliot would never read reviews, since talk of her books hampered her

20. *Interim*, the fifth of Dorothy Richardson's novel sequence *Pilgrimage*, was reviewed in the *TLS* on 18 December 1919, not by VW.
21. Clemence Dane (d. 1965), popular novelist and playwright. Her book had been called 'a really original book' in the *TLS* of 13 November 1919. Ethel Mary Smyth (1858-1944), composer, author and feminist. Her early memoirs, *Impressions that Remained*, were published in two volumes in 1919.
1. LW had contracted malaria when he was serving in Ceylon. He had been to Oxford on Friday 28 November to speak to the Oxford Union Socialist Society on Socialist Foreign Policy.

writing. I begin to see what she meant. I don't take praise or blame excessively to heart, but they interrupt, cast one's eyes backwards, make one wish to explain or investigate. Last week I had a cutting paragraph to myself in Wayfarer; this week Olive Heseltine applies balm.[2] But I had rather write in my own way of 'four Passionate Snails' than be, as K.M. maintains, Jane Austen over again.

Saturday 6 December

On Tuesday I lunched with the Cecils. Perhaps this is my first appearance as a small Lioness. The Bibescos wished to meet me. Lord Cranborne has a great admiration for me.[3] Elizabeth was nicer, & less brilliant than I expected. She has the composed manners of a matron, & did not strain to say clever things. I thought her slightly nervous when we drew into the window to talk. Perhaps she does not like the woman's eye to rest upon her. She is pasty & podgy, with the eyes of currant bun, suddenly protruding with animation. But her animation is the product of a highly trained mind; a mind trained by living perpetually among more highly trained minds. "Memory comes to take the place of character in the old" she said, discussing Lady D. Nevill.[4] Again, its a help to write things down; but there's a gulf between writing & publishing. This was said, I remember, owing to my rash abuse of Lady Glenconner & Wyndham Tennant.—her Aunt of course.[5] She turned round, a little uneasily, to disclaim all admiration for Lady G. I suppose she wishes to stand well with the intellectuals. Bibesco is handsome, amiable, a man rather too much of the smooth opulent world to be of particular interest, & his English is too difficult to let one get straight at him. Like all foreigners, he says serious priggish things—"I prefer to believe nothing save what my reason can confirm"—or words to that effect. Lord Robert was congenial

2. In his 'Wayfarer's Diary' (*Nation*, 29 November) H. W. Massingham, using a suggested comparison between the author of *Night and Day* and Jane Austen, pokes fun at VW's preoccupation with tea-drinking and taxis, and calls her main characters 'Four Impassioned Snails'. In the next issue, Olive Heseltine supported the comparison, and charged 'Wayfarer' with obtuseness and superficiality.

3. Lord and Lady Robert Cecil. Lord Cranborne (1893-1972; later 5th Marquess of Salisbury) was Lord Robert's nephew. Prince Antoine Bibesco (see 27 January 1918, n 43) had in April 1919 married Elizabeth Asquith, the only daughter of the ex-Prime Minister and his second wife, Margot, *née* Tennant.

4. Lady Dorothy Nevill (1826-1913), daughter of the 3rd Earl of Orford, published a history of the Walpoles and several volumes of reminiscences; *The Life and Letters of Lady Dorothy Nevill* by her son Ralph Nevill was the subject of a review by VW in the *Athenaeum* on 12 December 1919 under the title 'Behind the Bars' (Kp C179).

5. See above, 19 October 1919, n 3.

as usual, long, loose, friendly & humorous, in spite of the crucifix on his watch chain. Lord Cranbourne much of a Cecil in appearance, modest & gentle, with a long sallow face, no chin, & shiny blue coat & trousers. He had been to a lecture at the London School of Economics. I stayed talking with Nelly when the rest were gone—about adders, about servants, George Eliot, & Night & Day.

Sunday 28 December

Probably the last entry this year, & not likely to be the most articulate. Twenty two days gap to be accounted for chiefly by illness: first L.'s which dribbled on; then much in the same way I was attacked—8 days in bed, down today on the sofa, & away to Monks House tomorrow. It was influenza—what they call a low type, but prolonged, & sponging on the head as it always does. Not much to say therefore, even if I could say it. Indeed since L. started his malarial type, we've seen few people; & I, for the last 10 days, none at all. But I've read two vast volumes of the Life of Butler; & am racing through Greville Memoirs—both superbly fit for illness.[6] Butler has the effect of paring the bark off feelings: all left a little raw, but vivid—a lack of sap though; & a stage so thinly set as to be dull & bone dry towards the finish. I'm struck by the enormous space his 'fame' & books played in a life so bare of human relations. Isn't this 'reputation' the deepest of all masculine instincts? Almost at the end, when people began to praise, his life put forth a little flower; but too late. For such a critical & contemptuous mind, the value attached to reviews seems queer. Why, I dont think half or quarter so much of mine! But then he had indifference & silence for his lot; perhaps the most trying. It dont (the Life I mean) increase one's respect for human nature. Here was someone I expected to admire greatly; & the pettinesses are therefore more devastating than in the case of another. Festing Jones apes him to perfection. An effective style in its way; save that it becomes too mechanical.

Here I run on, but must stop. Oh yes, I've enjoyed reading the past years diary, & shall keep it up. I'm amused to find how its grown a person, with almost a face of its own.

L.'s book not yet out; but we have six copies in advance.[7] Nego[tia]tions proceeding for the sale of Hyde Park Gate & the purchase of this &

6. *Samuel Butler, Author of Erewhon (1835-1902): A Memoir* by Henry Festing Jones, was published in two volumes in 1919. Festing Jones had been a close friend of Butler's. The memoirs of Charles Greville (1794-1865), edited by Henry Reeve, had been published in three series in 1874, 1885 and 1887. VW had inherited her parents' copies, or at least the six volumes of the first two parts. (See *Holleyman*, VS I, p. 24.)

7. *Empire and Commerce in Africa* was published early in January 1920. See above 7 March 1919, n 11.

Suffield. Servants determined to stay for ever & ever. No news of the sale of N. & D. Reviews a good deal affected by Massingham, but private opinion highly pleasing to me. I see the public becomes a question. I.R. amalgamated with Contemporary, & L. to keep his office & his virgins. We think we now deserve some good luck. Yet I daresay we're the happiest couple in England.

APPENDIXES

APPENDIX 1

The Diaries of Virginia Woolf

The thirty diaries written by Virginia Woolf after her marriage, now in the Berg Collection of the New York Public Library, are here enumerated. Some of them are written in exercise or note books bought ready-made from a stationer's; numbers VII and IX to XV may well have been bound up and covered by Virginia herself; several others consist of loose-leaf pages once fastened into a ring- or spring-back binder; numbers XIX to XXV are books specially (and professionally) bound up for Virginia's use, and covered with the patterned or marbled paper used in the Hogarth Press. The writing, in blue-black or purple ink, is normally confined to the *recto* pages, within an area limited by a left-hand margin ruled by hand or mechanically in red or blue, though there are sometimes dates, additions, later comments or jottings in the margin or on the opposite *verso* page.

In this list, the address where each book was mainly written, and the dates of first and last entries, are given. Other locations and dates are indicated; these, when not self-evident, are derived from Leonard Woolf's record. The total number of pages devoted to journalising is noted; this does not include title-pages but does include additional pages which in some cases have been pasted in or otherwise inserted.

I   1915   17 THE GREEN, RICHMOND. 1 January–15 February 1915
     40 pp. Entries 1 January–2 February inclusive on attached leaves of ruled white paper, 28 × 22·5 cm; entries for 13, 14 and 15 February on three loose sheets plain paper, 32 × 20 cm.

II   1917   ASHEHAM HOUSE. 3 August 1917–6 October 1918
     65 pp. 8d notebook, 15·5 × 10 cm.

III   1917   HOGARTH HOUSE, RICHMOND. 8 October 1917–3 January 1918
     66 pp. Hard cover exercise book, 22·5 × 18 cm.

IV   1918   HOGARTH HOUSE, RICHMOND. 4 January–23 July 1918
     114 pp. Hard cover exercise book, 22 × 18 cm.

V   1918   HOGARTH HOUSE, RICHMOND. 27 July–12 November 1918
     75 pp. Hard cover exercise book, 22·5 × 17·5 cm.

VI   1918 HOGARTH HOUSE, RICHMOND. 16 November 1918–24 January 1919
25 pp. Hard cover exercise book, 22 × 18 cm. (Written at the opposite end to 21 pp. reading notes, begun 14 January 1918.)

VII   1919 HOGARTH HOUSE, RICHMOND. 20 January–28 December 1919
99 pp. Soft cover, 26·5 × 21 cm.

VIII   1919 MONKS HOUSE, RODMELL. 7 September–1 October 1919
16 pp. Soft cover notebook, 21 × 17 cm.

IX   1920 HOGARTH HOUSE, RICHMOND. 7 January 1920–2 January 1921
90 pp. Soft cover, 27 × 21 cm. Onto the first four pages are pasted pages torn out of VIII, written at *Rodmell*. Entries 2 August–1 October inclusive also written at *Rodmell*.

X   1921 HOGARTH HOUSE, RICHMOND. 25 January–19 December 1921
80 pp. Soft cover, 27 × 21 cm. 2 pp. inserted written in *Cornwall* 28 March. Entries 8 August–28 September inclusive written at *Rodmell*.

XI   1922 HOGARTH HOUSE, RICHMOND. 3 January 1922–3 January 1923
83 pp. Soft cover, 27 × 21 cm. Entries 3 August–4 October inclusive written at *Rodmell*. At opposite end are 4 pp. draft review (cf. Kp C221) dated 18 May 1921, and 17 pp. drafts for portions of *Jacob's Room*, dated 7 and 12 October 1921. 15 pp. have been cut out of the book, leaving stubs with some writing visible.

XII   1923 HOGARTH HOUSE, RICHMOND. 7 January–19 December 1923
71 pp. Soft cover, 27 × 21 cm. Entries 6 August–18 September inclusive written at *Rodmell*.

XIII   1924 HOGARTH HOUSE, RICHMOND, and 52 TAVISTOCK SQUARE, WC1. 3 January 1924–6 January 1925
56 pp. Soft cover, 27 × 21 cm. Entries from 5 April written at *Tavistock Square*; entries 2 August–29 September inclusive written at *Rodmell*. At end, 1 p. draft connected with *The Common Reader*, 1 p. explanatory PS dated 18 March 1925.

XIV   1925 52 TAVISTOCK SQUARE. 18 March 1925–19 January 1926

55 pp. Soft cover, 27 × 21 cm. Entries 5-30 September inclusive written at *Rodmell*. 4 pp. writing (not diary) towards end.

XV   1926 52 TAVISTOCK SQUARE. 8 February 1926–23 January 1927
88 pp. Soft cover, 27 × 21 cm. Entries after 27 July–30 September inclusive written at *Rodmell*.

XVI   1927 52 TAVISTOCK SQUARE. 3 February–22 December 1927
59 pp. on loose-leaf paper, 26 × 20·5 cm. Entries 8 August–5 October inclusive written at *Rodmell*.

XVII   1928 52 TAVISTOCK SQUARE.17 January–18 December 1928
63 pp. on loose-leaf paper, 26 × 20·5 cm. Entries 9 August–22 September inclusive written at *Rodmell*.

XVIII   1929 52 TAVISTOCK SQUARE. 4 January–15 June 1929
28 pp. on loose-leaf paper, 25·5 × 20·5 cm.

XIX   1929/30 52 TAVISTOCK SQUARE. 15 June 1929–2 September 1930
111 pp. Hard cover, 26·5 × 20·5 cm. Entries 5 August–2 October 1929 inclusive; 26 December 1929–4 January 1930 inclusive; 3 March 1930; and 6 August–2 September 1930 inclusive, all written at *Rodmell*.

XX   1930/31 MONKS HOUSE, RODMELL. 8 September 1930–1 January 1932
125 pp. Hard cover, 26·5 × 20·5 cm. Entries 8-29 September inclusive written at Rodmell; 11 October–23 December at *52 Tavistock Square*; 27 December 1930–2 January 1931 at *Rodmell*; 7 January–11 April at *52 Tavistock Square*; 17 pp. white paper inserted, recording journey to *La Rochelle*, 16–27 April; 3 May–19 July at *52 Tavistock Square*; 7 August–30 September at *Rodmell*; 5 October–17 November at *52 Tavistock Square*; 25 December–1 January 1932 at *Rodmell*.

XXI   1932 52 TAVISTOCK SQUARE. 13 January 1932–3 January 1933
110 pp. on blue paper. Hard cover, 26·5 × 20·5 cm. 28 pp. white paper pasted in, recording journey to *Greece*, 18 April–11 May; entries 5 August–16 September inclusive written at *Rodmell*.

XXII   1933/34 52 TAVISTOCK SQUARE. 23 December 1932–8 May 1934
128 pp. on blue paper. Hard cover, 26·5 × 20·5 cm. Entries

23 December 1932–15 January 1933 inclusive written at *Rodmell*; 17 pp. white paper pasted in, recording journey to *France and Italy*, 9-23 May; entries 30 July–6 October inclusive written at *Rodmell*; 25 pp. white paper pasted in, recording journey to *Ireland*, 30 April–8 May.

XXIII   1934   52 TAVISTOCK SQUARE. 18 May 1934–11 January 1935 69 pp. on blue paper. Hard cover, 26·5 × 20·5 cm. Entries 27 July–5 October inclusive written at *Rodmell*; 30 December 1934–11 January 1935 inclusive, 9 pp. pasted in, written at *Rodmell*.

XXIV   1935   52 TAVISTOCK SQUARE. 19 January–20 December 1935 155 pp. Hard cover, 26 × 20·5 cm. Entries 20-23 April inclusive written at *Rodmell*; 32 pp. inserted, recording journey to *Holland, Germany, Italy and France*, 6-31 May; entries 3 August–2 October inclusive written at *Rodmell*.

XXV   1936   52 TAVISTOCK SQUARE. 28 December 1935–30 December 1936
58 pp. on blue paper. Hard cover, 27 × 21 cm. Entries 28 December 1935–7 January 1936 inclusive written at *Rodmell*; also 30 December 1936.

XXVI   1937   52 TAVISTOCK SQUARE. 10 January–18 December 1937 104 pp. mostly blue loose-leaf paper, 26·5 × 21 cm. Entry 10 January written at *Rodmell*; 5 pp. typewritten notes inserted, recording journey to *France*, dated 25 May; entries 6 August–27 September inclusive written at *Rodmell*.

XXVII   1938   52 TAVISTOCK SQUARE. 9 January–19 December 1938 92 pp. on blue and white loose-leaf paper, 28 × 21·5 cm. Entries 3-11 June inclusive written at *Rodmell*; 4 pp. typewritten account of journey to *Scotland* dated 16 June inserted; entries 4 August–14 October inclusive written at *Rodmell*.

XXVIII   1939   52 TAVISTOCK SQUARE and MONKS HOUSE, RODMELL. 5 January–18 December 1939
72 pp. on loose-leaf paper, 28 × 21·5 cm. Entries 5-8 January inclusive written at *Rodmell*; entries 25 July–18 December inclusive written at *Rodmell*.

XXIX   1940   MONKS HOUSE, RODMELL. 3 January–29 December 1940
109 pp. white and some blue loose-leaf paper, 28 × 21·5 cm.

XXX   1941   MONKS HOUSE, RODMELL. 1 January–24 March 1941 11 pp. ring-back notebook, white paper, 25.5 × 20 cm.

APPENDIX 2

First version of Diary entries for 20, 22 and 24 January 1919
(see p. 233)

Monday 20th January

I mean to copy this out, when I can buy a book, so I omit the flourishes proper to the New Year. It is not money this time that I lack, but the capacity, after a fortnight in bed, to make the journey to Fleet Street. Even the muscles of my right hand feel as I imagine a servant's hand to feel. Curiously enough, I have the same stiffness in manipulating sentences, though by rights I should be better equipped mentally now than I was a month ago. The fortnight in bed was the result of having a tooth out, & being tired enough to get a headache, a long dreary affair that receded & advanced, much like a mist on a January day. One hour writing daily is my allowance for the next few weeks; & having hoarded it this morning, I may spend part of it now, since L. is out, & I am much behindhand with the month of January. I note, however, that this diary writing does not count as writing; since I have just re-read my years diary, & am much struck by the rapid haphazard gallop at which it swings along, sometimes indeed jerking almost intolerably over the cobbles. Still, if it were not written rather faster than the fastest typewriting, it would never be written at all; & the advantage of the method is that [it] sweeps up accidentally several stray matters that I should exclude if I took thought; & it is these accidents that are the diamonds in the rubbish heap. If Virginia Woolf, at the age of 50, when she sits down to build her memoirs out of these books, is unable to make a phrase as it should be made, I can only condole with her, & remind her of the existence of the fireplace, where she has my leave to burn these pages to so many black films with red eyes. But how I envy her the task I am preparing for her. There is none I should like better. Already my 37th birthday next Saturday is robbed of some of its terrors. Partly for [the] benefit of this elderly lady (no subterfuge will then be possible: 50 is elderly, though, I agree, not old) partly to give the year a solid foundation I intend to spend the evenings of this week of captivity in making out an account of my friendships & their present condition, with some account of my friends characters; & to add an estimate of their work, & a forecast of their future works. The lady of fifty will be able to say how near to the truth I come; but I have written enough for tonight. (Only 15 minutes, I see).

I admit I dont like thinking of the lady of 50. Courage however. Roger is past that age, & still capable of feeling & enjoying & playing a very considerable part in life.

. . .

325

Today is Wednesday January 22nd. Two days more were spent in bed, & today counts as my first of complete health. I even wrote a sentence of Alterations & Additions this morning. I have a book on Meredith to do for the Times, & we walked this afternoon, so I am back again nearly in my old position. As I cant get up to London & only see little framed pictures of Alix & Fredegond sitting by the fire here, I might attempt that solid foundation which I think necessary.

How many friends have I got? Theres Lytton, Desmond, Saxon; they belong to the Cambridge stage of life; very intellectual, cut free from Hyde Park Gate, connected with Thoby; but I can't put them in order, for there are too many. Ka & Duncan: for example both come rather later; they belong to Fitzroy days; the Oliviers & all that set are stamped as the time of Brunswick Square. Clive I put a little aside; later still there are the cropheads, Alix, Carrington, Barbara, Nick, Bunny. I must insert, too, the set that runs paralell, but does not mix, distinguished by their social & political character, headed perhaps by Margaret, & including people like Goldie, Mrs Hamilton, & intermittent figures such as Matthaei, Hobson, the Webbs,—no, I cant include either the darkies or Dr Leys, though they stand for the occasional visitor who lunches & retires to L's room to talk seriously. I have not placed Ottoline, or Roger; & again there are Katherine & Murry, & the latest of all Hope Mirrlees, who recalls Pernel & Pippa, & outlying figures such as Ray. Gertler I must omit, for reasons which if my account gets written I might give; & Eliot I liked on the strength of one visit, & shall probably see more of, owing to his poems which we began today to set up. This is a very partial account, but I shall never place half of them accurately unless I begin straight away. Lytton & Desmond & Saxon then. Well, I cherish a considerable friendship for each of them; the worst of it is how seldom we meet. With Lytton at Tidmarsh, & Desmond till last month tethered to a stool, months pass without a sight of them. The season of letter writing is over for all of us, I think; or perhaps we need different correspondents. Brilliant letters we wrote each other once, partly for the sake of being brilliant, & we were getting to know each other, & there was a thrill about it (I speak of my own feelings.) But when we do meet there is nothing to complain of. Lytton is said to be more tolerant & less witty; Desmond, they say, needs a glass of wine; Saxon has his rheumatiz & his hopeless love. Lytton again is famous these last six months, but as that was a matter of course since he was six months old there is not much surprise or change in that. Moreover, I hear he has abandoned his Asquiths, or they are provided with some one else. Nothing is easier, or more intimate than a talk with Lytton. If he is less witty he is more humane. Presumably, he is now preparing to fly, but as his alliance is not with me, the direction he flies in makes very little difference. I like Carrington though. She has increased his benignity. O yes, if he were to walk in this moment we should talk about books & life & our intimate feelings as freely as we ever did; & with the same sense of having hoarded a great deal peculiarly fit for the other.

. . .

24th Jan. Oddly enough, the day after writing this sentence I got into touch with Lytton unexpectedly on the telephone, & he is to dine here next Friday. But to resume. There are three words knocking about in my brain to use of Stracheys—a prosaic race, lacking magnanimity, shorn of atmosphere. As these words have occurred almost automatically, I daresay there is some truth in them. All the unpleasantness that I wish to introduce into my portrait of Lytton is contained in them as if in deep wells. I shall only need a drop or two for his portrait; but I fancy something of the kind is perceptible in him too; far more in James, Oliver & Marjorie. Roger's version is that all, except Lady S., lack generosity. There, or thereabouts, lie their faults. But then one must combine them with a great variety of mental gifts so that the faults are spread fairly thin. One might attribute what I mean in Lytton's case at least, to lack of physical warmth, lack of creative power, a failure of vitality, warning him not to be spendthrift but to eke out his gifts parsimoniously, & tacitly assume his right to a superior share of comfort & opulence. In matters of emotion this has a slightly ⟨ungenerous⟩ stingy appearance, nor is he ever unthinkingly generous & magnanimous at the risk of himself. Mentally, of course, it produces that metallic tone & almost conventional style which prevents his writing from being first rate. It lacks originality; it is brilliant journalism; it is a superb rendering of the old tune. Written down these words are too emphatic; one does not get them tempered & combined with all those charming subtle & brilliant qualities which make him as he is in the flesh. But when I think of a Strachey, I think of someone infinitely cautious, elusive, unadventurous. To the common stock of our set they have added phrases, gestures, & witticisms, but never any new departure; never an Omega, a Post impressionist movement, nor even a country cottage, or a printing press. We Stephens, yes, & even Clive with all his faults, had the power of initiative, & the vitality, to carry our wishes into effect, because we wished too strongly to be chilled by ridicule or checked by difficulty. Even in the matter of taking Tidmarsh, Lytton had to be propelled from behind, & without Carrington to drudge through the chaotic stages he would never have left Hampstead, or ceased to flit dismally from his study to the British Museum, & from there to Cambridge.

ABBREVIATIONS

CH, Camb.	Charleston Papers deposited in the Library of King's College, Cambridge
Holleyman	Holleyman & Treacher Ltd: *Catalogue of Books from the Library of Leonard and Virginia Woolf, taken from Monks House, Rodmell, and 24 Victoria Square, London, and now in the possession of Washington State University.* Privately printed, Brighton, 1975
Holroyd	Michael Holroyd: *Lytton Strachey. A Biography.* Revised edition, Penguin Books, 1971
Kp	B. J. Kirkpatrick: *A Bibliography of Virginia Woolf.* Revised edition, Hart-Davis, London, 1967
LW	Leonard Woolf. Five volumes of his *Autobiography*, Hogarth Press, London
I LW	*Sowing:* . . . *1880-1904.* 1960
II LW	*Growing:* . . . *1904-1911.* 1961
III LW	*Beginning Again:* . . . *1911-1918.* 1964
IV LW	*Downhill all the Way:* . . . *1919-1939.* 1967
V LW	*The Journey not the Arrival Matters:* . . . *1939-1969.* 1969
MHP, Sussex	*Monks House Papers.* University of Sussex Library Catalogue, July 1972
QB	Quentin Bell: *Virginia Woolf. A Biography.* Hogarth Press, London, 1972
I QB	Volume I: *Virginia Stephen,* 1882-1912
II QB	Volume II: *Mrs Woolf,* 1912-1941
TLS	*The Times Literary Supplement*
VW	Virginia Woolf
VW Letters	*The Letters of Virginia Woolf.* Edited by Nigel Nicolson. Hogarth Press, London
I VW Letters	Volume I: *The Flight of the Mind (1882-1912).* 1975
II VW Letters	Volume II: *The Question of Things Happening (1912-1922).* 1976
VW/GLS Letters	*Virginia Woolf & Lytton Strachey: Letters.* Edited by Leonard Woolf and James Strachey. Hogarth Press, London, 1956

NOTE

Unless otherwise stated, the *Uniform Edition* of the Works of Virginia Woolf, and the 4-volume *Collected Essays*, both published by the Hogarth Press, are used for reference purposes.

FAMILY TREE

Showing the Antecedents
and Relations of
Virginia Woolf

FAMILY

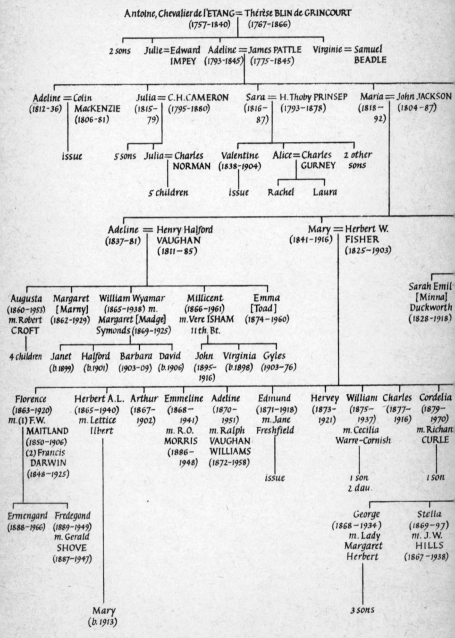

Antoine, Chevalier de l'ETANG = Thérèse BLIN de GRINCOURT
(1757-1840)   (1767-1866)

2 sons   Julie = Edward   Adeline = James PATTLE   Virginie = Samuel
        IMPEY   (1793-1845) (1775-1845)   BEADLE

Adeline = Colin   Julia = C.H.CAMERON   Sara = H.Thoby PRINSEP   Maria = John JACKSON
(1812-36) MacKENZIE (1815- (1795-1880)   (1816- (1793-1878)   (1818- (1804-87)
      (1806-81) 79)   87)   92)

issue   5 sons Julia = Charles   Valentine   Alice = Charles   2 other
             NORMAN (1838-1904)   GURNEY   sons

      5 children   issue   Rachel Laura

Adeline = Henry Halford   Mary = Herbert W.   Sarah Emil
(1837-81) VAUGHAN   (1841-1916) FISHER   [Minna]
      (1811-85)   (1825-1903) Duckworth
                               (1828-1918)

Augusta Margaret William Wyamar Millicent Emma
(1860-1953) [Marny] (1865-1938) m. (1866-1961) [Toad]
m.Robert (1862-1929) Margaret [Madge] m.Vere ISHAM (1874-1960)
CROFT   Symonds (1869-1925) 11th. Bt.

4 children Janet Halford Barbara David John Virginia Gyles
       (b.1899) (b.1901) (1903-09) (b.1906) (1895- (b.1898) (1903-76)
                          1916)

Florence Herbert A.L. Arthur Emmeline Adeline Edmund Hervey William Charles Cordelia
(1863-1920) (1865-1940) (1867- (1868- (1870- (1871-1918) (1873- (1875- (1877- (1879-
m.(1) F.W. m.Lettice 1902) 1941) 1951) m.Jane 1921) 1937) 1916) 1970)
  MAITLAND Ilbert   m. R.O. m.Ralph Freshfield   m.Cecilia   m.Richard
  (1850-1906)   MORRIS VAUGHAN   Warre-Cornish CURLE
  (2) Francis   (1886- WILLIAMS
  DARWIN   1948) (1872-1958)
  (1848-1925)   issue   1 son   1 son
                                     2 dau.

Ermengard Fredegond   George   Stella
(1888-1966) (1889-1949)   (1868-1934) (1869-97)
       m. Gerald   m. Lady   m. J.W.
       SHOVE   Margaret HILLS
       (1887-1947)   Herbert (1867-1938)

       Mary   3 sons
      (b.1913)

TREE

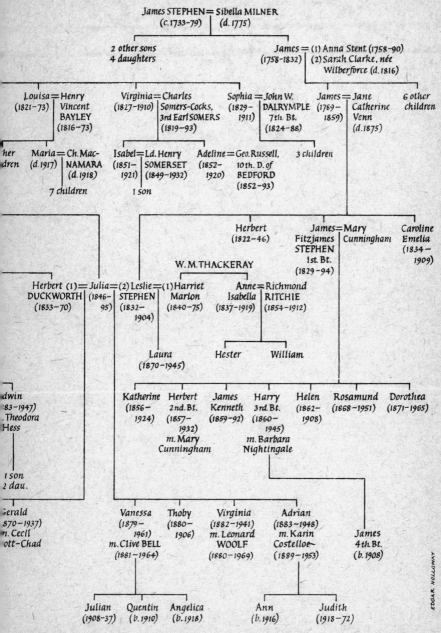

James STEPHEN = Sibella MILNER
(c. 1733–79)   (d. 1775)

2 other sons
4 daughters

James = (1) Anna Stent (1758–90)
(1758–1832) (2) Sarah Clarke, née
              Wilberforce (d. 1816)

Louisa = Henry   Virginia = Charles   Sophia = John W.   James = Jane   6 other
(1821–73) Vincent   (1827–1910) Somers-Cocks, (1829– DALRYMPLE   (1789– Catherine children
           BAYLEY   3rd Earl SOMERS 1911) 7th. Bt.   1859)   Venn
           (1816–73)   (1819–93)   (1824–88)   (d. 1875)

...her   Maria = Ch. Mac-   Isabel = Ld. Henry   Adeline = Geo. Russell,   3 children
...dren   (d. 1917) NAMARA   (1851– SOMERSET   (1852–   10th. D. of
                         (d. 1918) 1921) (1849–1932)   1920)   BEDFORD
              7 children   1 son   (1852–93)

                                              Herbert   James = Mary   Caroline
                                              (1822–46)   Fitzjames Cunningham Emelia
                                                               STEPHEN   (1834–
                                   W. M. THACKERAY   1st. Bt.   1909)
                                                               (1829–94)

Herbert (1) = Julia = (2) Leslie = (1) Harriet   Anne = Richmond
DUCKWORTH   (1846–   STEPHEN   Marion   Isabella RITCHIE
(1833–70)   95)   (1832–   (1840–75)   (1837–1919) (1854–1912)
                      1904)
                                   Laura   Hester   William
                                   (1870–1945)

...dwin
...83–1947)   Katherine Herbert   James   Harry   Helen   Rosamund   Dorothea
..Theodora   (1856–   2nd. Bt.   Kenneth   3rd. Bt. (1862–   (1868–1951) (1871–1965)
  Hess   1924)   (1857–   (1859–92)   (1860–   1908)
                                1932)   1945)
                                m. Mary   m. Barbara
...son   Cunningham   Nightingale
..dau.

..erald   Vanessa   Thoby   Virginia   Adrian   James
..870–1937)   (1879–   (1880–   (1882–1941) (1883–1948)   4th. Bt.
.. Cecil   1961)   1906)   m. Leonard m. Karin   (b. 1908)
..ott-Chad   m. Clive BELL   WOOLF   Costelloe–
                      (1881–1964)   (1880–1969) (1889–1953)

              Julian   Quentin   Angelica   Ann   Judith
              (1908–37) (b. 1910) (b. 1918)   (b. 1916) (1918–72)

EDGAR HOLLOWAY

INDEX

This index is not exhaustive: certain place names—as for instance England and Clapham Junction, which it seemed could be of little help to readers—have been omitted; so too the names of domestic animals, of military engagements, and battleships.

Footnotes have been indexed but only in so far as this is necessary to an understanding of the text; thus, a footnote relating to Rosa Allatini is indexed under Allatini, but her pseudonym A. T. Fitzroy, which appears only in a footnote, is not indexed; neither are authorities, supportive information, or works of reference cited only in the footnotes.

Reference to the page and footnote giving biographical details about individuals prominent in the diary immediately follows their name, and is printed in italics prefixed by *B*, thus: Bell, Clive: *B 9 n22.*

Titles of publications or works referred to by VW are listed at the end of their author's entry.

Familiar names, nick-names, abbreviated designations, are included in the index and cross-referenced to their proper names.

n . . footnote; *ref*: . . referred to; ax 2 . . Appendix 2.

Ewer, William Norman: 245 & n
Exhibition of works representative of the new movement in art, An: 61n

Fabian Research Department: 18n
Fabian Society: well worth hearing and seeing, 26; *ref*: 18 & n
Fabians, the 'Fabian type': 276
Fabre, Henri: 134 & n
Farrell, Sophia: 5 & n
Father *see* Stephen, Leslie
Fawcett, Henry: xxi
Ferguson, Inez: 176 & n, 264
Fergusson, Dr D. J.: 119, 159 & n
Fielding, Henry: *Tom Jones*, 107 & n
Firle, Sussex: 41, 44, 45, 46, 49, 50
First Post-Impressionist Exhibition, 1910-11: xxvi
Fisher, Herbert Albert Laurens: *B 88 n21*; in all papers, 88, 88n; brings inside story of victory to VW, 202, 203, 204-5; Minister for Education, 263, 264; *ref*: 207, 223-4
Fisher, Herbert William: 200 & n
Fisher, Hervey: 16 & n, 87, 88n
Fisher, Lettice, *née* Ilbert: doesn't like London, 88; *ref*: 88n
Fisher, Mary (Aunt Mary), *née* Jackson: *B 16 n46*; conceals low birth of son's fiancée, 16 & n; run over, 88 & n
Fishmonger's Hall, military hospital: 84 & n, 91
Fitzroy Square, No. 29: 18n, 205, 226, 234; ax 2
Fitzroy Street: 260
Flaubert, Gustave: 94
Fleet Street: 33, 233; ax 2
Foch, Marshal: 203, 204
Foreign Office: 306
Forster, E. M. ('Morgan'): *B 120 n5*; to read Defoe, 263; approves of *Kew Gardens*, 276; whimsical, vagulous, 291, 295; reception of *Night and Day*, 307, 308, 310; his novel, 310-11, 311n; *ref*: xxv, 120 & n, 213, 262 & n, 272, 285, 294, 295, 307; *A Passage to India*, 311n
Foundling Hospital: 10 & n
Fox, Miss: 252
France: 21, 121, 123, 169, 189, 195, 208
Franck, César: *Symphony in D*, 20n
Freda *see* Major, Freda
Fredegond *see* Shove, Fredegond

Freshwater, The Porch: 27 & n, 247; potential for comedy, 237 & n
Freud, Sigmund: 110 & n, 221 & n
Frodsham, Charles, & Co, clockmakers: 30 & n
Froude, Anthony: xxi, 223 & n
Fry (family): 91
Fry, Agnes Pamela: 227 & n, 274
Fry, Sir Edward: 208, 209n
Fry, Margery: 274 & n
Fry, Roger: *B 53 n12*; early career and character, xxvi, 10n, 53 & n; his quarrel with Ottoline, 62 & n; relish for French manners and language, 72; embarrassing to talk art in front of, 75; VW dines with, essentials of art, texture and structure, world's gloomy future, 80; success as portraitist, 86; bristling with ideas, 134 & n, 225; translation of *Lysistrata*, 136-7; examines a Cézanne, 140; on Clive Bell, 151; gloom and grievances, 152, 227, 228; on Stracheys, 235-6; most hated man, 261; and *Kew Gardens*, 273, 276; *ref*: 54, 59 & n, 61n, 73, 80n, 86n, 139, 140n, 152n, 159, 173 & n, 198, 201, 208, 224, 228n, 234, 235, 237, 252, 260, 265, 269, 274, 285, 288, 295; ax 2; *Lysistrata* of Aristophanes trans., 134n, 140
Fulham, verge of civilisation: 239
Fuller, Margaret: 23 & n

G. L. D. *see* Dickinson, Goldsworthy Lowes
Galsworthy, John: 213 & n, 225
Gardiner, Samuel Rawson: *A Student's History of England from the Earliest Times to 1885*, 70 & n
Garland's (formerly Garlant's) Hotel: 246 & n
Garnett, David ('Bunny'): *B 40 n5*; his socialism, 183; brings honey, sprouting docks and nettles, 191; writes novel in copy books, 249 & n; *ref*: 40 & n, 41, 43 & n, 69, 94, 106, 121, 182, 191n, 234; ax 2
Garnett, Edward: 43 & n, 182
Garsington Manor, home of Philip and Ottoline Morrell: gossip from, 75; week-ends at, 78, 173, 284; *ref*: xxvii, 58, 100, 176, 182, 284n
Gaskell, Mrs: 213n, 247; *Cranford*, 213 & n

Gatti's Restaurant: 246 & n
Gaudier-Brzeska, Henri: 90 & n
Geall, Mr: 197 & n, 298
George see Duckworth, George
George III: 14 & n, 220
George V: relationship with Walter Lamb, his false teeth, 14; *ref*: 14n, 64
Georgian Poetry, anthology: 95 & n
Gertler, Mark: a powerful spring, 158; an underworld figure, 159; a resolute young man, 175; his notions of painting, 183; talks about himself for some 30 hours, 198; VW in hot water owing to, 208 & n; *ref*: 154, 174, 180, 202, 235, 272, 284, 285; ax 2
Gibbon, Edward: 306
Gibson, Hugh: 263
Gilbert see Murray, Gilbert
Giotto: 69, 80
Gissing, Robert: 91
Glenconner, Lady: 316
Glyn, Elinor: 71 & n
Glynde, Sussex: 41, 42, 45, 49, 50, 52, 121, 177, 197, 250
Goethe: 194
Goldie see Dickinson, Goldsworthy Lowes
Gordan, Dr John D.: viii
Gordon Square, a social entity: 27, 65, 73, 86, 225, 260, 299, 305
Gordon Square, No. 41: 237, 284
Gordon Square, No. 46: a cheerful environment, xv; a scene of vice, xxii; Maynard at, xxvii; a party at, VW stays away, 9-10; atmosphere alien to LW, 65; party at, 73, 86; leased by Maynard, 73n; Delacroix and Cézanne on show, 140; *ref*: 9n, 17, 35, 75, 86n, 172, 173, 200, 202, 233, 246 & n, 260, 261, 288, 290
Gosse, Sir Edmund: xxi, xxv, 300 & n, 302
Grant, Duncan: *B 5 n12*; friendship with VW, character and reputation, xvi, xxiv, xxvi, xxvii; compared to G. E. Moore, 155; his fame, 183; inspires laughter, 187; his change in style, 208; a shaggy interlude, 240; domestic difficulties, 248; makes VW's bed, sets up canvas amid turmoil, 249; in bath with Vanessa, 260; *ref*: 5 & n, 7n, 55, 69, 72, 87, 94, 95, 119, 120, 130, 140, 151, 182, 198, 199, 209, 228n,

233, 234, 252, 253, 261, 288, 295, 297; ax 2
Grant, Jane Maria see Strachey, Lady
Gravé, Madame, dressmaker: 284
Gray, Thomas: 299
Greco, El: 228
Greek Anthology, The: 105 & n
Green, Minna: 254 & n, 309
Grenfell, Gerald: 108 & n
Grenfell, Julian: 108 & n
Greville, Charles: his memoirs, 317 & n
Grey, Sir Edward (Viscount Grey of Falloden): 19, 200 & n
Grote, George: 23 & n
Grotius: *De Imperio Summarum Potestatum Circa Sacra*, 167 & n
Guild see Women's Cooperative Guild
'Gumbo' see Strachey, Marjorie
Gunn, Frank: 42 & n, 46, 248, 302
Gunter's, tea rooms: 283 & n

Hague Conference: 207 & n
Hakluyt, Richard: 224
Hallett, Mrs: 3, 6, 7
Hamill and Barker, Misses: vii, viii
Hamilton, Mary Agnes ('Molly'): farewell party for Bertrand Russell, 137 & n; her character, 174, 175; *ref*: 173, 181, 228, 234, 255 & n, 258, 289, 296, 305, 311, 312; ax 2
Hamilton, Molly see Hamilton, Mary Agnes
Hamlet (fict): 193
Hammond, Mrs: 50 & n, 51, 54
Hamnett, Nina: 59 & n, 202
Hampstead: provides a third variety of human being, 83, 110; Woolfs Hampstead afternoon, 213; immaculate and moral heights of, 312; *ref*: 8 & n, 25, 30, 31, 60, 82, 94, 147, 214, 216, 222, 247, 281, 295; ax 2
Hampton Court: 100, 144
Handel, George Frederick: 5n
Hanwell Gazette & Brentford Observer: 121 & n
Harcourt, Lord: 201 & n
Hardy, Thomas: VW writes to concerning his poem on Leslie Stephen, 22; replies to VW's letter, 26; *ref*: xxi, 11, 57, 84 & n, 129, 151, 188, 238, 247, 291; *Moments of Vision*, 84n; *Satires of Circumstance*, 22n; *The*

Isham, Lady, *née* Millicent Vaughan: 87 & n
Isham, Sir Vere: 88
Isham, Virginia: milks cows, 88; *ref*: 88n
Isola Bella Restaurant: 259, 261

Jacks, L. P.: 101 & n
Jackson, Dr John: 107 & n
Jackson, Julia *see* Stephen, Julia
James *see* Strachey, James
James, Henry: 'Jacobeans', admirers of H. J., 125 & n; *ref*: xxi, xxiii, 27 & n, 57 & n, 224 & n, 300; *The Middle Years*, 57n
Janet *see* Case, Janet
Jayatilaka, D. B.: 60n, 122
Jebb, Sir Richard Claverhouse: 184 & n
Jeune, Lady *see* St Helier, Lady
John, Augustus: 184 & n
Johnson, Dr Samuel: xxi, 19, 56 & n, 161 & n, 278 & n; *The History of Rasselas*, 161 & n
Jones, Henry Festing: 317 & n
Jonson, Ben: 106
Jos *see* Wedgwood, Josiah Clement
Joyce, James: his new novel, 136 & n; his ms read by Desmond, 145; *ref*: xxv, 140, 151, 219 & n, 247; *Ulysses*, xxv, 136n
Judith *see* Stephen, Judith

K. M. *see* Murry, Katherine
Ka *see* Arnold-Forster, Katherine
Kaiser *see* Wilhelm II
Karin *see* Stephen, Karin
Katie *see* Cromer, Lady
Kay-Shuttleworth, Lawrence: 7 & n
Keats, John: 104 & n, 111, 113, 180
Kemble (family): 19
Kemble, Frances (Fanny): 23 & n
Kensington, a social entity: milieu of VW's youth, xviii-xxii, xxiii; *ref*: 25n, 206
Kensington, High Street: the whole poured into one room, 68; never seeing beyond, 206
Kerensky, Alexander: 160 & n
Kew: 14 & n, 77, 85, 116, 123, 147, 282
Kew Gardens: 28, 81 & n, 82, 114, 127, 148, 252, 263, 264, 304
Keynes, John Maynard: *B 17 n47*; in commune with VW, xvi; his ability, xxv, xxvi; his optimism, 17, 24; his

scepticism, 25; and 'society', 121; hires brougham for Vanessa, 201 & n; resigns over peace terms, 280 & n; his disillusionment, 288; *ref*: 17n, 73n, 86 & n, 94, 105, 106, 119, 139, 167, 181, 183, 233, 295
King, (Joseph?): 65 & n
King, The *see* George V
Kingston Barracks: 56, 67, 72
Kitchener, Lord: his portrait in National Gallery, 168 & n
Koklova, Olga *see* Picasso, Mme
Kot *see* Koteliansky, S. S.
Koteliansky, Samuel Solomonovitch ('Kot'): *B 106 n24*; a good deal to be said for, his views on K. Mansfield, 108; his general sordidity, 176; *ref*: 106 & n, 154, 158, 159
Kühlmann, Richard von: 146 & n

L. E. L. *see* Landon, Letitia Elizabeth
L. G. *see* Lloyd George, David
LM *see* Baker, Ida Constance
Labour Party: 41 & n, 137, 160 & n, 186, 229 & n, 262
Lacket, The, Lockeridge: 21n
Laforgue, Jules: 165 & n
Lalo, Edouard: *Symphonie Espagnole*, 20n
Lamb, Charles: 275 & n; *Essays of Elia*, 275
Lamb, Henry: 156 & n
Lamb, Walter ('Wat', 'Wattie'): *B 14 n36*; fresh from the King, 14; his character, 18, 35; his alabastrine baldness, 34; his success, tact, prosperity 64; dashed by VW's snobbery, 84; unbearable alone, spruce, suspicious, 93; slightly above usual level, 137-8; the ideal of manhood, 262; *ref*: 55, 71
Landon, Letitia Elizabeth (L. E. L.): 180 & n
Landor, Walter Savage: 304 & n
Langdon-Davies, Bernard Noel: 135 & n
Langston, Mrs, member of Women's Coop Guild: 76 & n, 90, 104, 112, 165
Lansbury, George: 284, 285n
Lansdowne, Lord: 86 & n
Laura *see* Stephen, Laura
Lawrence, D. H.: Woolfs in treaty for his house, 112 & n; 'Grantorto', 265 & n; *ref*: 176, 191 & n
Leconte de Lisle, Charles: 178 & n

Lee, Vernon: 266 & n
Le Grys, Mrs, landlady: best-tempered woman in England, 35; *ref*: 4, 15 & n, 16, 25, 31, 32
Leopardi, Giacomo: 126 & n
Lewes (Sussex): 19, 39, 40, 42, 43, 45, 50, 51, 52, 53, 54, 55, 170, 177, 178, 179, 198, 279, 296, 300, 302, 303
Lewis, Wyndham: 219 & n, 247
Leys, Dr Norman: 222 & n, 234; ax 2
Lichnowsky, Prince Charles Max: 146 & n
Lightbody, Hilda: 87 & n
Lil, N. Boxall's niece: 261 & n
Lilian *see* Harris, Lilian
Lily, a servant: her misadventures, 3, 6, 8; *ref*: 11, 19
Lister, C. A.: 108 & n
Little Folks, magazine: 47n, 277
Little Talland House, Firle: 51 & n
Liz, N., Boxall's sister: 56 & n, 65, 188, 227, 228
Lizzie, maid of all work: sets house on fire, 15 & n, 16; nearly bursts boiler, 17; smashes crockery, 18; bursts pipes, 25; leaves, 30; *ref*: 28, 31
Llewelyn Davies *see* Davies
Lloyd George, David: 128 & n, 203, 204, 218 & n, 251
Lock, Bella Sidney, *née* Woolf, *quo* Southorn: *B 47 n1*; 161, 277
Lock, Mr: 68 & n
Lockeridge, Wilts.: 21 & n
Logan *see* Smith, Logan Pearsall
London: effects of air raids, 65; exodus from, 68; seen through Defoe's eyes, 263; peace celebrations, 292; *ref*: xvii, xxvi, xxvii, 5, 9, 11, 23, 24, 29, 31, 32, 33, 35, 41, 44, 55, 66, 71, 75, 82, 94, 102, 111, 116, 121, 123, 134, 136, 146, 148, 156, 168, 171, 172, 176, 177, 183, 195, 198, 199, 204, 207, 208, 209, 212, 216, 217, 234, 254, 265, 270, 278, 283, 288, 293, 296, 298, 300, 302, 303, 304; ax 2
London Group, The: 308 & n
London Library, The: a stale culture smoked place, 25; LW and Desmond saddened by the thumb marks in slang dictionary s.v. 'f——', 82; *ref*: 16 & n, 17, 20, 32, 33, 35, 58, 65, 71, 101, 113, 121, 125, 169, 177, 225, 263
London Mercury, The, periodical: 309

London School of Economics: 24 & n, 28, 29, 317
Longleat, Wiltshire: 309
Lopokova, Lydia, later wife of J. M. Keynes (*quo* Signora Randolfo Barocchi): 246 & n, 290 & n
Lottie *see* Hope, Lottie
Lowes Dickinson *see* Dickinson, Goldsworthy Lowes
Lubbock, Percy: 125 & n
Lucretius: 192
Lynch, Barbara: 283, 284n
Lytton *see* Strachey, (Giles) Lytton

M. H. *see* Hutchinson, Mary
Mabel *see* Selwood, Mabel
Macaulay, Lord: his Life, 163 & n; *ref*: 101, 105, 165
Macbeth, Lady (fict): 193
McCabe, watchmakers: 30 & n
MacCarthy, children: 49n
MacCarthy, Desmond: *B 27 n77*: on Shakespeare and Thackeray, 114; the 'Ireniad', 115 & n, 218; wants VW to review him, 138; VW unwilling, 142; his character, 145, 150, 156, 206, 235, 238, 241-42, 267; and *New Statesman*, 218 & n; questions T. S. Eliot, 219; *ref*: xxv, xxvi, 27 & n, 51, 52, 82, 121, 144, 145n, 148, 206, 234, 238n, 239, 257, 263, 267n, 306; ax 2; *Remnants*, 138n, 241
MacCarthy, Mary ('Molly') *née* Warre-Cornish: *B 27 n77*; a sense of failure, 156; saved by 'Bloomsbury', 206; setting up house at Oare, 267; *ref*: 27 & n; 29, 51, 73, 93, 114, 119, 150, 155, 206n, 311, 312 & n; *A Pier and a Band*, 93 & n
MacColl, Andrée Desirée Jeanne and D. S.: 225 & n
McCurdy, Charles Albert: 157 & n
McDermott, Mr (MacDermott), printer: fails to deliver press, 104; generally invisible, 207; surrenders £7, 216; printing estimate, 229; blots Murry's poem, 257; *ref*: 77n, 109, 221, 227
MacDonald, Ramsay: LW and his treachery, 226 & n; *ref*: 162 & n, 171 & n, 190
Macmillan, New York publishers: interested in *Night and Day*, 280 & n, 297, 298, 305

MacNaghten, Malcolm: 72 & n
Macnamara, Maria ('Mia'): 88 & n
Maitland, Ermengard: 143 & n
Major, Freda: 208, 211
Manchester Guardian: 65, 115
Mandril, nickname for VW
Manners, Lady Diana, *see* Cooper, Lady
   Diana
Mansard Gallery, Heal & Son: 61 & n
Mansfield, Katherine *see* Murry, Katherine
Manus, Marjorie: 135 & n, 223, 225
Marble Hill House, Twickenham: 111
   & n
Margaret *see* Davies, Margaret Llewelyn
Marlborough, Duchess of: 166, 171 & n
Marny *see* Vaughan, Margaret
Marsh, Edward: editor of *Georgian
   Poetry*, 95n; 170n
Mary, Queen, consort of George V: 64
Massingham, Henry William ('Way-
   farer'): 182 & n, 316 & n, 318
Matthaei, Louise Ernestine (Matthew):
   her character, 135; her salary, 143;
   ref: 135n, 190 & n, 225, 234, 254 & n;
   ax 2
Matthew *see* Matthaei, Louise
Maud, a servant: 30, 31
Maxse, Kitty, *née* Lushington: xxiii, 87
   & n
May, Henry John: 65 & n
Mayfair, a social entity: xxiii, 286, 310
Mayne, Clarice: 201 & n
Mayor, Beatrice ('Bobo'), *née* Meinertz-
   hagen: 50, 51n
Mayor, Robert John Grote ('Robin'): 50,
   51n
Mecklenburgh Square: 11, 15, 22
Melville, Herman: 291 & n
Meredith, George: xxi, xxiii, 165 & n,
   191, 234 & n, 300; ax 2; *The Tragic
   Comedians*, 165 & n
Merrick, Leonard: 149 & n, 161
Meynell, Alice: 62 & n
Meynell, Viola: 140 & n
Michelet, Jules: *Histoire de France*, 10 &
   n, 23, 31, 34
Mill, J. S.: *On Liberty*, 126
Milman, Enid: 25 & n
Milman, Henry, Dean Milman: 25 & n
Milman, Ida: 25 & n
Milman, Maud: 25 & n
Milman, Sylvia *see* Whitham, Sylvia
Milner, Alfred, Viscount: 203 & n

Milton, John: 185, 186, 193; *Paradise
   Lost*, 192, 193
Mirrlees, Hope: *B 186 n15*; objects to
   being addressed as darling, 191; her
   character, 258; *ref*: 186 & n, 188 & n,
   235, 244, 282, 295, 301 & n; ax 2;
   Paris. A Poem, 282 & n
Molly *see* MacCarthy, Mary; *see also*
   Hamilton, Mary Agnes
Mongoose, nickname for LW
Monks House, Rodmell: acquired by
   Woolfs, 286-8, 287n; sale of contents,
   295; *ref*: 291, 295, 298, 302, 304, 317
Mont Blanc, restaurant: 172 & n
Moore, George: 264
Moore, G. E.: compared to Christ and
   Socrates, 155; *ref*: xxiv, 155n, 264
Moore, Lesley *see* Baker, Ida Constance
Moore, Thomas: 180 & n
Moralt, Dr Marie: 249n
Morgan, Evan Frederic: 78 & n, 125
Morley, John, Viscount: xxi, 83, 84n, 103
   & n, 119, 300 & n; *Recollections*, 103
   & n
Morrell, Lady Ottoline ('Ott'): *B 21 n58*;
   plurality of her social worlds, xxiv;
   at Garsington, xxvii, 175; introduces
   Marjorie Strachey to Jos Wedgwood,
   21, 22; old, languid, weary, 61,
   62, 66, 66n; vitality, velvet and
   pearls, 78, 79; imitated by Vanessa,
   129; on love, 175; rebuffed by
   Vanessa, 183; garish as a strumpet,
   201; her spirit, 245-6 & n; her
   character considered, 272-3; three
   hours on a hard seat with, 285; *ref*:
   62n, 75, 79, 81, 115, 117, 147, 153,
   202, 235, 273, 275, 284, 285n; ax 2
Morrell, Philip: *B 21 n58*; efforts to
   entertain Jos Wedgwood, 21; encased
   in best leather, 78; long-suffering, 79;
   his attack on Murry in defence of
   Sassoon, 174 & n; finds VW heartless
   and terrifying, 285, 286n; *ref*: 21n, 49,
   149
Morris, Emmeline, *née* Fisher: wraps dog
   in knickers, 104 & n
Moss, Henry: 120 & n
Mother *see* Stephen, Julia
Mozart, W. A.: badly played, 142; *ref*: 33,
   310; *Don Giovanni*, 157 & n; *Figaro*,
   a vindication of opera, 83; *Magic
   Flute*, 153

Mudie's Library: sickens VW of reading, 165; *ref:* 61 & n, 75, 83, 90, 99, 121, 126, 176, 215, 261

Muir-MacKenzie, the Hon. Mrs: 220 & n

Murray, Gilbert: 25, 210 & n, 221, 224

Murray, Lady Mary: 210 & n

Murray, Rosalind, *see* Toynbee, Rosalind

Murry, Arthur: 227 & n, 268

Murry, John Middleton: *B 58 n 14*; a good mind, 129; pale and sad, 156, 288; review of Sassoon, 174 & n; the shadow of the underworld, 159, 222; his poem hard to read, 223 & n; buys a press, 226, 227 & n; editorship of *Athenaeum*, 243 & n, 254 & n, 256-7, 260, 265; VW's manner towards, 265, 271; *The Critic in Judgment* badly printed and reviewed, 257, 281 & n; *ref:* 58 & n, 151 & n, 155, 159, 177, 179, 216 & n, 229, 235, 256n, 257, 257n, 258, 262, 267, 268, 290, 295, 305, 308, 315; ax 2; *The Critic in Judgment* ('A Fable for Critics'), 223 & n, 227, 257, 271 & n, 281 & n

Murry, Katherine (Katherine Mansfield, K.M.), *née* Kathleen Beauchamp: *B 43 n18*; gossip concerning, 67 & n, 75; her soul explained by Kot, 108; very ill, 129; marmoreal, married, 150 & n; 'failure' of *Prelude*, 169; writes that she is ill, 177 & n; *Bliss*, 'she's done for', 179 & n; VW visits, 226; a friend?, 242-3; inscrutable, 257; a true writer, 258; hurt by not being invited to party, 265; stories rejected, 265; VW likes more and more, 291; VW irritated by her review, 314; her health, 216, 243, 268, 281, 288 & n, 315; *ref:* 43 & n, 44, 56, 58 & n, 120, 151 & n, 159, 160, 163, 167, 216n, 222, 228, 235, 257n, 258 & n, 267, 271, 295, 314n, 315, 316; ax 2; *Bliss*, 179 & n; *Prelude*, 56 & n, 160n, 164, 165 & n, 168

Mutton's, Brighton restaurant: 189 & n

N. *see* Bell, Vanessa

N & L, Nelly Boxall and Lottie Hope

Nation, The: 174 & n, 181, 182

National Gallery: 168, 187, 206, 228

Nelly *see* Boxall, Nelly

Nelson, Geoffrey: 284, 285n

Nessa *see* Bell, Vanessa

Nevill, Lady Dorothy: 316 & n

Nevinson, C. R. W.: 240 & n

Newbolt, Sir Henry: 'slim greyheaded weasel', 113; and music, 244, 245; *ref:* 113n, 244n

Newcastle, Duchess of: 23 & n

Newcastle, Duke of: 70

New English Art Club: 154 & n, 240

Newnham College, Cambridge: 135, 135n, 160, 188 & n

New Republic, periodical: 290 & n

New Statesman, periodical: 15, 15n, 20, 27, 30n, 178, 218, 268

New Statesman, office: 17, 66 & n

Nick *see* Bagenal, Nick

Nightingale, Florence: 166

1917 Club: its birth, 57 & n; dinner, 94 & n; a success, 99; something of a lure, 102; quite a family party, 115; general meeting, 129; LW on committee, 153; LW speaks on Austria-Hungary at, 209 & n; and Forster on Egypt, 272; *ref:* 101, 113, 118, 121, 122, 125, 127, 134, 136, 137, 139, 141, 144, 148, 158, 161, 162, 164, 168, 170, 172, 173, 176, 208, 212, 214, 215, 217, 221, 222, 225, 228, 237, 238, 251, 256, 258, 261 & n, 263, 270, 280, 293 & n, 305, 307

Noble, Mrs Saxton: 64 & n

Northcliffe, Alfred Harmsworth, Lord: his press, 199, 200; and influenza, 209; *ref:* 254

Norton, Henry Tertius James: all that brain, 86; *ref:* 86n, 202, 237, 261, 273

Nutt, David, bookseller: 126 & n

Oare, Wiltshire: 155 & n, 238, 267, 306

Olivier (family): 234; ax 2

Olivier, Brynhild *see* Popham, Brynhild

Olivier, Daphne: xxiv, 143 & n

Olivier, Margery: xxiv

Olivier, Noel: xxiv, 131, 132 & n, 139, 141, 309

Omega Workshops: disloyalty to, 228 & n; *ref:* xxvi, 10 & n, 11, 25, 72, 75, 99, 134, 136, 140, 164, 173, 208, 236, 237; ax 2

Osborn, Frederic James: 309 & n

Ott *see* Morrell, Lady Ottoline

Owensmith, Edward and Elizabeth: 261

'Oxford': superiority, 77; death and decay, 315; *ref:* 75, 211, 264

Oxford, town: 31, 79

Oxford, University of: xviii, 204, 211, 264
Oxford Street: 111, 176, 264

'Painters', Vanessa Bell and Duncan Grant: smooth broad spaces in their minds, 69
Palladium, theatre: 142
Pall Mall Gazette: 24 & n
Pamela *see* Fry, Agnes Pamela
Pangbourne, Berkshire: 171
Pargiter, Thomas: 39n, 301
Paris: 191, 203, 221, 236, 283, 308
Park, Mungo: 300 & n
Parker, H.: *Village Folk Tales of Ceylon*, 4 & n
Parliament: ridiculous, 173; women eligible for, 207; *ref*: 222, 288
Partridge & Cooper, stationers: 99 & n, 132
Pater, Walter: 264, 300
Paton, Emily: 249 & n
Pattle (family): xx, xxi, 107
Pattle, James: xx, 107 & n
Peace Celebrations: 292, 294
Peace Conference, also Peace Congress (Versailles): 'a degrading spectacle', 288; *ref*: 221
Peace Debate, at Women's Coop Guild: 11
Pearsall Smith, Logan *see* Smith, Logan Pearsall
Pelican Press: 280 & n
Pepys, Samuel: 128 & n
Percy, Lord Eustace: 245 & n
Perera, E. W.: VW avoids him, 71; to see LW, 90; to consult once more, 93; *ref*: 60 & n, 122
Pethick-Lawrence, Mrs Emmeline: her gymnastics, 125
Petronius: 105-6, 106n
Phillimore, Mrs: 182 & n
Picasso, Pablo: 285 & n, 290 & n
Picasso, Mme, *née* Olga Koklova: 290 & n
Piccadilly: 63, 65, 71, 300
Pitcher, Dan: 249 & n, 270
Plato: and Lilian Harris, 151; *ref*: 192, 299
Poland Street: 135, 137
Police Strike: 211 & n
Ponsonby, Arthur: 222 & n
Pope, Alexander: 24n, 25n, 28, 29; *Epistle* ('Letter') *to Dr Arbuthnot*, 25 & n; *Essay on Criticism*, 24 & n; *Rape of the Lock*, 23

Popham, Brynhild, *née* Olivier: xxiv, 129, 130n, 139, 141, 143
Post-Impressionists, The (movement): xxiv, 236; ax 2
Post-Impressionist Exhibition: 1910-11 *see* First Post Impressionist Exhibition; 1912 *see* Second Post-Impressionist Exhibition
Pound, Ezra: 219 & n, 247; *Gaudier-Brzeska. A Memoir*, 90n
Powell, Harry J.: 237, 238n
Powell, Humphrey: 250 & n
Prime Minister, The (David Lloyd George): 'needs our prayers', 128 & n
Prince William of Sweden: *In the Lands of the Sun*, 34n
Prinsep (family): Prinsep's Pier wrongly called Princes' Pier, 108 & n
Prinsep, Valentine: xxi
Printing House Square: VW loses way to, 82, 83
Promenade concert: 205, 305
Proust, Marcel: 140 & n

Queen Alexandra *see* Alexandra, Queen
Queen's Hall: 5 & n, 20, 33, 205
Queen Victoria *see* Victoria, Queen

R. L. S. *see* Stevenson, Robert Louis
Radcliffe, Jack: 144 & n
Rail Strike: 301 & n, 302, 303, 304
Raleigh, Sir Walter: 166 & n
Rat Farm, Telscombe: 301 & n
Rathbone, Elena *see* Richmond, Elena
Rathbone, Mrs: 220 & n
Ravel, Maurice: 226
Raverat, Jacques: xxiv
Rayleigh, Lord: his cows milked by Virginia Isham, 88 & n
Reading, Lord: 86 & n
Reconstruction Committee: 74 & n
Regent's Park: 224
Regent Square, No. 36 (Vanessa Bell's flat): 270 & n, 305, 308
Regent Street: 241
Rembrandt: 228
Ribblesdale, Lord: 176 & n, 273
Richardson, Dorothy: 257 & n, 315 & n; *Interim*, 315n; *Pilgrimage*, 315n; *Pointed Roofs*, 257n; *The Tunnel*, 258n
Richardson, L. F.: 100 & n

hot and imperfect, 193; a source of
pleasure, 248, 259; *ref*: 80, 114, 120,
186, 192, 193, 194, 283, 305; *Hamlet*,
193; *King Lear*, 75, 214, 296; *Othello*,
114

Sharp, Clifford Dyce: 15n, 269

Shaw, George Bernard: 33 & n, 248

Shaw, Lord: 157 & n

Shaw-Stewart, Patrick: 108 & n

Shearman, Sir Montague: 174 & n, 208

Sheepshanks, Mary: xxiv, 225-6, 226n,
267

Shelley, Percy Bysshe: xxi, 29, 79

Shelley House, Chelsea: 219, 220, 220n,
226, 251

Sheppard, John Tresidder: 139, 154, 202
& n, 261

Short, Captain, of St Ives: and Tregerthen
cottages, 258, 259, 268, 269

Shove, Fredegond, *née* Maitland: *B 78
n26*; on social conscience, 100, 101; at
Tidmarsh, 105; mimics Karin, 106;
relations with Alix, 109, 172; accusa-
tions against VW, 113, 122; talk at
1917 Club, 115; *ref*: 78 & n, 102, 103,
127, 128, 130, 143, 234, 237, 252, 261,
284, 295; ax 2; *Dreams and Journeys*,
172n

Shove, Gerald: *B 78 n26*; renounces
tobacco, 101; behaves like a pig, 101;
his scruples about capital, 106; driven
to the land, 143; bursts his buttons,
261; *ref*: 33, 105, 109, 127, 130, 143,
218, 252, 295

Sichel, Edith: 206 & n

Sickert, Walter Richard: 240 & n

Sidgwick, Ethel: *Duke Jones*, 32 & n

Siegfried (fict): 17

Sitwell, Edith: 201n, 202

Sitwell, Osbert: 201 & n

Sitwell, Sacheverell: 201 & n

Sloane Square, London: 202

Smith, Sir Henry Babington: 118 & n

Smith, Logan Pearsall: *B 125 n16*; his
character, 274, 277, 285, 306; his
anthologies, 283 & n; supposed
review of *Kew Gardens*, 280; Hogarth
Press to print, 306; *ref*: 125 & n, 149
& n, 220, 272, 274, 275n, 282 & n,
289, 304, 305; *Stories from the Old
Testament*, 282n; *Trivia*, 149 & n

Smyth, Ethel Mary: 315 & n

Society, The, *see* Apostles

Socrates: compared with G. E. Moore,
155

Somers, Countess, *née* Virginia Pattle:
xx, xxi

Somerset, Lady Henry, *née* Isabel Somers-
Cocks: xxi, 274 & n

Sophia, Princess: 278 & n

Sophie *see* Farrell, Sophia

Sophocles: 202, 214, 228, 277; *Ajax*, 291;
Antigone, 149, 237; *Electra*, 184

Souhami, Joseph, oriental textiles importer: 162 & n, 164, 215

Southease, Sussex: its church, 45 & n;
ref: 39, 41, 45, 49, 50, 51, 53, 196, 270

South Kensington, as a social entity: its
breath, 206; *ref*: 244, 245

South Place Ethical Society: 262 & n

Spectator, The, periodical: its office, 212
& n

Spence, Dr John Buchan, chief of
Colombo Lunatic Asylum: 10, 11 &
n, 15

Spender, J. A.: 157 & n

'Sphinx without a secret' *see* Young,
Edward Hilton

Spicer & Son, papermakers: 260 & n

Spikings, tea rooms: 34 & n, 58, 62, 78
& n

Spiller Ltd, opticians: 101 & n

Spring-Rice, Dominic: 59 & n

Squire, John Collings, pseudonym
Solomon Eagle ('Eagle'): *B 26 n74*;
contributor to *Georgian Poetry*, 95;
callous-throated Eagle, 133 & n;
stands for Parliament, 143 & n; *ref*:
26 & n, 30, 58, 81, 93, 149, 218n, 278,
309, 314

Stacey, James: 248 & n

Stacey, Trissie, *née* Selwood: 57 & n,
158, 160, 188 & n

Stagg, Mrs: 205 & n, 242

Stanhope, Lady Hester: 23 & n, 264 & n,
273

Star, The, newspaper: 127

Star and Garter Home, Richmond: 294 &
n

Stawell, Florence Melian: 190 & n

Stephen (family): xiv-xv, xix-xxii; the
Stephen brain, 149; egoism proper to
all Stephens, 221; initiative and
vitality of, 236

Stephen, Adrian: *B 18 n48*; his frescoes,
10, 11n; his improvidence, 18, 20; no

longer to work on the land, 68 & n; political attitudes and activities, 119, 157, 158, 161, 165, 186; ties of blood, 149, 152, 187; frightened by faces on Heath, 153; happy, 185; too shy to write about *The Voyage Out*, 255; the right sneer for every occasion, 276; to become a medical student, 282 & n; *ref*: xiv, xvi, xxv, 14, 17n, 24 & n, 87, 137, 162 & n, 169, 183 & n, 186, 188, 275

Stephen, Ann: 186n, 253

Stephen, Harriet Marian ('Minnie') *née* Thackeray: xx

Stephen, Harry: 149 & n, 150, 221

Stephen, Sir James Fitzjames: xx

Stephen, Judith: 221 & n, 253

Stephen, Julia (Mother), *quo* Duckworth, *née* Jackson: xiv, xix, xxi, 269 & n

Stephen, Karin, *née* Costelloe: *B 24 n70*; her character and appearance, 106, 152, 186 & n, 188; her politics, 118-19, 161; a capable American, 185 & n; why Adrian married her, 187; to study medicine, 282 & n; *ref*: xxv, 18n, 24 & n, 162 & n, 165, 183 & n, 192, 253, 275, 276, 281

Stephen, Laura Makepeace: xv

Stephen, Sir Leslie (Father): *B 23 n64*; xiv, xv, xix, xx, xxi-xxii, xxv, 5n, 8n, 16n, 22 & n, 23, 28, 84n, 181, 225; *Hours in a Library*, 28n

Stephen, Thoby: xiv, xv-xvi, xxvii, 9n, 234; ax 2

Sterne, Laurence: xxi

Stevenson, Robert Louis (R. L. S.): xxv, 295

Stockholm Conference: 41n, 146

Stocks, Hertfordshire home of Mrs H. Ward: 207 & n

Stokoe, Frank Woodyer: 309 & n

Strachey (family): character, 235, 236, 312; their minds a source of joy, 264; *ref*: 153, 187, 209, 241, 305; ax 2

Strachey, household: denuded, 93

Strachey, (Giles) Lytton: *B 43 n17*; at Asheham, 43, 44; and Carrington, 89 & n, 105, 153, 176, 183; Lady Strachey's pride in, 107; and British Sex Society, 110-11; and review of *Eminent Victorians*, 128, 131-2, 142; health, 131, 208, 209; compared to G. E. Moore, 155; Mrs Ward's attack on, 166 & n; reflections on his character and attainments, 235, 236, 238, 264, 273, 277, 280, 281, 305, 311, 312; much hated, 261; praises *Night and Day*, 307; *ref*: xv, xvi, xxv, xxvi, xxvii, 21, 23, 64, 78, 101, 103 & n, 113, 176, 183, 209n, 213, 215, 234, 235, 236, 237n, 264n, 265, 272, 311; ax 2; *Eminent Victorians*, 64n, 131, 153, 238, 273, 280; *The End of General Gordon*, 90 & n, 101; *Queen Victoria*, 277; *The Son of Heaven*, 176 & n, 273n

Strachey, James Beaumont: *B 92 n27*; his 'iron will', 132; pursued by Alix, 212n, 237, 270; and Freud, 221 & n; dramatic critic, 254, 257; at 41 Gordon Square, 237n, 263, 284; his books, 305; *ref*: 92 & n, 99, 106, 122 & n, 131, 132n, 137 & n, 149, 172, 173, 212, 235, 263, 273, 280, 295; ax 2

Strachey, Lady, *née* Jane Maria Grant: *B 21 n59*; reminisces, 106-8, 108n; and poetry, 107, 187; *ref*: 21 & n, 188, 236; ax 2

Strachey, Marjorie ('Gumbo'): *B 15 n40*; emotional entanglement with Jos Wedgwood, 20, 21 & n, 22, 24, 27, 94, 153; a failure?, 252; her vivacious and commanding style, 262; *ref*: 14, 15 & n, 181, 235, 261; ax 2

Strachey, Oliver: *B 26 n76*; a new mistress, 153; described, 264; *ref*: 26 & n, 27, 33, 64 & n, 73, 91, 272; ax 2

Strachey, Pernel: *B 48 & n*; at Asheham, 48, 49, 188 & n, 189; *ref*: 235, 295; ax 2

Strachey, Philippa ('Pippa'): *B 117 n2*; untidy, old fashioned, 117, 118; and women's work, 170; *ref*: 154, 235, 252; ax 2

Strachey, Rachel ('Ray'), *née* Costelloe: *B 26 n76*; lectures to Guild, 155 & n; stands for Parliament, 220 & n, 229; *ref*: 26 & n, 73, 94, 162, 235, 281, 282; ax 2

Strawberry Hill, Twickenham: 294

Sturgeon, Flora, *née* Woolf: 5; 6 & n, 68 & n, 133 & n, 198

Sturgeon, George: his dramatic reception, 68; *ref*: 133n

Suffield House, Paradise Road, Richmond: the Woolfs consider buying, 313 & n, 318; *ref*: 19 & n

Turgenev, Ivan: 75
Tyrrell, Sir William: 145 & n

Union of Democratic Control (U.D.C.):
LW's profitable evening at, 76n, 77
Unwin, Stanley: 124 & n, 171

Valcheras, Richmond restaurant: 199 & n
Vanbrugh, Irene: 273 & n
Vandervelde, Lalla: to act Lytton's play,
166-7, 167n
Vanessa see Bell, Vanessa
Vaughan, Emma ('Toad'): *B 57 n9*; 56,
57n, 87
Vaughan, Halford: 88 & n
Vaughan, Janet: 88 & n
Vaughan, Margaret ('Madge'), *née*
Symonds: *B 88 n20*; 13n, 88 & n
Vaughan, Margaret ('Marny'): *B 86 n13*;
visits VW, her talk recorded, 86-9,
88n
Vaughan, William Wyamar: 13 & n, 88
Vaughan Williams, Adeline, *née* Fisher:
87 & n, 220n
Vaughan Williams, Hervey: 220 & n
Verrall, Arthur Woolgar: 165 & n, 169 &
n
Verrall, Jacob: 287
Verrey's, café-restaurant: 240 & n
Venizelos, Eleutherios: 253 & n
Victoria, Princess (2nd d. of Edward VII):
14 & n, 64
Victoria, Queen: 246, 277, 283
Victoria and Albert Museum ('Albert
Museum'): 205 & n
Voltaire: 205, 312
Vorticism: xxvi

W.G. see Women's Cooperative Guild
Wadhams, Judge Frederick Eugene: 139
& n
Wales, Rev F. H.: 88 & n
Waley, Arthur: 116 & n
Waley, Hubert: 209 & n
Walpole, Horace: 294 & n, 295 n
Walter see Lamb, Walter
Walter family, and *The Times*: 254 & n
War and Peace: periodical: 66n, 99n, 153
Ward, Arnold: 62 & n
Ward, Mary Augusta (Mrs Humphry
Ward), *née* Arnold: *B 57 n11*; attack
on Lytton Strachey, 166 & n; eligible
for Parliament, 207 & n; her writing

a menace, 211; her memoirs, 299-300,
300n; *ref:* 57 & n, 62 & n, 109, 204;
Marcella, 300 & n
'Wat' see Lamb, Walter
Waterlow, Alice see Williams, Alice
Waterlow, Margery ('Marg', 'Dawks'),
née Eckhard: *B 4 n2*; and conditions
at Asheham, 3, 7, 8, 12; her capacities,
155, 306; *ref:* 18, 18n, 110, 154, 305,
306n
Waterlow, Sydney: *B 6 n15*; and conditions at Asheham, 6 & n, 12, 12n; in
very good feather, 92; mellowed, taking to literature again, 155; needs
praise, 271; pleased with himself, 225,
306 & n; on *Night and Day*, 310; *ref:*
7, 8, 18, 18n, 22 & n, 33, 49, 110, 154,
305
Watts, George Frederic: xix, xxi, 237 &
n
Watts, Mary (Mrs G. F. Watts): 237 & n
Wayfarer see Massingham, Henry
William
Weaver, Harriet: 136 & n, 139-40, 140n
Webb, Beatrice and Sidney (the Webbs):
B 18 n51; Beatrice like an industrious
spider, 26 & n; luncheon with, 74;
her committees, 74 & n; LW to dine
with, 145-6; their visit to Asheham,
193-7; her opinions on great men and
women, 194; her snores and his
attempt to conceal them, 194; Sidney
on the future work of Government,
194; their shower baths of information, 195; on landscape beauty and
nature, 195; her private words with
VW, 196; how consistently *sensible*,
196; Sidney admires LW's book,
250; her 'little story', 251 & n; lunch
with, and her idea of municipal
bricks for children, 276; *ref:* 18 & n,
29, 139, 147, 215, 234, 272, 280; ax 2
Wedgwood, Ethel Kate, *née* Bowen: 21
& n, 22
Wedgwood, Josiah Clement ('Jos'): *B
21 n57*; his affair with Marjorie
Strachey, 21 & n, 22, 24, 27, 94,
252; marries 'his deaf governess', 153
Wells, H. G.: chief jingo, 157 & n; *Joan
and Peter*, 195 & n
Westminster Gazette, periodical (the
'Saturday Westminster'): 120 & n
White Hart Hotel, Lewes: 286 & n, 287

ence, 41n; the 'Ceylon affair', 60n, 71, 109 & n, 263; League of Nations, 127, 157-8; 1917 Club, 57, 129-30, 261; on Russia, 95; Antislavery Society, 137n; briefs Margaret Llewelyn Davies, 100; 'activities beyond counting', 152; tribulations, 171; parliamentary candidature?, 173 & n; to accompany Gilbert Murray to Versailles?, 221; General Election, 229; socialism and private wealth, 100, 194; ax 2

Works mentioned: *Cooperation and the Future of Industry*, 72n, 171, *Empire and Commerce in Africa*, 71n, 229n, 317 & n; *International Government*, 22 & n, 28, 139n; *The Three Jews*, in *Publication No 1* (with VW) 31 & n; *The Wise Virgins*, 32 & n

Woolf, Marie (Mrs Sidney Woolf), *née* de Jongh (LW's mother): never grown up, 161, 277; *ref*: 29 & n

Woolf, Philip: *B 7 n16*; army discontents, 7, 34, 123; wounded, 83; in hospital, 84, 90, 92; wound breaks out again, 111; printing Cecil's poems, 123, 128; back to the front, 167, 200; his character, 248; 277 & n

Woolf, Sidney (LW's father): xvi, 29n

Woolf, Sylvia (Mrs Edgar Woolf): 68 & n, 163, 277

Woolf, Virginia. Entries are divided into eight sections thus: (1) Early life and relationships. (2) Character, personality and health. (3) Literary activity and opinions. (4) Relationship with LW. (5) Public affairs and political activities. (6) Diversions, art and music. (7) Domestic (house hunting, house-keeping, shopping, etc., and financial). (8) The Hogarth Press.

(1) *Early life and relationships*: childhood and youth, xiv-xvi, marriage, xvii, social background—early, xviii, xxii, and later, xxii-xxviii; her mother's family, 106-8, her death, 269; Aunt Minna, 161; Jack Hills, 163; Harry Stephen, 149, 150, 221; never baptised, 225; Aunt Anny, 247; all much happier, 261; reunion with Violet Dickinson, 273-4

(2) *Character, personality, and*

health: insanity, xv, xvi, xvii, 39, 148, in others, 13; conservatism, xxiii; condemned as a slut, 7, as a tale-bearer, 208 & n; clothes and confidence, 35, 103-4, 284; dental treatment, 39, 83, 119, 216, 224, 233, 250, 311, menstrual periods, 66 & n, 104, 144, spectacles, 101, loss of weight, 119, ill in bed, 119, 233, 234, 317, rheumatism, 307; a bookbinder, 57n; love of parties, 59 & n, but not Webbs', 74, party manners, 261-2; memory, 102; ignorant of geography, 144; happy, 121, 267, 269, 283, 318, middle-aged and flustered, 295, depressed, 298, childless, 298, not a success, 305

(3) *Literary activity and opinions*: this diary, including Asheham Diary, xiii-xiv, 3, 29n, 39, 55, 119, 130, 179n, 198, 233-4, 295, 304, 311, 315, to be kept, 317; *The Voyage Out* begun, xvi, accepted for publication, 3, compared with *Eminent Victorians*, 238, with *Night and Day*, 259, Clive Bell on, 307, E. M. Forster on, 310, American offers for, 313, 314; *ref*: 29 & n, 214, 225, 259, 280, 298, 308; 'poor Effie's story' (*The Third Generation?*), 4 & n, 19 & n, 22; mediates a work upon eccentrics, 23 & n, 260 & n; assessments of Mrs Asquith, 71, Clive Bell, 95; Strachey too like Macaulay, 101; Mr Whitham on Eng Lit, 113-14; literary gossip, 115-16, 254; Cecil Woolf's verse, 124; not a Jacobean, 125-6; lure of book buying, 126; rejected by *TLS*, 127; not rejected, 128; Mrs Ward makes writing disgusting, 211; difficulty of reviewing friends, 129, 132, 138, 142; literature, morality and Janet Case, 213-14; T. S. Eliot, 218-219; reviewing, 224; comic possibilities of Freshwater, 237; dark world of gas, 250 & n; *Night and Day*, hopes Katherine Mansfield won't review it, 257, LW approves, 259, a pleasure to write, 259, Duckworth to publish, 269, offered to America, 280, 297, 314n, publication, 306 & n, E. M. Forster doesn't like, 307-8, 310, *The Times* on, 308, Katherine Mansfield on, 314-15, attacked and defended,

316, no news of sales, 318; *ref*: 76n, 224, 250, 261, 280, 302; to write for *Athenaeum*, 256; *Kew Gardens*, printed off, 229, published, 271, praised, 273, 276, production criticised, 279, success, 280, 284; *ref*: 216, 227; literature discussed, 271, with Clive Bell, 290; Lewes Public Library, 300; Margaret Llewelyn Davies and Janet Case prefer VW's criticism, 313; not to review Dorothy Richardson, 315

See also under individual authors

(4) *Relationship with LW*: VW on LW's family, xxiv, xxv, 6, 16, 29; his modesty, 9; his views on cooking in bed, 17; her belief in him, 22, 23, 25, 28-9; his birthday presents, 28, 113; quarrels, 31, 72-3; his care for VW when mad, 39; 'Mandril'—a term of endearment, 40 & n; LW to contribute to diary, 55; menaced by conscription, 56, 58, 59, 67; pleasure of his company, 70; real life with him, 70; testy—'some antics', 73; joins in his triumph, 124; unreasonable, 135; shocked by her ignorance, 144; bets 1/- he will be made editor, 167; dispute over fat bacon, 183; the wife of an editor, 190; admires his speech on Austria, 209; he brings comfort and reassurance, 223; his depression due to 'my wretched family', 259; a quarrel, 280; sympathetic explanation of Katherine Mansfield's criticism, 314; the 'happiest couple in England', 318

(5) *Public affairs and political activities*: Women's Cooperative Guild, 11-12, 76, 90, 112, 141, 165; VW a Fabian, 26; effect of bombing on London, 65, 71; air raids, 70, 84-5, 93-4, 116, 124, 144; Russia and the Future, 95; hope of peace, 99, 205-6, 215; wartime shortages, 100, 126; a meeting in Hampstead, 83; personal conduct of socialists, 101; impressed by Lloyd George, 128; achievement of the suffrage, 124-5, 207; gunfire and daffodils, 131; League of Nations debate, 157-8; LW for parliament? 173; the Webbs and the future, 193-6; Sir Edward Grey, 200; Herbert Fisher the horse's mouth, 202-4 armistice, 216; General Election, 229; coal strike postponed, 257; VW vague about Armenians, 271; Keynes and Versailles, 280, 288; distaste for the Fabian type, 276; Peace celebrated, 291, 292-4; Mrs Besant on India, 293; rail strike, 301, 302, 303; revolution anticipated, 309-10

See also under Fabian Society, Peace Conference, Webb, B. and S., and Woolf, L., section 4.

(6) *Diversions, art, and music*: public concerts, 5 & n, 20 & n, 63 & n, 77, 142, 205, 206 & n, 305, 306n, 311; Gordon Square parties, 9, 10, 73, 86; picture palaces, 18, 28; music halls, 19-20, 20n, 28, 144 & n, 201n, 222n; dinner parties in Soho, 59, 172, 259-60; Mozart operas, 83, 153, 157; 1917 Club dinners, 94, 293; Hampton Court, 100, 144; Cézanne, 140; The National Gallery, 168 & n, 228; a Brighton treat, 189; Russian Ballet, 201 & n, 222n, 288; a Sitwell party, 201-2; Victoria and Albert Museum, 205 & n; Peace Celebrations, 216, 292-3, 294; Shelley House concerts, 219, 220 & n, 226, 245n, 251, 309; Sickert exhibition, 240; Richmond Horse Show, 288

See also under Bell, C., Bell, V. and 1917 Club

(7) *Domestic affairs*: shopping, 5, 35, 100, 112, 126; house hunting, 9, 10, 11, 15, 24, 31-2, 33; domestic catastrophes, 15, 17, 25; windfalls, 60; Lottie rewarded, 67; trouble with, 91; a bad journey, 94; more trouble with Lottie, 143; Vanessa Bell's servant problem, 158, 188, 238, 262-3; servants' holiday after a row, 197; no money for new diary, 217; Asheham, notice to quit, 248; house hunting, 248, 278; in treaty for Tregerthen cottages, 258-9, 268, 269-70; Stephen children and nurse unacceptable, 253; Round House bought, 279; to be sold, 287; Monks House bought, 286-8, move to, 295; Nelly apologises, 304; gives notice, 313-14; proposed purchase of Hogarth House and Suffield House, 313

(8) *The Hogarth Press*: printing *Prelude*, 56; Alix starts work and gives up, 57, 60, 61; trouble with the machine, 76, 77n; Barbara Bagenal as apprentice, 79, 84, 85, 90, 91; trouble with the printer, 102, 104, 113; offer of *Ulysses*, 136, 140; buying type, 141; a gigantic effort, 142; Lottie spills the type, 143; *Prelude* completed, 164; *Kew Gardens* set up, 216; practically finished, 227; possibilities of the press, 229; Logan Pearsall Smith would be agent, 275; and suggests assistant, 289; work by him to be published, 306; *Kew Gardens* badly produced, 279, glut of orders for, 280; Altounyan brings a thick ms, 276; quantity of mss submitted, 282

See also Caslon's, McDermott

Works referred to: *Asheham Diary*, 39-55, 179, 198; *A Writer's Diary*, vii, viii; *Freshwater*, 237n; *Kew Gardens* (see 3 above); *The Mark on the Wall* (included in *Publication No. 1*), 31n, 240n, Clive Bell's praise, 240-1, VW's doubts, 271, 276, 280; *Night and Day* (see 3 above); *To the Lighthouse*, xiii; *The Voyage Out* (see 3 above); *The Waves*, xiii; *The Years*, 39n

Wooller, Sussex family: 41 & n, 44, 53, 301

Wordsworth, William: 131 & n, 180

Wortley-Montagu, Lady Mary: 81 & n

Wright, Harold: 109 & n, 132, 143 & n

Wright, Dr Maurice: 56 & n

Wycherley, Lewes estate agent: acts for Woolfs, 287, 288; *ref*: 279

Wycherley, Mrs: 279

Y.M.C.A. (Young Men's Christian Association): 213

Young, Edward Hilton ('The Sphinx without a Secret'): 21n, 130 & n, 172, 194

Young, George: 194 & n, 195

Zennor, Cornwall: 112 & n